John S. Conway was born in London and
educated at St. John's College, Cambridge.
After taking his doctorate in modern
German history, he taught for two years at
the University of Manitoba. For the past
ten years he has been a member of the
History Department of the University of
British Columbia in Vancouver, and is at
present Associate Professor of History there.
He is the author of numerous articles and
reviews dealing with twentieth-century
affairs, and is a contributor to *The Times
Literary Supplement* and other journals.

The Nazi Persecution of the Churches
1933-45

The Nazi Persecution of the Churches 1933-45

J. S. Conway

Weidenfeld and Nicolson
5 Winsley Street London W1

Church and state - Germany - history, 1933-45

Printed by C. Tinling & Co. Ltd, Liverpool, London and Prescot

To all my friends in the
World Student Christian Federation

We have all of us – the whole Church and the whole community – been thrown into the Tempter's sieve, and he is shaking and the wind is blowing, and it must now become manifest whether we are wheat or chaff! Verily, a time of sifting has come upon us, and even the most indolent and peaceful person among us must see that the calm of a meditative Christianity is at an end. . . .

It is now springtime for the hopeful and expectant Christian Church – it is testing time, and God is giving Satan a free hand, so that he may shake us up and so that it may be seen what manner of men we are! . . .

Satan swings his sieve and Christianity is thrown hither and thither; and he who is not ready to suffer, he who called himself a Christian only because he thereby hoped to gain something good for his race and his nation, is blown away like chaff by the wind of this time.

MARTIN NIEMÖLLER, *Sermon for the Fourth Sunday before Easter, 1934*

Contents

List of Illustrations

Acknowledgements

The publishers wish to thank the following for
permission to reproduce plates in this book:
Press Illustrationen Hoffmann, Berlin, plate 1; Hagel
Foto Service, plates 3, 4, 5, 6, 7 and 8; Fritz P. Krueger,
plate 14; and Südd. Verlag Bild-Archiv, Munich, plate 15.
The originals of plates 2, 9, 10, 11, 12, and 13 are to be
found in the Bundesarchiv, Koblenz.

Preface

My object in adding to the vast number of books on the Nazi era is to provide for the English-speaking reader an account of the methods by which Hitler and his followers sought to deal with the Christian Churches. For this purpose I have examined many of the documents dealing with Church affairs from the Nazi archives which survived the collapse of the Third Reich in 1945, and which were scattered in all directions by the fortunes of war. The principal sources used are the archives of Hitler's Reich Chancellery, the various German government records, the Nazi Party archives, the papers of individual Nazi leaders and the files of documents produced during the Nuremberg trials. Unfortunately all of these collections are incomplete, since some papers were deliberately destroyed, others were lost in the evacuation period, others were mislaid after capture and others have vanished without trace. By means of careful collation it is now possible to reconstruct much of the story; more could undoubtedly be found if the archives of the German Democratic Republic in Potsdam were freely open to western scholars. Large quantities of these papers have now been microfilmed, but reliable and complete indices are still lacking. Others of a more personal kind belonging to Nazi participants may yet be found, which, for obvious reasons, are still unavailable. But the main features of Nazi policy I believe are now apparent.

My gratitude is due in the first place to my colleagues of the University of British Columbia: so too, for financial help, to the Canada Council and the Humboldt Stiftung of Bad Godesberg. I am especially grateful to the help received from Institut für Zeitgeschichte in Munich, the Bundesarchiv in Koblenz, and the American Document Centre in Berlin. I am particularly indebted for her assistance to Miss B. Phillips of Liverpool University.

Preface

Very helpful suggestions were given to me by Dr Wilhelm Niemöller of Bielefeld, Dr Klaus Scholder of Tübingen University, Dr Friedrich Zipfel of the Free University of Berlin, Father Robert Graham S.J., Dr H. Boberach of the Bundesarchiv, and Professor Guenter Lewy. While I am sincerely appreciative of their help, the opinions contained in this book are not necessarily in agreement with their published views. The shortcomings are my own.

I acknowledge with gratitude permission from the editors of *The Journal of Bible and Religion* to reprint certain sections of an article which was published in July 1964, 'The Historiography of the German Church Struggle' (Copyright 1964 by the American Academy of Religion); and to reprint in translation a portion of Alexander Hohenstein, *Wartheländische Tagebuch 1941–2* (Munich 1963), which is to be found in Appendix 4B. I am grateful to Wm. Hodge Ltd. of Edinburgh for permission to use the quotations from Pastor Niemöller's sermon and to McGraw Hill Book Company and Weidenfeld and Nicolson Ltd. for permission to reprint four passages from *The Catholic Church and Nazi Germany* by Guenter Lewy—copyright 1964 by Guenter Lewy.

I should like to acknowledge the encouragement and co-operation of the Ryerson Press of Toronto and of the staff of Weidenfeld and Nicolson in London.

University of British Columbia   J. S. CONWAY

Introduction

It is a regrettable fact that in almost all the accounts by English-speaking authors of the Nazi era in Germany only slight attention is paid to the affairs of the Churches. So much attention has been paid, and so much discussion focused, on the military and political events of the years of the Nazi tyranny that the internal developments, with the exception of the Resistance movement and the construction of the notorious concentration camps, have largely been overlooked. Only in recent years have studies been made of the methods by which the Nazis were able to impose their totalitarian rule over one hundred million people, and the consequent results to all established institutions both within Germany and within the conquered territories. Among these institutions must be counted the Churches, in particular the Roman Catholic and Protestant Churches which together commanded the loyalty of ninety-five per cent of all Germans. This fact alone makes it remarkable that so little attention has been paid to the impact of Nazism upon institutions which had been part and parcel of German life for centuries. Even in the one area of the Churches' life which might seem to be of particular significance to political historians, namely, the Churches' involvement in the political life of Germany, most treatments are very brief. For example, William Shirer, whose history of the Third Reich stretches to over twelve hundred pages, devotes only seven meagre pages to Church affairs, and these are given over to the story of the Churches' persecution and their attempts at resistance to Nazi tyranny. J. L. Snell, in his short survey of *The Nazi Revolution* in the D. C. Heath series, makes no mention at all of the Churches, not even of their share in the Resistance movement. Even in the more specialized studies of the Resistance itself, little or no analysis is given of the contribution of the Churches, even though it is acknowledged that both in the case of the active conspirators, such as those who partook in the 20 July 1944 revolt, and in the more passive but ideologically-oriented forms of opposition to Nazism, Christian ideals and idealism played a formative role. It seems to have been assumed that the individuals concerned took their ideas from a substratum of Christian belief left over from pre-Nazi days, and that the witness of the Churches throughout the Nazi period is of little account. It is possibly noteworthy that, since the end of the war, a recently published book by an American nun, Mother Gallin's study, *The German Resistance: Ethical and Religious Factors* (Washington, D.C. 1961), is the only work in English explicitly on this topic.[1] There is therefore clearly scope for a more extended study of the life and witness of Christians of all denominations during those years when the Churches, like all other sections of German society, were faced with a totalitarian challenge unprecedented in recent history.

This gap in the English-speaking histories of Germany's recent past is all the more remarkable considering the very numerous and very thorough studies of the Churches' life which have appeared in German. A bibliography compiled in 1958 by Otto Diehn contained no fewer than six thousand items. In 1955 the Council of the Evangelical Church in Germany, recognizing that the Nazi period had brought about a revolutionary change in the history of the Church, appointed a Commission for the History of the Church Struggle in the National Socialist Period, under the chairmanship of Professor K. D. Schmidt of Hamburg. The Commission has already published several studies of great importance, from the point of view of the Evangelical Church, mainly by men who took an active part in the events of that time. Almost all of these have devoted considerable attention to the social and political developments involved in the relationship between the Nazi state and the Evangelical Church. Some Roman Catholics have also been concerned to undertake studies of the same developments. In the last few years notable publications have brought to light new documents, and fresh interpretations have been given to previous accounts. It is now possible to make a preliminary survey of the various historiographical trends discernible in this considerable mass of material, which, as explained above, is not generally familiar to the English-speaking reader.

The first motive behind these writings was undoubtedly somehow to come to terms with the recent events in German history. It will be readily admitted, as has already been pointed out, 'that the true story of the Church in Germany is not an unrelieved epic of faith and courage; it is to a large extent a sad tale of betrayal, timidity and unbelief. Even amongst those most faithful to the gospel, there were "none righteous, no, not one".'[2] Despite this conclusion, or perhaps because of it, historians have tried to see how it was possible that the land of Luther, Bach, and Charlemagne should also have been the land of Adolf Hitler and Adolf Eichmann. Even though Nazism is no longer either an active political force, or even a danger ideologically, the memory of its all-destroying impact cannot be expunged. More importantly, the Churches continue to play a vital role in the life of present-day Germany. Both the theological and socio-political exigencies of today demand and have demanded since 1945 a thorough analysis of the part the Churches can and ought to play in the reconstruction of Germany in the post-war world.

The second motive which prompted histories of the Church struggle was undoubtedly a desire to place on record the witness of all those who fell victims of the Nazi tyranny. The activities and achievements of such martyrs as Dietrich Bonhoeffer, the Scholls, or the Catholic priests murdered in Dachau, prompted a number of commemorative biographies and studies, such as the well-known edition of Bonhoeffer's *Letters and Papers From Prison* (London 1953 – later expanded into a four-volume collection of Bonhoeffer's writings); Dietmar Schmidt's biography of Pastor Niemöller (Hamburg 1959); the edition of letters written by prisoners in Germany on the verge of execution, translated as *Dying We Live* (London 1956); the biography by Inge Scholl of her brother and sister, *Die Weisse Rose* (Munich 1955); or Benedicta Kempner's *Priester Vor Hitlers Tribunalen* (Munich 1966). Such pictures of courageous but impotent resistance against the overwhelming power of a police state were complemented and strengthened by the historical studies of Pastor Wilhelm Niemöller, the brother of Pastor Martin, who has built up the archives of the Church Struggle in his rectory at Bielefeld. His book, *Kampf und Zeugnis der Bekennenden Kirche*, published in 1948, was a fuller and more historical study, supplementing his outline of the Church Struggle already published in 1946, *Kirchenkampf im Dritten Reich*. Besides the numerous studies since published by the Historical Commission under the title *Arbeiten zur Geschichte des Kirchenkampfes*, mention must be made of the seven-hundred-page collection of documents edited by Heinrich Hermelinck, *Kirche in Kampf – Dokumente des Widerstands und des Aufbaus in der Evangelischen Kirche Deutschlands von 1933 bis 1945* (Tübingen 1950).

These compendious studies have done much to clarify the historical outlines of a very involved and much disputed period of German church history. Nevertheless it is also apparent that these studies were motivated as much by the desire to justify the actions of the small but highly significant group who steadfastly opposed the Nazi tyranny, namely the 'Bekennende Kirche', as by an historian's interest in recent events. All the authors were members of or sympathizers with the 'Bekennende Kirche'. They were at pains therefore to point out the significance of the policies and attitudes of this group within the Evangelical Church, and in particular to dissociate themselves from the views both of the Nazi state and of their opponents within the Evangelical Church who more or less openly had shown their sympathy with the Nazis, and who were chiefly to be found within the rival movement of the 'Deutsche Christen'. The burden of all these studies has been to point out the errors, theological and political, of the 'Deutsche Christen', and to document the manner in which the 'Bekennende Kirche' struggled against the whole weight of the Nazi state machinery to preserve the truth of the Christian Gospel.

A very similar movement was to be found in the Catholic Church. Already by 1945 the steadily mounting opposition to the Nazi régime, and the wave of persecution which the Catholic Church suffered, provided the material on which the record of opposition to the Third Reich could be documented. Johann Neuhäusler's *Kreuz und Hakenkreuz*, published in 1946, was a compendious list of all the attacks upon the Catholic Church by the

Nazis, and of the vigorous if ineffectual opposition practised by the Catholic authorities.[3]

A fourth motive, moreover, was undoubtedly the desire of these authors in both of the Churches to demonstrate to the outside world that not all Germans had fallen for the errors of Nazism. In the immediate circumstances of the post-war world, when Germany lay defeated, occupied and divided, they sought to show that in the Churches at least were to be found those 'good Germans' in whom liberals abroad had hoped to find the examples of another and a better Germany, and that these were the people who could now be looked to in the task of rebuilding the shattered nation. In the exigencies of the occupation régime, all the military occupation forces were eager to find some non-tainted groups of Germans to whom the work of rehabilitating Germany could be delegated. Co-operation with the constituted hierarchies of the Catholic Church and the several Protestant Churches in the *Länder* was dictated, in all except the Russian Zone, by reason of the wish to return to 'normality' as soon as possible. There was little desire or opportunity to question the version of events as described by these historians in the name of the reconstituted Churches of the new Germany. Yet it cannot be denied that this enabled these writers to seize the opportunity to strengthen their case. This attempt, not merely to win the favour of Germany's new masters, but also of influential ecclesiastical circles abroad, particularly in England and Switzerland where interest in such questions was most lively, certainly met with considerable success. It was the members of the 'Bekennende Kirche' who were personally best known to Church leaders abroad, especially in English-speaking countries and in the circles of the ecumenical movement. The historic meeting, for example, between Bishop Bell of Chichester and Dietrich Bonhoeffer in Stockholm in 1942, when the latter revealed the resistance hopes of the 'treacherous' opposition of the 'Bekennende Kirche', had kept alive the hope that here the true soul of Germany was to be found. The English-speaking public was all the more disposed to give every credit to the 'Bekennende Kirche' because all the books published in English before the war were wholeheartedly on their side. The best of these was A. S.

Duncan Jones's *The Struggle for Religious Freedom in Germany* (London 1938). Both the theological and political inclinations of such authors as S. W. Herman, Arthur Frey, Paul Means, Dorothy Buxton, and Nathaniel Micklem, and the publicly expressed statements of hostility towards the Nazi state made at the Oxford Conference of the ecumenical movement's Life and Work Committee in 1937, prove the unanimity of this opinion.[4] The universal sympathy with Martin Niemöller throughout his eight years of incarceration very naturally led to approval of his theological and church-political opinions. Indeed the English-speaking authors unanimously if one-sidedly saw the struggle as one of Church versus State, good versus evil, 'Bekennende Kirche' versus Nazi storm-troopers or racialists. It was also natural that to them the political aspects of the Church Struggle should be more significant than the theological. Undoubtedly, too, the ever-increasing importance of the theological writings of Karl Barth in English-speaking countries, and his well-known championing of the 'Bekennende Kirche', meant that after 1945 this interpretation of events within the Evangelical Church was virtually unchallenged.

Lastly, and probably most importantly, a further motive would seem to have been present in the minds of these historians at this time. In writing the history of the Church Struggle, they were conscious of the need to direct and guide the pattern of their Churches' life and thought for the future. Since the writers of the 'Bekennende Kirche' were so imbued with the ideas of Karl Barth, they sought to direct the new thinking of the Church into Barthian channels. The history of the Church Struggle was therefore a vehicle for proving the validity of their theological viewpoints. Indeed, as one or two historians were constrained to point out, the Church Struggle was not primarily, as all the English-speaking writers assumed, the struggle between Church and State, but rather between rival theological parties within the Church. In their view it was a conflict between the true and the false Church, and therefore of more consequent significance to the life of the Church long after the political persecutions of the Nazis had been forgotten. Historiographically this has been a one-sided battle since 1945, as not a single theologian or Church historian has sought to defend in general the opponents of the 'Bekennende Kirche', in particular the 'Deutsche Christen' or the theological deductions they made from their political decisions. One short study of conditions in Schleswig-Holstein has been written by a layman, Dr. Christian Kinder, who played for a time a significant role in the ranks of the 'Deutsche Christen'. The book is tendentious and apologetic, and avoids many crucial issues. Dr Kinder claims that he was able to prevent any sharpening of the Church Struggle in Schleswig-Holstein due to his subtle compromises with the Nazi rulers. His work brings out clearly his refusal to adopt any stand on principle, his opportunistic collaboration with the Nazi hierarchy, and his refusal to support in their hours of need those who did oppose Nazism relentlessly. Hans Buchheim has made a brief study of the political position of the 'Deutsche Christen' in his *Glaubenskrise im Dritten Reich* (Stuttgart 1953) and Dr Ellen Flessemann in an unpublished dissertation has examined the contradictions of their supposedly theological fantasies. But neither supports the 'Deutsche Christen'. At the same time it is worth mentioning that not a single work has been written which describes or analyses the position of the majority of the pastors of the Evangelical Church, who refused to join either the 'Bekennende Kirche' or the 'Deutsche Christen'. These men of the 'middle', these 'Neutrals', tried to stand aside from the Church Struggle, for a vast variety of motives which are now only too likely to be misunderstood. They have therefore thought it wiser to keep silent about their thoughts and actions during the Third Reich. It should not, however, be forgotten that throughout these men outnumbered the committed participants of the other factions. Eberhard Klügel in his *Die lutherische Landeskirche Hannovers und ihr Bischof 1933–45* (Berlin 1964) and his supplementary volume of documents has come closest to describing the attitudes of this section of the Evangelical clergy, though only for one provincial Church. The hero of his book is Bishop Marahrens, whose role in the Confessing Church was never as resolute as the followers of Niemöller and Barth would have liked. Klügel claims that the Church struggle would not have led to such personal sufferings if the flexible attitude and tactical manoeuvring of Bishop Marahrens had been more widely practised, but avoids any mention of the pro-Nazi declarations which the Bishop gave in his support of Germany's war aims and in the persecution of the Jews.

The acceptance of Barthian views by the staunchest members of the Confessing Church, however, was not merely in the realm of 'pure' theology, since the Barthians drew explicitly political conclusions from their theology. They based their stand upon the famous Barmen Declaration of 1934 (excellently analysed by A. C. Cochrane in his book *The Church's Confession Under Hitler*), for which Karl Barth had provided the theological justification. Since 1945 some of the theologians of the 'Bekennende Kirche' have continued to plead for a new political orientation – in secular terms a 'left-wing' orientation – and even for a complete dis-establishment of the Church, the adoption of full synodical (and possibly democratic) organization of the Church, and a determina-tion not to become once again the obedient servants of the political rulers of the State. This attempt has contained elements of enormous risk, as the subsequent life-stories of Pastor Niemöller and Karl Barth have shown. Furthermore it must be noted that in 1945 the opportunity was not taken to establish the Church on a completely free basis, but rather the Church in the Federal Republic of Germany now has the same established status as it had in 1932. In East Germany, of course, there could be no question of an established church, but hardly because of the successful acceptance of Barthian views!

All these reasons, therefore, the historical, the hagiographical, the apologetic, the political, and the theological, in both the Evangelical and the Catholic Church gave rise to this almost unanimous corpus of historiography. Nevertheless in seeking to demonstrate their opposition to the Nazi state and to those in the Churches who had shown sympathy with Nazi aims, these historians were not free from the grievous fault of suppressing certain facts and of blurring over the record of their own former sympathies and their own participation in the political processes which had brought the Nazi state into power. For this reason, neither Wilhelm Niemöller nor Johann Neuhäusler made significant mention of the attitudes of their respective groups in the crucial year of 1933, or rather the first eight months, when the totalitarian control of the Nazi régime was fastened upon Germany. Instead both sought to show that the 'Bekennende Kirche' and the Roman Catholic Church had been uninterruptedly the opponents of Nazism, that they were now worthy of undertaking to govern the Church in the post-war world, and that the events of history had justified their previous political and theological stand.

It was not until very recently that these interpretations have been challenged or disputed. But now a new group of mostly younger historians has grown up which has raised important objections to these received views of the Church Struggle in the Nazi period. Three main reasons would seem to lie behind this 'revisionism', which, it must be acknowledged, is equally motivated by present concerns. First, there is the motive of historical accuracy. There are still enough people alive to remember the course of events as they actually happened, and who are therefore reluctant to allow the version of events as described by the 'Bekennende Kirche' or the officially-approved Catholic historians to go unchallenged. One might mention Friedrich Baumgärtel's *Wider der Kirchenkampflegenden* (Neuendettelsau 1959), which draws attention to such unwelcome facts as Wilhelm Niemöller's active support of the Nazi SA before 1933, or Martin Niemöller's telegram of congratulations to Hitler on the occasion of Germany's desertion of the League of Nations! Younger historians find difficulty in understanding how it was possible that the Churches which were so apparently united in their opposition to the Nazis could have allowed the Nazi state to be imposed on them so easily. Especially among Catholics, a feeling of bewilderment has led to a desire for fuller knowledge.

This feeling has only been strengthened by the second motive, which might be described as a 'political' desire for a revision of the received version of the Church Struggle, again especially among Catholics. The present strongly-entrenched position of Catholicism in the councils of the West German government, and the apparent endorsement by the Catholic hierarchy of the policies of

German rearmament, of the staunch maintenance of the 'established' position of the Churches, and of the approval given to the present forms of economic development in Western Germany, have caused uneasiness among a significant minority. The historians among them have been alarmed by what appears to be a recurrence of the kind of 'political Catholicism' which was apparent during the Weimar Republic, and from which the Church Struggle had supposedly liberated the Church. Was the Church, and is the Church, bound to be politically subordinate to the wishes of the State? Turning their attention to the events of the 1930s and particularly to the developments which led to the Reich Concordat of July 1933, these historians have raised a whole series of serious charges against the Church leaders of those days and by implication against their interpretations of the Church's witness during the Nazi era. The most significant of these new 'revisionist' attempts is to be found in Hans Müller's *Katholische Kirche und Nationalsozialismus* (Munich 1963). Müller's views were strongly supported by a biting attack on the Catholic policies of 1933 by E. W. Böckenförde in the issue of the liberal Catholic journal *Hochland* of February 1961, and substantiated by Kurt Sontheimer in a lengthy and well-argued introduction to Müller's book. All these authors seek to show that the Catholic hierarchy was far from solidly opposed to Nazism in 1933, and that indeed the contrary was the case. Although up to the time of the Nazi takeover of power, Catholics had been forbidden to have anything to do with Nazism, a sudden and disastrous change took place. Not only did the leaders of the largely Catholic Centre Party voluntarily lead their party into self-immolation, with their support of the Enabling Law of March 1933 which extinguished the last hopes of democracy in Germany, but the Catholic hierarchy welcomed all too readily the signing of the Concordat in July.[5] Cardinal Faulhaber, indeed, sent a letter of congratulations to Hitler, praising him for achieving in six months what the old parties and parliaments had failed to achieve in sixty years. By compromising themselves in this way, the Catholic hierarchy was never able to lead the Catholic Church in wholehearted opposition to the Nazis, even after the hostile intentions of the latter were all too plainly revealed. Müller, Sontheimer, and Böckenförde therefore reject as misleading, and even deliberately so, the picture of Catholic opposition as shown by Neuhäusler. They point to such unwelcome facts as the Catholics' endorsement of the war, the signal absence of any attempt to defend the democratic way of life, the lack of protest against the Nazis' expansionist aims, and the absence of any opposition to the Nazis' violent and murderous policies against the Jews. Suffice it to say that their documentation of their case is ample. On the other side of the Atlantic, the political scientist Professor Guenter Lewy has used a wider variety of Catholic sources to give a very full, if one-sided, account of the manner in which German Catholics, and in particular the German episcopate, were prepared to collaborate in the establishment of the Nazi totalitarian power. He stresses the similarity of outlook in the common factors of anti-communism, anti-semitism, dislike of democracy, liberalism and pacifism, and the positive support of the Nazis' nationalist ambitions. Lewy's corrective is valuable for its diligent pursuit of evidence from all over Germany, and reveals clearly enough the illusions which all too many of the Bishops maintained about the true nature of the Nazi régime. Professor Gordon Zahn has raised exactly the same questions in his book *German Catholics and Hitlers' Wars*, in which he comes to the depressing conclusion that the German Catholics were never taught at any time during the whole Nazi era to recognise the demonic nature of the Nazi régime. The implication of this 'revisionism' would appear to be the hope that the Catholic Church will not allow itself to be fobbed off with the reassuring belief that it was all along on the right side, that it was always more sinned against than sinning, and that it could have done nothing further against the evil power of Nazi aggression. Such a desired re-examination might then lead to a more radical critique of the Catholic Church's present involvement in the political life of Western Germany today.

Thirdly, these 'political' revisionists have been matched by others whose objections to the received views of the Church Struggle may be said to be based on theological rather than on political grounds. Against all the self-justifying of a Church, ready to compromise with political evil for the sake of expediency, these critics raise the uncompromising claims of the Gospel itself. The most notable of such revisionists is Rolf Hochhuth, whose play *Der Stellvertreter* has raised exactly this issue in the most agonizing manner possible.[6] Although the chief target of his indignation is Pope Pius XII, the fact that he is a German and that his play concerns the events of the Nazi period clearly touched on the sorest possible point in the whole attitude of the German Catholics towards the Nazi state. There are many in Germany today – and by no means only non-Catholics – who are not willing to accept any longer the reassuring version of events produced by Neuhäusler. This attitude of frustration and disappointment has been excellently analysed by Carl Amery in his book *Die Kapitulation* (Hamburg 1963). As his title suggests, he follows the same line of criticism as Müller and Böckenförde, and gives an excellent sociological analysis of the reasons why the Catholic Church in 1933 and still today is prepared to avoid at almost all costs a real commitment to a Church Struggle. His suggestions as to the reasons for the German Catholics' willingness to abandon democracy and the weapons of political protest, for collaboration with the Nazis, and for their half-hearted resistance and failure to oppose the evils of Nazism more vigorously thereafter, are enlightening.

There is evidence that a very similar critique can be made against the received version of events in the Evangelical Church. Protestant revisionism is less radical than, say, Hochhuth's attack on the Roman Catholic Church, if only for the reason that the historians of the 'Bekennende Kirche' were themselves fierce critics of their own denomination. Their histories all along stress the fact that only ten per cent of the Evangelical pastors were supporters of the 'Bekennende Kirche', that their attitude to Nazism (in contrast to the other ninety per cent) was unrelenting, and that the martyrs of the Evangelical Church were almost all from their ranks. Nevertheless the same questions are being asked of the 'Bekennende Kirche' too. What protests did they make against the overthrow of democracy in Germany; what was their attitude towards the course of German expansionism; and what, apart from the heroic witness of Provost Grüber, did the 'Bekennende Kirche' do to

xxiv

succour and relieve the Jews?[7] These questions are directed all the
more pointedly by those of the younger generation of church
historians who openly express their bitter disappointment that the
Evangelical Church of Western Germany today seems to reflect
none of the prophetic vision and readiness to proclaim the uncompromising claims of the Gospel, which the historians of the
Church Struggle were so ready to point to as the hallmarks of the
'Bekennende Kirche'. Can it be wondered that doubts are now
being raised about the fight of the 'Bekennende Kirche' for
political independence, when the two best known bishops of the
Evangelical Church, themselves prominent in the 'Bekennende
Kirche', today appear as the willing spokesmen of the West
German government, and even have earned from their opponents
the epithet of NATO bishops? Can the leopard change his spots?
Has the Evangelical Church failed to draw the lessons which the
historians of the Church Struggle so meticulously pointed out?
Was the 'Bekennende Kirche' no more than an isolated example
of the independent proclamation of unwelcome truths? Or were
the historians possibly misinterpreting and distorting the record
of events to justify their own personal views and rationalizations?
Certainly the attempts of Martin Niemöller in the postwar years
to subject the Evangelical Church to the spirit of radical criticism
based on his reading of the Gospel, in the tradition, as he believes,
of the 'Bekennende Kirche', can hardly be described as successful.
And the almost perceptible complacency and self-satisfaction of a
Church, whose income is tied to the rising tax revenues of the
State of which it is now all too willingly and uncritically a part,
constrained even Karl Barth to ask in a recent issue of the *Ecumenical Review*:

Do we Protestants share in the experience and the fructification of a
shaking of the foundations? Or are there not among us all too many
offensive movements that have made no progress, for instance in the
Evangelical Church in Germany and its spiritual paralysis that began
such a short time after the brief awakening during the time of the
Church Struggle, so that now the 'progressive' elements form a minority
with its back to the wall? Does there not exist among us an express
enmity against all genuinely disturbing factors? And as a complement

to this, is there not far too great a measure of conformism with respect to the powers that rule in the people, state, and society?[8]

These dissatisfactions and disappointments have driven the younger historians to take a further and deeper look at the history of the Church Struggle. They seize upon the remark that the Church Struggle was not so much an issue between the Church and the State, as between two rival factions within the Church, to ask whether or not the leaders of the Church were ever seriously trying to rouse the nation in opposition to Nazism, or whether they were not all along led by motives of expediency to seek to protect the Church and to safeguard its institutions regardless of the consequence to the nation as a whole. This question is particularly apposite with regard to the Concordat of 1933. Can Catholic historians such as Neuhäusler really maintain that the leaders of the Church were not aware of the dangers of Nazism? Were they naive in accepting Hitler's promises at face value and thereafter claiming that they were betrayed? In the face of their very strong and definite opposition to Nazism before 1933, on very sound theological and political grounds, such an interpretation would seem hardly credible. Or were they well enough aware that Hitler was not to be trusted, and that in all probability the Nazi seizure of power would lead to an all-out attack on the Church, but nonetheless, in the hopes of entrenching their existing situation, decided to come to terms with their new masters? In other words, were they opportunists in hailing the Concordat as the method which would give them the best tactical advantage in the inevitable conflict ahead? Such a view would interpret the later years of the Church Struggle only as the more or less unsuccessful attempt to preserve the Church intact by men who had been outmanoeuvred and outflanked by Hitler's more dynamic methods of attack. This interpretation as put forward by Müller and Böckenförde is certainly a radical revision of previous views. In reply Hans Buchheim in a later issue of *Hochland* has argued that these critics have paid too little attention to the climate of opinion in 1933. It was a time of the greatest confusion of opinions. The sudden vision of national renewal which the Nazis seemed to offer and the liberation of energies which their guarantee of political stability released, made everyone, the Catholic hierarchy included, believe that all sorts of new possibilities were now open. Hitler's staging of the service of national reconciliation at the Potsdam Garrison Church two days before the passing of the Enabling Act, and his speech on that occasion promising full support to both religious confessions in the country, appeared to many to draw a line under the unhappy divisions and uncertainties which had marked the Weimar period and had affected the life of the Catholic Church ever since the *Kulturkampf* under Bismarck. The whole Church was caught up in the spirit of the national revolution. How could the bishops have withstood the pressure of the average Catholic, anxious to ally himself with the tide of events, for an agreed settlement with the new State, on the basis of rendering unto Caesar the things that are Caesar's, and unto God the things that are God's?

The debate about this aspect of the Church Struggle has caused Carl Amery to raise equally fundamental questions which deserve consideration. Was not the condition of the Church itself in the 1930s more to blame for the half-heartedness of resistance to the Nazi onslaught than the alleged opportunism or betrayal of the Church leaders? To be sure some of the latter need not have been so impetuous in sending telegrams of congratulations to Hitler, but basically could the leaders have been expected to have adopted a more outspoken line of opposition and criticism? Was not their tactic of defending the interior life of the Church dictated by the fact that this is exactly what the average church-goer desired? What evidence exists that either the Protestant or the Catholic laity would have been prepared to follow a more heroic course? Would those who today believe, like Hochhuth, that the Pope should have denounced the Nazi policy towards the Jews, have actively followed his lead, if he had spoken out? Has the Protestant Church of today become a prophetic community responding to the call of Jesus Christ in outspoken opposition to political injustice, as the 'Bekennende Kirche' claims to have been in the Nazi era? If the Protestant Church has not learned the lessons of the Church Struggle, which its historians were at such pains to proclaim, then is it not necessary to look again at the life and witness of the Church in the 1920s and 1930s to see the reasons for such

widespread apostasy? Was not perhaps Pastor Gross, writing in
Die Wandlung in 1947, right in saying: 'For the prophets to recall
the Church to a higher standard of loyalty and behaviour is sure to
bring about the reaction of the priests against the prophets, of the
people against its origins?' There are surely all too numerous
occasions in the present scene which testify to the truth of this
assertion.

Pastor Gross also made another damaging assertion against the
historians of the 'Bekennende Kirche'. Were they not in fact
trying to dissociate themselves from policies and attitudes which
to a large extent were not just the invention of the Nazis, but which
the whole Church shared? If Nazism is to be seen as a diseased form
of the whole development of twentieth-century life, could the
'Bekennende Kirche' be justified in trying to isolate itself on the
rock of Barthian orthodoxy? Neither national aggrandizement
nor anti-semitism, nor anti-democratic ideologies, were the
product of the Nazis alone. All Germans, Evangelicals and Catholics
alike, shared these ideas to a greater or lesser extent. For the Church
Struggle to be seen in terms only of a conflict between the 'en-
lightened' 'Bekennende Kirche' and the 'diseased' Nazis is to
misjudge the issues entirely. A far more searching analysis of the
involvement of the Church in the life and thought of the Germany
of those days is needed, and it is one which will raise fundamental
theological as well as sociological questions. As Professor F. H.
Littell has so rightly pointed out, the present historiography which
depicts 'the heroic image of a tiny minority, valiantly and clear-
headedly resisting the Nazis, is like a well cultivated tropical plant
of brilliant colour. There remain, however, a number of unsettled
questions to which the vivid contrasts rather blind the eye. It may
be that a certain amount of "demythologising" of the Church
Struggle will be necessary before the true view begins to emerge.'[9]
It would seem that here is the area of debate about the history of
the Church Struggle which is likely to be undertaken in the next
few years.

A remarkable omission in all of this literature has been the lack
of any thorough analysis of the policies advanced and adopted in
the ranks of the Nazi hierarchy on the future place of the Churches

in the Third Reich. This is in part due to the fact that the majority of books have been written by historians of the Church, who sought to defend, or attack, the actions of their denominations, and who availed themselves primarily of church records and archives. In part it is also due to the difficulty of access to the records of the Nazi Party and State after the defeat of 1945. Only in recent years have these records been returned to German hands, and some are still not available for private study. Only Friedrich Zipfel in his book *Kirchenkampf in Deutschland 1933–45* (Berlin 1965) has made partial use of documents discovered in the American Document Centre in West Berlin, but he did not see other collections available in the Bundesarchiv at Koblenz, or on microfilms available from Washington. Although his work appeared as one of a series produced under the auspices of Historical Commission for Berlin, he does not confine himself merely to events in the capital city. Unfortunately his self-imposed limitations prevent this from being regarded as a fully satisfactory study.

Despite the destruction at the end of the war, many of the records of the ReichChancellery, the Foreign Ministry, the Nazi Party headquarters, the *Reichssicherheitshauptamt*, as well as Himmler's personal files and large quantities of Rosenberg's papers survive. (The files of the Ministry of Church Affairs are believed to be intact but unavailable in the hands of the East German authorities at Potsdam.) Examination of these sources reveals a much more complex attitude to the Churches in the ranks of the Nazi Party than is generally supposed and throws new light on the processes by which Nazi totalitarianism sought to impose its rule on all aspects of German life.

By use of these sources, it has been my object in this book to look at the tangled skein of Church–State relations from 'the other side of the hill', and to outline the various factions within the Nazi Party, the considerations they adopted, and policies they advocated towards the Churches.

The omission of such an examination heretofore is all the more remarkable in view of the fact that throughout the whole Third Reich the initiative lay with the Nazis. Their determination to enforce their will on all aspects of German life was decisive in their conduct of affairs from the moment of achieving power. The Churches, like all other institutions, were to be moulded to the Nazi will, they were thrust into a passive position, in part voluntarily and in part unwillingly, and they were constantly assailed with propaganda or police measures, designed to cajole or enforce their submission. The whole debate on the extent of the Churches' collaboration with or resistance to Nazism, or on the validity of the Church struggle, needs to be placed in its full context. On the one hand, it is now possible to see in its entirety the extent of the Nazi persecution and the deliberate policies of repression under which the Churches suffered. This may prevent too easy a condemnation of churchmen for failing to resist the onslaughts of tyranny. On the other hand, the limited successes of the Churches can be seen to be due less to their heroic defence of their beliefs, than to the divisions amongst their foes. Within the ranks of the Nazis, strong differences of opinion over tactics developed, never to be finally resolved. It is my hope that this book will shed light on these varying policies, so that a clearer picture of the confrontation between the Christian Churches and totalitarianism will be possible.

My intention is in no way to seem to destroy the reputation of the heroes or to make the villains less villainous. No one who has perused daily the papers of the Nazi hierarchy can derive anything but a feeling of intense distaste at the enormity of inhumanity revealed therein – indeed a positive physical effort is required to overcome the revulsion which any civilized scholar must experience. And yet at the same time doubt must be cast on some features of the received and popular versions in the interests of historical accuracy and integrity.

In conclusion, a few wise words of James Joll, from his essay on 'The Historian and the Contemporary World' in *Geschichte und Gegenwartsbewusstsein: Festschrift für Hans Rothfels* (Göttingen 1963) might be cited, which, though written in a general setting, none the less have especially fitting reference to the Church Struggle:

There are episodes in our recent past so charged with emotion that they can only be studied by treating them as if they were part of the remoter historical past and not part of our own direct experience. This

can perhaps be shown by the Germans' attitude to their own immediate past. For a German who was grown-up before 1945 it must be
almost unbearable to take a steady look at the Nazi period; and it must
be impossible to do it without a personal examination of conscience.
Thus, while it is admirable that German historians, such as the excellent
team associated with the Institut für Zeitgeschichte in Munich should be
producing detailed, detached, scholarly, almost dessicated studies, it is
also inevitable that this should be a process of anaesthesia, a deadening
of the pain, which enables the patient to achieve a temporary illusion
of detachment from the operation on his own body. There are, in fact,
aspects of contemporary history which are so living and painful that
they are falsified if treated in too cool and scholarly a way.

1 The Seizure of Power

'Hitler was born at Braunau. Braunau is in
that part of Upper Austria which went
Protestant at the Reformation. After that it
was forcibly Catholicised by the forces of the
Counter-Reformation, the Hapsburgs and the
Jesuits. Since then there has been no religion
in that part of the world.' – CHANCELLOR
BRÜNING

When Adolf Hitler was appointed Reich Chancellor of Germany
by President Hindenburg on 30 January 1933 and took the oath to
defend the constitution of the Weimar Republic, he had, so far as
is known, no clear policy on the relations between Church and
State. The suddenness of his rise to power, his constant manoeuvr-
ings between the existing political groups, the frequency and
fervour of his speechmaking, and his pre-occupation with the
political and economic conditions of Germany, had pushed less
significant matters into the background.

There can, however, be little doubt that his fundamental hostility
to Christianity long preceded his rise to power. Born and brought
up in a Catholic household and educated at a Catholic school, he
had quickly abandoned whatever Christian principles he had learnt
in childhood, in favour of ideas prevalent in the early years of the
century, which derived, albeit in a perverted form, from Darwin,
Nietzsche and Gobineau. It was, in fact, during his years as a partially employed labourer in Vienna, and in the bitter experiences
and disillusionments of the First World War, that Hitler worked
out his personal creed and rejected both Christianity and the
Christian Church.

In this he was not alone. Millions of men and women throughout
Europe had likewise come to realize that for them the doctrines of

the Christian faith no longer held meaning or truth. The confident optimism of nineteenth-century liberal theology withered and died before the stark reality of the Flanders trenches. Christian values no longer seemed tenable in the bloody circumstances of total war. The Churches' all-too-willing support of nationalist war-time aims, on both the warring sides, appeared uncommonly like hypocrisy. And the inability of the Christian Churches to explain why the religion of the Prince of Peace was powerless to prevent the catastrophic disasters of 1914–18 finally destroyed all Christian belief in the hearts of a generation that had watched its comrades die so tragically in the belief that they were defending their country's Christian heritage.

Nevertheless, a longing for some faith to replace the disillusionments of the post-war world was in everyone's heart, and when Adolf Hitler appeared in Germany with a programme and a promise calculated to appeal to the defeated and discouraged, and offering what appeared to be a vital secular faith in place of the discredited creeds of Christianity, the time was ripe for its acceptance.

Hitler, on his own admission, was in no way a religious reformer.[1] He was basically indifferent to all theological questions and regarded Christian religious experience as a delusion possibly because of the association between Christianity and the 'Jewish spirit' which, from the earliest days of his political career, was the chief target of his hatred. The ready acceptance of Nazi ideology as a substitute for Christian beliefs in the years following Germany's defeat in 1918 was due, not to Hitler's persuasiveness as a political philosopher, but to a profound revolution in the spiritual life of the country. Nazism filled a vacuum in the lives of countless Germans, by offering, in emotional and semi-religious language, both a dynamic political creed and a plausible explanation of Germany's post-war predicament. National Socialism was to become far more than an alternative political party offering a programme suited to the times: it was, in Hitler's own words, 'a form of conversion, a new faith'.[2] While the democratic parties advocated self-discipline and acceptance of Germany's new position in the world, Hitler promised apocalyptic victory over all her

2

enemies. By their speeches, their parades, their songs and their music, the Nazi leaders sought to arouse a national hysteria which would sweep away all sober counsels and unite under one banner all the elements of society in a crusade for Germany's national regeneration. The elements of the campaign were not invented by Hitler, nor even 'systematized' from the rambling prognostications of *Mein Kampf*. Rather, it was the work of the Nazi propagandists, who welded together the various trends already existing within Germany into one *völkisch* ideology. Because it satisfied the aspirations of millions of Germans who were unwilling to face the reality of their situation, the people embraced the new idolatry of this latter-day Pied Piper of Hamelin.

It is a matter of speculation how far Hitler himself believed in the ideology which so successfully won for him the popular support he needed. Certainly he rejected many of the more extreme forms of Nazi ideology, and even maintained that he had never read Alfred Rosenberg's *The Myth of the Twentieth Century*, the book commonly held to be the ideological handbook of the Nazi Movement. That he was ready to adopt any attitude that suited his immediate political purposes is particularly true of his relations with the Christian Churches, though there can be no doubt of his fundamental antagonism to the 'satanic superstition' of the 'hypocritical priests' who, he held, were interested only 'in raking in the money' and 'befuddling the minds of the gullible'.[3] Even if he at one time thought, like his associates Dietrich Eckart and Alfred Rosenberg, that a 'true' Christianity, purged of its Jewish elements, could be combined with a belief in the superiority of the so-called Aryan race, such ideas were later replaced by a cleverly disguised hostility to Christianity *in toto*.

Hitler's opposition to the Church was, however, not so much ideological as political. He saw in the Church an organization whose power he resented. Indeed his antagonism to the Roman Catholic Church contained a strong element of envy, coupled with a sort of respect for a body that had preserved its influence for two thousand years. To his mind, the unity, continuity and authority of the Church were due, not to any spiritual cause, but to its well-organized control over its followers, a control which

3

the Nazi Party would do well to emulate. By contrast, the disunity, rivalry, and consequent lack of authority of the Protestant Churches made them despicable in his eyes. Both Catholics and Protestants could, however, be used for his own purposes. If they were prepared to participate in his work of national renewal and to become subordinate to his political ends, so much the better. Consequently, throughout the 1920s Hitler refused to campaign against the Christian Churches, fully realizing that, by professing support for the Churches' position in the state and by emphasizing the nationalist aspects of his programme, Catholics and Protestants alike could be persuaded to assist his rise to power.

It was this combination of national appeal and tactical deceit which led thousands of Christians in Germany to lend Hitler their support even before his accession to power, and which sustained millions more in his armies of conquest and terror in their imposition of the Nazi 'revolution of nihilism' from one end of Europe to the other. The skill with which he conducted his political campaign during his meteoric rise to power cannot be denied. It was no accident, but a deliberate policy to avoid the risk of offending substantial groups of potential supporters, which led him to refrain from challenging the Christian churches. After his abortive attempt to seize power in 1923, he realized that the citizens of Munich who had failed to support him in his *Putsch* would have to be persuaded by other means. He would therefore use the machinery of democracy to bring about its own overthrow. In his tireless campaigning and speech-making in the ensuing years, Hitler indulged in no recriminations over the 1923 débâcle, concentrating instead on a positive appeal to the electorate, by offering a programme of nationalism, racialism, and leadership exactly in tune with the aspirations of the German population. Direct attacks on Christianity, to which the masses were still attached, were most carefully avoided.

How deliberate this decision was can be seen in the contrast between Hitler's conduct and that of Germany's leading general of the World War, General Erich Ludendorff. Ludendorff, who had also been implicated in the 1923 coup d'état, drew a conclusion exactly the opposite of Hitler's. If the Bavarians clung too loyally to their Catholic heritage, they must first be persuaded of its worthlessness. Under the influence of his wife Matthilde, Ludendorff from 1924 onwards threw the whole weight of his prestige into a violent anti-Christian campaign and established the Tannenberg League as a centre for the propagation of belief in a German God combined with radical nationalism. Like the Nazis, Ludendorff believed that Germany's defeat in 1918 had been due to a combination of the international forces of Marxism, Freemasonry, Jewry and the Catholic Church, all seeking to enslave Germany. But when he challenged Hitler on his lack of explicit anti-Christian condemnation, Hitler merely replied:

I entirely agree with His Excellency, but his Excellency [Hitler spoke to the General always in a servile and devoted way and addressed him always in the third person as he had learnt to do as a corporal] can afford to announce to his opponents that he will strike them dead. But I need, for the building up of a great political movement, the Catholics of Bavaria just as the Protestants of Prussia. The rest can come later.[4]

For the same reason Hitler included in his party programme the ambiguous phraseology of Point 24:

We demand freedom for all religious denominations in the State so far as they are not a danger to it and do not militate against the customs and morality of the German race. The Party as such stands for positive Christianity, but does not bind itself in the matter of creed to any particular denomination. It fights the spirit of Jewish materialism *inside* and *outside* our ranks and is convinced that our nation can achieve permanent health from within only on the principle: 'Common welfare comes before individual welfare.'[5]

Frequent appeals to Hitler to elucidate these terms met with no success, for, as he frequently declared, 'he was completely uninterested in questions of faith'. It was hardly surprising, therefore, that many Germans interpreted Point 24 in their own way, and that few stopped to question its ambiguities. Practising Christians who were drawn to Hitler for nationalistic reasons, and who in increasing numbers saw the Nazi movement as a bulwark against the anti-Christian forces of Communism, were confident that this Point was proof of the Christian foundation of Nazi policies. By

1933 churchmen of all denominations believed that, just as Hitler had abandoned the more extreme policies of some of his followers such as Dinter and G. Strasser in the economic and social fields, so he would disavow the very hostile feelings against the Church and clergy expressed from time to time by the more radical of his followers. The fact that *Mein Kampf*, though full of statements contrary to Christian doctrine, nevertheless avoided direct attack upon the institutions of the Church, appeared to many sincere Churchmen to be 'proof' of Hitler's reliability in this respect. Attention was consequently focused less on the more extreme aspects of Hitler's racial policies as on such phrases as: 'The task of the Party was not to seek a religious reformation of our people, but a political reorganization. The party sees in both religious denominations valuable props for the values of our people and therefore attacks those parties which seek to degrade the moral and religious foundations of our community by using them as an instrument for their party's interests';[6] or 'in the ranks of our movement the most faithful Protestant can sit next to the most faithful Catholic without coming into the slightest clash of religious convictions'.[7] This intimation of religious tolerance was popularly associated with the then widely-held slogan that 'Everyone can be saved in his own fashion'.

As for the Churches themselves, it was not until 1930, the year in which the Nazi Party made phenomenal electoral gains and the then chief editor of the Nazi Party's newspaper, Alfred Rosenberg, published *The Myth of the Twentieth Century*, that they began to pay serious attention to this new political force. And with their wakening interest striking differences of attitude became apparent between the denominations. In the Catholic Church, a number of clearsighted theologians saw the incompatibility between Christian doctrine and the Nazi ideas of so-called 'positive Christianity'. In several parts of Germany Catholics were explicitly forbidden to become members of the Nazi Party, and Nazi members were forbidden to take part in such Church ceremonies as funerals. The Bishop of Mainz refused to admit Nazi Party members to the sacraments. In his New Year's message on 1 January 1931, the Presiding Bishop in Germany, Cardinal Bertram of Breslau, issued a warning against false prophets and agitators, declaring that extreme nationalism, by overglorifying the Race, could lead only to a despisal of the revelation and commandments of God. 'Away therefore with the vain imaginings of a national religious society, which is to be torn away from the Rock of Peter, and only guided by the racial theories of an Aryan-heathen teaching about salvation. This is no more than the foolish imaginings of false prophets.'[8]

Nevertheless, despite these warnings, large numbers of devout Catholics were giving their support to Hitler. In the previous decade, the political trend among Catholics had been towards the Right. In Bavaria particularly, the stronghold of Catholicism, the forces of conservatism had encouraged the spread of nationalistic and anti-democratic ideas, which in the 1920s meant the rejection of the Treaty of Versailles and the demand for the reversal of the verdicts of 1918, both internal and external. Some Catholics had romantic visions of their country as the focal point of a new Reich, which would rebuild the might of medieval Germany out of the political disorders and dissensions of the Weimar Republic. The promise of an organic state, free from the divisions of a politically pluralistic society, appealed to many Catholic thinkers, while others openly expressed their dislike of the whole tide of events since the French Revolution, which had introduced what they considered the dangerous heresies of liberalism, individualism, and democracy.[9] Fear of Communism and the rejection of everything that smacked of Marxist heresies became a standard feature in the pronouncements of Catholic speakers on political developments in Germany. Furthermore, some groups were led to support the growing claims of nationalist propaganda by a determination to show that they too could be as loyally German and nationalistic as anyone else. Such groups were peculiarly susceptible to the appeal of authoritarianism in the Nazi programme, and were not unsympathetic to the view that one of the chief beneficiaries of developments since 1918 had been the Jew.[10] Hitler did nothing to disillusion these potential supporters.

The Nazis, however, were not prepared meekly to suffer the official disapproval of the Catholic Church. Already the Party in

7

the provincial parliaments had opposed the introduction of Concordats for Baden and Prussia. When challenged to explain their
opposition in view of the Party's stand for 'positive Christianity',
their reply was that it was necessary, not because of religious
differences, but purely for political reasons. By this shrewd distinction between the spiritual and the political side of Catholicism,
Hitler was able to drive a wedge between the Catholic forces in
the country. The Catholic politicians of the Centre Party, and its
associate the Bavarian People's Party (BVP), no longer enjoyed the
full support of the Catholic episcopal hierarchy. The political
leaders of the Centre Party viewed with a mixture of distaste and
alarm the development of nationalistic right-wing tendencies in
German Catholicism. The aim of the Centre Party was to play a
moderating and mediating role in Germany's political life. Under
the leadership of Heinrich Brüning, Reich Chancellor from
1930–2, Catholic politicians, realizing that the very existence of
German parliamentary life was threatened by the growth of
extremism, whether of Right or of Left, formed during the 1920s
a coalition with the moderate Social Democrats, in a vain attempt
to halt the tide which eventually was to sweep away both the
Weimar Republic and the whole structure of democracy.

This coalition, however, was regarded with grave suspicion by
the German bishops. Under the influence of the Papal Nuncio,
Eugenio Pacelli, later Pope Pius XII, the German bishops had
discouraged any support of 'socialist' tendencies in the Church.
They regarded the politicians as playing with fire and as insuf-
ficiently under control. They therefore took no action to prevent
the overthrow of Chancellor Brüning in 1932, and raised no
protest when the Prussian Provincial government was forcibly
displaced by the nominally Catholic Reich Chancellor von Papen
a few months later. Indeed, the suspicion cannot be avoided that the
German bishops were not wholehearted in the defence of democracy, or indeed of the maintenance of their political associates.

Pressure on the bishops was also brought to bear by laymen who
supported parties more nationalistically inclined than the Centre
Party. Some were of the opinion that National Socialism might be
rescued from its anti-Christian attitude if Christian laymen were to

support its campaign for national renewal and the overthrow of the Bolshevik menace, and some Catholic priests encouraged their flocks to join Nazi organizations in order to Christianize them from within. Moreover, after 20 January 1933, many leading Catholics saw in the inclusion of von Papen as Vice-Chancellor in Hitler's Cabinet a convincing proof that an authoritarian system could be established on Christian lines. The hierarchy was therefore inclined to take issue with the Nazis only on ideological questions, at the same time stressing their own nationalistic sympathies, which were in general similar to those of the Nazis. Following the defeat of Brüning in 1932, the hierarchy received some comfort when the chairmanship of the Centre Party was placed in the hands of an ordained priest, Monsignor Ludwig Kaas, who might be expected to be susceptible to episcopal, and indeed to Papal, influence. From 1930 onwards Catholics were increasingly influenced by the Nazi propaganda, which claimed to be rescuing the Church from Communism, and many were carried away by the 'spirit of national renewal' which Hitler and his party appeared to embody.

Nevertheless, the official attitude of the Catholic Church on 30 January 1933 was one of reserve. With a few minor exceptions,[11] the Catholic clergy and laity had given no open support to the Nazi movement, and the Catholic doctrinal position remained unaltered.

A very different position prevailed in the Evangelical Churches. Here the Nazi Party had gained a substantial following not merely for its political ambitions, but, from a sizeable group of the Evangelical clergy, in the theoretical field as well. Taken as a whole, the Evangelical clergy were politically conservative, patriotic and paternalistic. Many were ardent monarchists; few had reconciled themselves to the establishment of the Weimar democracy and few had taken advantage of the new autonomy under the Weimar constitution. Increasingly they exerted their influence in the campaign to correct the so-called injustices of the Versailles Treaty, pouring scorn on the failures and weaknesses of the parliamentary government under which they were reluctantly obliged to live. Some, believing that democracy was, deservedly, a lost cause, were ready with theological arguments to justify the revival of authoritarianism.[12] Others welcomed the Nazis' overthrow of democracy as a first step towards the reintroduction of government by Christian authorities, affirming, with St Paul (*Romans* 13), that 'the powers that be are ordained of God'. Theologically, the events of the First World War had led to confusion and uncertainty among the Evangelicals. The prevailing liberalism of the school of Harnack had challenged the authority of Lutheran orthodoxy; yet the war had posed such doubts of liberal optimism that its proclamation could no longer be effective. A few theologians had adopted the rigorous neo-orthodoxy expounded by Karl Barth, but to the majority his theology was suspected because of his Calvinist background. Others had espoused the young ecumenical movement, but this too was suspected because of its possible 'socialist' and 'internationalist' connections. The desire for some new doctrine that would be conservative but not outdated, Lutheran but not tied to the sixteenth century, and above all German, prepared the way for a new theological attitude that could take into account the pulsating political forces which were affecting the whole life of the German people.

The search for a new and politically relevant theology had begun early in the 1920s, when a group of right-wing nationalist clergy had formed the Federation for a German Church (*Bund für eine Deutsche Kirche*), aimed at the theological justification of their country's aspirations and its desire for a restoration of national glory. Eagerly swallowing the nationalistic propaganda which ascribed Germany's recent defeat to internal enemies, principally the Jews, the Federation sought to give a purely German character to the Christian gospel. Under the continuing influence of the former Lutheran Court Preacher Adolf Stöcker, they believed that the future of German Lutheranism lay in obliterating the Jewish background of Christianity, and in creating a national religion based on the traditions of German Christianity. They repeatedly stressed Luther's anti-semitic statements and his abhorrence of democracy.[13] They believed that only by a return to the authoritarian patterns of former times could a renewal of national forces be achieved under Christian auspices. As early as 1931, Karl Barth, then

Professor of Systematic Theology in Bonn, had attacked what he described as hyphenated Christianity, in which the role of Christ Himself was linked with nationalist feelings. The nationalists claimed that twelve centuries of Christianity had left an ineradicable imprint on the German community, giving it its own particular identity and mission, and sealing it as the creation of Almighty Providence. It followed that not only in the Bible, but in the community also, could be found the measure of the truth of God's revelation. A national renaissance was possible only if the latent forces for good in the German community were re-mobilized: Luther's reformation would be finally completed by a national and spiritual re-assertion of Germany's power and strength.

Even more radical was the group known as the Thuringian German Christians (*Thüringer Deutsche Christen*). Here the most extreme nationalist claims found a home, largely because of inadequate Church discipline. The leaders of the movement, Pastors Julius Leutheuser, Joachim Hossenfelder and Siegfried Leffler, strove to convince their fellow clergy that only a completely new interpretation of Christianity, divested of the old orthodoxies, bureaucracies and rigidities of the Lutheran Church, could meet the needs of the new age. They sought to rid the Church of its 'pre-scientific' mentality and its archaic liturgies, and to substitute the new revelation as found in Adolf Hitler. The essential need was not Christian orthodoxy but Christian activism, that would follow the example of the 'heroic' Jesus. In place of pietistic preaching, they demanded the Church's complete commitment in political affairs. In the new creation of the Nazi Party, they saw a vehicle for their programme that offered the fellowship which they believed to be the characteristic of true Christianity. If Hitler could perform what they called Christian deeds, then orthodoxy could be abandoned. The Führer, they said, was 'the redeemer in the history of the Germans. Hitler stood there like a rock in a wide desert, like an island in an endless sea. In the darkest night of our Christian church history, Hitler became for our time that marvellous transparency, the window through which light fell on the history of Christianity.'[14] 'We put our trust in our God-sent Führer who was almost blinded when he heard God's call: "You must save Germany", and who, once his sight was restored, began that great work which led us to the wonderful day of 30 January 1933.'[15]

This uncritical devotion to the Nazi cause led Leutheuser and his followers to believe that they themselves would be the spiritual leaders of the Nazi political crusade for Germany's rebirth. They contrasted the Nazi appeal to the masses with the establishment-arianism and provincialism of the existing churches. They believed that the Nazi Party and the Church should hand in hand present themselves to the people to offer them one People, one God, one Nation and one Church.

More limited in their aims were the members of the 'Christian German Movement' (*Christlich Deutsche Bewegung*) founded by the Prussian pastor Werner Wilm, whose aim was to arouse in the Evangelical Church interest in political questions and support for right-wing politics. They were the first to welcome Nazi forma-tions to their churches and to take over chaplaincy responsibilities to such paramilitary organizations as the SA (*Sturmabteilung*).[16] Their efforts, however, incurred the disapproval of the Prussian Evangelical Church authorities, and in order to combat this opposition, an association under the direction of the Prussian Nazi leader, Wilhelm Kube, was formed to campaign in the 1932 Church elections. Joining forces with the Federation for a German Church and the Thuringian German Christians, the group, at Hitler's suggestion, became known as the Faith Movement of German Christians (*Glaubensbewegung Deutsche Christen*). In April 1932 Pastor Joachim Hossenfelder was made Reich leader of the movement, and in June their manifesto was published.[17]

For a time Hitler regarded this Faith Movement as a useful ally which served to disrupt the official establishment of the Churches and to sow confusion in the minds of their congregations. But their over-exuberant loyalty to himself and to the Nazi party was never reciprocated. Hitler continued to despise the whole body of Evangelical clergy without distinction, perceiving, quite rightly, that many of the leaders of the 'German Christians' were oppor-tunists who hoped to gain by political means the prizes of office which they had otherwise failed to secure. Nevertheless, he considered them as temporarily valuable to the Nazi cause and worthy of some appearance of support in order to foster their activities and so to disrupt the ranks of the Evangelical churches.

It was this widespread support from individual Christians that encouraged Hitler to hold in check the more extreme of his anti-Christian and anti-clerical followers. These reforming zealots were eager to profit by the campaigns against the rival political parties, and especially against the Centre Party, as a means of expressing their opposition to the Churches and the clergy. During 1931 and 1932 so much alarm had been caused in church circles by the nihilistic tendencies of the SA that Hitler was at some pains to explain these excesses as due to 'spontaneous' outbursts of resentment against the Catholic Church's prohibition of membership in the Nazi Party. So long as the Catholic Church adopted such a hostile line towards the Nazi Party, he declared, such unfortunate occurrences were bound to occur. He was, moreover, equally ready to disavow Rosenberg's *Myth of the Twentieth Century*, which he described as a purely personal work, unsupported and unauthorized by the Nazi Party.[18] Hitler openly refused to support one of his staunchest lieutenants, the Thuringian *Gauleiter*, Arthur Dinter, in his efforts to propagate his own ideology under the title of a 'German People's Church'. Nor, as we have seen, did he in any way encourage the activities of his former partner, General Ludendorff. As for the rest of Hitler's followers, their opinions varied from complete rejection of Christianity to indifferent approval of the Churches' claims. It was not until later that significant differences with regard to the future place of Christianity in Germany were to occur within the Nazi Party.

Conscious of the appeal which his anti-Communist crusade was making amongst churchmen, Hitler repeatedly stressed the need for both Catholics and Protestants to stand side by side with the Nazi Party in bringing about a national revival against the forces of 'international Communism'. In contrast to the revolutionary atheism of Communism, Nazism appeared to offer an authoritarian Christian structure which, modelled on the example of

13

Mussolini's Fascist Party, would come to terms with the Church as Mussolini had done in the Lateran Treaty of 1929. Many churchmen were thus able to harbour the illusion, even after the assumption of Nazi power in 1933, that the anti-clerical outbursts, the suppression of the freedom of the individual, the employment of spies, the creation of forced-labour and concentration camps, and the censorship of the press, were only temporary measures necessary in a time of revolution, all of which would disappear once a strong authoritarian government had been established.

It is therefore understandable that 30 January 1933 was regarded as a day of liberation by large numbers of German Protestants who had long despised and rejected the democracy of the Weimar Republic. Hitler was widely believed to be more moderate and more responsible than his followers. Indeed, in many nominally Protestant households there was the innocent belief that Hitler, like Bismarck, was essentially a 'pious' man, piety being a characteristic of all Germany's historic leaders.[19] Hitler was careful to foster such illusions. He never officially 'left' the Church and he continued to pay the compulsory Church taxes. In the first years of power he attended several Catholic Church services, including the Requiem for the Polish dictator Marshal Pilsudski in Berlin Cathedral in 1935. Photographs of his presence on such occasions and his frequent references to 'Providence' in his speeches were designed to show his respect for Christian values. For the large majority of Protestants and Catholics, such manifestations justified them in resuming their traditional attitude of support for the State, an attitude which had been shaken by some aspects of the Weimar régime. The 'protective authoritarianism' of the Nazi state and the 'pious' qualities of its leaders were regarded as safeguards against political atheism or subversion.

In seeking to understand the almost incredible blindness of churchmen to the spread of Nazi totalitarianism, this attitude of mind, so deeply ingrained, particularly among the Protestants, must be taken into account. It alone explains the pathetic confidence which innumerable churchmen could maintain, even as late as 1945, that Hitler had never meant the Church any harm. As a contemporary American witness reported in 1934:

There is almost unanimity [among churchmen] in standing by Hitler. Many reasons for it appear. They have confidence in him. They feel the need of a strong hand upon the nation. They believe in his sincerity and in his unselfish interest in nation and people. More than one churchman emphasized Hitler's personal integrity and his belief in a moral character for the State, his success in breaking down classes and in developing unity among them. . . . It was interesting to hear a lifelong National Liberal like Walter Simons, former President of the Republic and former Chief Justice of the Supreme Court[20] express confidence in Hitler, adding that 'National Socialism, with all its errors, has saved us from Bolshevism'. There you have the main ground for Christian support of Hitler or of National Socialism or of both.[21]

It was to strengthen such confidence that Hitler on 1 February 1933, among many reassuring promises of continuity between the old and the new régimes, declared that

the National Government will support and defend the foundations on which the strength of our nation is built. It will seek firmly to protect Christianity as the basis of our whole morality, and the family as the nucleus of the life of our people and our community.[22]

That his true intentions were quite different can be gathered from the following conversation with his associate Hermann Rauschning shortly after his assumption of power.

Neither of the denominations – Catholic or Protestant, they are both the same – has any future left. At least not for the Germans. Fascism may perhaps make its peace with the Church in God's name. I will do it too. Why not? But that won't stop me stamping out Christianity in Germany, root and branch. One is either a Christian or a German. You can't be both.[23]

Early in 1933, while he still maintained that his task was not that of a religious reformer, Hitler's strategy against the Churches was evolved on a pragmatic basis. As he later remarked:

In my youth, I took the view: dynamite. Later I realized that one can't break the Church over one's knee. It has to be left to rot like a gangrenous limb. . . . But the healthy youth belong to us.[24]

In the first months of his power, Hitler was influenced in part by the possible dangers of an immediate policy of 'dynamite', and in

15

part by his belief that a campaign against the Church would not be needed. As an ideological opponent the Church was, he believed, no longer relevant and could be left to die. He saw it only as a society for fulfilling certain spiritual needs which would not be required by the stronger, more heroic, Germans of the future. In his view, the Christian faith was long out of date, its ethical position no longer tenable, its customs the relics of a bygone age. As an institution the Church was useful only for the propagation of certain desirable policies.

Do you really believe the masses will ever be Christian again? Nonsense! Never again. That tale is finished. No one will listen to it again. But we can hasten matters. The parsons will be made to dig their own graves. They will betray their God to us. They will betray anything for the sake of their miserable little jobs and incomes.[25]

It was not until later, when he encountered unexpected and stubborn resistance from the Churches, that Hitler's indifference turned to a hatred that led him to decide on their complete destruction. For the moment it was only the extreme anti-Christian members of the Nazi Party who called for a campaign against the Church. Tactical considerations, and the confident belief that the Churches would be ready to make terms with the new régime, dictated Hitler's policy during the first months of his power.

The month of February 1933 was spent by the Nazis in taking over the key positions of government, particularly in the police forces, from which they were later to dominate the whole country. Their first moves, as might be expected, were directed to the consolidation of their political control. With characteristic astuteness, at the same time as their first measures were taken against their political opponents, including the leaders of the Communist Party, they announced the holding of new elections on 5 March. Confidently believing that the elimination of the Communists from active politics would be welcomed by the majority of Germans, Hitler justified his measures by stressing the need to defend Christianity and the Christian culture of Germany by the removal of such atheistic and materialistic elements. As Bernhard Rust, the newly-appointed Minister for Education in Prussia, proclaimed in his inaugural address:

For one hundred and fifty years, during the wars of religion, we were, as a people and empire, almost destroyed. Today we find ourselves in a bitter struggle for our existence against Bolshevism. I appeal to Christians of both denominations to join us against this enemy in defence of their living faith, their values and their customs.[26]

What Hitler needed from these new elections was not merely a working majority in the Reichstag, but total control. There can be no doubt that the Reichstag fire of 27 February was exploited for that purpose alone. With great skill the Nazi propagandists set themselves to demonstrate that here was a diabolical attempt to reduce Germany to anarchy while Hitler was appealing for national unity at the polls. Even more significantly, on 28 February, the day after the Reichstag fire, Hitler persuaded President Hindenburg to issue, under the emergency powers of the Weimar Constitution, an ordinance which was effectively to remove personal freedom from all German citizens. Under the plea of preventing Communist terrorist activities, the ordinance annulled the seven articles of the Weimar Constitution which safeguarded the freedom of the individual, the rights of free speech, the rights of meeting and assembly, and the security of the citizen from house searches or from interference with his postal, telegraph and telephone communications. This was the measure which was later used to justify most of the police measures against the Churches.

Nevertheless, despite the intensive propaganda that followed the Reichstag fire, Hitler failed to gain an absolute majority in the March elections. This decided him to adopt the still more revolutionary plan of doing away with Parliament altogether, by means of an Enabling Bill that would give the government the entire legislative powers in the country. To pass such a bill the support of at least two-thirds of the Reichstag was required, and the Nazi Party and Hugenberg's right-wing National Party together could not muster the necessary numbers. Despite the incarceration of the Communist members and the promise of Goering that a sufficient number of socialists would likewise be put out of the way, Hitler was anxious to obtain more positive support. The Centre Party, for long the stronghold of the Catholics of Germany, which, together with the Bavarian People's Party, represented 13.9 per cent of the voting population, he regarded both as an obstacle to be overcome and as a group to be seduced. He shrewdly and rightly calculated that the best method of achieving both these ends was to influence the men behind the Centre Party, namely the bishops of the Catholic Church, and even the Vatican itself.[27] If he could prevail upon the bishops to induce the Centre Party to support the proposed Enabling Bill, or even to drop their support of the Centre Party in favour of the Nazis, then the necessary legislation could be passed in a blaze of national unity.

The bishops, however, were not yet convinced of the sincerity of the Nazis' intentions. Their pastoral letters before the elections almost unanimously condemned Nazism, at least in theory. The first month of the Nazi régime had brought in a flood of reports of illegal and near terroristic activities against political opponents, including the Catholics. Officials were dismissed to make room for members of the Party; the Press was brought under control; the radio stations were directed to support the Nazi election campaign; and the tone of Nazi speeches was both alarming and intimidating. On 10 March, Cardinal Bertram wrote to President Hindenburg expressing the growing concern and fears of the Catholic population over what he described as 'the precipitate events of recent days'.[28]

Such doubts, however, were not voiced in public, and the leader of the Centre Party, Monsignor Kaas, proved to be more pliable than had been expected. His motives have still to be fully clarified.[29] Undoubtedly he was influenced by the desire of the Vatican that the anti-Communist front should not be disrupted by an open breach between the Nazis and the Centre Party. Undoubtedly, too, he saw that there was no future for an opposition party in the authoritarian society at which he believed Hitler to be aiming. On the day after the March elections, he approached Papen and offered to draw a line under the past, so that the Centre Party too could join in the work of national renewal. Although some members of the Centre Party, like ex-Chancellor Brüning, were sceptical of any such collaboration, Kaas was able to persuade most of his colleagues to agree to a discussion with Hitler over possible terms. This discussion took place on 20 March. By promising to set up a small committee to review the effects of the proposed Enabling Bill, Hitler was able to gain assurance of the Centre Party's support. Whether or not any mention was made of suitable concessions to the Catholic Church is uncertain, but the hope, at any rate, was sufficient to lead Kaas to recommend to his party that they should give the new government a chance. In a further conversation with Kaas, Hitler was ready to promise that there would be no alteration in the powers of the provincial governments, and no interference either with the judiciary or with more than the minimum of civil service posts (promises which were all repudiated within a year) but he made it clear that he intended to take strong measures against Communists and fellow-travellers wherever they might be, and he hoped that Kaas and the Centre Party would not be found on the wrong side. Furthermore, should the Centre Party want any further assurances, he promised to include them in his first Reichstag speech if they were submitted in time. Accordingly, in the late evening of 22 March a letter, formulated by Kaas and Brüning and containing demands for the safeguarding of the constitutional status of the Church, and of the Weimar Constitution, was sent to Hitler. No reply was ever received.[30]

On the previous day, 21 March, Hitler had arranged an impressive spectacle for the opening of the new session of the Reichstag in the Garrison Church at Potsdam. The aim of the occasion was to strengthen the hopes of the conservative classes of Germany that the new régime even if authoritarian, was ready to act with responsibility. There can be no doubt that its object was triumphantly achieved. The pomp and splendour of the ceremony, the honour and respect paid to the aged President, the address by General Superintendent Dibelius, and the parades with all the nationalist insignia were convincing evidence that, despite all contrary indications of the previous weeks, National Socialism was demonstrating its national conservatism. In the ranks of the Churches, doubts over the Nazis' racial ideas and political nihilism were allayed by the impression of national unity. The 'Day of Potsdam' was looked upon as the beginning of a fruitful restoration of the unity of Church and State.

This favourable impression was further strengthened when, two days later, in his first statement on Government policy to the new Reichstag, Hitler pronounced the assurances for which many had long been waiting.

By its decision to carry out the political and moral cleansing of our public life, the Government is creating and securing the conditions for a really deep and inner religious life. The advantages for the individual which may be derived from compromises with atheistic organizations do not compare in any way with the consequences which are visible in the destruction of our common religious and ethical values. The national Government sees in both Christian denominations the most important factor for the maintenance of our society. It will observe the agreements drawn up between the Churches and the provinces; their rights will not be touched. The Government however hopes and expects that the task of national and ethical renewal of our people, which it has set itself, will receive the same respect by the other side. The Government will treat all other denominations with objective and impartial justice. It cannot however tolerate allowing membership of a certain denomination or of a certain race being used as a release from all common legal obligations or as a blank cheque for unpunishable behaviour or for the toleration of crimes. [The national Government will allow and confirm to the Christian denominations the enjoyment of their due influence in schools and education.] And it will be concerned for the sincere cooperation between Church and State. The struggle against the materialistic ideology and for the erection of a true people's community (*Volksgemeinschaft*) serves as much the interests of the German nation as of our Christian faith . . .
The national Government, seeing in Christianity the unshakable foundation of the moral and ethical life of our people, attaches utmost importance to the cultivation and maintenance of the friendliest relations with the Holy See . . . The rights of the churches will not be curtailed; their position in relation to the State will not be changed.[31]

Hitler fully realized the risk he was taking by such conservative utterances, the very success of which might prove to be a hindrance to his later freedom of action. Indeed, had the Churches been able to insist that his promises were kept, the whole Nazi claim to total power would have been challenged if not prevented. As Hitler himself acknowledged later, he had had to face this danger at the time.[32] Nevertheless, with his intuitive understanding of the political forces at work among his opponents, he calculated, quite rightly, that he would be able to outflank the Church's leaders, and in his own time, when his political grip was more secure, would be able to revoke the concessions which he now appeared to offer so generously.[33]

The immediate effect of his pronouncements was to place the Catholic bishops in an extremely difficult position. In face of these far-reaching promises, could the opposition of the Catholic Church to the Nazi revolution be maintained? Only a few days previously, Cardinal Bertram had expressed his confidence that it could. On 18 March he told Papen that the Church had clearly stated its reasons for opposition:

1. Because certain parts of the official party programme, as they are stated and must clearly be so interpreted, contain errors of doctrine.

2. Because the statements of numerous representatives and publicists of the Party are of a hostile character in that they oppose fundamental teachings and doctrines of the Catholic Church, and these statements have never been denied or withdrawn by the highest officers of the Party; in particular this was in regard to the questions of the denominational schools, Christian marriage and other matters.

3. It was the united opinion of the Catholic clergy and the loyal Catholic defenders of the Church's interests in public life, that if the Nazi Party succeeded in gaining the so hotly desired totality of power in Germany, that this would only offer the gloomiest prospects for the Church interests of the Catholics. . . .

In short, he added, if there is to be any revision of attitudes, these must come from the leader of the Nazis himself.[34]

Within a week, the situation had changed. The leaders of the Centre Party had made their peace with the régime; Cardinal Faulhaber, after a short visit to Rome, had brought back no hopes of support for opposition from the Vatican;[35] and now continued resistance would be very difficult to explain to the Catholic masses, who implicitly accepted Hitler's pledges. Moreover, it appeared likely that the mass appeal of the Nazi campaign might succeed in persuading thousands, even millions, to leave the

Church. In the face of such promises, continued opposition could serve only to brand the Bishops as the 'black reactionaries' which the anti-clericals had always considered them to be. In a word, opposition would drive the Catholic Church into a sort of ghetto and force it into a *Kulturkampf* similar to that which it had experienced under Bismarck. Indeed, as many Catholics pointed out, Nazism contained the same combination of nationalist slogans, humanistic anti-clericalism and utopianism as had been used by the Church's enemies under Bismarck. The bishops shrank from another such experience. The Church, they believed, was incapable of surviving such a challenge, particularly against a government potentially far more powerful than Bismarck's. Only in recent years had they succeeded in overcoming the feelings of persecution and inferiority which the years of the *Kulturkampf* had induced. Perhaps, they felt, Hitler could after all be trusted. Perhaps he could be persuaded of the value of Catholic support in a joint campaign against Communism and moral decadence. Perhaps he might be prevailed upon to accept the assistance of the Catholic Church and its many associated organs, in the reconstruction of an ordered unified society.

In view of the heated political atmosphere it was impossible to sit on the side-lines and wait. Accordingly on 25 March, only two days after Hitler's Reichstag speech, Cardinal Bertram addressed a circular to all the bishops, seeking their advice:

The necessity for instructions to the clergy has become urgent. The number of questions asked about our attitude in the present stage of the Nazi movement are everywhere flowing in ... Motives for haste: (1) To wait and see whether the Government will fulfil all the excellent promises made in the Chancellor's programme speech could lead to a delay of years before any clear attitude was taken. Nothing worse than that. That is why I believe it is good for us to use this opportunity to go as far as we can without contravening the faith or canon law. (2) In Catholic cities, where closed formations of the SA are now not allowed to attend Catholic church services, church attendance is none the less made obligatory by their commanders. The Catholic members, in as far as they are dependent upon the SA for their bread and their clothing, go in great crowds to the Protestant Churches. This will only increase.

(3) In the enclosed suggestions nothing should be included against the faith or the canon law. Purely disciplinary standards can be adapted for the better saving of souls.

Please reply by Wednesday afternoon . . .[36]

Three days later sufficient agreement had been reached for a joint statement to be issued:

The Bishops of Germany's dioceses, for good reasons which have been repeatedly explained, in their dutiful care for the purity of the Catholic faith and the protection of the tasks and rights of the Catholic Church, have in recent years adopted a negative attitude towards the Nazi movement, through prohibitions and warnings, which are to remain in force so long as the reasons for them continue.

We can now recognize that the highest representative of the Reich government, who at the same time is the authoritarian leader of his movement, has given open and impressive declarations, in which the inviolability of the Catholic doctrines and the immutable tasks and rights of the Church are acknowledged. So too the treaties made by the individual provinces with the Church are explicitly guaranteed in their entirety. Without revoking the judgments of our previous statements against certain religious and ethical errors, the episcopate nevertheless believes it can now cherish the hope that the previous general warnings and prohibitions need no longer be considered necessary.[37]

Whether this sudden change of attitude was dictated by an effort to save the Church from persecution or by the hope of influencing the Nazi régime towards a national rather than a revolutionary goal, there can be no doubt that Hitler was exultant. For Hitler too feared a *Kulturkampf*, particularly so soon after his assumption of power. Not only did this expression of collaboration open the way for Nazi infiltration into the Catholic ranks, but it also meant that the Church hierarchy, having adopted their new position, would be unable to recreate the kind of political organization that had been used to mobilize the Catholic opposition to Bismarck. Deprived of the support of the Catholic Bishops, the Centre Party could be dealt with effectively. Equally significantly, without the Centre Party the Catholic bishops could be driven out of the political arena for ever. That was the first of Hitler's goals.

It is now easy to see that political resistance by the German

Catholics against the Nazis was never a practical proposition. But to Hitler, in 1933, it appeared a very real danger. 'Political Catholicism' was to his mind the only reason why the Church had survived for so long. The power of the Church, both in Germany and throughout the rest of the world, was a factor which he had to take into account. The readiness of the Bishops to make concessions had therefore to be seized upon as the opportunity to clip their political wings. Cardinal Bertram had already stated in his letter to President Hindenburg that 'The Church for her part holds herself aloof from purely political affairs and has no associations with political campaign organizations'[38]; Hitler had noted this disclaimer even if he did not believe it. Now was the time to put it to the proof.

It was in this atmosphere that Papen approached Hitler with the suggestion that the Nazi government should re-open the question of a Concordat with the Vatican.[39] In his memoirs Papen declares that he was motivated solely by the desire to strengthen the guarantees given by Hitler on 23 March, and to safeguard the future policy of the new government from the anti-clericalism of his extremer Nazi comrades. A Concordat, covering the whole Reich, would give the Catholic Church a legal status never before enjoyed, and would strengthen the impression abroad that the Nazi régime was to be trusted as a staunch member of the anti-Communist front.[40] Hitler concurred with Papen's idea, and agreed that Papen should himself go the following week to Rome. If resistance were encountered in the Vatican, the whole attempt could be disavowed as a personal effort on Papen's own initiative; if, on the other hand, in return for a few tactical concessions on minor points, which Hitler would not consider binding if inconvenient, the Papacy could be induced to sign a Concordat, the resulting political gains, both at home and abroad, would be considerable.

Papen's efforts were certainly due in part to his desire to justify to his fellow Catholics his over-enthusiastic support for the Nazi Party – upon which, it must be remembered, the prohibition of the Church had lain until 28 March, and in part to his hope of raising his own status in Hitler's régime. To his surprise his reception in Rome was extremely favourable. The former Papal Nuncio in Germany, Cardinal Pacelli, now advanced to the position of Cardinal Secretary of State, declared himself ready to enter into negotiations with the Nazi government. His readiness to consider Papen's suggestions was undoubtedly influenced by the presence in Rome of Msgr Kaas, who on 7 April had abandoned Germany and the Centre Party for ever.[41] Papen's instructions as to the concessions which could be made to the Church were vague, but on the demand that the clergy should be prohibited from intervening in political affairs they were specific. Kaas and Pacelli, on the other side, were ready to agree that the Centre Party's position could hardly be maintained after the passing of the Enabling Law. To Pacelli, at least, the Church's interests were far better defended in the ecclesiastical than in the political field. Both sides, however, were ready for mutual accommodation. Pacelli therefore produced a draft agreement similar, if not identical, to the one proposed by Rome, but refused by the Reich government in 1929. To everyone's surprise it was almost completely accepted in Berlin, and negotiations were immediately set in train to cover the numerous technical points.

In order to maintain the pretence of benevolent interest in the renewal of Church life, Hitler issued instructions that nothing must be done to jeopardize the possible conclusion of a Concordat with the Vatican. The reversal of the German Bishops' previous attitude of hostility must be confirmed by fair words and promises. Accordingly, on 26 April Hitler granted an interview to Bishop Berning of Osnabrück, a firm, nationally-minded Conservative. He was 'most hurt', Hitler told the Bishop, 'to hear accusations that he was opposed to Christianity', for he was convinced that without Christianity neither personal life nor a State could be built up, and the German State without the Christian Church was unimaginable. 'I am personally convinced of the great power and deep significance of Christianity, and I won't allow any other religion to be promoted. That is why I have turned away from Ludendorff and that is why I reject that book by Rosenberg. It was written by a Protestant. It is not a Party book. It was not written by him as a Party man. The Protestants can be left to argue with him . . . As a Catholic I never feel comfortable in the Evangelical Church or its structures. That is why I will have great difficulty if I try to regulate the affairs of the Protestant churches. The evangelical people or the Protestants will in any case reject me. But you can be sure: I will protect the rights and freedoms of the churches and not let them be touched, so that you need have no fears about the future of the Church.'

Hitler was also ready to discuss with the Bishop his views on the Jewish question: 'As for the Jews, I am just carrying on with the same policy which the Catholic church has adopted for fifteen hundred years, when it has regarded the Jews as dangerous and pushed them into ghettos etc., because it knew what the Jews were like. I don't put race above religion, but I do see the dangers in the representatives of this race for Church and State, and perhaps I am doing Christianity a great service.'[42] The Bishop's answer is not recorded.

The same fair words are evident in a letter from Hitler to Cardinal Bertram two days later. He promised the Cardinal the good will and support of the new government, expressed his regrets at the attacks on the priests – which were solely the result of the bitter experiences of the Nazis before 1933 – and undertook to carry out an investigation of all complaints.[43]

It is significant of the attitude of the Bishops at the time that they allowed these specious promises to allay whatever doubts they may still have had on the desirability of a Concordat. The more enthusiastic among them were prepared to believe that Hitler had 'revealed' his true attitude to Bishop Berning, that the Nazi Government would soon settle down to a conservative authoritarianism, and that a relationship with the church could be established along Italian lines. The more sceptical hoped that the terms of the Concordat would be sufficiently specific on the legal rights of the Church as to pin the Nazis down. Both enthusiasts and sceptics were reconciled to the abandonment of their political influence through the Centre and Bavarian People's Parties. As already suggested, there was some tension on this point between the clergy and laity. On 3 May Cardinal Bertram sought to reassure the clergy that the new government sincerely desired the aid of the Church in a joint campaign against Marxism, atheism and immorality. 'The Church is not to be pushed back into the sacristy, but it is expected to accomplish through its own intellectual and spiritual resources what the state seeks to do for the recovery of the nation by way of the political power at its command. To do such Catholic work no new invitation is necessary for us.'[44] Three days later the Cardinal informed Hitler that the Church was 'aware of its sacred duty to deepen in the hearts of the faithful that respect and obedience towards the constituted authorities which was a religious virtue, and to lead all segments of the people to make sacrifices and to participate in the promotion of the common good'.[45]

Undoubtedly the prospect of substantially improved conditions for the Church in the non-political field encouraged the clergy to accept what they regarded as a loss of lesser significance. Moreover, many of them were alarmed by the progress of events in the Evangelical Churches. The efforts to promote a new Reich Church that would combine the various Lutheran and Reformed groups might be a stepping-stone to the proclamation of a single established Reich Church, with the consequent extinction of the other churches, or at any rate their reduction to a position of inferior legal status. This indeed was what the more extreme of the 'German Christians' were already demanding, remembering the slogans of Bismarck's days. In order to combat such dreams of Protestant supremacy, the Catholics must hasten the signing of a Concordat, in the hope that it would give them a hitherto unrecognized national status.[46]

Hitler, on his part, was interested in promoting a Reich Concordat solely for the sake of political concessions from the Vatican. In the telegrams from Berlin to the German negotiators in Rome the need for prohibiting the clergy from any activity in political matters was repeatedly stressed.[47] On 2 July Papen in Rome was able to report to Hitler as follows:

Article 32: Finally brings the solution which you have wished, Chancellor, whereby the Holy See issues regulations for excluding membership and activity in political parties for all members [of the clergy] and people belonging to Orders [*für alle Mitglieder und*

27

Ordensleute]. In this regard it is simply stated that similar regulations are to be made for the other denominations . . .[48]

The German negotiators also insisted on the inclusion of an article narrowly defining the role of the Catholic organizations. Only if they were dedicated to purely religious activities could they receive the protection and legal status afforded by the Concordat. This, as Papen gleefully pointed out, would apply only if such associations were declared by the Episcopate to be members of Catholic Action, an organization which excluded all but non-political and purely religious associations. The wording of the paragraph left for later definition the grounds on which an association could be designated as purely religious – a fatal omission, which enabled the Nazis to proceed forthwith against such organizations as the Catholic Trade Unions and youth and professional groups before they could be protected under the terms of the Concordat.

These negotiations with the Catholic Church were not welcomed by the more fanatical element of the Nazi Party, which consisted of two distinct groups. On the one hand there were those who objected to Christianity for ideological reasons, and whose doubts were restrained only by the conviction that Hitler's support for a Reich Concordat or indeed for any form of Christianity, was no more than a temporary disguise for his real intentions towards the Churches and the clergy.

Much more virulent, however, was the hatred expressed by the revolutionary wing of the Party, which had its stronghold in the ranks of the SA. The leaders of the SA had imagined that the take-over of power by the Nazis would lead to a wholesale destruction of the existing order in State and society. Particularly in Bavaria, where the SA had its strongest support, this revolutionary corps of armed thugs wanted to establish itself as a vigilante group whose function would be 'to guarantee the success of the Nazi revolution, by acting forcibly against any persons or institutions not sufficiently active in propagating Nazi views'. In many parts of the country, SA commanders installed themselves as Commissars, and exercised jurisdiction unlimited by established law or the established organs of government. They claimed to be the most loyal followers of the Führer and to possess a kind of telepathic understanding of his desires and purposes, which made their persons sacrosanct, their decisions infallible, and their demands the consequence of the categorical spirit of the revolution. These revolutionary elements saw in the priests and laity of the Catholic Church the agents of reaction and the old social order, whose intimidation and persecution would be essential. The close association of the Catholic Church with the former Centre Party gave a political justification to which was added the endemic anti-clericalism of their nihilist origins.

These coercive acts were strengthened and supported by the swiftly-growing Bavarian Political Police, now taken over by Heinrich Himmler, and his assistant Heydrich, who had already laid their plans for a wholesale attack upon the Catholic clergy. These men were not so convinced, as Hitler appeared to be, that the Catholic clergy would follow the example of so many of their Evangelical brethren and become the willing mouthpieces of Nazi policy. More decisive measures were needed. Some well-known opponents of Nazism amongst the Catholic clergy had already been arrested and manhandled. Rectories had been searched by the police. Catholic organizations had been inhibited or forced to go into voluntary liquidation. Attempts had been made to abolish Catholic parish schools.[49] Diocesan property had been confiscated, and anyone who protested had been openly abused. Catholic civil servants had been dismissed, and the Catholic press had been compelled to conform to Nazi requirements. A particularly blatant example of the inconsistency between Nazi professions at Rome and their practices at home was witnessed on 8 June when a large meeting of the Kolping Society, a Catholic Young Men's Organization, which was to be addressed in Munich by no less a person than von Papen himself, was broken up and finally abandoned because of attacks upon the members by units of the Hitler Youth, the SA, and the Bavarian Political Police. A few days later, under the provisions of the President's Order for the Protection and Safety of the Reich of 28 February, Himmler ordered all public meetings in Bavaria to be forbidden until further notice. There can be no doubt that this order was aimed at the Catholic Church in anticipation of some form of political protest against the imminent demise of the Centre Party and the conclusion of a Concordat.

In a second instruction to the police authorities dated 20 June, Himmler stipulated that two exceptions could be made to the general prohibition: (i) for meetings of the Nazi Party and its organizations, and (ii) for purely religious church activities, such as pilgrimages or processions, but not for activities of a secular nature.[50] On 1 July Dr Ley, the head of the newly established German Labour Front, launched a violent attack against both Evangelical and Catholic labour unions, charging them with hostility to the State, and demanding their immediate liquidation.[51] To hasten the imminent dissolution of the Bavarian People's Party, orders were issued on 28 June for the arrest of nearly 200 prominent Catholics including over 100 priests. They were not released until after the Bavarian People's Party was dissolved on 4 July.

Hitler, though recognizing that these moves against the Church might endanger the negotiations in Rome, nevertheless did nothing to stop them. He calculated that such assaults might be a useful means of bringing pressure to bear on the Vatican to hasten the conclusion of the Concordat. As Cardinal Pacelli himself acknowledged two months later, 'A pistol had been pointed at his head and he had had no alternative. The German Government had offered him concessions ... wider than any previous German Government would have agreed to, and he had to choose between an agreement on their lines and the virtual elimination of the Catholic Church in the Reich.'[52] This threat to the spiritual and physical welfare of twenty million German Catholics induced Pacelli to sign the Concordat, while Papen smoothly promised that in return Hitler would effect a complete reconciliation between the Catholic populace and the Reich Government, and put an end forever to the conflicts of the past. It is unlikely that either side believed that such a promise would be kept, but it served to secure for Hitler his desired goal of eliminating the Catholic Church as an effectual political force.[53]

In the meantime, Hitler's early professions of support for the Churches were being received with enthusiasm in the ranks of the Evangelical churches. The 'German Christians' believed that their aspirations were about to be realized and that a new dawn for the Church had begun. Now they felt, was the hour for the re-Christianizing of Germany; now was the time when backsliders who had sunk into a state of apathy or hostility – particularly those who had been seduced by the claims of Marxism – could be led to see that their true loyalty was to Hitler, to Germany, and to the German Church. The 'German Christians', not unnaturally, read far more into Hitler's words than they warranted. The State, they hoped, would support the revitalization of the Church, and in return the Church would loyally support the revitalization of the State. On 3 April the first National Conference of the 'Faith Movement of German Christians' met in Berlin, at which enthusiasm for national renewal was expressed by speaker after speaker. The concluding resolution was formulated to affirm both the loyalty of the 'German Christians' to the new State and the tasks which they saw ahead:

God has created me a German, the German way of life (*Deutschtum*) is the gift of God, God wills that I should fight for my Germany. War service is in no case a forcing of the Christian conscience, but obedience before God. The faithful Christian has the right to practise revolution against a state which is promoting the powers of darkness ... For a German, the Church is the community of believers who are obligated to fight for a Christian Germany. The aim of the Faith Movement of German Christians is an Evangelical German Reich Church. Adolf Hitler's State appeals to the Church, the Church must obey the appeal.[54]

The sort of appeal that would be made by Adolf Hitler's State had been adumbrated only a few days earlier, when on 1 April the first Nazi measure against citizens of Jewish origin was begun by the organization of a boycott of all Jewish shops throughout the country. The 'Central Committee for the Prevention of Jewish-organized boycotts or Atrocities', whose leader was Julius Streicher, *Gauleiter* of Nuremberg and editor of the violently anti-semitic and pornographic journal *Der Stürmer*, was given the task of establishing action committees. Goebbels, the newly appointed

Minister of Propaganda and Public Enlightenment, mobilized his staff for this dissemination of anti-semitic propaganda, and Hitler declared in the Cabinet meeting of 28 March that 'these preventive measures had to be organized, or else the people would take it upon themselves to show their feelings, and this could easily lead to undesirable developments'.[55]

Accordingly, on 1 April, in all the major cities placards were placed on Jewish shop windows: 'Don't buy from the Jews; Germans take care!' Uniformed men of the SA and the SS stood on guard outside the shop entrances. Columns of SA men marched through the streets, seizing Jews and subjecting them to physical violence. Goebbels spoke in inflammatory terms, justifying the boycott, and in thousands of 'spontaneous' gatherings, in cities and towns and even in the smallest villages, anti-semitic feelings were aroused and excited by Nazi agitators. That such lawlessness and anarchy so blatantly promoted would be condemned by the Churches seemed inevitable. Yet two days later General Superintendent Dibelius, in a broadcast to the United States, appeared, not to condemn, but to excuse what had happened. He gave expression to a widely-held opinion among Evangelical Churchmen that the measures against the Jews were perfectly justified in view of the agitation against Germany's new government roused abroad by people who were still filled with the hatred engendered by the World War. The boycott was conducted, he said, 'in conditions of complete law and order', and, he contended, was the best way to put an end to anti-German feelings held by persons who did not personally know the conditions in Germany.[56]

The boycott met with only a limited response from the German people. Nevertheless no opposition ensued, and within a week, under the Enabling Act, the Nazi government passed the Civil Service Reconstruction Law, which prohibited the employment of Jews in the Civil Service. This was the law that later led to indignant protests from sections of the Evangelical Church when its application to the pastors was demanded.

It is an indication of the widely varying attitudes in the Nazi ranks towards the Evangelical Church that, at the same time as many high-ranking Nazis, including Goering and Frick, the

Minister of the Interior, were openly giving support to the Faith Movement of German Christians, the more radical wing of the Nazi Party was engaged upon plans for a very different future for the Church. In many areas, the local Nazi leaders had already begun to wage a campaign against the Churches. In eastern Pomerania, the SA were conducting an anti-clerical propaganda campaign supported by members of Ludendorff's Tannenberg League. In Bavaria, incidents against Catholic priests and Catholic institutions were increasingly frequent. On 18 April, the new Reich leader of the German Farmers, Darré, an ardent disciple of Rosenberg, published in the Nazi paper of the small province of Mecklenburg, an article by a certain Walther Bohm entitled 'Farmers, conquer the Church!'[57] This piece of pamphleteering, designed to arouse the farmers against payment of the customary church dues and accusing the clergy of living off the fat of the land without a care for the needs of the people, would ordinarily have gone unnoticed; but it was used by the Governor of Mecklenburg, Granzow, as an excuse for an immediate take-over by the State of all the Church's affairs. For this purpose, on 22 April Granzow appointed none other than the author of the article in question as State Commissioner for the Evangelical Church in Mecklenburg–Schwerin, to co-ordinate the church authorities with those of the State. This usurpation of power for such a revolutionary purpose, in contravention of Hitler's promises of less than a month before, brought a wave of protests not only to Hitler and Frick, but to President Hindenburg himself as the 'Protector' of the Church. Hitler probably knew nothing of his subordinates' plans, which in no way coincided with his own shrewder calculations of the political odds; and, as he was not yet ready to abandon his tactical placating of the Churches, Frick was instructed to restore the situation to 'normal' and to reverse the Governor's appointment. Hitler himself received the Bishop of Mecklenburg and promised him full independence in the running of the Church's affairs. The Bishop in reply issued a long statement expressing his full confidence in Hitler's assurances and his intention of joining the Nazi Party immediately.[58]

The incident is noteworthy in that it contained all the elements of the future confrontation. The extremists in the Nazi Party were prepared to use force to obtain their ends, regardless of law or tradition; Hitler was actuated solely by motives of political opportunism; and the Church leaders, clinging to the desperate hope that such events were merely isolated incidents and not part of a deliberate policy, ruled that it was the Church's duty to obey the nation's rulers and not to protest.

Mecklenburg was only a small province and far away from the centres of church life. Far more attention was being paid to a movement which since January 1933 had been sweeping with increasing force through all the provinces of the Evangelical Church, calling for their unification and 'nationalization'. All earnest churchmen hoped for the achievement of a better state of affairs both within the churches and in their relations with the State if the narrow age-old provincialism of Church life could at last be overcome. Instead of twenty-eight separate provincial churches, they foresaw the creation of a single Reich Church, with a single Reich Bishop at its head. In this way the Church would follow the State in its efforts for renewal and reconstruction, in the interests of joint national and spiritual renaissance.

Such ideas were altogether acceptable to Hitler. There was, of course, a danger that a united Reich Church might become politically much stronger than the twenty-eight separate churches, and to combat such an eventuality, the leadership of the Church must be politically reliable. Once that leadership was established, political control could then be applied to make the whole Church an instrument of the Nazi party.

In considering whom to select as a suitable candidate for such leadership, Hitler shrewdly chose, not Joachim Hossenfelder, the leader of the Faith Movement of German Christians, whose extremism was bound to arouse opposition, but Ludwig Müller, a seemingly more moderate man, with whom he had become acquainted some years before. Müller, then aged fifty, had spent most of his career as a chaplain, serving in naval and military units in East Prussia. He was a man of no account, but he was a fervent Nazi, an ardent admirer of Hitler, and, while wholly devoid of the humility to acknowledge his own unfitness to lead the Church, could be relied upon to turn the Church into an organ of Nazi propaganda whenever Hitler so desired.

At Berchtesgaden on 17 April Hitler had a long conversation with Müller and outlined his ideas for the next stage in the Nazi Party's relations with the Evangelical Church. He supported the establishment of a Reich Church, provided that it did not become an independent organization. The methods of its creation must be non-controversial, inoffensive to the Church leaders, and such as to give rise to no unwelcome comments in the foreign press. Above all, the leaders of the Church must be prepared to accept the political leadership of the Nazi Party and to regulate their affairs accordingly. It was Müller's task so achieve these ends diplomatically and quickly, and to prevent any break-away movements towards independence. Eight days later, Müller was officially appointed Hitler's 'Delegate and plenipotentiary for all questions concerning the Evangelical Churches'.

These plans, however, met with considerable opposition in the ranks of the Evangelical Church. Although the church authorities were agreed on the desirability of a united Reich Church led by a Reich bishop in accordance with Nazi leadership principles, no agreement had been reached on the candidate for the office. The 'German Christians', in order to show their loyalty to Hitler and to ingratiate themselves with the Party, supported Ludwig Müller, who openly boasted of his backing by the highest political quarters. Other groups in the Church, however, supported Friedrich von Bodelschwingh, the director of a large Church hospital and welfare centre in Bethel, Westphalia. When a vote was taken on 27 May, under rather dubious constitutional procedures, Müller was defeated by a large majority.

The 'German Christians' at once launched a vigorous campaign, demanding the revocation of the election and the substitution of Hitler's approved candidate. Meetings were organized throughout the country; radio and press propaganda poured out, all linking the establishment of a united and renewed Reich Church with the choice of Müller. Hitler was well aware that a Church led by such a pacific character as Bodelschwingh, whom he refused to meet, would not be an instrument subservient to the Nazi state. Through

Müller, Hitler expressed to the Church authorities 'his extreme regrets that the efforts for the reconstruction of the German Evangelical Church had taken a difficult and decidedly unloveable turn'.[59] When this expression of his displeasure proved ineffectual in forcing the Church leaders to change their minds, more direct methods of pressure became necessary, though, as Hitler stipulated (bearing in mind, no doubt, the fiasco in Mecklenburg), the Nazi Party as such was not to be involved. The Church itself must find its own solution.

The 'German Christians' were in a difficult predicament. They did not command a majority of the clergy, still less of the ruling church authorities, and they could only hope to win the day by seeking help from outside the Church. In the Prussian Minister of Education, Rust, they found a ready ally. Rust, as one of the civil servants in the Reich Ministry of the Interior remarked, 'soon gathered round him a collection of dilettantes, fools and rascals',[60] including his deputy and State Secretary, the thirty-one year old Wilhelm Stuckart, whose sole qualification was a fanatical devotion to the Nazi creed. It was to these men that the 'German Christians' appealed for aid in dealing with the Evangelical Church in Prussia, the largest and most important Evangelical Church of all. When the President of the Prussian Church Council resigned at the end of June, Rust announced that the affairs of the Prussian church would henceforth be run by the Prussian provincial government.

On 24 June, at Stuckart's instigation, the appointment was announced of Dr August Jäger, his former law teacher, also a fervent Nazi, as Commissar for the Evangelical Church of Prussia. Jäger was narrowminded, presumptuous, arrogant and mean; he was also a thorough-going bureaucrat who obeyed orders regardless of the human consequences – qualities which were perhaps regarded by his superiors as a suitable contrast to Müller's evasiveness.

Jäger never pretended to have any theological understanding of the Church, which to him was simply a corporation to be administered. As an enthusiastic supporter of the Nazi cause, he at once set to work to bring the Prussian Evangelical Church into line with Nazi ideas by removing as many as possible of the Church's administrators and replacing them with 'German Christians'. The offices of the Evangelical News Agency were searched by the police; the Central Executive of its chief charitable agency, the Inner Mission, was replaced by two Nazi commissars who described themselves as 'trustees of Jesus Christ'; and all the Prussian General Superintendents were suspended. Dr. Dibelius learnt of his replacement by the thirty-four year old Hossenfelder, by reading the announcement in the newspapers, and Bodelschwingh, in despair, resigned his office as Reich Bishop-designate.

With the help of the SA, Müller, proclaiming himself as Reich-Bishop elect, was installed in the Prussian Church offices, and Hossenfelder issued a decree that on the following Sunday, all Prussian Churches should hold a service of thanksgiving for their deliverance from the 'anarchy' which had previously prevailed.[61] In Koblenz, Pastor Krummacher, Jäger's representative for the Rhineland, standing on the steps of the swastika-covered Church House and flanked by SA troops, addressed the throng as follows:

For the first time . . . a German in a brown shirt enters the offices of the Church Consistory. On the State's orders he was called . . . to work for the creation of a unified German Evangelical Church. . . . The State is today Nazi, and the People's thinking is Nazi. And so it was his task to bring together the Church, which like all human institutions had to change with the times, into line with the new Nazi spirit which was now inspiring the people.[62]

The protests which followed these arbitrary and illegal actions were legion. President Hindenburg was urged from all sides to intervene with Hitler for the restoration of the Churches' independence. On 29 June, at an interview with Hitler, the President warned him of the dangers which might result if the extremists among his supporters were allowed to go unchecked. Hitler replied that the protests only came from those who refused to align themselves with the spirit of the national revolution, and that all would be well once the new constitution of a unified Reich Church was prepared and implemented.

Nevertheless the warning was not lost on him. On the previous day, in an interview with a certain Pastor Backhaus, he denied all knowledge of the steps taken by the 'German Christians' in his name, and stated that he had not given his approval to Müller's self-appointment as Reich Bishop.[63] A few days later he remarked to Frick, the Minister of the Interior: 'Our task will be greatly endangered if talk is still allowed about the completion of the revolution, or about a second revolution. Whoever talks in this way, should realize that he is mutinying against the Führer and will be treated accordingly.'[64] Müller was instructed to hasten the preparation of the new constitution, and worked with such effect that Hitler was able to telegraph to President Hindenburg on 12 July:

Following the conclusion of the work on the constitution of the German Evangelical Church yesterday, negotiations have been concluded today on the settlement of the Prussian church conflict in a way equally satisfactory to the State and the Church. The internal freedom of the Church, for which I am specially concerned, will doubtless be assured by the withdrawal of the Commissars and Assistant Commissars of the State. The internal reorganization of the provincial Churches will be brought to an early conclusion by a free election of the Evangelical Church people in accordance with Church Law.[65]

The Commissars accordingly were 'retired' on 14 July and the suspended Church officers were reinstated.

These moves were taken as a sign of compromise by Hitler. In fact, they marked a significant difference of opinion between him and the 'German Christians', which as time went on grew gradually wider. As Dr Jäger later wrote,[66] the 'German Christians' wanted to make the Church a part of the State's machinery, to be dedicated to National Socialism and to be directed by Nazi leaders. They strongly opposed any separation of Church and State, and sought to bind together Church and State into an indissoluble whole, in which the Church, though subordinate to the State, would be the means of permeating the whole with the spirit of 'positive Christianity'. Such a State Church would incorporate the principle of authoritarian leadership, and would abolish, as out-of-date liberalism, any system of church elections. The outmoded divisions within the Churches would thus be swept away, and so too would the dangerous division of a man's religious life from his secular life. In the view of Dr Friedrich Wieneke, a prominent 'German Christian', religion was too deeply imbued in the German people's character to be easily overthrown; it was a mistake to draw a line between religion and the secular life, as some Nazi members tried to do, leaving the one to the Churches, while claiming total loyalty to the other. Indeed, Wieneke averred, only if the whole man were dedicated to Nazism could its total outreach be made effective; religion was not in opposition to Nazi totalitarianism, but was rather its presupposition.[67]

These ideas meant nothing to Hitler. His indifference to all religious questions, and his view that the Church's only function was to satisfy the 'religious' needs of those who still relied upon them, led to his contemptuous rejection of the ideas of the 'German Christians'. His objection to any State Church was simply political. Mussolini had been entrapped into making concessions to the priests, and had consequently been obliged to defer to the Church. A State Church on the Italian model led to divided loyalties, and Hitler would tolerate no such limits to his totalitarian claims.

As his appetite for power grew with the consolidation of his régime, he became more and more inclined to listen to the views of the anti-Christian forces in the Nazi Party, who held that both the 'German Christians' and their ecclesiastical opponents should alike be eliminated, or at the very least left to die out. In the meantime, 'German Christian' enthusiasm must be held in check and the supremacy of the Nazi Party re-emphasized.

The 'German Christian' organization was never given any status in the Nazi régime, nor was its leader Hossenfelder ever appointed to any office in the Nazi Party or received personally by Hitler. While tactical considerations alone determined how far these groups should be exploited, the support of the Evangelical Christians, especially in northern Germany, was a matter of some importance, and their willingness to co-operate with the new régime was therefore to be encouraged rather than repelled by too rapid or too violent measures. Consequently, while general support could be given to the pro-Nazi activities of the 'German Christians', the measures of Rust and of Jäger were to be countermanded, and a much closer control was to be maintained over the campaign to win the whole Church and its administration over to the Nazi Party.

14 July 1933 marks a significant advance in the consolidation of Hitler's power over the Churches. At a Cabinet meeting held on that day approval was given both to the new Constitution of the Reich Church and to the Reich Concordat.[68] The formal recognition by the leaders of Germany's two main churches and by the Vatican of the Nazi revolutionary régime was seen by Hitler as the vindication of his policy to gain control of the Churches through a process of promises and tactical concessions. He told his Cabinet colleagues that

he saw three great advantages in the conclusion of the Reich Concordat: 1. that the Vatican had negotiated at all, while it operated, especially in Austria, on the assumption that National Socialism was un-Christian and inimical to the Church; 2. that the Vatican could be persuaded to bring about a good relationship with this purely national German state. He, the Reich Chancellor, would have considered it impossible even a short time ago that the Church would be willing to obligate the bishops to this state. The fact that this had now been done was certainly an unreserved recognition of the present régime; 3. that with the Concordat the Church withdrew from activity in associations and parties, e.g. also abandoned the Christian labour unions. This, too, he, the Reich Chancellor, would not have considered possible even a few months ago. Even the dissolution of the Centre Party could be termed final only with the conclusion of the Concordat, now that the Vatican had ordered the permanent exclusion of the priests from party politics ... This agreement with the Curia was such an indescribable success that all critical misgivings had to be withdrawn in face of it.[69]

Nevertheless Hitler regarded the Reich Concordat as merely a stepping-stone to further achievements. How little he intended to honour the spirit of the agreement is shown by the fact that at the same Cabinet meeting approval was given to the Nazi Sterilization Law, publication of which was delayed until after the announcement of the conclusion of the Reich Concordat.[70] Furthermore, pressure was brought to bear on the Vatican – and not resisted – to include a Secret Annex to the Concordat, dealing with the position of the clergy 'in the event of a reorganization of the present German military system by the introduction of general military service' – a step in complete contravention of the Treaty of Versailles.[71] Such a frank declaration of the German intention unilaterally to break the terms of one international treaty boded ill for the future of the other, which was signed with much ceremony in Rome on 20 July.

Only one further step was needed to complete the process of the voluntary co-ordination of the Churches with the Nazi State. The selection of suitable persons to take over the leadership of the Evangelical Reich Church, as envisaged by the new constitution, and in particular the promotion of a politically reliable Reich Bishop, was the next object of Nazi Church policy. To take advantage of the hope kindled by the announcement of the promulgation of the new constitution, Hitler announced that elections would be held to fill the whole range of administrative posts and synodal vacancies on 23 July, i.e. in nine days' time. Such a short interval left no time for adequate preparation, for not even the parish voting lists were ready. But it did allow time for Goebbels to mobilize the Nazi propaganda machine behind the candidates proposed by the 'German Christians'. Officially, the State stood aside for a free election; but in practice the now familiar mixture of blandishments and threats served to encourage both the uncritical optimism of some churchmen and the tactical opportunism of others. Hitler had learnt from earlier experience that the imposition of State power served only to unite the Church against interference. Elections, however, would give a semblance of legality upon which to effect, within the Church, a political revolution of the same sort as had occurred within the State six months previously, while the backing of the Nazi Party would be sufficiently pervasive to hold in check the more extreme of the 'German Christians'.

The holding of the elections testified to the recognition by Hitler that church policy was of sufficient importance to warrant his personal attention. It was no longer a matter of complete indifference to him who administered the Church, even though, as before, he regarded doctrinal questions as nothing more than mere 'parsonical squabbling'. The subordination of the Church to Nazi ideology was to be achieved by a resounding campaign on behalf of the 'German Christians'.

The 'German Christians' were naturally delighted at this massive support. Riding the crest of the wave, they were encouraged by the increasing number of clergy and laity who were joining their ranks, and they were eager to demonstrate that the Churches, no less than the universities and the political parties, were loyal to the Nazi movement. The majority did so with little or no theological introspection, being intoxicated by enthusiasm for the 'German Christian' identification of Christianity and Nazism, and uncritically accepting the arguments disseminated by the press and radio for their cause. Hossenfelder proclaimed that 'the German Christians are the SA of Jesus Christ in the struggle to do away with bodily, social and spiritual distress . . . Our people need the social creation of a Church of German Christians in order to build the Third Reich . . . We regard as holy these laws of God's creation: marriage, family, race, people, state and authority'.[72] It is doubtful whether such sentiments could be called Christian at all, but the attempts of the other Protestant groups now united under the name 'Gospel and Church' and looking for a church free from political pressure, were overwhelmed by the wave of enthusiasm for the 'German Christians'. Threats were made against the candidates for 'Gospel and Church'; accusations of disloyalty to the Nazi state were accompanied by the enforced dissolution of election meetings; and even declarations of the 'Gospel and Church' party's political loyalty to Adolf Hitler, so long as the Church was left to God, were unavailing.[73] Even Pastor Martin Niemöller himself, who was later to be a leader of the Church's resistance to Nazism, said at the time:

We are at present in the midst of a large-scale reconstruction of our Protestant Church. The newspapers devote columns to it, and the forces which are pressing it forward are animated by an honest purpose and by an enthusiasm which is contagious and irresistible. Among many sections of our people the hope has sprung up that there will now be a new meeting between our nation and the Christian Church, between our nation and God. And we will hope from our hearts that through the movement which is at present developing in our Church, obstacles will be swept away and the way made clear.[74]

Against such contagious enthusiasm, the efforts of the 'Gospel and Church' party were unavailing. Too late they discovered how weak was the theological reasoning of those who saw no contradiction between the propaganda of the 'German Christians' and the doctrines of Christianity. After years of nationalist indoctrination, most of the clergy were no longer able to distinguish between the true and the false in political affairs, and in the confused and turbulent situation of the time their emotions overruled their judgment. Like many other Germans, under the 'inspiration' of the Nazi propaganda machine they 'thought with their blood'.

On 17 July Hossenfelder sent a letter to all Nazi Party *Gauleiters* urging them to encourage their party offices to help the 'German Christians' in the forthcoming struggle. All Party comrades were urged to do their duty and to register on the parish voting lists before 20 July, whether or not they were 'active' in the parishes. On 19 July, the Nazi newspaper, the *Völkischer Beobachter*, proclaimed that:

> Every Evangelical member of the Nazi Party should use the opportunity to vote on Sunday, the day of the Church elections. This is simply a matter of course. And it is equally a matter of course that his vote should be given to the 'Faith Movement of German Christians'.[75]

Nor was action limited to mere propaganda. On 17 July, Jäger, who still retained his position as the official responsible for Evangelical Church affairs in the Prussian Ministry of Education, ordered the Berlin Gestapo to raid the campaign offices of the 'Gospel and Church' party. The raid was duly carried out and more than 620,000 pieces of election material were confiscated.[76]

The most substantial support for the 'German Christians' came, however, from Hitler himself, who, in a broadcast to the nation, expressed his wish that the church elections would bring victory to the forces within the Church who supported the renewal of the nation and the new policies of the State. He compared those who, unable to recognize the great events of the day, turned away from the world only to be caught in a condition of religious

43

petrification, with those who belonged to a living movement. 'I see those forces marshalled in that section of the Evangelical population which has taken its stand in the "German Christian" movement on the ground of the National Socialist state.'[77]

The results of the elections were a foregone conclusion. With the aid of voters who had hitherto shown no interest in Church affairs, the 'German Christians' won an overwhelming victory in almost every part of the country. Forgetful of their previous repudiation of elections, the 'German Christians' could now claim that the result had incontrovertibly demonstrated that their campaign had been approved by the Almighty. State, People and Church could now unanimously declare their unity, and their dedication to the inspired leadership of Adolf Hitler.

2 The Rise and Fall of the 'German Christians' and the growth of the Churches' disillusionment

'The Swastika on our breasts, and the Cross in our hearts.' – Slogan of the 'German Christians'

The criticism has frequently been levelled against the leaders of the German Churches that they failed in their Christian duty by not making a firm stand against the Nazi movement from its inception. They are accused of having been so busy with their task of saving souls that they remained silent while their people were being seduced by Nazism; by grossly underestimating the Nazis' nihilistic designs against Christianity, and by their subserviency of 1933, they let slip the opportunity of resistance while resistance was still within their power. Alternatively, they are charged with following the Lutheran tradition of obedience to the State at a time when such an attitude was no longer justified, and of continuing to advise submission despite the accumulating evidence of Nazi oppression. Either from cowardice, it is said, or from an inability to understand the logic of events, they struggled to avoid a head-on clash with the ruling powers when they should have been fighting them with all the resources at their command. Indeed, they are even accused, by their predisposition to authoritarianism, of having encouraged the Nazi régime, particularly in its assumption of dictatorship, its racialist persecution, and its expansionist foreign policy. In a word, they are blamed for seeking to defend the Church's existence as an institution at the expense of their doctrine.

There is at least some justification for all these charges. The German Churches were trapped in a situation which exposed their every weakness and encouraged every temptation. Humanly speaking, their leaders, by collaborating with the Nazis, were no more and no less guilty than the rest of their fellow countrymen. But, as custodians of the Christian Gospel, their conduct must be judged by different standards. Their readiness to allow the truths of the Christian faith to be distorted for the purposes of political expediency, and their failure to denounce the crimes so openly committed in their society, place a heavy burden of guilt upon them.

It must, however, in fairness be recognized that this is not the whole truth as regards either the Evangelical or the Roman Catholic Church. In both there were always a few – though only a few – who recognized the Nazi régime as the evil thing it proved to be, and who never ceased to appeal to the foundations of Christian teaching to stem the 'contagious and irresistible enthusiasm' with which so many Christians greeted the Nazi movement in 1933. Upon these few was built the core of resistance which saved the Church from total apostasy to Nazism.

In August 1933, however, those who pleaded for the upholding of Christian doctrine as set forth in the Scriptures, the Church's traditions, or the Confessions of the Reformation, received scant attention. The 'German Christians', having obtained the backing of the Nazi Party by their demonstration of loyalty and usefulness to Adolf Hitler, were determined to press ahead with their programme of revival and renewal within the Church. Their guiding principles, laid down a year before, included an intensive campaign against Marxism, coupled with a demand for racial purity and a positive Christianity which would correspond to the German spirit of Luther and to a heroic piety.[1]

The Church must enter completely into the Third Reich, it must be co-ordinated into the rhythm of the National Revolution, it must be fashioned by the ideas of Nazism, lest it remain a foreign body in the unified German Nazi community.[2]

The self-confidence of these militant churchmen was abundantly demonstrated at the provincial synods which were summoned to put into effect the provisions of the new constitution. So much so that on 1 August the Swedish newspaper *Svenska Morgenbladet* carried the following report on the synod of Brandenburg, one of the provinces of the Evangelical Church in Prussia:

It is completely inconceivable, under Swedish conditions, to imagine a synod of 200 clergymen dressed in brown uniforms, riding boots, body and shoulder straps, with all sorts of swastikas, badges of rank and medals, meeting in the legislative buildings. These brownshirts were 'German Christians', and the synod had been called to hand over the legislative authority of the synod to a new executive for Brandenburg. The observer must report that the spiritual climate of Germany has so changed in recent times that, for a Swede, no South American republic could have been stranger. It was a shameful experience, but the reporter was not the only one who found it so; he observed that several of those present exchanged glances during the proceedings which said more than words . . .

The first item of business was the discharge of the previous Chairman of the Synod. His successor was Provost Grell, a man in a brown shirt with a military bearing and a corresponding voice. He declared that now a German faith and a German God was needed. The marvellous revolution had now ensured that it was a joy to be living and revolutionary times were not for weaklings. Whoever could not liberate himself from his old ways was not fit to take part in the work of the renewal. His speech was greeted by the Brownshirts with loud cries of 'Heil Hitler' . . .

The second item on the agenda was the adoption of the Aryan paragraph, with its provision for the dismissal of non-Aryan ministers and officials. Dr. Jacobi of the Memorial Church in Berlin read out a statement declaring that the use of secular standards was inappropriate in the interests of the Church. This was greeted with cries of ridicule, and a vote was called at once without any discussion. The Brownshirts began to call for an open vote by name, and proceeded to greet all those who voted 'No' with ironic cries of 'Bravo', 'Aha' and the like . . . The meeting closed with 'Deutschland, Deutschland über alles' and the repulsive Horst-Wessel Song. The whole thing could only be described as religious barbarism. And the impression was not improved when the reporter was twice challenged in the hallway because he had neglected to give the Hitler salute.[3]

On 4 September, the General Synod for the whole of Prussia, most of its members dressed in Nazi uniforms, convened to confirm Ludwig Müller as its bishop, and to establish ten new bishoprics in place of the General Superintendents. These bishoprics were promptly conferred on Nazis, nearly all of them inexperienced and mostly very young, including Hossenfelder, who was made Bishop of Brandenburg. A motion was adopted declaring that, in recognition of the desirability of authoritarian leadership in church government, there was no need for further synods. Another law was passed embodying the 'Aryan' paragraph and calling for the dismissal of all non-'Aryans' from the Church's staff. Müller's final victory came at Wittenberg, the home of the Lutheran movement, where, at the National Synod held on 27 September, his election as Reich Bishop was confirmed by a large majority of faithful 'German Christians'. In his acceptance speech, Müller declared:

The whole German movement for freedom with its leader, our Chancellor, is for us a present from God, given in a time of decision, when the enemies of Christ were doing their best to destroy our people both inwardly and outwardly. In the triumph of this German freedom movement we hear the call of our God, and it is our honourable and sincere duty to listen to this call and to act accordingly ... The old has passed away. The new has begun. The political struggle in the Church is over. Now begins the struggle for the soul of the people.[4]

This was exactly the work which the 'German Christians' were waiting to undertake. Having established themselves in office, the radical wing of the 'German Christians' were eager to complete the task of co-ordinating the Church with the Nazi State, recognizing no limitations to the totalitarian claims of Nazism and striving to identify the claims of Nazism with the tenets of Christianity. On 30 August, Pastor Leutheuser declared:

Christ has come to us through Adolf Hitler. He was the decisive figure when the people were just about to go under. Hitler struck out for us, and through his power, his honesty, his faith and his idealism, the Redeemer found us ... We know today the Saviour has come ... We have only one task, be German, not be Christian.[5]

48

To this astonishing outburst it was a logical corollary that anyone who did not commit himself completely to the Nazi Party and to Nazi ideology was unfit to be a priest of the Evangelical Church. To cling to the old orthodoxies was a sign of disbelief in the new age which had been created by the Nazi Revolution under Hitler's leadership. The missionary work of the German Church was now to be undertaken with the same zeal as the supporters of the Nazi Party had shown in the secular sphere, and with the same fervent devotion to Hitler as the regenerator both of the Church and of the nation.

Not unnaturally, so radical a departure from the orthodox teachings of the Evangelical Church provoked some opposition from within the Church. Dr Martin Niemöller, pastor of Berlin's fashionable Dahlem Church, was seriously alarmed by the trend of events in the Prussian Synods, particularly by the secular demands for the introduction of the 'Aryan' paragraph, which flagrantly violated the Church's confession of faith. On 21 September he addressed a circular letter to all German Evangelical pastors inviting them to join a 'Pastors' Emergency League', the members of which would commit themselves in their preaching 'to be bound only by Holy Scripture and the Confessions of the Reformation'. The response was immediate. Within a week two thousand pastors had offered their support, and the less revolutionary of the 'German Christians', led by Müller, were jolted into realization that, if the unity of the Church was to be maintained, this opposition must be placated. Accordingly Müller quietly dropped the 'Aryan' paragraph from the agenda of the Wittenberg Synod when he was elected Reich Bishop on 27 September, counselling patience and caution to his radical wing and advising them against inflammatory and revolutionary agitation – an attitude that was greeted with dismay and incredulity by the more militant radicals of the 'Faith Movement of German Christians'.

What was more disconcerting, however, was the fact that they now found themselves dropped by the hierarchy of the Nazi Party. In Hitler's view, the 'German Christians' had served their purpose: the Church had been put under the control of Müller, and further radicalism was undesirable. Moreover, Hitler decided that no group should be allowed to build up such a following that the authority of the Nazi Party might be challenged. The 'German Christians', he decreed, were in no circumstances to be allowed to become a rival 'movement within a movement', with their own political basis and their own claims to 'spiritual leadership'. A sharp reminder was therefore sent from the Nazi Party headquarters in Munich to the leaders of the 'German Christians' forbidding them to make use of Nazi nomenclature or of such titles as 'Führer'.[6] Furthermore, many of Hitler's anti-Christian associates resented the 'German Christians' usurpation of ideological leadership and their claim to be the best Nazis of all. It might be true that all Christians ought to be Nazis, but it was not true that all Nazis ought to be Christians. Led by Rosenberg and Dinter, the Party members who had no desire either to be associated with the parsons or to tolerate competition in the ideological sphere, brought pressure to bear for some form of dissociation, or at least of disengagement, from what was becoming an embarrassment. On 16 August Rosenberg, in the *Völkischer Beobachter*, argued that it was not the Nazi Party's task to support one or other group in the Churches; according to Point 24 of the Party Programme, the Party was impartial towards all denominations, and the various churches must be left to argue amongst themselves without political support for any individual claim.[7] On 6 October this view was officially approved by Martin Bormann, the Chief of Staff to Hitler's Deputy, Rudolf Hess, who sent a circular letter to the Nazi Party offices stating that Party members who had not supported the 'German Christians' in the July elections, i.e. who had contravened Hitler's express desire, would not be penalized by exclusion from the Party or from the Womens' organizations. 'The purpose of the Church elections has been reached', he stated. 'The Führer sees no point in carrying the matter further.'[8] The dissociation was finally completed by a Decree issued by Hess on 13 October, which stated bluntly:

No Nazi is to suffer any disadvantage for not belonging to a certain denomination or church party, or because he belongs to no denomination at all. Faith is a very personal matter which each person must decide in his own conscience. There must be no forcing of consciences.[9]

This was a severe blow to the 'German Christians' who had so readily affirmed that Nazism and Christianity could never again be separated and that the idea of religion as a private matter was a 'thoroughly Marxist' concept. Hitler himself, however, was still not averse to the Nazi Party assisting the Church to fulfil its tasks. Speaking to a visiting American churchman, Dr C. A. Macfarland, on 31 October, he declared that the Nazis had no wish to interfere either with the Church's administration or with its doctrine. Adopting the position of a detached observer, Hitler assured his visitor that his only desire was for peace and unity within the Church, and that he was always ready personally to act as an intermediary between disputing parties.[10] In view of the events of June and July these assertions marked the extent to which Hitler was prepared to withdraw from all-out support of the 'German Christians' and to allay the fears of foreign visitors from North America and elsewhere.

Meanwhile, the radical 'German Christians', finding themselves now opposed by a sizeable group of their clerical colleagues and deserted by their political comrades, became even more extreme in their views and more violent in their expression.

Was the whole idea of our struggle just to put a new set of Bishops and Provosts in well-paid positions? Just to see ourselves delivered into the hands of our old ideological enemies in the parishes with our hands tied? What happened to the introduction of the Aryan paragraph? Where is the pure-German Christianity? Where is the religious renewal?[11]

It was not enough for Hossenfelder's assistant, Pastor Loerzer, to declare on 26 September that the degree of stagnation which appeared to have set in was in reality only the calm before the storm.[12] Under the leadership of a layman, Dr Reinhold Krause, the more fanatical elements decided to organize a mass rally at the end of October to initiate a great propaganda campaign that would overwhelm their enemies within the Church as the Nazi Party had overwhelmed its 'reactionary' opponents, and that would at the same time publicly confirm their loyalty and indispensability to the Nazi Party.

The Nazi Party, however, had other business on hand. Germany's delegation had just been withdrawn from the League of Nations Disarmament Conference at Geneva, and Hitler had announced that Germany would have no further contact with the League, but would make her way in the world independently and by her own efforts.[13] To offset the effects of this international isolation, Hitler was anxious for a public demonstration of his popularity at home. A plebiscite was accordingly ordered to be held on 12 November, and the campaign was opened with speeches throughout the country delivered in an atmosphere of frenzied and mounting enthusiasm. At such a time it was obviously not in Hitler's interests that ecclesiastical differences should be allowed to dispel the picture of national unity and harmony. The 'German Christians' were ordered to postpone their meeting until after the 'election'.

It was therefore not until 13 November that twenty thousand men and women, clergy and laity, assembled in the Berlin Sports Palace, in the presence of Reich Bishop Müller and other leading churchmen, to open the campaign for the religious renewal of the people through the spirit of the Nazi revolution. The most important speech was delivered by Dr Krause, in which he called for a departure from the old ways and for the creation of a new Church in line with the new State: 'not a Lutheran, nor a Reformed, nor a United, not a synodical or consistorial Church, not an episcopal or a church with General Superintendents, but one mighty, new, all-embracing German people's Church.' The first step in the creation of their new indigenous Church was to get rid of 'the Old Testament with its Jewish morality of rewards, and its stories of cattle-dealers and concubines'. All perverted and superstitious passages were to be removed from the New Testament, and the whole theology of the Rabbi Paul, with its ideas of scapegoats and its sense of inferiority, was to be expunged. Exaggerated views of the Crucified were to be avoided and a 'heroic' Jesus proclaimed.

Krause's speech was received with tumultuous applause. In a spirit of jubilant enthusiasm, sixty new flags of the 'Faith Movement of German Christians' were dedicated, with the words: 'Let us always be revolutionary to the core, revolutionary against anything which restricts life or fetters the spirit.' To formulate the programme a resolution was proposed calling for the discharge of ministers who were unwilling to co-operate in the completion of the Reformation in accordance with the spirit of National Socialism; the rapid implementation, without compromise, of the 'Aryan' paragraph in the provincial churches, the transfer of all Christians of alien blood to separate parishes, and the founding of a separate Jewish Christian Church; the removal of all un-German elements in the Church services and creeds, particularly in the Old Testament; the freeing of the Gospel from its oriental 'distortions' and their presentation of a 'heroic' Christ; and the creation of a single people's Church to complete the Reformation of Martin Luther and to do justice to the totalitarian claims of the Nazi State.[14] The resolution was passed with only one opposing vote.

The effects of this meeting were immediate. Protests poured in from the defenders of Church Orthodoxy. To large numbers of clergy and laymen the results of their uncritical support of the 'German Christians' now became apparent, and the enthusiasm displayed for this confusion of political fanaticism with religious intolerance shocked them out of their misguided complacency. Thousands of clergy transferred their allegiance to Niemöller's Pastors' Emergency League. Reich Bishop Müller was forced to withdraw his patronage of the 'German Christian' movement and to suspend the introduction of the 'Aryan' paragraph into the Church. And Hossenfelder was obliged, albeit reluctantly, to resign his position as the 'German Christian' Reich Leader and member of the National 'Spiritual Ministry'.

Nevertheless, despite these doubts and defections, most of the pastors still preferred to remain loyal to the Nazi State, unable or unwilling to believe that responsible men, especially in the legally established government, could agree with such views. Nor could they understand that by their attacks on the orthodox Evangelical churchmen the 'German Christians' were serving the purpose of disrupting any unified stand against Nazi pretensions. Even had they realized the position, the consequences would have been so disturbing that they could only be ignored, in the fond hope that they could not be true.

On the Nazi side the reaction was equally strong. National unity was being destroyed by 'parsonical squabbles'. The Party had no wish to be implicated in the plans of the Church, to which it was indifferent, but it would not tolerate a 'mighty new all-embracing people's Church', which might become a dangerous rival. Krause, the Nazis contended, had no right to claim the support of the Party, and by so doing had contravened the Party's orders to maintain peace in the Church. Opposition to his extreme demands might even be directed against the Party itself, which might thus find itself on the defensive on a battlefield where it had no desire to fight. The Nazi press denied that it had been in any way involved, and reiterated the Party's declared resolve never to become a religious movement.

The Führer has always refused to become a religious reformer . . . A preference for this or that theological position cannot be adopted since such questions lie outside the State's sphere . . . Nazism is today an idea of the State, which has to encompass the whole people and must not be drawn into matters which threaten the unity of the country.[15]

The extremism of the 'German Christians' left Hitler in no doubt as to its potential danger, and decided him to complete the process of dissociation for which the anti-Christian Nazis had been pressing. The Party, he decided, must revert to its policy of strict impartiality in Church affairs. At the end of November, the Minister of the Interior, Frick, was ordered to forbid interference in Church affairs. The current disputes in the German Evangelical Church were, it was stated, purely ecclesiastical, and no group could call on the State's support. On 1 December Goebbels instructed the press to treat the news of Church disputes with the greatest reserve. Even *Gauleiter* Kube, who in July had been one of the strongest supporters of the 'German Christians', was obliged to acknowledge the desirability of separating the affairs of church and state.[16]

This was not the first time that Hitler had had to stifle the enthusiasm of his more fanatical followers. To withdraw support from Churchmen, for whom only a few months before he had personally campaigned, might throw doubt on the consistency of

Hitler's policies and so damage the Party's interests, and there was even a danger, as Goebbels was quick to point out, that the decline of the 'German Christians' might be hailed as the beginning of the end for the Nazi Party. But it would be even more dangerous to be involved in unwanted disputes. Hitler's support for the 'German Christians' had never been more than lukewarm. He could see no reason why these Churchmen should seize ecclesiastical power as the Nazis had seized political power. His policy on Church matters had been an experiment, unsupported by resolute indoctrination and propaganda through all the Party units. Having encountered so much resistance and so many set-backs, the policy was now to be abandoned and Hitler quickly lost interest.

Nevertheless, the problem of the Church as an organization remained. The 'extremists' of the 'German Christians' were no more acceptable than the 'reactionaries' of the Pastors' Emergency League. The likelihood of a united approach from the Church was rapidly receding, and if a satisfactory solution were to be achieved more time was needed. Reich Bishop Müller was peremptorily instructed to put an end to internal disputes and to bring matters under control, so that the Government should no longer be embarrassed by further regrettable developments in the Evangelical Church. The Evangelical Church should pay more attention to pastoral care and to support of the 'Winter Help Programme'.[17]

It was clear that the Evangelical Church had not proved a practical instrument for the strengthening of the Nazi ideological hold on Germany. If the Evangelical clergy refused to put themselves unreservedly at the disposal of the Nazi Party, or if they attempted to develop a rival movement of their own, they would not serve Hitler's purposes. If the Church as an institution refused to conform to the needs of the political situation, or to put its resources for popular education behind the Nazi cause, then other means would have to be found for the ideological leadership of the people.

The implications of this dissociation were realized only slowly, and then not by all Nazi adherents. The official governmental policy remained as before, but the way was now open for the Party, through its local organizations, to intensify its propaganda campaign to exalt a purely Nazi ideology. Anti-clerical attacks were no longer discouraged, and lip-service ceased to be paid to Christian traditions. This was the beginning of the attempt to eliminate Christian influence, particularly from education and youth work, and with it came the publication of books and pamphlets by anti-Christian writers praising the 'new heathenism' including Rosenberg's *Myth of the Twentieth Century* which on 5 December was recommended by the official 'Central Gazette of the Curriculum Administration for Prussian Schools' for use by all teachers and pupils.[18] It also marked a notable – if short-lived – rise in the fortunes of Alfred Rosenberg, who, having persuaded Hitler to give him a greater share of responsibility in the ideological field, on 24 January 1934 was appointed the Führer's Delegate for the Entire Spiritual and Philosophical Education and Supervision of the Nazi Party.[19]

The 'German Christians' never regained the support of the Nazi Party. Despite their repeated pledges of loyalty and their frequent reiteration of the true fulfilment of Christianity through the Nazi movement, they were eventually completely abandoned by the Nazi hierarchy. Never again, even for tactical reasons, did the Nazi leaders seek to strengthen their position by the support of a 'German Christian' group in the Church. After 1934, the Nazi policies developed along quite different lines, exploiting the political support of the 'German Christians' but ignoring their theological views. As the Nazi hostility to Christianity became more apparent, the 'German Christians' found that their unity in 1933 had been but a temporary phenomenon based on political expediency. The leaders were consequently torn with dissension. The pastors who had supported the Nazi cause for nationalist reasons while still striving to maintain the truth of the Gospel, were increasingly obliged to retreat into 'neutrality' or to join the Confessing Church. The radical wing, on the other hand, complained that the tempo of the Nazi revolution in the Church was decreasing and that Nazi favour could only be regained by the Church's wholehearted commitment to Nazi racial ideas and by following the lead of Hitler, the source of its modern revelation. An attempt to reformulate the policy of this group was made by an appeal on 10 December, in the Twenty-Eight Theses of the Saxon People's Church for the inner reconstruction of the German Evangelical Church.[20] The incompatibility of these two parties soon reduced the movement to a state of impotent sectarianism, with its leaders, both local and national, increasingly dependent for the maintenance of their position on the favour of the Nazi Party bosses.

No one was more aware of this disruption than the hapless Reich Bishop Müller. Deserted by his supporters and attacked on every side, his attempts to gain time or to rely on the support of the Nazi Party served only to increase the suspicions of the Pastors' Emergency League as to his fitness for office. And the few attempts that he made to meet his opponents' wishes earned him only further distrust from both his former supporters and from the Nazis who had relied on him to bring the Church under control. Müller attempted to buy his way back into Hitler's favour by undertaking to demonstrate the unity of 'his' Church with Nazism. Since, however, a direct move in the field of Church order would inevitably evoke yet another wave of protests from his opponents, he decided to sacrifice part of 'his' Church by ordering the integration of its youth work with the Hitler Youth. On 12 December 1933 the Executive Committee of the Youth Commission was dismissed and on 19 December an agreement was reached between Müller and Baldur von Schirach, the Nazi Reich Youth Leader, for the incorporation of the 700,000 members of the Evangelical Youth with the Hitler Youth. Previous promises were ignored; consultation with the Church authorities was passed over; but the move merely proved that the Reich Bishop's support no longer came from any Church grouping or party, but was merely based on his usefulness to the Nazi leaders.

It was the same story with the later development of the 'Faith Movement of German Christians'. The movement's sole advantage lay in the fact that its members were more acceptable to the Nazis than their opponents who had formed themselves into the Confessing Church. By suitably ingratiating tactics, the 'German Christians' were rewarded by their Nazi friends with appointments to vacancies in Church bishoprics, Church administration and theological professorships. The opportunists among them were not slow to realize their chances. A typically notorious case was that of Pastor Wolf Meyer-Erlach, erstwhile Radio Padre in Bavaria, whose sermons were a mixture of anti-Communism and anti-semitism 'in the defence of our Christian way of life'. Though without academic qualifications, he was appointed in 1933 to the post of Professor of Practical Theology in the University of Jena, which boasted that it had become the 'brown heart' of Thüringen and the prototype of a Nazi university. In 1934 he was made Dean of the Theological Faculty, and in April 1935 he stood as candidate for the Rectorship (Presidency) of the University. He received eight votes to his opponents 108, but, in accordance with Nazi anti-democratic practice, the votes were 'not counted but weighed'. Meyer-Erlach was appointed Rector and forthwith proceeded to install fellow-Nazis into other professorial positions, including Walter Grundmann, Professor of New Testament, who later became the Head of the Research Institute into the Removal of Jewish Influences from the Christian Church, and the author of a lengthy series of anti-semitic publications.[21]

So long as these men had the backing of the local Nazi Party leader, they were able to defy all criticism of the abandonment of Christian principles in the administration of the Church. They actively associated themselves with Nazi designs to rid the Church of 'undesirables'. They justified the persecution, arrest and imprisonment of their fellow clergy by accusing them of disloyalty to the Nazi State. They condoned the persecution of the Jews as a proper punishment for the crime of the Crucifixion and for Jewish obstinacy in refusing to be converted to the German revelation of Christianity.

Nevertheless all these gestures availed them little. The 'German Christians' were placed under the same restrictions and limitations as the other clergy. Compromised by their pro-Nazi attitude, they tried to convince themselves that such actions were not directed by Hitler but could be justified by the circumstances of 'national emergency'. In 1935, in Regensburg, their meetings were prohibited by the Gestapo.[22] In July 1935 Reich Bishop Müller himself was prohibited from addressing any secular gatherings.[23] And in

1938 the use of the swastika alongside the Cross as the symbol of the 'German Christians' was forbidden by Hitler's Deputy and by the Chief of the Security Police, 'lest the suspicion be aroused that the Party and State stood behind the activities of the "German Christians", whereas the Party lays the greatest stress on remaining independent towards all Church groups'.[24] A year later Bormann issued a directive to all *Gauleiters* prohibiting contact with any 'German Christian' pastors who offered their services to Nazi Party members who had 'officially' left the Church.[25]

Incredible as it may seem, there were still a few idealists among the 'German Christians' who continued to believe that Nazism and Christianity were ideologically linked, and that the increasing hostility of the Nazi Party was due only to the undue influence of a minority of anti-Christian 'heathens', such as Rosenberg, within the Party. They clung to the belief that this influence was hampering the efforts of the Christian majority of the Nazi Party to defend themselves from the attacks of the Confessing Church, and was indeed harming the Party's image abroad. In spite of all the evidence to the contrary, some of these idealists continued to the end to believe that Nazism and Christianity were basically compatible and that all that was needed to effect a lasting union was a statement from Hitler supporting the Party's stand for 'positive Christianity'.

A typical case is that of Professor Cajus Fabricius, Professor of Systematic Theology in Breslau from 1935, who claimed to be 'one of the oldest Party members among the German professors'. He wrote several works glorifying the 'positive Christianity' of the Third Reich, one of which was translated into English and Japanese at the Nazi Party's expense, and proved useful for deluding foreign visitors, including the Bishop of Gloucester, as to the actual state of religious life in Germany. In 1936 he complained to Hitler of the radical anti-clericalism and new 'heathenism' that were spreading in Germany, and suggested that, if these could be suppressed, it would be easier to turn the Catholics into friends of the Nazi state. Later he issued a series of mimeographed letters entitled *Reich im Kampf*, quoting examples of how the 'Christian' reputation of the Nazi Party was being sullied by dangerous free-thinking elements. A copy of his *Inner Re-armament*, a twenty-six page indictment along the same lines, was circulated to leading government and church offices in September 1939. When it fell into the hands of Goebbels' Propaganda Ministry at the end of October, Fabricius was arrested by the Gestapo and threatened with life imprisonment in a concentration camp. Despite his protestations of unswerving loyalty to the Nazi cause, he was held for two months and released only when he had signed an undertaking to take no further part in political activity. Thereafter he was excluded from the Nazi Party, without the option of appeal, and placed under local arrest. His repeated complaints of unfair treatment, after all his loyal services to Nazism and as a Professor of Theology, were ignored. The file on Professor Fabricius closes with the following abrupt letter:

National Socialist German Workers' Party
Berlin   Munich
Wilhelmstr. 64   The Brown House

The Führer's Deputy   12 December 1940

To   Strictly Confidential
Reich Minister and
Head of the Reich Chancellery   Personal
Dr. Lammers,
Berlin W.8
Vosstrasse 2–6.

Re: Professor Dr. Cajus Fabricius
  For your information, I can inform you that Fabricius because of his activities, was, on the personal order of the Führer, to have been put in a concentration camp. He would probably still be there now, but for the fact that he was pardoned because of his advanced blindness.
                                                                      Bormann.

  The same process of disillusionment and disengagement was repeated during the latter part of 1933 in the relations between the Nazis and the Roman Catholic Church. Although there was never a substantial number of Catholic equivalents to the 'German Christians', there were numerous Catholics who saw in the

Concordat a means for joint collaboration in the work of national renewal. Cardinal Faulhaber, offering his congratulations to Hitler on 24 July, four days after the signing of the Concordat, wrote:

Your statesmanlike far-sightedness has achieved in six months what the old parliaments and parties failed to achieve in sixty years . . . This agreement with the Head of the Church can bring for the inner life of the German people, through the securing of religious freedom, an increase of faith and with it an increase of the ethical power of the people.[26]

Most German Catholics were ready to believe Hitler's public assurances, and to rejoice that under the terms of the Concordat they could continue their traditional political obedience. Indeed, so anxious were they to cause no 'difficulties' that all activities, clubs and newspapers that might appear hostile to the Nazi Party were brought to an end or readjusted to a state of *Gleichschaltung* (co-ordination). On 3 May the Catholic Trade Union dissolved itself, and in the course of the next few months many Teachers' Federations did likewise. Catholic Student organizations issued avowels of loyalty to 'the Nazi State, which, growing so powerfully out of the Revolution, is the only way to restore Christianity to our culture. . . . Long live the Great German Reich. Hail to our Führer Adolf Hitler.'[27] Many Catholic newspapers adopted a friendly tone towards the Nazi revolution even before the Concordat was signed, and once its terms were published a wave of pro-Nazi enthusiasm broke loose.[28] Laymen were encouraged to join the SA and the SS,[29] the children were instructed to give the Hitler salute, and Nazi flags were carried into the Churches. It seemed only a matter of time before all the Catholic organizations would be incorporated in the Nazi structure as an expression of Catholic support for Hitler's 'inspired leadership'. The aims of the new Government were described as being the aims of the Church.[30] On 24 August, to celebrate the signing of the Concordat, a Mass was held outside the Catholic Cathedral in Berlin by the Papal Nuncio, Msgr Orsenigo, at which a sermon calling for Germany's resurrection was preached, a telegram was dispatched to Hitler, and the Horst Wessel song was sung.

The attitude of the Nazi Party, however, was unmoved. It was an essential point of Nazi policy at the time that all rallying points of possible political opposition were to be eliminated, and in the continuance of the Catholic professional, youth and laymen's organizations, of which each diocese had a number, the Nazi policy-makers saw dangerous focus points which must be removed. They had purposely been careful not to stipulate in the Concordat which organizations would be allowed to continue and which would be dissolved, under the terms of Article 31. The final protocol had left the question to be decided by later consultation and the Nazi leaders were not long in deciding that Article 31 was too great a concession, and that its provisions must be circumvented by the forcible extinction of as many of the Catholic organizations as possible before the final terms were agreed upon. Even the professional organizations with no political implications found themselves jeopardized by the pro-Nazi enthusiasm of their members and the pressure of the authorities. Many organizations decided on 'voluntary' dissolution or merged with an associated Nazi body. By the end of August the German bishops were becoming seriously alarmed. A number of Catholic organizations had had their property seized and their contributions confiscated. Others that showed unwillingness to be 'voluntarily' *gleichgeschaltet* were accused of political unreliability, or even of hostility. The leader of the German Labour Front, Dr Ley, issued a decree prohibiting dual membership in the German Labour Front and in a denominational professional organization, knowing full well that such prohibition would cripple the denominational movements.[31] Pressure was brought to bear on individual Catholics not to continue membership of such organizations. Catholic teachers were urged to persuade their pupils to join the Hitler Youth.[32] Catholic civil servants were branded as enemies of the State. The attacks on the Church press became so frequent that the Bishops realized that if the persecution and pressure were to continue on the same scale, there would soon be no Church press left.[33] On 20 July, the very day on which the Concordat was signed, the Reich Minister of the Interior issued a decree to all newspapers forbidding them to describe themselves as Catholic, on the grounds that denominational differences amongst the people must cease: no longer was there to be a Catholic press or an Evangelical press, but only a German press.

Yet Cardinal Bertram, writing to Cardinal Pacelli in Rome on 2 September, still maintained that these were only temporary disruptions, that would disappear with the final ratification of the Concordat.

A retardation of the ratification of the Reich Concordat is not desirable for the following reasons:
1. Many voices have been raised against the Concordat. Including those who say that the Reich Chancellor is only interested in the foreign policy prestige success of the Concordat and doesn't wish to keep the internal side of the bargain.
2. Wide circles declare that the government made too many concessions; a return movement would be desirable. Such views would be heard more loudly if ratification were delayed. And that would disturb our Catholic people.
3. With ratification we shall have the chance of proceeding more vigorously against numerous anti-Catholic actions. But if ratification is delayed, the bishops' position will be made more difficult.[34]

Pacelli was less sanguine. In conversation with a British diplomat, he expressed grave concern over the course of events in Germany, and frankly admitted his doubt about future developments, though he too believed that the signing of the Concordat would improve the lot of the German Catholics.

If the German Government violated the Concordat – and they were certain to do so – the Vatican would have a treaty on which to base a protest. In any case, the Cardinal added with a smile, the Germans would probably not violate all the articles of the Concordat at the same time.[35]

It was, as we have seen, against the Catholic organizations that the Nazi attention was first concentrated. Despite the Government's explicit promises to Cardinal Pacelli before the ratification of the Concordat on 10 September, it was only nine days later, on 19 September, that Himmler's deputy, Heydrich, informed the Bavarian Political Police that the signing of the Concordat made no difference to the Nazi determination to stamp out activity in the secular sphere that could be construed as a demonstration against the Nazi state. The only activities left to the Church were to be limited to purely 'religious' functions held within the Church buildings. All other activities and all such gatherings as group expeditions, sports meetings, theatre visits, or parades were forbidden. In no circumstances would the wearing of uniforms be permitted. Any organization which was suspected of trying to keep alive the political spirit of the Centre Party must be ruthlessly suppressed.[36] On the grounds of information obtained from letters captured in police raids, Himmler ordered that the Catholic organizations *Neudeutschland, Deutsche Jugendkraft, Kreuzschar* and *Sturmschar* were to be excluded from the safeguards of the Concordat's Article 31, and subsequently liquidated.[37] Such drastic measures, taken so soon after the signing of the Concordat, an instrument expressly designed to eliminate tension, led to an outburst of resentment from the Catholic clergy. But still the Bishops wavered. Handicapped by their previous declarations of loyalty to the Nazi state, they knew not how to act, and in their uncertainty they finally compromised by leaving the initiative to the Vatican.

In November, Cardinal Pacelli, deeply shocked by the many cases of persecution reported to Rome, threatened to issue an official protest from the Vatican, well aware that such a protest would add to Germany's already considerable international difficulties caused by her defiant attitude towards the League of Nations. In a note despatched to the German Foreign Ministry, Pacelli complained bitterly of 'difficulties and persecutions, carried to a virtually intolerable degree, which the Catholic Church in Germany is now enduring in open violation of the Concordat'.[38] An official from the Ministry of the Interior was hastily sent to Rome to smooth the matter over and to persuade the Vatican into silence. But even as he went the disillusionment of the Bavarian bishops found utterance: in a statement on the Plebiscite of 12 November they expressed themselves so forcibly and in such uncompromising terms that their words were banned by the Bavarian Government from appearing in the public press and even from being read in the pulpits.[39]

This conflict between Nazi public promises of support and their open persecution of the Churches brought endless confusion to the minds of the Catholic populace. Having so readily greeted the first months of Nazi rule as the coming of national renewal, having so lightly accepted the abandonment of democracy and the rule of parliamentary law, and having so plausibly found excuses for the persecution of the Communists and Jews, the Catholic clergy and laity now found themselves among the victims. Moreover, the religious grounds upon which any protest should have been made had, by their own actions, long since been lost. Their experience during the previous generation had led them to think only in terms of achieving their rightful status in the national community – a status which the Reich Concordat had seemed to ensure. Political involvement for other ideals had become alien to them, although the tradition and discipline of the Catholic Church had enabled them still to maintain their unity. Recognizing this, the Nazis knew that it would be virtually impossible to gain from the Catholic clergy the same degree of compliance that they hoped to win from the Evangelical Church under Reich Bishop Müller. The influence of the Catholic priesthood must therefore be circumscribed. As Hitler expressed it in a speech on 24 October:

We have brought the priests out of the Party political conflict, and led them back into the Church. And now it is our desire that they should never return to that area for which they were not intended.[40]

The Catholic laity, however, were a more significant target. So long as the Catholic organizations existed under Catholic control, they would be subject to clerical influence. If they could be persuaded to dissolve themselves or be amalgamated with Nazi associations, then the danger of the Church as a rallying point for political discontent would be substantially reduced.

The priests, however, in contrast to the clergy of the Evangelical Church, were known to be well aware of the danger of losing control over their lay organizations – always a strong vehicle of influence in the Church. Especially in Bavaria, where the chances that the Catholic lay organizations might be captured for Nazi purposes seemed remote, a policy of persistent circumscription and restriction was believed to be the most effective means of silencing Catholic opposition. Every unguarded remark was therefore seized upon by the Gestapo as evidence of 'political' opposition and as justification for punitive measures.

Himmler and Heydrich, however, were clever enough to realize that too sudden a departure from the 'official' policy of the Reich Concordat would be likely to stir up a hornet's nest, and not in Germany alone.[41] The power of the Roman Church was far reaching, and therefore all the more dangerous to Nazi ambitions. Accordingly, Himmler was determined to deal more shrewdly with the Catholics than with the Evangelical Church, and on 2 November, an order was issued that no individual action was to be taken by the police without instructions. Compliance with Nazi wishes would not be gained by appeals for the 'conversion' of Catholic doctrine to Nazi ideology nor by assertions that they were identical, but by a series of subtly-planned police measures designed to awaken fears for the position of the Catholic Church in the new German community.

3 'Politics do not belong in the Church'

'Saboteurs must be rendered innocuous even
if they do their nefarious work in the disguise
of a Servant of God.' – *Völkischer Beobachter*

I

At the beginning of 1934 the Nazi campaign against the Churches
was concentrated on limiting the Churches' influence and popularity and, by prohibiting the activity of such lay organizations as
might be used for political agitation or opposition to Nazi totalitarian claims, to drive a wedge between clergy and people. Despite
all the gestures of good-will and compliance made by the Churches
in the first twelve months of Nazi rule, a basic antagonism and
suspicion continued on the Nazi side, with a determination to
forestall any clerical opposition by branding it as 'political' and by
subjecting it to police supervision or suppression. The slogan used
to justify this attitude was that 'politics do not belong in the
church'.

The conflict engendered by these totalitarian measures was felt
most severely in Bavaria. In Munich the hostility to the Church
displayed by Martin Bormann in the Nazi Party Headquarters
was matched by that of Himmler and Heydrich in the Police
Headquarters. For these three men, the appetite for power indeed
grew by what it fed on. They were determined to break once and
for all the strongly entrenched position of the Catholic Church in
Germany's most Catholic province. On 13 October 1933 Bormann
wrote from Munich to all the Nazi *Gauleiters* as follows:

It is reported to Party headquarters that some individual Catholic priests more or less openly are working against Nazism and its leaders both in and outside the Church. The same is reported about certain Catholic organizations. I hereby request you to report *concrete and provable cases* of this nature immediately to this office.[1]

In a similar vein on 21 February 1934, the Special Controller for the Highest SA Leaders in Bavaria circulated a memorandum to all SA leaders on the attitude of the Catholic clergy:

The numerous cases from the various parts of Bavaria, particularly from Franconia and the Palatinate, give a concrete, if unfortunately unwelcome, picture of the attitude of a large part of the clergy against the new State. I have therefore allowed myself to point out that it is not a case of dealing with individuals by police methods, but rather the need for a fundamental change of attitude by the clergy as a whole, with the possible intervention of the Ministry of Education with the Bishops, in order to bring about a change towards the State. For it can be seen that the Catholic clergy, especially those who were formerly so active for the Centre Party or the Bavarian People's Party, cannot realize that they cannot use their position any more for political purposes. But again and again there is evidence that attempts are being made to win back the lost political influence. Particularly in the matter of education, for many clergy the Hitler Youth and the *Bund Deutsche Mädel* are a thorn in the flesh. It would seem time to remind the clergy of the limitations accepted by them in the Concordat, which did not give unlimited rights over against the State, but rather defined their obligations. This particularly applies to the Bishops whose task it is to instruct the clergy to carry out the obligations for the welfare of the State, and to avoid damage to the State's interests. As part of these sworn obligations, in my view, is the duty to discipline clergy who did not give enough respect to the State and those who, along with the majority in their parishes, have set themselves up in total hostility to the State. Such elementary demands have so far not been fulfilled by the Bishops ...[2]

The Nazi strategy for dealing with this suspected hostility was first to restrict all the public activities of Catholics outside their Church buildings, and secondly to obtain detailed information on every aspect of Church life, particularly on the attitude of the clergy as shown in their sermons. On 6 January, a further order to all Bavarian police offices was issued by Heydrich, who, while

claiming to be preserving peaceful relations between Church and
State as established by the Concordat, stated:

> Strict measures are to be taken against anyone who might destroy
> trust in the integrity of the Church treaty partners. . . . Any general
> order for permission for Church meetings must be refused. Only
> individual permits for Church meetings are to be given out and never
> more than for those meetings which can be watched and placed under
> surveillance. . . . The activities of the Catholic organizations cannot be
> entirely refused, but prohibitions can be made on local grounds only.
> . . . Any priests who openly oppose the Government and fail to teach
> their children to give the German greeting [Hitler salute] are destroying
> the educational work of the Nazi State and consciously undermining
> the State's authority. In such circumstances the Bavarian Political Police
> should be informed of the details, along with the names of reliable
> witnesses. . . . A report should be submitted on the 25th of each
> month.[3]

From then on, all church services were placed under regular surveillance. The activities of priests who were suspected of anti-
Nazi sympathies were strictly supervised, and every kind of
obstacle was placed in the way of their work.[4] Nor was the campaign restricted to the inferior clergy. Cardinal Faulhaber of
Munich, who in a series of sermons in November had condemned
the exaltation of race above all other obligations, including those
owed to the Church, was publicly and persistently denounced by
the Nazis as a political reactionary disloyal to Germany.[5] The work
of the Catholic lay organizations and especially of the youth
groups was made increasingly more difficult. The persecution was,
however, sporadic and limited. No general assault was launched,
though many of those attacked had been ardent supporters of the
Centre Party, and hence were vulnerable to a charge of aiding
'political Catholicism'. Most of the clergy acquiesced in their
changed status. Their instinctive desire to support the national
cause, and their sympathy with many of the Nazis' objectives,
reconciled them to the loss of direct political influence. So long as
no direct attempt was made to interfere with the ministrations of
Word and Sacrament, many of the Bishops and the clergy were
content to leave political affairs to the Nazis, having no wish to

circumvent the express provisions of the Concordat which denied them political acticity.

The same attitudes were prevalent amongst the former active members of the Centre and Bavarian People's Party. Dispirited by the turn of events in 1933, abandoned by their leader, Prelate Kaas, and compromised by the signing of the Reich Concordat, most of the Centre Party leaders retreated into silence, or joined the ranks of the Nazi Party to demonstrate their sympathy with the national revolution, or perhaps to preserve their posts in the civil service and elsewhere. Only a few of them attempted to keep 'political Catholicism' alive with the idea of seizing power again when a suitable opportunity arose. A letter from a prominent member of the Catholic Laymans' Organization 'New Germany', dated 21 June 1933, which was captured by the Gestapo during a search of the home of the Duke of Wrade, provided the Nazis with sufficient proof of the dangerous disloyalty of the 'political Catholics' to justify the institution of extreme measures against all such potential opponents.

Tasks and Possibilities of Political Catholicism between the First and Second Wave of the National Revolution in Germany.

The Catholic Church has missed the bus again, always being in opposition to the movements which grip the Germans – liberalism, socialism, national socialism. Despite the Bishops' recantation, it is now too late ... all too probable that we shall now be pushed back into the pre-war Ghetto. Only the Catholic academics have found it a bit easier to creep into the N.S.D.A.P. Flight into the sacristy is a sell-out for the Church ... What we need is our own political leadership. If we get this, it won't matter if we take on the name or the protection of some Nazi formation ... The reason for this firm policy:

a) Naked self-preservation and maintenance of the Catholic milieu, including the position of the Catholic Church in the Third Reich.
b) A Movement which believes in itself and its objects does not dissolve. (Against the so-called infiltration or leavening policy which hopes to win over the N.S.D.A.P. from below.)
c) The need to preserve pluralism of the State and against totalitarian single-race, single-power policies ...

At the present moment, the Bishops, the politicians, and the Catholic

Youth Organizations are all marching in different directions hoping for a Deus Ex Machina to give them directions. We need to combine in order to claim the right to exist. The dynamic lies with the Youth, the leadership is with Brüning and the moral reinsurance with the Bishops ...[6]

But the dissolution of the Centre Party, the signing of the Concordat and the determination of the Nazis to allow no form of 'political Catholicism' to survive made such plans little more than dreams. The retreat into the sacristy began, in part reluctantly, in part not unwillingly. The clergy believed that their hold over their people was safest from within the bastion of the Church's stronghold. They did not perhaps realize that they could also be imprisoned therein.

II

In the meanwhile, a similar disillusionment was growing between the Evangelical Church and the Nazi Party. Not only had Reich Bishop Müller failed to unite the Church behind the Nazi state, but the events of 1933 had unmistakably revealed the differences of opinion within the Evangelical Church itself. By the beginning of 1934 the Pastors' Emergency League had grown to 7,000 members, Goebbels had issued instructions that no further mention of Church conflicts was to be made in the press, and Hitler had ordered a policy of complete reserve on the part of state officials. Despite the restrictions already placed on the Church press, it was accused by *Gauleiter* Florian of harbouring treasonable and separatist elements; while on 26 January 1934 the Bavarian Political Police called for a report on the activities of the Pastors' Emergency League and prohibited all expressions of opinions against Nazism or the State that might endanger public safety.[7]

The focal point of resentment amongst the Evangelical clergy was the ill-fated Reich Bishop Müller. Unwilling to abandon their confidence in Hitler's promises and unaware of the more extreme Nazi plans, the majority of the clergy took exception only to the 'German Christians' ' confusion of politics and religion and to the arbitrariness of Müller's edicts. Protests against Müller's continued holding of the highest spiritual office, despite his evident unworthiness, flowed in from all sides. Having succeeded in protesting against the excesses of Krause's speech, the Pastors' Emergency League now concentrated upon bringing about Müller's resignation. They issued a vote of non-confidence which amounted to an ultimatum.

With a complete lack of any sense of moral obligation, however, Müller refused to resign. Not merely did he secretly arrange in December for the transfer of the Evangelical Youth Groups to the Hitler Youth, but on 4 January 1934 he issued on his own responsibility an edict reimposing the 'Aryan Paragraph' and forbidding the clergy to take a stand on the Church's political situation either in their sermons or by means of circulars and memoranda. This 'muzzling decree', as it became known, served only to aggravate the position. Thousands of pastors defied the Reich Bishop's ban, and at the risk of suspension protested from their pulpits against Müller's authoritarian and illegal actions – protests which, of course, were banned from publication in the press.

On 8 January the Gestapo instructed the police throughout Prussia to report any demonstrations or attacks in speech or writing against the authority of the Reich Bishop. As a result, pastors in Berlin, Thüringen, Brandenburg, Brunswick and Altona were denounced to the Gestapo by Nazi members of their congregations and suspended from office for reading to their congregations the text of the Pastors' Emergency League's reply to the 'muzzling decree'. In Berlin on 24 January an anti-'German Christian' pastor was dragged from his bed and beaten up by five youths. On the same day further fears were aroused by Rosenberg's appointment as the Führer's Delegate for the Entire Spiritual and Philosophical Education and Supervision of the Nazi Party.

Appeals were made both to Hitler and to Hindenburg. On 12 January Hindenburg sent for the Reich Bishop to express his concern at the measures taken. Müller's attempts to justify his conduct were not convincing. A later report to the Reich Chancellery recorded Hindenburg's opinion that the Reich Bishop, partly on health grounds, partly because of lack of authority, was not in a position to rectify the very confused state of affairs of the

Evangelical Church or to restore unity to the Church.[8] The Minister of the Interior, Frick, also expressed a lack of confidence in Müller, to whom hints were dropped that if he could not restore order to his Church, the state subsidies to his office would be stopped.

Hitler, though unwilling to admit that his choice of Müller had been wrong, did not hide his vexation at the intractability of the Evangelical Pastors. On 5 January he stated that he wanted to hear no more about the Evangelical Church and refused to see either Müller or any of the Bishops.

Three weeks later, however, he revised his attitude and decided to intervene personally to bring the issue to a head. On 25 January he interviewed twelve of the most prominent leaders of the Evangelical Church, ostensibly with a view to ascertaining whether or not they were prepared to continue to work with Müller, and in the hope of ending his first year of office with this particular trouble-spot resolved. But the meeting took a very different course from that which the Church leaders had hoped. At the very beginning Goering read out the text of a telephone conversation monitored earlier on the same day by secret microphones, between Pastor Niemöller, who was present, and one of his colleagues.

In the rush of preparations for meeting Hitler, Niemöller had used an unguarded phrase about the influence of Hindenburg on Hitler in the matter of Müller's dismissal. This was seized upon by Hitler as grounds for accusing Niemöller, and with him the whole Pastors' Emergency League, of disloyalty to the Nazi state by trying to drive a wedge between himself and Hindenburg. The other church leaders, shocked by this revelation of Niemöller's impetuosity and fearful of offence or apparent disloyalty to the rulers of the State, hastily dissociated themselves from the activities of Niemöller and his friends. How far the scene had been engineered beforehand remains uncertain. Accusations of disloyalty and of misuse of foreign contacts were nothing new in attacks against the Church leaders, but Goering's presentation of the alleged evidence had exactly the effect upon the pastors which Hitler wanted. Describing the event eight years later he said:

The representatives of the Evangelical Church were so shaken with terror that they literally collapsed, to the point of becoming dumb and invisible.[9]

Niemöller alone answered back – an event of such rarity that Hitler never forgot it – but in the circumstances there was no more talk of forcing Müller's resignation, but only of unswerving loyalty to Germany, to Hitler and to the Nazi State. On the same evening Niemöller's home was searched by the Gestapo for evidence that might incriminate the Pastors' Emergency League with hostile circles abroad, and a few days later, a crudely made bomb exploded in the hallway of his house.

Müller lost no time in reasserting himself. He summoned a meeting of all the provincial bishops, including those hitherto opposed to him, and announced his intention of establishing what was virtually an Episcopal dictatorship over the Prussian Church, thereby dispensing with the need for collaborators in a 'Spiritual Ministry'. Intimidated by the savagery of Hitler's attack and by the supposed 'disloyalty' of Niemöller, the bishops unanimously withdrew their opposition to Müller. They resolved to give no further support to the Pastors' Emergency League, but, in order to restore unity and peace to the German Evangelical Church, to follow obediently the leadership of Hitler's agent, Müller, and to collaborate fully with him. The communiqué issued after the meeting ran as follows:

Under the impression of the great occasion on which the leaders of the German Evangelical Church met with the Reich Chancellor, they unanimously affirm their unconditional loyalty to the Third Reich and its Leader. They most sharply condemn any intrigues or criticism against the State, the People or the [Nazi] Movement, which are designed to endanger the Third Reich. In particular they deplore any activities on the part of the foreign Press which seek falsely to represent the discussions within the Church as a conflict against the State. The assembled Church leaders stand unitedly behind the Reich Bishop and desire to carry out his measures and directives in the manner he has laid down, to prevent opposition against them from within the Church, and to strengthen the authority of the Reich Bishop with all the constitutional means at their disposal.[10]

At Müller's suggestion this declaration was immediately sent to the Press, 'in order to avoid any possible misunderstandings'.[11]

A flood of disciplinary measures followed, coupled in the majority of the provincial churches with suspensions, dismissals, and the retirement of members of the Pastors' Emergency League by Müller and by the 'German Christian' bishops. The opposition was to be compelled into silence. On 27 January Niemöller was given leave of absence, and on 10 February was superannuated without leave to appeal. The leader of the Pastors' Emergency League in Saxony was placed in a concentration camp, and in Prussia Pastor Rzadtki of Schneidemühl was likewise sent to a concentration camp for five weeks for refusing to endorse the opinion of the local *Gauleiter* Kube that Faith arises out of Blood.[12] Meanwhile, services of celebration and thanksgiving were held in many Evangelical Churches on 30 January, to mark the first anniversary of the Nazi assumption of power.

III

Hitler had thus given Müller another chance to restore order in the Evangelical Church. Party officers were warned not to interfere with church affairs, nor to introduce religious matter into Party activities. In a directive issued to Reich Leaders and *Gauleiters*, Hess stated: '. . . I have . . . also heard that at some Party meetings there have been discussions of religious problems, even hymns sung from hymn books. According to my instructions of 17 October 1933, this is all forbidden. Church affairs should have no place in the Party.'[13] In early March, Heydrich instructed the Bavarian police forces to avoid any action which might disturb the work of unity and growth of a united Evangelical Church, now that the Evangelical leaders had agreed to support the Reich Bishop and his measures. 'The attitude of the State authorities is also important in this respect. We must keep to the instructions of the Führer not to interfere in church quarrels within the Evangelical Church. After the agreement reached on 27 January 1934, this attitude is even more necessary. The authorities must take great care not to mix themselves in purely theological questions, though of course in cases of political activity suitable measures must be taken. But since any mistake might be dangerous, action against Evangelical priests is only to be taken by permission of the Bavarian Political Police.'[14] Caution was still to be the watch-word of state policy. In order that there should be no martyrs in the church, the Pastors' Emergency League was not prohibited, despite pressure from the 'German Christians' and an evident readiness on the part of the Minister of the Interior.[15]

Hitler's innate hostility to the Church, however, tempered though it was by political expediency, was clearly shown in his interview on 13 March with the two South German Evangelical Bishops Meiser and Wurm, who came to complain that, despite the declaration of solidarity which the bishops at Hitler's request had given to the Reich Bishop on 27 January, Müller's subsequent actions had only further demonstrated his untrustworthiness. Confronted with such criticism, Hitler was sharply belligerent. His words, as recorded by Bishop Meiser, are in significant contrast to the display of supposed sympathy assumed for the benefit of Bishop Berning less than a year before:

Christianity will disappear from Germany just as it has done in Russia. The churches were not able to prevent either the French Revolution, or Bolshevism, or Marxism, or the Revolution of 1918. He had offered the Evangelical Churches the greatest opportunities. If the Church would not take advantage of them, the people would not suffer. But it would be another question whether the Church as an institution would not be broken by such behaviour. The German race had existed without Christianity for thousands of years before Christ and would continue to exist after Christianity had disappeared. The Church had failed to recognize its epoch. Instead of seizing their opportunities and involving themselves in history with all their energies, the bishops and priests had gone off into quarrels about dogma. He wasn't going to involve himself in doctrinal questions. All he was interested in was that there should be a firm authority in the Church. It was highly regrettable that the Evangelical Church had no firm doctrine. Some interpreted God's Word in one way, others quite differently. The Orthodox were accused even by the 'German Christians' of heresy. He had had to tell the 'German Christians' that they should forego all quarrels over doctrinal matters. First of all the exterior of the building

must be constructed. After that there would be plenty of time to enter-
tain themselves with dogmatic questions. He knew the people and how
they were annoyed at the way in which these old quarrels were being
dragged up again in these times. The Church left him alone when he
was fighting for power. He had expressed his desire for a National
Church. Instead of that, there were all these attempts to maintain the
provincial churches and to prevent the creation of a strong central
authority. He would suggest to the Churches that they had been unable
to grow out of their provincialism, even though Luther had long ago
expressed himself in favour of a National Church. Luther would today
be standing on the side of the 'German Christians'. The Pastors' Emergency League was nothing but a lot of reactionaries. He knew the
people who belonged to it. They were all his old opponents. As for the
criticism against Ludwig Müller, it was all a lot of rubbish. Everybody
had moral failings. Even the Kaiser had moral failings, but he was
supported loyally. We (the Evangelical Churchmen) had elected Müller
ourselves and now we had to put up with him.

He was not going to be bothered with doctrinal questions which
didn't interest him at all . . . The Church must get used to the teachings
about Blood and Race. Just as the Catholic Church couldn't prevent the
earth from going round the sun, so the Churches today could not get
rid of the indisputable facts connected with Blood and Race. If they
couldn't recognize these, history would simply leave them behind.
He never went to a Catholic Church, but still less did he want to go to
an Evangelical Church which was so riven with disputes . . . about the
'German Christians' he said they must also put an end to theological
bickering . . . Müller was not to be pursued for the sake of revenge. He
had shown himself loyal during all the years before the revolution and
already then had been thinking about a National Church. If he – Hitler
– had known how matters would develop, he would never have bothered
with the Evangelical Church at all.

Despite this violent outburst, the two bishops remained uncon-
vinced. If such was Hitler's view, Meiser averred, then they could
only look forward to being the proponents of Hitler's most loyal
opposition. At which Hitler, in a fury of rage, retorted: 'You are
not my most loyal opposition, but traitors to the people, enemies
of the Fatherland and the destroyers of Germany.'[16]

The reaction within the Evangelical Church was both confused
and confusing. Though appalled by the fanaticism of the extreme

'German Christians', the majority of the pastors were equally disinclined to remain in association with Niemöller if he were indeed 'disloyal' to the established government. Many of them were so deeply shocked by the tumultuous course of events in the first year of Nazi rule that their only wish was to withdraw from political involvement of any sort. Both their sense of loyalty to established power and their theological leanings, strongly influenced by the Pietistic tradition, inclined them towards a purely 'spiritual' ministry, concerned only with individualistic salvation and ethics, and a readiness to obey the government's orders under all circumstances.[17] On that account they were prepared to accept the Nazi dictum that 'politics do not belong in the Church'. But their voluntary flight into the sacristy inevitably led to a passive acceptance of the measures taken against the Church by the Nazi forces. And their naive confidence that the Nazis could be trusted to order the 'temporal' affairs of the nation in the best interests of all was matched by an illusion that in the 'spiritual' realm the Church would continue respected, supported, and inviolate.

IV

With the beginning of 1934, the Nazis began more openly to attack the position of the Church in their public speeches. Goebbels, Rosenberg, Goering and Schirach in particular repeatedly referred to the Church question and made no secret of their hostility. Whereas the Nazi Party, they claimed, had saved the Church from extinction at the hands of the Marxists and had established its status by means of the Reich Concordat, the Church had shown its gratitude by becoming a breeding-ground of political disaffection, creating, by its doctrinal differences, a disunity among the people which was a danger to the unity of the German Reich.[18] The Churches, they maintained, would do far better to concentrate on charitable works than on dogmatic squabbles. Politics must be wholly separated from the Church, and the clergy would do well to remember the words 'My kingdom is not of this world'. No longer could the Church believe that it could play a part in the political education of the people; its role was rather to stand in solidarity behind the new State and to limit itself to its spiritual functions—matters which the Nazis were prepared to tolerate because they were irrelevant to the Party's present concerns.

Consequently, any move suggestive of 'political activity' provoked a sharp reaction among the Nazi leaders. For example, the attempts of the Catholic Action to consolidate the work of the Catholic organizations was stigmatized by Goering as demonstrating the existence of 'a firm block within the Catholic clergy which continues to oppose the aims and schemes of the Nazi State'.[19]

In contrast, the reserve of the Catholic leaders was notable. In fact they were deeply divided. Many believed that the Nazis sincerely intended to keep the promises made by Hitler in March 1933 and outlined in the provisions of the Concordat. Did not the Church and the Nazi government share a common belief in the need for strong national leadership, and were they not equally opposed to the radical tendencies of rationalistic philosophies? Did they not stand united against the menace of Communism? Sooner or later the Nazi Party must surely realize that the Church was equally dedicated to the values of an authoritarian society, and would not the agitation then die away when it was realized how staunch a pillar of the Third Reich the Catholic Church would become?[20] Other Catholic thinkers were less optimistic, in view of the course of events in the Evangelical Churches. They feared that the anti-Christian element in the Nazi Party was in the ascendant and that the Reich Concordat had been little more than a delusion from the start.

From the distance of Rome, such fears were very strong. As early as December Cardinal Pacelli had expressed to an official of the German Ministry of the Interior the dismay felt by the Pope at the inadequate fulfilment of the Concordat and at the restrictions laid upon Catholic clergy, including the attempt to impose the 'Aryan' clause on Catholic teachers of theology. Indeed, the Cardinal spoke openly of his fear of a new *'Kulturkampf'*.[21]

So sharp was this antagonism that, only a few days after the appointment of Rosenberg as the Führer's delegate, the Vatican responded by placing *The Myth of the Twentieth Century* on the Index, thereby setting in motion a huge wave of Catholic propaganda against the evils of the New Heathenism. While no names were mentioned, though the meaning was clear, this counterattack served to clarify at least some of the issues. But even the thunder from Rome was insufficient to combat the onslaught of Goebbels' Ministry of Propaganda, with all its machinery geared to engender a quasi-religious belief in Hitler's infallibility and to create, even among Churchmen, a fanatical enthusiasm for the Nazis' 'successes'.

Those amongst the Catholic leaders who were pessimistic over the prospects for the Church were soon to have their fears confirmed. But they were in a quandary: only a few months earlier they had given their approval to the Concordat; to revoke their stand now would be both illogical and unpatriotic. More or less reluctantly, therefore, they were obliged to allow themselves to be persuaded, both by their more optimistic colleagues and by the pressure of their parishioners, to adopt an attitude of reserve towards the current political events, which excluded intervention in matters not specifically ecclesiastical.[22]

In the early months of 1934 the Nazis began to devote particular attention to their campaign for control of the Catholic Youth Organizations. In this they were encouraged by Müller's voluntary transfer of the Evangelical Church Youth, and they hoped for some similar arrangement with the Catholics. The willingness of the priests to abandon their political activities and to acknowledge that politics were not the proper concern of the Church would, the Nazis hoped, be matched by a readiness to co-operate with the new government in leaving the political education of German youth entirely in the hands of the Party. The *Gleichschaltung* (co-ordination) of the Catholic Youth organizations would, of course, give the Nazis a stranglehold over the future of Catholicism in Germany, for it would enable the Party so to indoctrinate the younger generation that they would accept the Nazi teachings of racialism, nationalism, and aggression unquestionably and without reserve. But the Catholic youth groups were a large and indispensable part of the Roman Church, and opposition to the Nazi plans were therefore inevitable. The Nazi tactics for dealing with such resistance were to repeat, on an even more effective scale, the mixture of blandishments and threats which a year ago had been used to secure the Concordat. In towns and villages where the Hitler Youth was already established, its members were openly encouraged to organize scuffles and brawls with the 'Black Youth'.[23] Defamation of Catholic Youth Groups became more and more frequent, and priests were denounced for failing to urge their young people to join the Hitler Youth. Baldur von Schirach, the Reich Youth leader, appealing to the patriotism of the childrens' parents, urged them to accept loyalty to Germany as a claim superior to their denominational ties. His call to the Catholic Youth on 15 March 1934, was designed to contrast the 'disloyalty' of Catholic sectarianism with the bright future ahead for those who joined the victorious Nazi throng.[24]

Meanwhile, in the Evangelical camp, the Reich Bishop had laid plans to gain control of all the organs of government in his Church. The first stage of his strategy – that of unifying the different regional Evangelical Churches – had been achieved by July 1933. The agreement of 27 January 1934, had marked the second stage; and now the third was to be begun.

On 7 March, Müller issued a new ordinance on the administration of the German Evangelical Church, and on 13 April, he granted a general amnesty to all pastors who had been subjected to disciplinary action because of current disputes. A new 'Spiritual Ministry' was to be appointed, and the restrictions imposed on 4 January were to be removed. The sting in the tail of this announcement, however, was the appointment of the notorious August Jäger to be the legal member of this 'Spiritual Ministry' and legal administrator of the Church.[25] His task was to destroy the individual provincial Church administrations which had so far refused to acknowledge Müller's leadership and to subordinate them all to Müller's central direction. Those of the twenty-eight provincial churches which already had 'German Christian' bishops, synods and administrators promptly handed over their executive authority to Müller and Jäger. At Jäger's suggestion, membership of the reconstituted National Synod was limited to those 'who at all times have shown themselves wholeheartedly on the side not only of the German Evangelical Church but also of the Nazi State'.[26] In other parts of the country Synods which resisted Müller's plans were quickly dissolved, often by the police, and more compliant assemblies were convened in their place, and voted their powers into the hands of the Reich Bishop.[27]

There was, however, some resistance within the churches. Freely-chosen Synods were set up, which claimed to be the voice of the 'true' Church and refused to accept the authority imposed upon them from Berlin. And in certain churches, notably in Bavaria and Württemberg, the Church authorities refused to hand over the reins of office to Müller, and took council with others of like mind to resist this attempt at episcopal subjection.

To subdue this insubordination Müller decided to make an example of the Bishop of Württemberg. On 16 April, an announcement was made on the radio – obviously at the inspiration of Müller and Jäger – that Bishop Wurm no longer enjoyed the confidence of his Church Council and was no longer acceptable as a public figure in the new Reich. Müller and Jäger arrived in Stuttgart on the following day to 'restore unity' to the Evangelical Church in Württemberg, but they found that public support was entirely behind the Bishop, who refused to be coerced into silent obedience. By this time Bishop Wurm had realized the full implications of his pledge of support to Müller made at the end of January, and he had now decided to support new efforts towards a common action against further attempts by Müller at arbitrary dictatorship within the Church. On 22 April, in Bishop Wurm's Cathedral at Ulm, a conference was gathered from the whole country, to consider the structure of an alternative Church government. The Declaration issued by the conference boldly stated that:

We, the assembled representatives of the Württemberg and Bavarian Provincial Churches, of the Free Synods in the Rhineland, Westphalia, and Brandenburg, as well as of many confessing congregations and Christians throughout Germany, make this declaration before this congregation and the whole of Christendom as the constitutional Evangelical Church of Germany.[28]

With this bold claim the Confessing Church can be said to have come into being. Its affairs were to be conducted by a Reich Council of Brethren, most of whose members had already been engaged in the affairs of the Pastors' Emergency League.

Müller and his Nazi supporters were scandalized and alarmed at this public repudiation of the Reich Church government and at the establishment of a rival authority with considerable backing within the Church. Nor was the subsequent news of the calling of a rival National Synod at Barmen any more welcome. But Hitler was still unwilling to sanction a large-scale persecution of Müller's opponents, partly because of the damage to Germany's reputation abroad likely to be caused by such a manifest lack of harmony. That Germany's reputation indeed was suffering was made known to him by a long report prepared by the Foreign Ministry in June 1934, detailing the reactions to events in the Evangelical Church as sent in by German Embassies abroad and which affirming bluntly that 'conditions in the Evangelical Church in the Reich have developed during the last few months in a manner likely to jeopardise seriously the Reich's political and economic relations abroad'.[29] For example, the German ambassador in London, it was stated, had had a forthright interview with the extremely well-informed Bishop of Chichester, Dr George Bell, who had declared that Müller's acts of arbitrary repression had caused very great concern throughout all the European Protestant Churches, and indeed throughout the whole Ecumenical Movement.

The Reich Council of Brethren, under the guidance of Professor Karl Barth, recognized the need for a definition of what constituted theological as distinct from political concerns – what, in fact, was to be rendered to Caesar and what to God. In their eyes, the unscriptural acceptance of Nazi views by the 'German Christians' on the one side was matched by the ineffectualness of the 'Pietists' on the other. The concepts of Christian involvement in politics and the limits of Christian loyalty to the State now had to be distinguished. In a series of meetings held during the months following the capitulation of the Church leaders to Hitler's pressure, the task was undertaken. It terminated in the writing of the famous Barmen Confession of May 1934. The six articles of the

Confession recalled the German Church to the central truths of Christianity and totally rejected the false doctrines of the 'German Christians'. Indeed, Article 5 went so far as to reject the totalitarian claims of the State both on the Church and in the political field.

We reject the false doctrine that the State, over and above its special commission, should and could become the single and totalitarian order of human life, thus fulfilling the Church's vocation as well.

We reject the false doctrine that the Church over and above its special commission, should and could appropriate the characteristics, the tasks, and the dignity of the State, thus itself becoming an organ of the State.[30]

This trenchant rejection was aimed both at the Nazi Party's claims to undivided loyalty and to Müller's attempt to use the State's power to enforce his decisions on the Church. But, couched as it was in general terms, the Declaration was of considerably deeper significance. It became indeed the basic statement of the whole Confessing Church, a theological life-line in the stormy seas which lay ahead, forged to hold the Church true to its mission and to allow it neither to become a propaganda weapon of a political movement nor a society for the propagation of views about the next world.

It must be emphasized, however, that the Confessing Church did not intend to use the Barmen Declaration as a programme of political protest. Neither in 1934 nor at any time afterwards was it the aim of the Confessing Church to become the spearhead of political opposition to the Nazis or the organizers of resistance to the tyranny which was to engulf the whole country. Nor did they take a stand in the early years against such crimes as the murders of 30 June 1934, the persecution of the Jews or the erection of concentration camps. For this, there are three principal reasons. In the first place, these men were theologians not politicians. Their concern was to maintain the integrity of the Gospel against the distortions and misuse of the 'German Christians'. Their call was to preserve the heritage of the Christian faith against evident heresy. In this they enjoyed the support of many people especially laymen, who were supporters of Hitler and even Nazi Party members, in whose minds a protest against heresies of the 'German

Christians' was completely dissociated from political circumstances. For instance, even in Niemöller's church, while denuncia-
tions of Reich Bishop Müller were made from the chancel steps,
Nazi flags hung on the walls and the Hitler salute was given by the
congregation. Throughout the Confessing Church loyalty to
Hitler was professed by clergy and by laity, and even the more
clear-sighted long continued to believe that a compromise was
possible by which the Church could be freed from 'German
Christian' regimentation, the concomitant intervention by the
state could be checked, and the energies of both could be united
for the benefit of the German nation.

Secondly, most of the Evangelical clergy refused to be committed to any political involvement, either with the 'German
Christians' or with the Confessing Church. Indeed, those in the
Confessing Church who sought to establish a connection between
theological and political resistance were constantly hampered by
the reluctance of the majority to accept what to the exponents of
resistance was the urgent need for a stand against the Nazi totalitarian claims, at the very least in matters which directly affected
the Church.

Thirdly, the Lutheran tradition of respect for the ruling power
was too deeply engrafted to be lightly overthrown. The popular
image of the pastor in German society was one of loyal support to
the ruling classes, never of dissent or opposition. How difficult this
tradition was to break can be seen in the deliberate decision of the
Confessing Church not to set itself up as a rival free Church. This
decision was taken both for social and for theological reasons. The
clergy had no wish to lose the social advantages of the establishment, only a few of them recognizing that in a Nazi State the
pastors were bound to be regarded as citizens of the second rank.
Theologically, they had a hatred of sectarianism. The Confessing
Church stoutly affirmed the mission of the 'true' Church, and
regarded the Nazi and 'German Christian' innovations as merely
temporary, if heretical, phenomena. The orthodoxy of the
Christian Gospel had to be defended, but not by abdication or the
establishment of another sect.

Some of the pastors, it is true, realized that their plans to represent the 'true' Church by establishing a 'Provisional Church Administration' for the whole German Evangelical Church could not hope to succeed even if a majority of the Evangelical clergy supported them – which unfortunately was never the case. The 'official' Church government under Reich Bishop Müller had no intention of resigning and still apparently enjoyed the official support of the Nazi Party and the State. The Confessing Church's only hope of establishing its right to be the effective government of the Church would have been that Hitler would withdraw his support of the pro-Nazi 'German Christian' movement and appoint their nominees instead. But these were the men, Barth, Niemöller, Jacobi and Dibelius, who had already challenged him on the Nazis' most salient and sensitive issue namely by their rejection of the 'Aryan' clause for the ministers of the Church. Alternatively, the Confessing Church might have succeeded by compromising for the sake of national unity, and by working their way into the Church government by glossing over theological difficulties and ignoring the political issues at stake.

This temptation indeed occurred, and led to still further divisions within the Evangelical Church – divisions which were promptly exploited by the Nazis. With the refusal of most Churchmen to follow a course of political and theological 'disloyalty', hopes for a centre of resistance to Nazism quickly faded, while Luther's supposed teaching of obedience to the state was extended and misinterpreted to cover the submission of increasing numbers of Churchmen.

Fundamentally, the reason for the lack of political resistance in the churches lay in the fact that the same political outlook and attitude were shared by the German people as a whole, Churchmen and others alike. Like the lawyers, the doctors and the university professors, churchmen were carried away by nationalist emotions and became too bemused to make a stand in defence of democracy and the rights of the individual. As time was to prove, Protestants and Catholics, in common with most other Germans, condoned Hitler's course of aggression and expansion, believed in Germany's mission to save the world from Communism, suffered bitter disillusionment by the events of the War, and were divided in conscience over the loyalty of the Resistance Movement. The majority of the clergy were probably never convinced Nazis; but neither were they more than passive resisters to Nazi tyranny. Their attempts to create an effective opposition were doomed to failure from the start – indeed, considering the psychological obstacles in their way, it is perhaps surprising that an opposition existed at all. For most Germans, national loyalty dictated their political outlook, even in the Confessing Church. As for the Catholics, Professor Zahn has justly pointed out that:

At no time was the German Catholic population released from its moral obligation to obey the legitimate authority of the National Socialist rulers under whom those Catholics were placed by the 1933 directives of their spiritual leaders; At no time was the individual German Catholic led to believe that the regime was an evil unworthy of his support.[31]

The illusion that Hitler could do no wrong, even if his subordinates openly persecuted the Church and clergy, faded only when events in the last years of the war forced all Germans to see that their idol had feet of clay.

v

To the more militant Nazis, the weaknesses in the Church's stand were merely matters to be exploited for their own ends. The only acceptable attitude was total submission; anything less called for prompt and effective counteraction. Both the objections of the Catholic bishops and the deliberations of the Confessing Church were regarded as dangerous focus points of opposition and as evidence of a hostility to the Nazi State which could not be disregarded. The publication of the Barmen Confession was immediately followed by the confiscation of the text by the Gestapo in many parts of the country, and by threats of the concentration camp for those who possessed a copy. Since the police restrictions already in force had proved insufficient to tame the Churches into submission, 'localized' campaigns designed to terrorize the Church into silence must therefore be extended and intensified. Behind the scenes, even more comprehensive plans were in preparation. In May 1934 Himmler's personal 'security service', in a 32-page report on the relations between the Catholic Church and National Socialism, recommended an all-out attack against the Catholic Action, the leading layman's organization,[32] whose hostility to the Nazi movement could, the report alleged, be considered 'proved' by its self-appointed mission to take over the 'political' life of the Church after the exclusion of the clergy under the provisions of the Concordat. On 5 June another report was submitted to Heydrich, the executive head of the 'security service', containing lists of Catholic priests in the strongly Catholic Rhineland who were opposed to the Nazi movement.

And a few days later, on 21 June, a long report appeared from the same detachment under the title 'Suggestions for Counter-Measures Against the Large-Scale Operations of the Catholic Action.[33] The purpose of the increased activity of the Catholic Action could not, the report stated, be for the reasons given, namely, to strengthen Catholic faith and to combat the new heathenism of Rosenberg or Ludendorff.

It becomes ever clearer that the chief reason for the struggle is a campaign against Nazism. It concerns the maintenance of positions from which the Church in the past exercised her power and importance in public life and which she is determined to continue to exercise; . . . in particular the maintenance of the large Catholic professional and youth organizations which will demonstrate the Church's special position against the organizations of the Nazi State and the separate leadership of the Catholic people dividing them off from the great German people's movement . . . the Catholic organizations used to be the auxiliaries and the actual strength of the Centre Party. . . . Now in the difficult economic situation of the last few months these experienced politicians believe that they see the right moment has come to attack Nazism by arousing a general unrest among the people in the Catholic areas of the country.

Counter-measures against this political opposition were alleged to be not only necessary but justifiable on the grounds that, according to Catholic Canon Law, the Concordat was valid only so long as its conditions, both explicit and implicit, were upheld. Hitler categorically stated that a complete withdrawal from politics by the clergy and their open and active support of the Nazi State were an essential condition of the Concordat. The attitude of the Catholic organizations and of certain priests, coupled with their encouragement of political opposition by means of mass meetings and other gatherings, 'proved' that this condition was not being fulfilled. The Concordat could therefore be considered invalid as regards these 'disloyal' groups and no justifiable objections could be raised against disciplinary measures by the State.

In any case a far-reaching regulation of the activities of Church organizations would appear necessary to all right-thinking persons, after these affairs during the liberal era had grown up like weeds far too much. This regulation in the last resort would not only be in the interests of the *Volksgemeinschaft* but of the Church itself since it would define clearly the relationship of Church and State in extra-Church activities.

Precise plans were accordingly proposed for the control of the Catholic organizations, still widely held to be the spearhead of subversive activity and the breeding-ground of 'political Catholicism' aimed at separating the Catholic population from the rest of the German people. It would be necessary to ensure that the Catholic organizations which in the past had been politically incriminated, and which now were stirring up opposition, must be excluded from the provisions of the Concordat. The professional organizations, in particular, must be dissolved because of their claim on the allegiance of their followers 'in areas of life which in a unified people's community could only belong to the State'. This would include the labour unions, the civil servants' associations, the Catholic Academics' Association and the Catholic Women's Auxiliary, as well as associated organizations for young people and apprentices.

Mass meetings and rallies, it was suggested, could be prevented if each organization was allowed to meet only within the walls of the Church buildings. Processions and pilgrimages established by custom in the parishes could hardly be prohibited, but they could be limited to the parish concerned and should not be allowed to take place jointly with other parishes. The police must be exactly informed of all such gatherings. Detailed plans were also suggested for the handling of hostile priests.³⁴

The evidence that the Gestapo had made well-prepared plans for dealing with opponents within the Catholic Church is conclusive. Secret lists were prepared of high-ranking Catholics who should be 'liquidated', and as part of a wider action which Himmler was preparing to launch against political 'reactionaries' throughout the country, SS leaders were informed of measures to deal with turbulent priests.

By June 1934, political tension in Germany was rising rapidly. On the one side, the more radical Nazis were stridently demanding a 'second revolution', from which they hoped to gain the fruits of office which they had earlier been denied. They aimed at the destruction of the conservative hierarchy of the Army and the establishment of a people's Army in tune with the revolutionary spirit of Nazism, under the leadership of the chief revolutionary street-fighter of the movement, SA Commander Ernst Röhm. On the other side, the conservative forces, particularly in the ranks of the regular Army, relying on the support of the aged and ailing President, were ready even to withdraw their support of Hitler if he failed to quell his extremists and thereby to remove the danger of a second revolution.

Hindenburg was obviously dying. With his death, there was the possibility that Hitler might be deposed if he continued to encourage the SA and his extremist followers in the belief that they were 'Germany's destiny'.³⁵ A public protest had already been voiced by no less a figure than the Catholic Vice-Chancellor von Papen. In a speech at Marburg University on 17 June, Papen expressed all the fears and resentment of the conservatives in a spirited attack on the notion of a second revolution. 'It is time,' he declared, 'to join together in fraternal friendship and respect for all our fellow countrymen, to avoid disturbing the labours of serious men and to silence fanatics.' His speech had been drafted by a leading Munich lawyer, Edgar Jung, who for many years had been a prominent worker for Catholic Action and who doubtless welcomed this opportunity of reasserting the Christian foundation of the State and the need to avoid agitation and propaganda.

In the midst of the crisis, Hitler decided to bargain with the Army. He promised the Generals that he would put an end to the activities of Röhm and his SA storm-troopers and maintain the authority of the Army hierarchy, if in turn the Generals would support him in his determination to alter the Constitution on Hindenburg's death, and to proclaim himself President as well as Chancellor. Believing that this argument would enable them to exercise a dominant political influence thereafter, the generals accepted. Hitler, it need hardly be said, had no intention of allowing the 'reactionaries' to influence him in the future development of his plans, but he was anxious to avoid a head-long clash during the last days of Hindenburg's life. A similar caution also governed his attitude to the Churches. Rosenberg noted in his diary that Hitler had decreed on 27 June that no attacks were to be made needlessly against the Church. 'The "old Gentleman" should be spared every possible trouble, since he believes that Hindenburg cannot last much longer.'[36]

Nevertheless, to show the conservative forces that he was no mere pawn in their hands, Hitler personally ordered the arrest of Papen's speech-writer, Dr Jung, and his transfer to Gestapo head-quarters in Berlin. Papen's speech was banned from the press, and Goebbels furiously replied to it on 24 June with a fiery attack on the upper classes as the enemies of Nazism.

The long-delayed negotiations with the Catholic Episcopate were resumed on 25 June to settle the future implementation of Article 31 of the Concordat, and with it the status of the Catholic organizations. As the political crisis mounted on 27 June, the only day which Hitler spent in Berlin during the whole crucial period, he received representatives of the Catholic hierarchy in a long interview conducted in a most friendly tone. Hitler promised to make a personal announcement in the press to the effect that both Government and Party were favourably disposed towards the activities of the Catholic Church in her own sphere and that neither would have anything to do with the so-called 'third religion', the German National Church, or similar movements opposed to Christianity.[37]

It is not clear whether this show of friendliness was dictated by tactical considerations, in order to win the Catholic Church's support as he had won the Army's, or whether it was no more than a manoeuvre to placate the Bishops while plans were hatched for the ruthless liquidation of all opponents. The guise of friendliness was at any rate sufficient for negotiations to proceed smoothly between the representatives of the Catholic hierarchy under Archbishop Gröber, and members of the Reich Ministry of the Interior, the Nazi leaders of the Youth Movement, and the German Labour Front.

After four days, agreement was finally reached on a provisional settlement of the vexed question of the future of the Church organizations. The Bishops promised that the Catholic organizations would withdraw from all political activities, and the Nazis pledged themselves to respect the existence of the Catholic Youth Organizations, even of those whose extinction had already been ordered by Himmler.[38] On the following day, however, 30 June 1934, before their agreement could be ratified, news was received of the Röhm *Putsch* and of the terrible wave of indiscriminate assassinations which followed. The negotiations were broken off in the general panic that ensued, and were never resumed.

The blood-bath, which in the early hours of that fateful day began with the capture of Röhm and his lieutenants, was seized upon by the SS as a pretext for putting into effect their well-laid plans against the Catholic Church. On the afternoon of the same day, Dr Erich Klausener, a leading German Catholic layman, and the General Secretary of the Catholic Action, was shot dead in his office in Berlin by SS Leader Gildisch; it was later announced that he had committed suicide. The National Director of the Catholic Youth Sports Association, Adalbert Probst, was abducted and later found shot dead, allegedly while 'fleeing from arrest'. The bodies of the two dead men were not handed over to their relatives, but were cremated in defiance of Catholic doctrine. Dr Edgar Jung was shot in the cellars of the Gestapo headquarters. In Munich the editor of the Catholic weekly *Der Gerade Weg*, Dr Fritz Gerlich, who had been severely critical of the Nazis, was likewise murdered. The body of Father Bernhard Stempfle, editor of an anti-semitic Bavarian newspaper, who years ago had collaborated

in the drafting of *Mein Kampf*, was found in a wood in the
suburbs; he too had allegedly been 'trying to escape'.[39] And the
leading Catholic politician and former Chancellor of the Reich,
Dr Brüning, undoubtedly escaped a similar fate only because he
happened to be in London at the time.

These murders were not the result of a 'mistake'; nor can they
be explained away as a 'spontaneous improvisation' by undisci-
plined lower ranks of the Party. They are the final proof of the
SS leaders' long-prepared plot to eliminate all opponents of
Nazism, including those in the Church, or to force them into
obedience by terror and violence. Unlike those members of the
party who had sought to make political capital out of Catholic
support or who were restrained by the possibility of repercussions
abroad, the more extreme Nazis were determined to carry through
their policy of persecution by police measures, imprisonment and
if necessary, murder.

As Professor Trevor-Roper has rightly said:

The Blood-Bath of June 30th, 1934, set the tune for Hitler's rule. It
showed that it was not only a dictatorship, but a criminal dictatorship.
. . . Several hundred Germans were murdered without evidence, charge,
or trial. And to the astonishment of the civilized world, German society
not only acquiesced in this brutal slaughter, unparalleled since the
Massacre of St. Bartholomew, it applauded. The President thanked
the Chancellor, though a previous Chancellor, appointed by him, was
amongst the victims. The Vice-Chancellor, whose two assistants had
been murdered continued to serve their murderer. The German Army
obediently swore an illegal oath of personal allegiance to its blood-
stained master. The German people, on the next opportunity,
emphatically confirmed his regime.[40]

It is a sad fact that the leaders of the Churches also acquiesced in
this deplorable apostasy. The Catholic Hierarchy made no attempt
to condemn the atrocities carried out despite Hitler's promises to
the Bishops on 27June. Undoubtedly a tremendous relief was felt
at the sudden removal of the anarchistic threat posed by the SA,
which had been only too real to the Churches for the previous
eighteen months. Only Bishop Bares, the Catholic Bishop of
Berlin, refused to believe the lie about Klausener's suicide, and

wrote to Hitler for an explanation; but even he could go so far as to say: 'I do not doubt for a moment that Your Excellency did not include Klausener in the framework of those measures thought to be necessary against proven revolutionary elements, and that his death was only the result of an unfortunate chain of unforeseen events.'[41]

Nor did any word of condemnation come from Reich Bishop Müller in the name of the Evangelical Church. Indeed only a few days later, despite the Ministry of the Interior's prohibition on political utterances issued on 9 July, Jäger had the temerity to demand of his opponents in the Church 'to ask themselves whether they too were not in part guilty of the events which have lately shattered our people'.[42] Despite the bold statements made by the Confessing Church at Barmen only a month before, no protests of any sort came from its leaders. A much more typical reaction among large sections of the clergy was expressed by the Evangelical Bishop of Nassau-Hessen, Dr Dietrich, in a telegram to Hitler:

The Evangelical Church of Nassau-Hessen sends its warmest thanks for firm rescue operation, along with best wishes and renewed promises of unalterable loyalty. We pray for God's blessing on our beloved Führer.[43]

And in a circular letter, dated 4 July, while the reverberations of the blood-bath were scandalizing all Europe, the bishop followed up this telegram by writing to his clergy:

The events of June 30th, 1934, have opened the eyes of the blind, and demonstrated to the world, as I always affirmed, the unique greatness of the Führer. *He has been sent to us by God.*[44]

The reaction to the events of 30 June revealed all the weaknesses of the spiritual leadership of Germany. Who can doubt that the failure to condemn these enormities, and the lack of the moral integrity and courage to censure those who perpetrated them, paved the way for the Church's silence about the far greater Nazi crimes which lay ahead?

4 'The Church must be separate from the State'

'When we put on our brownshirts, then we
cease to be Catholics or Protestants, we are
only Germans.' – ALFRED ROSENBERG, in
Hanover, 22 January 1934

The Röhm *Putsch* brought home to all Germans who were not
completely intoxicated by Nazi aspirations of grandeur the utter
ruthlessness of the régime and the determination of its leaders, not
merely to obliterate opposition to their political hegemony, but
to treat as subversion deserving of imprisonment, or even of death,
many of the practices which had hitherto been regarded as of no
political significance. This is particularly true as regards the
Churches. The Nazi interpretation of the slogan 'Politics do not
belong in the Church' was far more comprehensive and more
damaging to the Churches' interests than was realized by the well-
meaning churchmen who had agreed to accept it in principle. The
slogan had been deliberately coined to conceal the Nazis' intention
of excluding the Church from involvement in any aspect of
political life. The only permitted role for the Churches was, as
we have seen, to cater for the support of the State and the Party.

From 1934 onwards the Nazi attack on the Church was conducted along three separate lines. The first line was designed to
win administrative control, whereby the Evangelical Church,
and later the Roman Catholic Church, would be brought under
the authority of the State. This conflict ebbed and flowed right up
to the outbreak of war, when Hitler declared a truce. It caused a
great deal of controversy and intrigue, but it was in fact never

more than a façade, only the actual participants believing that the administration of the Churches was the crucial concern at stake.

Secondly, there was the ideological struggle, the object of which, under the spur of Rosenberg's ideas, was to capture the heart and mind of the whole German nation and to establish a new cult to replace the two-thousand-year-old influence of Christianity. And thirdly, there was the campaign of terrorism and intimidation, to be so extended by secret police regulations and prohibitions that the Christian Churches would gradually be reduced to insignificant remnants, whose final extinction would only be a matter of time.

These three lines of conflict were conducted simultaneously. And it was part of Hitler's tortuous planning that he encouraged the protagonists of his three-pronged attack to rival and even to compete against one another, thus enabling him to maintain his own paramount position and to conduct his campaign according to whichever strategy seemed at the time to be the most advantageous. In this he was not original. The persecution of the Church under the Nazis had much in common with its persecution under Napoleon, Henry VIII, and the Emperors Diocletian and Julian. The attempts to brand the Church as hostile to the State, the use of spies and informers, the reluctance to create martyrs, the organization of the campaign in such a way as to make it appear that Hitler himself was above the struggle, which had arisen from the 'spontaneous' activity of the lower echelons, and the deliberate confrontation of churchmen with the choice between Christianity or Nazism, all stemmed from previous oppressions of the Church, modified to suit the present situation.

Unfortunately, few German churchmen were capable of setting up the kind of resistance which the earlier history of the Church has shown to be the most effective. Among the Evangelical churchmen in particular, as we have seen, the inbred qualities of obedience, loyalty and service to the State could not easily be discarded. Furthermore, at a time of inflamed nationalism, when more than ever an alternative viewpoint, drawing its support from contacts with the Church in other lands, was urgently needed as a corrective to the Nazi claims to represent the 'true' Germany, the narrowness of the Evangelical Church's theological thinking proved inadequate to the task. The majority of churchmen retreated into a passivity which both encouraged and assisted the Nazis in their plans for persecution and subordination.

For a time, the Nazis found it expedient to be cautious. World reaction to the Röhm *Putsch* was wholly hostile, and a violent speech by Dr Goebbels accusing the foreign press of hysterical hatred did nothing to improve world opinion of Germany. On 25 July 1934 the unsuccessful Nazi *Putsch* in Vienna, in which the Austrian Catholic Chancellor Dollfuss was murdered by terrorists supported by Germany, inflamed opinion still further.

A few days later, however, the event took place for which Hitler had long been waiting – on 2 August Field Marshal Hindenburg died. On the previous day, the Cabinet, by virtue of the Enabling Act, had resolved that, as soon as the Field Marshal was dead, it would be announced that Hitler would unite his own office with that of the Reich Presidency. A plebiscite to 'approve' the change in the constitution was to be held on 19 August, and, should any opposition arise, its sponsors would be brought before the newly established 'People's Court' for the trial of political crimes.[1]

All the conditions for the control of the State were now in Nazi hands. As Hitler took leave of Hindenburg at the graveside, with the 'positive Christian' farewell: 'Our dear dead General, go now to your Valhalla!', he must have felt himself at last the sole ruler of Germany.

The two churchmen most eager to take advantage of this situation and simultaneously to satisfy their power-hungry ambitions, were Reich Bishop Müller and his assistant Jäger. Both resolved to consolidate their control over such of the provincial churches that still refused to accept the authority of the National Church, and to take disciplinary measures against those who supported the separatism of the Confessing Church.

In a speech in Hanover, outlining his future plans, Müller went so far as to state that his aim was to establish a single united German Church – one State, one Nation, one Church. This was, not unnaturally, taken to mean an enforced amalgamation, not only of

E

all the Protestant Churches with their differing traditions, but also of as many Catholics, including the old Catholics, as could be incited to sever their connections with Rome. The vision of a German Church free from Rome was guaranteed to arouse the strongest opposition from both the Catholic and the Protestant sides. But as Müller said:

The struggle to renew the Church in the Third Reich must go on. Anyone who cannot join in with us should keep quiet or stand aside. If he does not, I will force him to do so.[2]

On 9 August a National Synod was convened which, as was to be expected from its all-Nazi membership, approved the previous unconstitutional acts of Jäger in 'co-ordinating' the provincial churches as the first step towards the creation of a National Church. Jäger promised, however, that no force would be used against the three churches of Hanover, Bavaria and Württemberg which still refused to be *gleichgeschaltet*. The final act of the Synod was to pass an ordinance obliging all pastors to take the same oath as the civil servants (and as shortly was to become obligatory in the Army) 'in loyal obedience to Adolf Hitler, the leader of the German people and State'.

The response of the Confessing Church was prompt. It denied the authority of the National Synod and instructed its supporters to refuse to take the proposed oath, on the grounds that political obligation could not supercede the higher obligation of ordination vows, which in any case could not be altered by a Church Synod.

At the same time, Müller and Jäger issued a proclamation calling on all Evangelical churchmen to vote in the plebiscite on 19 August.

The beloved Father of our Fatherland has gone to his long rest. Only the Führer remains to us as the Promised One and as the incarnation of our people's longing. He is sent to us by divine will as the moulder of German life . . . On August 19, our people and the Evangelical Church will therefore say 'yes' to the Führer in loyalty and trust.[3]

Jäger's promises were quickly broken. Less than a month after they were made he used the pretext of financial irregularities in the Church of Württemberg for ordering it to be placed under a special Commissioner, and later both the Württemberg and the Bavarian Churches were placed under the legal control of the German Evangelical Church in Berlin. On 14 September Bishop Wurm was ordered by Reich Bishop Müller to go on leave and was placed under house arrest for three days. Under police surveillance, the Church offices were occupied and searched. A decree was received from Müller in Berlin altering the constitution of the provincial Synod and summoning a new and purely 'German Christian' Synod. Formations of the police, the SA, the SS, the Hitler Youth and the Labour Corps were ordered to appear at the 'German Christian' Churches to give the appearance of popular support. On 6 October, Wurm was placed under protective custody in his Stuttgart home, and on 10 October the newly-convened Synod called for his immediate 'retirement'.

On the following day, Jäger launched his attack against the sister provincial Church of Bavaria, again despite promises from the Ministry of the Interior and from the Nazi Party offices that no coercive measures would be used. Jäger, accompanied by a number of Gestapo officials from Berlin and without previously informing the local authorities of his intentions, entered the Church offices in Munich and declared that henceforward all authority would be exercised by him, and that for purposes of administration Bavaria would be divided into three districts, to be placed under spiritual Commissioners. 'An end,' he said, 'must be put to the conditions of mutiny and rebellion.' On the following day Bishop Meiser was dismissed, and, like Bishop Wurm, was placed under protective custody in his own house.

These high-handed actions caused a fury of reaction. Demonstrations of sympathy and support for both Bishops took place throughout Bavaria and Württemberg.[4] Church services were used to rally the faithful behind their ordained Bishops. Only a tiny fraction of the clergy were prepared to support the newly-installed Commissioners, and even Streicher, the foul-mouthed *Gauleiter* of Nuremberg, who was anything but a friend of the Church, was obliged to withdraw the support of the local Party and the police for such lawless usurpation.

The reaction abroad was equally unfavourable. On 29 September the Foreign Minister, on instructions from Hitler, summoned Reich Bishop Müller and told him bluntly that if he could not unite the Evangelical Church by peaceful means, and if he were to continue to make speeches like the one delivered at Hanover, he would no longer receive the support of the Reich Chancellor, who would finish with him once and for all.[5] On 11 October the Pope summoned the German Ambassador to the Vatican and expressed his serious anxiety both for the Church, and for Germany as a whole. He had been alarmed, he said, by a whole series of events, including the persecution of the Evangelical Church, which he feared might be a rehearsal for a similar treatment of the Catholics.[6] On 12 October the Bishop of Chichester, speaking to a member of the German Embassy in London, expressed grave concern over the developments in southern Germany 'of which he was most fully informed, even to the minutest detail';[7] and four days later the Archbishop of Canterbury told the German Ambassador that 'it was in the view of the Anglican clergy intolerable that coercive measures of force with the assistance of members of the State Police [Gestapo] should be used against high Church dignitaries'.[8]

So many similar reports flowed into the Foreign Ministry that on 16 October Neurath insisted on a personal interview with Hitler to draw his attention to the need for an early settlement. Even two of the most prominent leaders of the 'German Christians', Dr Kinder and Pastor Christiansen, Director of the Press Department of the German Evangelical Church, appeared at the Reich Chancellery to demand the immediate dismissal of Jäger.[9] Hitler was left in no doubt that Jäger's activities were proving to be a liability, and that the Church question was increasingly becoming a question of the political prestige of the Reich itself.

In view of the position, on 26 October Hitler completely reversed his policy. Jäger was that day to 'resign' as Administrator of the German Evangelical Church and the two Bishops were to be immediately released from protective custody and reinstated in their offices. Together with Bishop Marahrens of Hanover, they were summoned to Berlin for an interview at the Reich Chancellery. The meeting took place four days later in the presence of

Hitler and Frick, the Minister of the Interior. Hitler was both affronted and embittered by the evidence of mass resistance by the Protestants of Württemberg and Bavaria, the core provinces of the Nazi movement. He said little and his attempts to deny that he supported the activities of the Reich Bishop proved his indecision and lack of policy. Nevertheless, he still refused to accept the Bishops' suggestion that Müller should be forced to resign, although even Frick made common cause with the Bishops in acknowledging the illegality of the previous proceedings.[10] The meeting closed with assurances that henceforward the Churches would be controlled only by measures in conformity with the constitution of July 1933.

This apparent victory for the anti-'German Christian' forces was widely welcomed both at home and abroad. But the victory was illusory. Hitler's reversal of attitude was not due to any arguments of legality or to any remonstrances of foreign church dignitaries. It was merely due to the fact that the actions of Müller and Jäger had become politically unacceptable. In the previous year Müller's dream of establishing a single church with himself at its head had failed to win the approval of the Nazi hierarchy; and now Hitler again saw no advantage for the Nazi Party in such a piece of self-aggrandizement. Other leading Nazis felt the same. Rosenberg noted in his diary:

The Rei-Bi [usual abbreviation for Reich Bishop] is any way at the end of his tether, the whole youth movement swears by me, the SS and the Farmer's Leaders [Bauernführung] are educating their men openly in the Teutonic spirit, i.e. anti-Christian, the schools of the Party Organization are clearly based on The Myth, the Churches are drying up. . . . Perhaps in ten years it will be time for a reformer to take possession of the Churches with a new message, aligning them with the heroic trend of the times. I imagine . . . that in place of many of these tormented 'saints' we could erect statues of the German heroes, while the buildings will no longer reverberate to Jewish 'words of prophecy' or Jewish songs of Jehovah.[11]

Even if not all his colleagues shared Rosenberg's zealous anti-Christianity, there was a sufficient feeling of jealousy to cause them to rejoice at Müller's discomfiture. In any case, most of the leading

Nazis agreed with Hitler's contemptuous view of the Evangelical clergy. The unification of the Churches was not a matter of political importance, and the plan could always be discarded if it proved unsuccessful.

To depose Jäger and to humiliate Müller were, however, no substitute for a policy. At first Hitler wavered. The alternatives were all undesirable. To mobilize the whole apparatus of the Party and the State to enforce Müller's policies was certain to arouse further internal opposition, and would commit the Nazi Party to an ideological course of action which most of its leaders rejected. Equally unattractive was the idea of seeking an understanding with Müller's opponents on their own terms. And even more intractable was the nihilistic antipathy felt by the Nazis for all sections of the old social hierarchy and its patterns of thought. Like the Army and the bureaucracy, the Church was a pillar of the old order, whose standing, though it might be exploited as a temporary measure, was fundamentally resented by the leading members of the Party. The Third Reich was to be built, not on this basis, but on the foundation of the new revolutionary Nazi organizations, the spearhead of the new ideas with which the whole German people were to be indoctrinated. If the clergy were prepared to collaborate, they would dig their own graves; if they were not, their graves would be dug for them.

Opinions in the Nazi hierarchy differed on the means by which the Churches' place in German life could most surely be undermined. Rosenberg believed that the people would be converted by ideological education in the heroic values of the Nazi *Weltanschauung*. Von Schirach believed in capturing the youth of Germany so that indoctrination would eventually infuse the whole country with Nazi ideals. Darré, the Minister of Agriculture, attacked the religious beliefs of the farming community by means of anti-Christian literature sponsored by his Ministry.[12] Himmler, wishing to avoid public conflict, preferred the use of police methods of intimidation progressively to curtail the freedom of the Churches and to eradicate Christian influence from the national life. Hitler's own opinion combined implacable hatred with practical flexibility:

I promise you that, if I wished to, I could destroy the Church in a
few years; it is hollow and rotten and false through and through. One
push and the whole structure would collapse. We should trap the
priests by their notorious greed and self-indulgence. We shall thus be
able to settle everything with them in perfect peace and harmony. I
shall give them a few years' reprieve. Why should we quarrel? They
will swallow anything in order to keep their material advantages.
Matters will never come to a head. They will recognize a firm will,
and we need only show them once or twice who is the master. Then
they will know which way the wind blows. They are no fools. The
Church was something really big. Now we are its heirs. We, too, are
the Church. Its day has gone.[13]

These, however, were all long-term schemes; the most pressing
problem was how to deal with the Church in the immediate
future. In a speech to his *Gauleiters* on 1 November Hitler outlined
his own views. It would do the Party no good to be embroiled in
the conflict in the Evangelical Church. If the 'German Christians'
could not unite the Church by their own efforts, they were
obviously not worthy of the Party's support. What could the
Third Reich expect from a Church which squandered its energies
in fruitless squabbles? All Nazis should maintain the utmost reserve
and neutrality, so that there should be no impression of support for
the policy of enforced unification of the Churches in Bavaria and
Württemberg. The conflict should be shown as due solely to
interdenominational bickerings and intrigues. The Church should
be left strictly alone and the clergy could stew in their own theological juice. Orders would be given prohibiting any discussion
of Church problems in public or in the press. In view of the forthcoming plebiscite in the Saar, which was due to be held in January
1935, care would be taken to avoid anything that might cause
unfavourable repercussions in the Evangelical or the Catholic
Churches and arouse hostility abroad. The interference of official
bodies in Church affairs was expressly forbidden.[14]

Accordingly, on 6 and 7 November Frick issued two decrees
peremptorily forbidding the daily press, Church newspapers,
parish news bulletins or other pamphlets to publish articles dealing
with the Evangelical Church other than official notices put out by

the National Church administration. Müller, seeking to safeguard his own position, announced that his responsibility was not to those who had elected him as Bishop, nor to the Evangelical Church as a whole, but solely to God. 'The Bishops,' he stated, 'have expressed to me their conviction that, if I were to resign, our whole German Evangelical Church would be engulfed in an unforeseeable conflict and chaos.' Thus armed, he felt himself safe enough to ignore the many strongly worded demands for his resignation, including a protest from 119 Professors of Theology.[15]

In the meanwhile, efforts were made by the Nazis to encourage the people to oppose the Churches on the grounds of their political unreliability. Frick, in a speech at Wiesbaden on 7 December, said:

> The State does not intend to interfere in Church affairs. But unfortunately there is good cause for thinking that under the disguise of a concern for the Church all sorts of hostile and traitorous elements have gathered in order to continue their 'politicking' in a supposedly purely ecclesiastical area, and so to cause difficulties for the Third Reich.[16]

Anti-clerical speeches were encouraged. Measures were put in hand to deprive the Churches of the long-held position of pre-eminence, especially in the fields of education and social welfare, and to curtail the financial support which they had long received. The slogan for the new campaign was to be 'The Church must be separate from the State'.

To Hitler, to whom all questions of theology were subordinate to practical politics, the problem still remained a political one. In December 1934 the need for a popular success in the forthcoming plebiscite meant that the largely Catholic population in the Saar must not be offended by open measures against the Church. In public Hitler declared himself ready to support the Christian Churches if they confined themselves to upholding the ethical values of the Nazi State, and to mobilizing the people behind the anti-Bolshevist crusade; but the political influence of the Churches must be suppressed, and every possibility of their interference must be prevented.

Neither in earlier times nor today has the Party the intention of waging any kind of war against Christianity. The Nazi State will however not tolerate under any circumstances any new or any continued political activity of the denominations. Let there be no misunderstanding about the resolve of the Party and the State on this matter! We attacked the political clergy once and got rid of them from the parliaments at a time when we had no power behind us and the other side had it all. But today we have the power and can defend these principles better. We will not conduct this struggle as one directed against Christianity or against only one of the two denominations. But we will ensure the purging from our public life of all those priests who have mistaken their profession and who ought to have been politicians and not pastors.[17]

His subordinates were eager to challenge the position of the Churches at once and on a much broader front, and Rosenberg, though he recognized the need for political caution, regretted that the atmosphere was not sufficiently ripe to allow him to lock up Cardinal Faulhaber for preaching against *The Myth of the Twentieth Century*. Rosenberg was eager to exploit his newly established position as ideological leader in the Party. He strongly resented the attacks made by the Churches against him, and in early 1935 published a tendentious pamphlet *An die Dunkelmänner unserer Zeit* which sought to refute the criticisms made of his earlier theories, and to accuse his opponents of obscurantism and political sabotage. A later work, put out in August 1937, entitled *Protestantische Rompilger* accused the Evangelical Church of betraying the German Reformation in favour of alien ideas imported from Rome or Jerusalem.

Once the Saar plebiscite was successfully over, the *National Socialist Monthly* was given orders to whip up propaganda against the Church, and the Party's *Schulungsbriefe* (Instruction Leaflets), that were being printed with a million copies each, were directed to conduct a systematic attack against the teaching of the Roman Catholic Church from the earliest times to the present day. Hitler Youth leaders were urged to refute the criticisms of the Bishops and the Jesuits,[18] and all anti-Christian activities were particularly to be encouraged. For this purpose, the Nazis found a willing tool in the person of Professor Jakob Hauer, the leader of the newly established 'German Faith Movement' (*Deutsche Glaubensbewegung*).

Professor Hauer, of Tübingen University, had for five years been a missionary in India where he had been greatly impressed by the spiritual mysticism of the Eastern religions. He returned to Germany determined to convince his clerical brethren and his congregations of the great spiritual potential of mystical and 'existential' living. Gradually he grew disillusioned with the narrow dogmatism of the Württemberg Lutheran Church, and in 1921 he abandoned his clerical work for a teaching post at Tübingen. In 1934 he set himself the task of bringing together all non-Christian or anti-Christian groups, from the Free Thinkers to the followers of the Nordic faith, with the objective of welding them into a powerful instrument to be used against the obscurantism of the established Churches. In Hitler he not surprisingly found the German archetype whose inspiration all should follow. Some idea of his intentions can be gathered from his Movement's Principles of Membership:

The members of the new Society are required to make the following declaration under oath.

a) That they are free from any taint of Jewish or coloured blood.
b) That they belong to no secret organization, nor Freemasons' Lodge, nor the Society of Jesus.
c) That they belong to no other community of believers.

Those who have joined the Movement but who are still members of another community of believers (Church) will have to fulfil the above-named requirements, and will provisionally be entered only as associate members. Only full members can use the designation 'Believers in Germany' (*deutschgläubig*). The leader of the German Faith Movement will select a circle of co-workers. Furthermore an Assembly (*Thing*) of official holders and a General Assembly (*Allthing*) will be constituted, to maintain the connections between the leader and the local units.

The emblem of the German Faith Movement is a golden sun on a blue background.

The basic principles of the Movement are:

1) The German Faith Movement seeks to renew the religious life of the people from the inheritance of the German character.
2) The German character in its divine origins has an eternal task to which we are obedient.

3) In its teachings and customs it is bound solely to this task. To obey these is to lead the German life.[19]

In February 1935 the German Faith Movement began a mammoth campaign for the dissemination of its views. Up to sixty meetings a week were held, culminating in a mass rally held at the Sports Palace in Berlin in April, at which Hauer was supported by a number of prominent speakers, including Count Reventlow. The Movement's flag, with its golden sun in conjunction with the Nazi swastika, typified the interweaving of naturalistic and national socialist principles which Hauer set himself to preach. The positive content of his Movement was too small to give it much weight, and its intellectual inconsistencies doomed it to early collapse, but by attacking the established position of the Churches, and with the active backing of the Nazis, the German Faith Movement temporarily occupied a prominent place on the public stage.

Hauer himself affirmed that he was not against Christianity but only against dogmatism and the un-Germanic nature of the Churches. But the radical wing of his Movement was openly demanding a complete break and the establishment of a new religion. It quickly adopted the Nazi rabble-rousing technique of agitation, and made its appeal to the lowest exponents of anti-clerical prejudice, as, for example, in a speech delivered at Munich, in May 1935:

Christianity has failed us in the social question, the racial question and in the educational question ... All that Cardinal Faulhaber can suggest is to introduce the denominational school. (Cries of 'String him up, Shoot him'.) The plain fact is that the religions are no longer suited to the new tasks of the people and must disappear, in Munich too. Only those should be trusted with education who are dedicated to the whole nation and no one else. (Cries of 'We don't want denominational schools'.) ... When one remembers how the confession boxes are used, it is only for treasonable purposes. (Cries of 'Boo'.) ... Can one imagine one of our Hitler Youth lads with a rosary? Or an SA or SS man taking part in a pilgrimage along with a lot of old women? (Loud laughter) ... Our faith is in blood and earth, we want to be pure heathen, not contaminated with Christian ingrafts. God is too great for us to be confined in churches. (Cries of 'We don't want any more churches'.) We don't need any priestly or spiritual midwives ... We won't stop until all the theological colleges disappear from our universities. (Loud applause.) We will get rid of those useless monasteries. The police will help them to learn about earthly values by putting them to work in Dachau.

For Rome or for Germany. That's the decision today. We don't talk about Christians or heathens, but only about Germans. We will close with a three-fold Hail to the genius of our people, Adolf Hitler. (Cries of 'To the gallows with the Cardinal, Shoot him, Throw them out of the Churches, Away with the monasteries, Shoot the priests, String up the nuns, We don't need Christianity, Away with Christ'.)[20]

Swept along by the impetus of his own delusions, Hauer began to aspire for his movement an equal status with the churches under the law and for an equal part in such matters as religious education. Like the 'German Christians' before him, he was also anxious to be accorded the support of the Nazi Party. This suggestion, however, was not favourably received by the Nazis, who had no intention of letting any faith movement become strong enough to build up a following of its own or to lay claims to any form of ideological leadership. Its function, so far as the Nazi Party was concerned, was the negative one of sowing doubt in the people's minds about the validity of the doctrines of the Christian Churches.

The interest which Himmler and Heydrich had shown in the early days of this Movement had cooled considerably by August 1935. In a decree issued to the Bavarian Political Police, Heydrich banned the holding of any more rallies or public meetings by the German Faith Movement, although it might continue to operate in private. In April 1936 Heydrich again intervened, this time to demand Hauer's resignation as the Movement's 'Führer', on the grounds that there was room for only one 'Führer' in Germany. The Movement thereafter lost most of its mystical appeal and was obliged to concentrate its efforts on propagating a political faith based on a purely racial and *völkisch* idea, with the slogan 'Germany is your Fate . . . Germany is the great Law above us all, one all-embracing Law of Fate and Salvation'.[21]

Meanwhile, intensive propaganda of a more explicit kind was being issued, in strict confidence, at the many indoctrination sessions of the Nazi Party and its subordinate organizations. A graphic account of the Nazi attitude at the time is preserved in the records of the *Nationalsozialistische Studentenbund* (Nazi Students' League). In July 1935, at the Reich School at Bernau, one speaker bluntly declared:

> One is either a Nazi or a committed Christian. We affirm *das Volk* as our inheritance, and commit ourselves to Life. Christianity today affirms *das Volk* at best as secondary, or sees it only as an accidental society. For Christianity the true community is that of the faithful. The only inherited characteristic is that of sinfulness (the doctrine of the Fall). Christianity therefore promotes the dissolution of racial ties (*Entrassung*) and of the *Volksgemeinschaft*. What the theologians teach springs from the defence of their own interests . . . But we do not need any churches, whether Baroque or Gothic; we will find our own places of holiness. Christianity sees the earth as a place of troubles and promises its followers their reward in the life hereafter. But we seek revelation not in writings but in *das Volk* and in our homeland. We must repudiate the Old and the New Testaments, since for us the Nazi idea is alone decisive. For us there is only one example, Adolf Hitler and no one else.[22]

The widespread popular support for the German Faith Movement and the reports of the Party's indoctrination sessions left no doubt in the minds of percipient churchmen of the direction in which Nazi Church policy was heading. The 'German Christians' were shocked and scandalized by what they considered to be a betrayal of the true Nazi position. They addressed innumerable appeals to Hitler to put an end to the anti-Christian propaganda which ran counter both to the Nazi Party programme's point 24 and to his own promises. Recalling their loyal devotion to the Nazi cause, and the fact that the great majority of Nazis were also Christians, they begged him to put an end to the minority of freethinkers whose activities, they submitted, could not be approved by him.

The Catholic Church and the Confessing Church had fewer illusions. The similarity between Hauer's ideas and those of Rosenberg was too close to be ignored. With *The Myth of the Twentieth Century* already on the 'Index', the clergy were instructed to lose no opportunity of attacking the falsehoods that were being so widely taught as truth, and of combating by every means at their disposal the new heathenism, the pseudo-scientific race theories, and the insulting attacks to which the Catholic Church was continuously subjected. Since 'official' Nazi policy had not so far openly approved Rosenberg's theories, since Hitler still protested that *The Myth* was merely a private work, and since Hauer had been given no official status, the Church was thus able to express its anger towards the political régime by attacking Hauer and the new heathenism. Its spokesmen used the opportunity to expound their ideas, obliquely but none the less clearly, about the new Nazi teachings and the new Nazi state. They named Hauer, but they meant Hitler. And by this means, they were able openly to express in unmistakable terms the incompatibility of Christian doctrines with the ideas of Nazism at a time when attacks upon the author of *Mein Kampf* were no longer permissible.

The Nazis were fully aware that open competition in the field of ideology would serve only to strengthen the Churches' hold upon their followers. Since on such terms it might take years for Nazi ideas to gain the ascendant, more instant measures were therefore imperative. In February and March 1935 the Bavarian Political Police were instructed that meetings within the church buildings arranged for discussion of Rosenberg's *Myth* were to be restricted, and that all copies of *Catholic Writings on Contemporary Problems* were to be confiscated.[23] In April, the police in the Rhineland forbade the Church to criticize the fundamentals of National Socialism.[24] And in the same month, a law was promulgated imposing a *de facto* censorship on anti-Nazi writings.[25]

In a strictly confidential report to the Ministry of the Interior and to Hitler's deputy the leader of the *Rassenpolitischen Amt* (Race-Political Office) of the Nazi Party wrote in June 1935:

According to my experience, it is possible with considerable success to make our point of view propagandistically understood even to those who are tied to their denominations, in so far as we are able to limit or prevent the systematic poisoning of the atmosphere by the other side. Our own propaganda will have only a limited effect so long as the Church is able to continue its operations without control in reaching out to large segments of the population. I believe it therefore necessary that the right of the State and the Party to supervise all racial-political utterances, which we have already imposed on the Evangelical Churches, should be extended to cover the Catholics too. Regard for the terms of the Concordat can no longer be maintained in circumstances where the Church has been proved to have been misusing the freedoms of the Concordat as an opportunity for unheard-of attacks upon the authority of the state and its laws.[26]

Himmler shared these opinions. Since in his view intimidation was more effective than persuasion, he considered administrative restriction to be the best method of putting a rope around the neck of the Churches without appearing to touch the 'spiritual' life of their members; and the not-so-subtle pressure of exclusion from participation in the life of the *Volksgemeinschaft* as the most effective method of bringing the Church laity to heel by obliging them to choose between their church and their country.

Police ordinances and decrees proved an effective method of limiting the Church's participation in any aspect of public life outside the walls of the Church. The breakdown of the June 1934 meetings and the failure to reach agreement over the future of the Catholic organizations, left the way open for further measures against them. At the end of November 1934, a directive to the Bavarian Political Police noted that the Catholic organizations had reached a scale of activity designed to cause trouble among the people. Orders had already been issued, as we have seen, on 6 January that only so many meetings should be allowed as could be kept under surveillance. The establishment of new groups was forbidden. No group banned since the national uprising or volun- tarily dissolved was to be revived. Only the State authorities had the right of decision over the dissolution of associations, the dis- position of property, and the prohibition or permission for meetings.[27]

On 20 December 1934 the notorious Conspiracy Law was promulgated, which gave the police almost unlimited powers of arrest and was increasingly used against the clergy. On the follow- ing day a ruling was issued by Himmler limiting public meetings to those which could be held indoors, and permitting old-estab- lished customary processions and pilgrimages to be held only under strict supervision. No secular gatherings which could be used as a means for church propaganda would be tolerated, and no mention of these restrictions was to be published in the press.[28]

The resultant sharpening of feeling was reflected in a circular issued by the Bavarian Political Police on 6 May 1935.

In recent months it has become clear that the clergy of both Christian denominations are more openly and more actively working against the State. In order to overcome this, it is necessary for each detachment to pay particular attention to the activities of the clergy. *But it is strictly ordered that there should be no interference under any circumstances in the services of the Church.* Immediate reports should be made on any important matter.[29]

This limitation of interference with Church services did not, however, prevent forcible action being taken by the police against individual priests whose actions were considered subversive. In April, three students of the University of Rostock called to see Msgr Leffers, their Catholic Chaplain, to ask his opinion of *The Myth of the Twentieth Century*. When he expressed his considered and well-grounded objections to its crude superficiality, he was promptly denounced by the students and sentenced by a Nazi court to eighteen months' imprisonment. In the same month, the police in Bavaria issued the following instructions to all local detachments and local government agencies, under the title 'Safeguarding against the Jesuits':

The Jesuits are instigating systematic and far-reaching activities in Bavaria to undermine the Third Reich and to bring contempt even on the Führer himself. In various semi-scientific lectures the philosophic principles of National Socialism are submitted to an acrimonious criticism which is nothing more nor less than disguised incitement against the Reich. These lectures, moreover, are so ambiguously and cunningly composed that a judicial punishment of the lecturer is possible in only very few cases.

In order to check this subversive and rebellious activity of the Jesuits and to dishearten their propaganda efforts in Bavaria, increased attention must be paid to their public appearances; public meetings are to be prevented by all means; private meetings are to be watched, and the severest penalties must be imposed on offenders, statements injurious to the State being ruthlessly punished by 'protective custody'. Further, political appearances of the Jesuits are to be reported immediately, and even if no activities are observed, a report is to be made on the 30th of each month starting from 30 May 1935.[30]

In May, the President of the Synod of the Confessing Church asked all parishes to include in their services intercessory prayers for 'Sixteen Saxon Pastors who have been taken to Sachsenburg concentration camp, five pastors from Hesse who have been in Dachau concentration camp for several weeks, two Saxon pastors, one pastor from Bremen, three Prussian pastors who are now in prison as well as seven pastors from Brandenburg and one from Silesia who have been ejected from their parishes. You are asked also to remember in your prayers these orphaned congregations.'[31]

The persecution disclosed by these prayers was, however, designed to go much further than merely to silence unwelcome criticism from the clergy. On 7 July Frick, the Minister of the Interior, in a speech at Münster, the See city of Bishop Galen, revealed the full measure of the Nazis' determination to root out the influence of the Churches altogether.

We Nazis demand a separation of Church and State in the entire public life of the country. What is the sense in still having Catholic associations of civil servants? We do not want Protestant or Catholic civil servants, we want German civil servants. What is the point of the Catholic Daily Press? We do not need a Catholic or a Protestant but only a German Press. The Catholic professional organizations and the Catholic youth organizations no longer fit into our age. They are often active in areas which the Nazi State claims for itself in fulfilment of its tasks. All these things are designed to disturb the unity of the German people, which Adolf Hitler created after fifteen years of struggle for the soul of Germany.[32]

A week later Goering, in his capacity as Premier of Prussia and Head of the Prussian Gestapo, issued a directive to all local governors that strict measures should be taken against any kind of revival of 'political Catholicism'.

It has to be fundamentally understood that all priests who are employed in the public service – as for instance in giving religious instruction in public schools – will be expected not merely to avoid any possible

negative attitude towards Nazism in their teaching, but also like all
other members of the public service to commit themselves positively on
Nazism's behalf, and thus stand without hesitation in Nazism's service.
Only then can Nazism allow the priests to participate in the religious
education of young people.[33]

The consequences of non-compliance were soon apparent. The
Governor of Hanover Province shortly afterwards ordered his
civil service employees to submit to him written statements
promising that they would give up membership of any denominational professional organizations to which they belonged, and
would withdraw their children from denominational youth
organizations. 'It is not intended to exercise any pressure on
conscience by this measure, for those who believe that they cannot
follow this directive are hereby notified that they must withdraw
from any further participation in the rebuilding of the State.'[34]
Faced with the alternative of dismissal from their posts or obedience
to the behests of their Nazi superiors, few men were ready to give
up their livelihood. By thus concentrating pressure on the individual, and by branding all opposition as prompted by political
motives, the Nazis sowed confusion in the ranks of churchmen.

Most people, even most Church leaders, were anxious to keep
their Church intact and at the same time, at whatever cost to their
theological principles, to support the new régime. But for the
Nazis that was not enough. The only sphere in which they were
prepared to tolerate Church activity was in purely 'spiritual'
matters concerned with the next world. The separation of Church
and State was designed to drive churchmen out of every activity
which contributed to the 'life and work' of the Church. Then,
and only then, could the clergy and the faithful remnant dispute
among themselves the vexed, but to the Nazis irrelevant, questions
of 'faith and order'.

The mixture of theological indifference and practical totalitarianism was a frequent feature in Nazi speeches. Goebbels, for
instance, on 4 August 1935 declared:

Everyone here can save himself in his own fashion. To educate the
young people into religious ways may perhaps be the task of the Church,
but to educate the young in politics is very much our affair. . . . The

youth belongs to us and we will yield them to no one. And the denominational press is equally superfluous. . . . For the Churches there is
only one solution, which will ensure peace: Back into the sacristy. Let
the Churches serve God; we serve the People.[35]

The Nazi campaign against the Churches' manifold participation in public life was conducted with many weapons – propaganda, administrative obstruction, individual pressure, and as a
last resort the concentration camp. If the desired end could be
achieved by lesser means, the blunter weapons were not used. But
the threat of their use was always there.

The Nazis were not content with the many signs of political
compliance which the Churches had already shown. Total submission was their aim. So long as the Churches showed any signs
of maintaining independent lives of their own, they were to be
harried and chased. After two years' experience, it was clear that
the Churches were not prepared to become fused with the Nazi
State as mere instruments for the Nazification of the people.
Separation, and if possible suppression, was therefore henceforward
to be the Nazi policy towards the Churches. Paradoxically, however, by the beginning of 1935 several prominent Nazis were
beginning to argue that the struggle against the Churches would
need to be placed under more effective centralized leadership if the
resistance of the Catholics was to be broken and the blunders of
the Nazi Evangelical Church leadership avoided. The methods of
Bismarck's *Kulturkampf*, with its desire to separate Church and
State and simultaneously to impose strict State supervision could
now be revived. To ensure the separation of Church and State, it
would be necessary for the government to intervene in decisive
fashion, and to decree by state authority the ever-diminishing part
in German life which the Church would be allowed to play.

5 The Establishment of the Ministry of Church Affairs

> 'True Christianity and True Nazism are
> identical. Since 1933 Hitler has hammered
> Jesus and His teachings into the hearts of the
> people ... The Pastors must march with the
> people.' – REICH MINISTER KERRL

I THE ORIGINS OF THE MINISTRY

It was one of the illusions of German churchmen that the centralization of Church affairs in the hands of Reich Bishop Müller and his associates would lead to a revival of Church life. What they failed to realize was that the rhetoric and the show of pectoral crosses by the 'German Christians' were no more than a façade screening what Rauschning rightly described as 'the hot rivalry of small men in the pursuit of posts and power and success'[1]. Müller and Jäger were only pawns in the Nazis' wider strategy. The ultimate object of the Nazi *Gleichschaltung* was to destroy, deliberately and systematically, all the social classes that had contributed to Germany's previous history, to abolish the existing order, and to force into conformity with its own ambitions every form of independent activity and association. All that could not be converted to Nazi uses was to be totally expunged. By 1935 the National Socialist revolution had already achieved sweeping successes. The capitulation of the Reichstag had been followed by the *Gleichschaltung* of the bureaucracy, of the press, of the provincial governments, of the Army, and of all the media of mass communication. The need to maintain the momentum of the 'permanent revolution' now obliged the Nazi hierarchy to extend its control yet further. The relative failure of attempts so far made to control the Churches provided an excuse for further measures to wipe out their resistance – a political motive which was reinforced by the equally dominant determination to destroy this last and most deep-rooted pillar of the conservative forces, in order that the way might be opened for the total control of the populace. The mobilization of effective means of organizing the masses into obedience to the Nazi leadership necessitated the elimination of any elements that might provide the German people with an opposing set of values. It was not enough, therefore, to declare the Party's lack of interest in 'theological squabblings'. As one leading Nazi said, 'National Socialism has conquered Marxism, it cannot and must not capitulate to the denominations'.[2] Spurred on by hatred and a lust for revenge, the Nazi leaders set themselves to destroy both the social achievements of past generations and the Christian Faith, as the most powerful influence in Western civilization.

After the defeat of Müller's ambitions in October 1934, while Hitler was seeking new ideas for the subjugation of the Churches, a memorandum was presented to him in January 1935 that seemed to answer the needs of the case.[3] This memorandum had been prepared by Dr Wilhelm Stuckart, the ambitious young *Staatssekretär* of the Ministry of Education, whose high-handed activities had already run foul of the Minister, Rust, and had led to his 'retirement' in September 1934. In an attempt to ingratiate himself with Hitler, Stuckart prepared a detailed review of the Church–political situation and drew up a plan for its 'purgation' in accordance with Nazi ideas. The Church question, he maintained, could be settled only if there were clarity of ideas and unity of purpose on the part of the State. Previous attempts to solve the problem by means of the Church's own administrators had failed, and any change in its leadership would merely assist the political reactionaries disguised as Christians who had formed the Confessing Church. The Confessing Church, on its part, was using the façade of the Evangelical Church simply to propagate its own political campaign, which went far beyond the limits of Church life and might even challenge Nazism itself – one of the reasons for its many friends abroad. The 'German Christians' had failed in their attempt to evangelize the masses because they had been interested only in seizing the chief positions and the emoluments of the Church.

The only way to settle the matter, Stuckart argued, was to create a single competent state authority which would deal with all Church questions, both Catholic and Evangelical, in every part of the Reich. A clear and unified state policy should be implemented promptly and rigorously, in such a way as to leave no doubt of the immutable purpose of the Nazi revolution to establish the *völkisch*-Nazi People's State. It was the duty of all institutions to serve that purpose, or at any rate not to hinder it.

Two possible ways of achieving this end, Stuckart noted, had already been suggested – total separation of Church and State, and increased control of the Churches by the State. The first of these methods would entail the ending of the State subsidies to the Churches, the abolition of the compulsory Church tax, the removal of the Churches' legal privileges, the cessation of religious instruction in the schools, and the suppression of the theological faculties in the universities. Such measures would have undoubted financial advantages for the State. The Evangelical Church would be reduced to the level of the lesser sects, it would be obliged to subsist solely on voluntary contributions, and would no longer benefit from its historic established position. But there were disadvantages: separation might prevent the effective disciplining of the Church through established links, and a sizeable amount of Church property would no longer be available for the general welfare. In fact, if the Church were to be disestablished, the secularization of a significant portion of Church property would have to be considered. As for the Catholic Church, separation from the State would be an open breach of the Concordat, which would undoubtedly cause trouble, and the Catholics and Protestants might even be driven to unite in a joint effort to resist the Nazi State and ideology. Against such a possible union, the German Faith Movement was an insufficient vehicle of counter-attack. Moreover, complete separation might be hailed by the Catholics as evidence that the State was opposed to religion altogether, and so be the cause of undesirable divisions among the people. In such circumstances, the Catholic Church, urged on by reactionary circles, indeed might emerge the only winner. For that reason, the separation of Church and State could not at the moment be recommended.

In Stuckart's view, greater advantage would be gained by a much stricter control over the Churches' temporal concerns. By bringing the administration of the Evangelical Church into line with the principles of the Nazi State authority the Church would be prevented from becoming the refuge of every politically hostile element in society. Without touching its so-called 'spiritual' life, steady and subtle pressure could be brought to bear upon the Church by means of a single authority for Church affairs set up within the Reich Ministry of the Interior. This would prevent the different provincial Churches from playing off one local state authority against the others. It would also enable a nation-wide policy to be enacted towards state subsidies to the Church by channelling them through a suitably controlled National Church administration. By suitably generous donations, not only would opposition be bought off, but the State's right to control all Church property would be established. Control of the purse-strings would soon bring the Churches to heel. The already established right of the State to give or withhold its approval of Church appointments could then be fully exercised. Every candidate for the pastorate would be required to have participated in the Reich *Arbeitsdienst* (Labour Service) and to have received instruction in History and Nazi ideology; and all appointments to bishoprics and theological professorships would need the approval of the appropriate Party officers.

Stuckart's memorandum concluded by pointing out that the office of Reich Bishop had not proved a success. A purely secular organ would be a more effective means of control, administered by an officer responsible for the finances, administration and legislative programme of the Church. The national administrator would be responsible solely to the Reich Ministry of the Interior. The legal position would be regulated by a new law cancelling all previously established rights of the provincial churches, a move that could be justified by analogy with similar processes in the secular provincial governments, whose functions were now to be centralized in Berlin. The first task of the Church administrator would be to restore clarity to the confused legal situation, in accordance with the needs of the new Nazi State. To the Reich Bishop would be left the purely pastoral supervision of his flock.

Stuckart's ideas made an instant appeal to Hitler. After a personal interview, Hitler remarked that Stuckart's talents ought not to be lost to the Nazi Party,[4] and that an iron fist in a velvet glove would be the best means of dealing with the Churches, at least temporarily. Nevertheless, the establishment of a new organ of control raised certain problems. The Minister of the Interior, Frick, advised by his civil servants, had, as we have already seen, consistently adopted a negative attitude towards intervention in Church affairs, and had thereby been accused by the Party fanatics of adopting too legalistic an attitude. His position in the Nazi hierarchy was under constant attack from Himmler, who had already succeeded in gaining control over the police and security forces, and in merging them with his own force, the SS. Frick did not favour the idea of adding a new division to his Ministry, which would almost certainly lead to further difficulties. In order to accommodate Hitler, however, he agreed to get rid of certain 'reactionary' members of his Ministry, to give Stuckart the position of *Ministerialdirektor* in charge of constitutional questions, where his views would be given a hearing, and, where possible, to take stricter measures against the 'indiscipline' of the Evangelical Church. In March 1935 Frick made two speeches in which he referred to the need for introducing new laws to obtain order in the Church. Yet, as he told a visiting Canadian journalist,

> I declared recently at a Party Rally in Thüringen that Frederick the Great's views still hold good for us, that everyone can be saved in his own fashion . . . On the other hand we cannot tolerate any attempt to influence youth through seemingly religious associations against the presently valid Nazi form of the state and legal constitution.[5]

A similarly negative attitude prevailed in the Ministry of Education, the other Ministry which traditionally held responsibility for relations with the Churches. The Minister, Rust, was fully occupied in defending his department against raids by such Party agencies as Rosenberg's office and the Nazi Teachers' League, and against Schirach's insatiable demands to control all youth affairs. Rust believed that an effective propaganda campaign was all that was needed to displace the old loyalties, and that further administrative or coercive measures were unnecessary. National Socialism, he wrote in an article designed for foreign consumption, meant a new religion just as it meant new politics, a new writing of history, even a new mathematics. The only question that was not yet finally decided was whether the new religion to be taught the Hitler Youth should be called Christianity or should be given some other name.[6]

Neither Frick nor Rust then, was anxious to involve his Ministry in the further complications likely to follow increased State intervention in Church affairs. The alternative of setting up a new Ministry was equally unwelcome to the civil service, whose members feared that such a move would afford yet another opportunity for the Nazi Party to seek further to influence the administration of government. The idea of placing the Churches under direct governmental control was also too revolutionary to commend itself to the existing administrators. Stuckart's scheme therefore received little backing. Nevertheless the ideas contained in it prepared the way for later developments.

II THE SITUATION CALLS FOR A NEW REMEDY

In the meanwhile, the situation in the provincial churches still remained eminently unsatisfactory to the Nazi rulers. Frequent attempts by Müller to reassert his authority were successfully challenged in the courts, and the Confessing Church continued to strengthen its 'Provisional Church Administration' (*Vorläufige Kirchenleitung*).[7] Müller sought to obtain a ban on the use of this title, but his plea was likewise rejected by the courts. A year later, on 6 July 1936, the Ministry of Church Affairs ordered the police to forbid the use of the term, but even in face of official prohibition it still continued to be widely used.[8] Despite the arrest of a number of pastors, the Confessing Church refused to be terrorized into compliance. The 'German Christians', for their part, found themselves confronted not only by the opposition of the Confessing Church but also by the militant propaganda of the widely supported German Faith Movement. Their appeals to the Nazi Party to support their most loyal followers fell on deaf ears. The Confessing Church, on its part, was increasingly aware that only a return to orthodox Christian tradition could prevent the growth of national apostasy in any one of its many pro-Nazi forms. When Rosenberg published his vitriolic attack against the Church in the pamphlet *An die Dunkelmänner unserer Zeit*,[9] the Confessing Church was constrained to protest strongly. In early March the Synod of the Prussian Union of the Confessing Church issued an uncompromising statement, to be read from the pulpits of all the Confessing Churches on 17 March, rejecting the 'new religion' as a heresy against the first commandment and an attempt to set in its place the Nazi racialist *Weltanschauung*, with its worship of blood and race and its exaltation of 'eternal Germany'.[10] This, the statement protested, had nothing to do with Christianity: it was nothing less than anti-Christ.

The Nazis reacted quickly. Spurred on by Rosenberg, the political police prohibited the reading of the statement. On the evening of 16 March all clergy were so informed; but the ban was widely defied and large-scale arrests were made. Within a few days five hundred pastors in Prussia alone were taken from their homes and families. Protests from other parts of the country against such intolerable measures led to over two hundred further arrests. Indeed, it was only after the personal intervention of Bishop Marahrens of Hanover at the approach of the Easter season that the Minister of the Interior agreed to release all but seven of the internees. The refusal of the majority of churchmen to accept the fantasies of the German Faith Movement established beyond doubt the failure of so puerile an attempt to indoctrinate the Church with Nazi ideas. Indeed it was clear that such attempts served to strengthen the opposition of the Confessing Church and to unite its followers more firmly together.

In the Catholic Church Nazi attempts to silence opposition met with similar resistance. Despite the terms of the Concordat, Nazi pressure on Catholic individuals to forsake their church organiza-

tions continued relentlessly throughout 1935. Dual membership
of Catholic associations and of the Hitler Youth, the German
Labour Front or such Nazi professional groups as the Nazi
Teachers' League was prohibited with increasing severity. Baldur
von Schirach, who in November 1934 had declared that 'The way
of Rosenberg is the way for the German youth', continued to denounce the Catholic youth organizations as separatist and political
in their intentions.

In our common irrefutable decision to lead and to unify the German
youth, we will not allow ourselves to be misled by anything, by any
power, or by any denomination. We, my comrades, know our enemies,
and even if they disguise themselves ... we will carry to victory the
flag of German unity, of the revolutionary socialist youth of Adolf
Hitler, despite all their plans ... They claim that they are serving the
cause of religious instruction, but they serve no God but their stomachs.
It is not a question of their religion but of their jobs. They want to
carry on with the denominational youth groups the same game they
played before with the Centre Party. They call us godless because we
will not tolerate this. But if the Centre Party was so beloved of God,
as they always claimed, why did the Almighty allow it to be broken up?
I tell you the Almighty wants to have nothing to do with those who
together with the Marxist traitors are stabbing their country in the
back, and who are conspiring with Marxists, traitors, and separatists to
carry on a policy of terror against National Socialism ... God is always
against the enemies of our people and was always with those who
recognized what we today, this hour, confess: Germany, our eternal
Germany![11]

A few days later, on 9 April, Schirach made even more definite
threats against the Catholic Youth Organizations:

It will be apparent in the coming weeks whether the Catholics will
possess enough sense to give up of their own accord this freakish and
disloyal system of theirs or whether it will be necessary to use force ...
And unless the devil himself is against us, we shall succeed in compelling
the Catholics just as we have compelled the hundred and one other
clubs and associations.[12]

These and similar speeches were obviously designed to drive a
wedge between the leaders and the members of the Catholic

Youth Organizations. In the Rhineland, Schirach proclaimed a 'spring offensive' which, by using both propaganda and terrorist tactics, would force the Catholic organizations to dissolve altogether. In the schools and the factories Catholic youngsters were coerced into 'voluntarily' joining the Hitler Youth; at home their parents were exhorted by members of the Party to do their 'duty' by their children; and in schools all over the country teachers were enjoined to devote themselves to promoting the idea of the Hitler Youth.

To support and recruit for the Hitler Youth is a part of the work and duty of all teachers at every school, and, therefore, all activity on behalf of denominational Youth Associations both inside and outside the school is forbidden. The same applies also to the Clergy permitted to teach religious lessons.[13]

Many of the employment exchanges made membership of the Hitler Youth a prerequisite to employment for school-leavers. By press articles, posters and wall-paintings the 'disloyalty' of the Catholic Youth Organizations was attacked. Nor were more forceful measures lacking. Bodily attacks were ignored by the police, and in Hessen the Police headquarters publicly posted a large placard which read: 'The Police support the Hitler Youth.'[14]

Yet, despite all these measures, the number of adherents of the Catholic Youth Organizations continued to grow. As a countermeasure, in July Heydrich issued an order to all police and Gestapo units in Prussia, and later throughout the whole country, forbidding the Catholic Youth Organizations to undertake any activities that were not purely religious in nature. Political or even sports meetings were thus banned, as well as parades, marches or camps, along with their accompanying bands, flags and banners. The wearing of distinctive uniforms and the carrying of insignia of the organizations were likewise forbidden.[15] In Württemberg, all the Catholic Young Men's Associations were compulsorily dissolved and their property was confiscated. In Baden the *Deutsche Jugendkraft*, the great Catholic gymnastic association, was proscribed and dissolved. And on 15 August the Ministry of Education prohibited all teachers of religious instruction in high schools from undertaking the responsibilities of pastoral care in denominational youth groups.[16]

A similar campaign against the members of the other Catholic organizations was likewise intensified. They were accused of harbouring both political reactionaries and atheist Communists, who, it was alleged, regarded their organizations as an instrument for conspiring against the Nazi State. In April, Dr Ley openly declared that the prohibition of dual membership was designed to eliminate his Catholic rivals entirely.[17] The German Labour Front, he said, was according to Hitler's decree, to be the sole organization for meeting the needs of every German; the Catholic Workers' Associations had therefore no further justification for their existence. The protests of the Bishops against this blatant breach of the Concordat, and their assurance of the willingness of Catholic workers to support the Nazi leaders in repelling Communism, were entirely disregarded.

Early in 1935, a new Nazi tactic was devised for stirring up anti-clerical feelings amongst the population. A campaign of vilification of the Clergy and of members of the religious orders was launched which, it was hoped, would prove more effective than the doctrinal disputes of the German Faith Movement. Priests, monks and nuns in particular were accused, among other things, of violating the complicated currency regulations, under which no German funds could be sent out of the country, even for the payment of long-standing debts or for the support of German missionaries abroad. Members of the religious orders were put on trial in a blaze of publicity, and unsubstantiated accusations were levelled against them that Jewish capital was being smuggled out of the country by their means. Whereas other offenders against the currency regulations were punished usually by the imposition of a fine, the Party insisted that every case, however minimal, in which members of the religious orders were involved should be prosecuted in the courts of criminal law.[18] The speeches for the defence and the public condemnation by the Bishops of all such attempts to evade the laws of the land, were not reported in the Nazi Press. Rather, these trumped-up charges of currency smuggling were magnified into irrefutable proof that the hostility of the Catholic Church was politically inspired. To give further offence, a ribald song current at the time was quickly seized upon by the Hitler Youth, and despite protests from some of the more moderate Nazis, was shouted out on every possible occasion.

Song of the Religious Life

Oh, the cloistered life is jolly!
Nowadays, instead of prayer,
Smuggling money is the business;
Forth on this sly sport they fare.

Swift they say a Pater Noster
Priest and monk and pious nun.
Swifter then with zealous purpose
Smuggling currency they run.

Laden with the goodly specie
Slinks the nun from place to place.
No one would suspect the creature
From her modest pious face.

To the monk she slips the packet
Puts the swag into his hand.
Out he sallies bold and merry,
From his German Fatherland.

One fine day the whole thing ended;
One fine day the racket crashed
And the news of this rare scandal
Far and near to all was flashed.

Priest and nun and holy friar –
What a horror, they're in clink!
From the labours of their smuggling
To a well-earned rest they sink.

To the priest the nun soft whispers,
'Glorious was the task and grand,
Backing up our Holy Father
Smuggling money through the land.'[19]

The virulence and scurrility of these attacks still failed, however, to produce the desired results. The laity refused to desert their clergy and rallied more strongly to their defence.[20] In fact, so offensive were the Nazi defamations that many of those who had previously supported the authoritarian pattern of development in Germany now began to protest against the trend towards the destruction of their established institutions. The Bishop of Münster, Count Galen, for example, who had shown little sympathy for the Weimar Republic, and who in 1934 had urged the country to co-operate with the new authority that had brought Germany out of chaos, now had second thoughts. At the end of May 1935 he wrote to the Governor of Westphalia protesting against a proposed Nazi rally in the city of his See, at which Rosenberg was due to speak. 'The overwhelming Christian population of Westphalia,' he said, 'could regard the appearance of Rosenberg only as an outright provocation, designed to pour contempt on their holiest and most cherished religious convictions.'[21]

The response of the Nazis to the Bishop's protest was as might have been expected. On 7 July a mammoth rally was held in Münster's main square, in front of the Bishop's palace, when Galen was denounced as a black reactionary and as a leader of the political brand of Catholicism which refused to recognize that times had changed. Frick used the occasion to make his speech, already quoted, demanding the separation of Church and State, and Rosenberg entitled his remarks, 'On German spiritual freedom' – a calculated challenge to the Catholic ethos. In his view, he declared, Nazism had done more for Christianity by overcoming the Bolshevik menace than all the other political parties altogether. Was Nazism intolerant? How could it be when the Bishop was allowed to write such disgraceful letters against the leader of the Nazi movement without being gaoled as a consequence?[22]

Similar demonstrations were organized by the Hitler Youth and the SA against the Bishop of Trier and the Archbishop of Paderborn, in furtherance of the policy expressed by the SA Chief of Staff, Lutze that, 'Whoever provokes us, we will attack, and whoever fights us we will smash.' But still the Catholics refused to be shaken from their allegiance. The Gestapo's prohibition of pastoral letters left no doubt in the minds of the clergy and laity that the very institution of the Church was in danger. The laity increasingly identified themselves as fellow warriors with their clerical leaders in the Church's defence, and as Gestapo reports from Aachen throughout 1935 showed, Church circles which had previously taken a passive attitude were now adopting a much more active role.[23] So strong was the resistance, and so unfavourable the impression created both at home and abroad by the Nazi attacks on the Church that Hitler was at length constrained to intervene and to reconsider the position.

III THE CHURCH MINISTRY, ITS PERSONNEL AND ITS FUNCTION

Shortly after the Münster demonstration, Hitler, while on a tour of inspection near Brunswick, discussed the unfavourable developments in the Church situation with one of his earlier supporters, Hanns Kerrl. In Hitler's view, hopes for a voluntary merging of the Churches into a Nazi State Church, under such Nazi Churchmen as Müller, had floundered. The affairs of the Evangelical Church were, according to Frick, in so confused a state, both legally and administratively, that disunity among them was increasing. Public order was being disrupted and the whole community of the people was being divided against itself. These developments had already caused severe criticism abroad.[24] Rosenberg's plans for victory by propaganda, and Himmler's attempts to achieve the complete subordination of the Churches, both Catholic and Evangelical, in the public life of the country, seemed to lead only to further difficulties. Perhaps the time had come for a complete change of policy, and for the use of new methods of control in order to knock some sense into the Churches. The ideas contained in Stuckart's memorandum now appeared more attractive than formerly, and worthy of further consideration. Kerrl, always eager to please, offered personally to carry out the provisions of the memorandum, and accordingly on 16 July 1935, it was announced that Minister Kerrl had been authorized to establish a new department in the Reich government to deal with all Church matters.

As Mr D. C. Watt has pointed out, the key to power in Nazi Germany lay in the ability to advance proposals that accorded with Hitler's ideas at the time of their expression. Hitler's ideas changed rapidly. They consisted of a few

settled convictions surrounded by a larger penumbra of ideas borrowed from his entourage, enterprises pressed upon him by those who sought power in the hierarchy he dominated, and his own reactions to the circumstances of the moment, and to the actions and statements of foreign statesmen and the foreign press.

Having gained the ear of Hitler, each member of the hierarchy sought first to

obtain a general authorization, a *Führerbefehl*, with which to found a personal office, title, and financial appropriation; and then, the most difficult task of all, to maintain sufficient intellectual initiative at least to protect these gains, if not to expand them, against the claims of . . . rivals. For Nazi Germany was the only state in which the war of the *diadochi* was allowed to proceed openly while its emperor was still alive.[25]

Hanns Kerrl, who for the next six years was to play an important part in the Nazi persecution of the Churches, was a man of decided but limited views. Born in 1887, a son of the headmaster of a school in Fallersleben, he had aspired to a legal career, but having no university education, he was obliged to content himself with the post of accountant in the Prussian law courts.[26] He joined the Nazi Party in its early days and by 1928 had been elected to the Prussian legislature. In 1933 he was awarded the post of Minister of Justice for Prussia, where he was instrumental in organizing a purge of the legal system designed to exclude Jews from legal practice in the courts. Unfortunately for him, the amalgamation of the provincial with the Reich ministries in 1934 led to his exclusion in favour of the Reich Minister Gürtner, a blow to his self-esteem which was not fully appeased when he was accorded the honorary title of Minister without Portfolio and put in charge of town and country planning. Kerrl's reason for suggesting himself as Hitler's agent to deal with the Churches was simply that as such he would have an opportunity of reinstating his authority and of exercising control over a section of German life which no one else had yet dominated. Within a few days he had conferred on himself the resounding title of Reich and Prussian Minister for Ecclesiastical Affairs, and had begun to recruit his staff.

There was never any clear definition of what this Church Ministry should do. As Kerrl conceived it, it was to be an instrument for the external control of the separate factions of the Evangelical Church and for insuring that the Catholic Church fulfilled its obligations to the Nazi State. Its object was to bring to an end the quarrels within the ranks of the Evangelical Clergy, and to regularize the legal and administrative situation. In no circumstances, Kerrl declared, would he allow himself to be caught up in theological squabbles or to interfere with matters of doctrine. He desired only to be the means of reconciling the different parties in the situation created by the Nazi revolution which had brought about fundamental changes in the relationships within the Evangelical Church. Since the Evangelical Church had demonstrated its incapacity to settle its own internal feuds, there was an urgent need to prevent the misuse of Christianity as a cover for hostility towards the State. Evangelical churchmen must, he declared, realize their historical duty to stand shoulder to shoulder with the rest of the people behind the Nazi State.

It was not the State, nor the Party, but Fate itself which is now knocking at the door of the Evangelical Church. Today it is confronted with the great decision, just as the whole people are and must reckon with the fact that a new age has been born and that men must be born again. The Church must march with these men since its field of operations lay with the German people. The mass of the people is marching today with the Führer. The Church has to decide whether to march too or whether to be left behind.[27]

Kerrl, according to his own words, was not interested in establishing a State Church; he desired solely to root out politics and factionalism from the councils of the Evangelical Church, and, by taking over the functions of its secular administration, to coordinate them with the policies of the Nazi State. It must, in all fairness, be said that Kerrl took up office with a sincere wish to consider the arguments of both sides in order to find a fair solution. But he soon made it clear that he intended to use all the weapons at his command to 'encourage' the co-operation of churchmen in developing a sense of community from the fact that they were German, and in acknowledging 'the duties of the race'. He was himself a firm believer in the 'positive Christianity' of the Nazi Party programme, and stoutly maintained that Nazi ideology could be reconciled with the maintenance of German Christianity. He derived most of his ideas from the books of Houston Stewart Chamberlain, a noted racialist, and seized every opportunity of quoting from Chamberlain's *The Foundation of the Nineteenth Century* to justify his view that a strong nation needed a powerful racialist ideology. Such an ideology, he believed, would heal the divisions caused by the Reformation, after which all sides could unite, for ideology and religion would be one.

With such views Kerrl was basically in sympathy with Müller and the 'German Christians', though, like the other Party leaders, he believed that Müller had failed in his task by allowing the fanatics in the ranks of the 'German Christians' to stir up obscurantism among the supporters of the Confessing Church. As the holder of a Government post, with all its resources at his command, he was determined to use his every power to bring into being a united Church dedicated to the service of the State. 'The damage done by the liberal Church policies of the past would have to be overcome, so that the Church would come to recognize the depth and breadth of the complete revolution brought about by the ideas and actions of the Führer.'[28] As for the Catholics, they too must be brought to see that their first loyalty was to Germany, not to Rome.

Kerrl's appointment was not altogether welcome to some of the Party's ideological strategists. They resented the fact that his post was a government appointment, and not of the Nazi Party. And, as Kerrl attempted to build up his 'empire' and to gain control over all aspects of Church policy, his actions were increasingly disputed by his rivals in the Party structure. They never accepted his identification of 'positive Christianity' with Nazi ideology. They made constant attempts to remove from his control whole areas of Church life, and violent quarrels arose over future policy. As time went on, Kerrl proved himself incapable of preventing his so-called colleagues both in the Nazi Party and in the State from indulging in activities which ran counter to his own tactics. He never succeeded in building up a following within the Party strong enough to intrigue successfully against his more ruthless rivals; nor did he gain any influence over the means of mass communication, which were controlled with increasing strictness by the anti-clerical associates of Dr Goebbels. On the one side, both Catholic and Evangelical churchmen regarded his appointment as yet another attempt to impose a Nazi-dominated policy over the whole Church, and to the Confessing Church in particular his activities were no more acceptable than those of Reich Bishop Müller. On the other side, Rosenberg, Schirach, Bormann, and Himmler were equally determined to continue their respective campaigns against the enemies of Nazism in the Churches, with the object of eliminating them completely. Kerrl was a highly volatile and irascible person, but he carried none of the political weight of his rivals. And when, at the insistence of Bormann in the Munich headquarters of the Nazi Party, a reliable Party henchman, Hermann Muhs, was appointed as the *Staatssekretär* of the new Ministry, to hold in check Kerrl's erratic outbursts, he was powerless to object.

Muhs was an opportunist Nazi. Born in 1894 in North Germany, he had joined the Party in 1929, and had been an active promoter of Nazism in Göttingen and Lower Saxony. In 1932 he was promoted to be *Gauleiter* of the South Hanover–Brunswick region. In the following year his services were rewarded with the government post of *Regierungspräsident* (Governor) of the same area, where his extremism made him very unpopular. In Church affairs he was known to be a supporter of the radical wing of the 'German Christians', and though he gained a seat on the Hanover Church Synod, he did so despite a protest from Bishop Marahrens of Hanover. It was hardly surprising that the Confessing Church should from the beginning have regarded him with suspicion, a suspicion which quickly spread to others in the Churches' ranks.

The methods which he used to intensify the Church struggle finally resulted in a complete loss of confidence in him and a repudiation of his authority by the whole Church.

At first Muhs sought to advance his career by sedulously cultivating the support of Goebbels and Rosenberg. In 1937, however, when he was put to work with Kerrl, one of Rosenberg's chief rivals, he began to develop his own policy for the successful *Gleichschaltung* of the Evangelical Churches into the Nazi State. In doing so, he revived the policies of the discredited Reich Bishop Müller, reinforced by such powerful agencies of the State as the Gestapo, to implement them. Although he had been appointed to act as a restraining influence on Kerrl in fact he caused so much resistance in the Church that Kerrl was obliged to limit the number of his public appearances. Only after Kerrl's death in 1941 did Muhs again assume control of the Church Ministry, which by then had been much reduced in scope and authority. Thereafter he proved to be a willing tool in the hands of Bormann, and as a result came to be regarded as one of the most implacable persecutors of the Church.

Another member of the Church Ministry was Hermann von Detten, one of Papen's associates who had earlier been placed in charge of the Nazi Party's department of Cultural Peace, an office originally designed to advise Nazi Party organizations on Church affairs, which was dissolved in November 1935 when its activities were transferred to the Church Ministry. Among the subordinate members was Dr Roth, a former Catholic priest from the Munich Diocese, who had accepted a post in the Church Ministry against the wishes of Cardinal Faulhaber; and Provost Ernst Biberstein, a highly active Nazi Pastor in Schleswig-Holstein, who was later transferred to the Gestapo, where he became the leader of an Extermination Group in Russia and was condemned to death at the Nuremberg Trials in 1947.[29]

The establishment by Hitler of the Church Ministry resulted in a curiously paradoxical position. At a time when Nazi Party zealots were working to separate Church and State with the object of squeezing out the Church from participation in the life of the State, the creation of the Church Ministry set in motion the organs of the official government to work in daily collaboration with the Evangelical Church and to maintain working relations with the Catholic Church. While the Party was decreeing a policy of elimination, Kerrl and Muhs were intent on bringing together the disparate elements of the Evangelical Church, a plan which Hitler was later personally to support by ordering new elections in the Church to secure a Synod favourable to its success. At the Nuremberg rally of 1935 Hitler stated categorically that the Nazis would never intervene against Christianity or against either of the two denominations. Yet the Gestapo's constant harassment of the clergy, of the Churches' organizations and of the church press went far deeper than the mere suppression of political influence within the Churches. Neither group, of course, wanted the Churches to be allowed to conduct their affairs in freedom. But while Kerrl and his Ministry were seeking means to establish a good relationship between Church and State, the Party organs were as busily undermining it. Each side thus cancelled out the work of the other. It is to be supposed that Hitler, in this case as in others, was ready to encourage the hostility and rivalry of his subordinates for the furtherance of his own ends.

On only one aspect of this sorry story did the Nazi State pursue a completely single-minded policy – to drive the Churches out of political life. On that ground the policy of suppression, and even of persecution, was to be justified, and it should be noted that many members of the Churches themselves were persuaded that some of the restrictions were not entirely unwarranted. Most Evangelical pastors denied the claims of the Confessing Church to dispute the concepts of authority within the Church. Many were ready to agree with the Nazis that opposition within the Churches was inspired by political motives. Many of the more pietistic Protestants had long suspected the Catholic Church of political aims designed to strengthen its own position. Others argued that the Nazi Party's drastic limitations of Church activities were to be regarded, not as a defeat, but rather as a liberation from a dangerous over-extension of ecclesiastical influence into the political arena. These limitations they contended, would now make possible a new strengthening of Church life in the field of personal evangelism and pastoral care. There was therefore considerable support for Kerrl's expressed aim of reuniting the Evangelical Church for its prime task of serving a united people and a united nation. And large numbers of Protestants were willing to accept at its face value Hitler's promise at the Nuremberg Rally of 1935 that the Party had no intention of waging war against Christianity. They assumed that Hitler had decided to repudiate the revolutionary views of his radical followers in Church matters just as he had sacrificed Röhm in favour of the regular Army. It was all part, they believed, of the process of his evolution from being merely the leader of an extremist political movement to becoming the statesman of Germany.[30]

IV THE CHURCH MINISTRY IN OPERATION

In accordance with this new move in Nazi policy towards the Churches, Kerrl, at the beginning of September 1935, issued a general amnesty for all pastors convicted or under discipline by the police for opposing the previous Church administration; and at the end of the month he decreed a 'Law for the Safety of the German Evangelical Church', which restored the authority of the provincial churches as outlined in the Constitution of July 1933 and later violated by the extreme measures of Müller and Jäger.[31] A few days afterwards on 3 October, he appointed a series of Church Commissions, both national and local, to establish some semblance of order in the external relations and administration of the Evangelical Churches following the arbitrary rule of the Reich Bishop and the 'German Christians'.[32] In view of the tangled legal situation left by the plethora of decrees issued by Müller, the Commissions were welcomed by many churchmen in the hope that they would at least establish who was in charge of which office and who was responsible for the payment of salaries. Many members of the Confessing Church also were eager to make a new start, despite the ominous passage in the declaration of the new National Commission which read:

We welcome the National Socialist popular evolution (*Volkwerdung*) on the basis of Race, Blood and Soil.[33]

The highly venerated General Superintendent Zöllner, who en-joyed much support in the ranks of the Confessing Church, accepted the chairmanship of the National Commission. His appointment, made with the authority of the new Ministry, meant the displacement of Reich Bishop Müller, and many hoped that it would also mean the end of the extremer policies of the 'German Christians'. Müller, who was left to associate only with the more radical wing of his former followers and was forbidden by the Gestapo to preach at public gatherings, finding himself consigned to a sort of ecclesiastical limbo, eventually wrote plaintively in April 1940 to Lammers, the head of Hitler's Chancellery, to inquire whether the position of Reich Bishop was to be liquidated.[34]

To some Churchmen, however, who, like Pastor Niemöller, were anxious to maintain the Church's autonomy, the establish-ment of a new authority to regulate the Church's affairs by edict of the Nazi State was a cause for alarm. At the end of July 1935 Niemöller sent a circular letter to his supporters in the Confessing Church stating that the recent developments in Church organiza-tion were not in accordance with the principles enunciated at Barmen.

We are in danger of losing God's grace through our own disloyalty. Therefore we must ask our brethren to examine their hearts to see if they are ready for the future struggle ... In recent months we have been waiting for the decisive success of our Church administration and for the official recognition by the State of the Confessing Church. But we have only received one disappointment after another. Many of us are therefore tired and despondent. But we must recognize that it is our faithlessness which has caused us to put our trust in men rather than in God.[35]

A letter from Bishop Marahrens protesting against the setting up of the new Ministry was regarded by Kerrl as a piece of impudence and was sharply rejected.[36] A lengthy meeting with Kerrl a month later failed to remove the misgivings felt by the leaders of the Confessing Church. But the seeming benevolence of Kerrl, despite his lack of theological qualifications, was enough to persuade others that the Confessing Church was demanding too much. And, because they were anxious to continue as loyal citizens in the new

Germany, large numbers of the Evangelical clergy were prepared to believe that a new era in Church policy had been inaugurated by Hitler and that further resistance would serve only to encourage Germany's enemies abroad by weakening internal unity under Hitler's leadership.[37]

These differences of opinion were clearly apparent at the Steglitz meeting of the Prussian Synod of the Confessing Church held at the end of September. A representative of Kerrl's Ministry, Dr Stahn, attended and addressed the delegates. Having admonished them to follow the advice given in the Apocrypha – 'My dear children, learn to hold your tongues; for if you do so you will insult no one' – Stahn stated that though Kerrl had not been pleased at the convening of the Conference, nevertheless he hoped that it would result in an increase in mutual confidence. Should his expectations not be realized, the delegates must expect unpleasant consequences to follow.[38] Caught in a conflict of loyalties, the Confessing Church split. Confronted with Kerrl's determination to bring order and unity into the Church's administration – a decision which he was later to reaffirm at the Prussian Brethren Council of the Confessing Church at the end of November – many leading Churchmen, including the Bishops of Hanover, Bavaria and Württemberg, felt obliged to dissociate themselves from the uncompromising stand of Niemöller. Niemöller and his supporters, however, stood by their resolve not to be dictated to by any secular agency: their commission could come only from the Word of God; it was impossible to separate freedom of doctrine, which Kerrl conceded, from the organization of the Church, which he was determined to control. In January 1936 the Confessing Church published a new pamphlet entitled *The State Church is Here!* Written by the former General Superintendent Dibelius but issued under Niemöller's name, it bitterly attacked the attempts of the Minister to enforce conformity within the Church and his use of the Gestapo to effect it. This, the pamphlet stated, was only another method of imposing the views of the 'German Christians' upon the Evangelical Church.

This conflict of views was discussed at a lengthy national Synod of the Confessing Church held at Bad Oeynhausen in Westphalia on 17 to 22 February 1936. But the opposing sides were irreconcilable. The leaders of the Church in Hanover, Bavaria and Württemberg, while believing that their affairs should be conducted in accordance with the teaching of the Gospel, were nevertheless prepared to co-operate with Kerrl and his National Commission. In opposition, a second Provisional National Administration of the Confessing Church was established, which refused to countenance any step that would lead to the abandonment of its claim to represent the true Evangelical Church. There can be little doubt that the fundamental theological differences which were here reflected were accentuated by personal animosities. But the disunity in the ranks of the Confessing Church gave the Nazis an excuse for accusing Niemöller and his supporters of being motivated solely by political obscurantism. It also prevented the Evangelical Church as a whole from looking beyond its immediate organizational concerns and from making a united stand against the Nazi imposition of totalitarian rule by the progressive establishment of a police state.

Kerrl was understandably impatient at all these controversies. He was desperately anxious to ensure the success of his Ministry by bringing the support of a united Evangelical Church behind the Nazi State. If the Churchmen would not be persuaded by his arguments, then stronger methods would have to be used. On 2 December 1935, he issued an executive order forbidding the Confessing Church to exercise authority in any of the areas where Church Commissions had already been established.[39] He also circularized all the local government offices and all branches of the Gestapo stipulating that nothing should be done to jeopardize the success of his efforts and that no measures, such as arrests, expulsions, prohibitions or confiscations against members of the Churches, should be made without his express permission.[40] This order appears to have been designed to restrain the activities of certain over-enthusiastic local Nazi elements, especially in Bavaria, where petty persecution of the clergy was a continued source of disquiet. Nor could Kerrl regard with equanimity the continuing attacks made upon the Churches by the German Faith Movement, by the leaders of the Hitler Youth and by outspoken anti-clerical elements in the Nazi Party. It was Kerrl's view, as he told the students of the University of Berlin, that the true Nazi must be religious, for otherwise he had not grasped the full depth of National Socialism. Christianity was not to be attacked, but was rather to be brought to completion through the 'positive Christian' achievements of National Socialism.[41]

Opposed on the one side by the anti-Christian forces associated with Rosenberg, Schirach, Bormann and Himmler, and on the other by the hard core of the Confessing Church, Kerrl's Ministry was under constant fire. While he never succeeded in convincing his Party members of the rightness of his policies, the extent and scope of the measures taken against the Churches by the various organs of the Nazi Party obstructed any possibility of successful collaboration either with the many branches of the Evangelical Church or with the Catholic Church. Kerrl's efforts to find new grounds for compromise were rejected and his motives were suspected. Unaware, perhaps, of the extent of the internecine feuds within the Nazi Party, the churchmen not unnaturally assumed that Kerrl was promoting or at least supporting the local activities of the Nazi Party organs which were causing such distress to the Churches. The refusal of the Nazis to abandon their totalitarian claims to complete control over all aspects of German life was matched by the Churches' refusal to be relegated to a position of irrelevant pietism, or of being simply the acquiescent applauder of Nazi achievements. In such a situation, there was no possibility of collaboration between Church and State, and hence no real future for the Church Minister. The ambitious plans with which Kerrl had entered office were progressively abandoned, until he was finally reduced to a policy of terrorizing his recalcitrant opponents by ever-increasing penalties, while trying unsuccessfully to ward off the attempts of his so-called colleagues to deprive him of large sections of his responsibilities. Kerrl's career in the Church Ministry was a dramatic demonstration of the empiricism, indecision and lack of understanding which formed the basis of the Nazis' official church policy in the first years of the Thousand Year Reich.

6 'Positive Christianity' or Nazi Cult: the Ideological Conflict

'The great miracle of God become man, a
stumbling block to the Jews and foolishness
to the Greeks, has found its true meaning in
the Germanic soul.' – AUGUST WINNIG

The Nazi ideology was never fully articulated or made systematic.
The writings of Alfred Rosenberg, the chief spokesman for the
movement, were diffuse and incoherent. Even the Nazi leaders
themselves were never fully convinced of the validity of the un-
examined and confused doctrines which were to be found in such
books as *The Myth of the Twentieth Century*. The claim to be the
representatives of a new paganism was, nevertheless, not just a
personal idiosyncrasy of a few minor figures in the Nazi hierarchy.
The conviction of being the vanguard of a new ideological force
in European culture was an integral part of all Nazi thinking.
Among the most prominent features of this new paganism can be
discerned the exaltation of the personality of Hitler, the propagation of the 'religion of the Blood' and the attempts to provide
pagan equivalents for 'outdated' Christian ceremonies.

The tactical restraints on the publicizing of such views, which
had been imposed during the years of struggle to achieve power,
were now progressively abandoned. Although some Nazi leaders
believed it necessary first to break the stubborn hold of long-
established traditions of German life, including those derived from
the Christian churches, others sought to take advantage of the
new optimism and new sense of purpose which, by 1936, took
hold of the German people. Now was the time, these Nazi leaders

believed, to launch more striking efforts to indoctrinate the people with the Nazi ideology and to campaign for the abandonment of beliefs belonging to the discredited past. It was in the years 1936 and 1937, therefore, before the efforts of Germans began to be harnessed to Hitler's military ambitions, that the ideological campaign against the Churches was to reach its zenith. An examination of some of the more prominent features of this campaign may be relevant to an understanding of the Nazi ambitions in this sphere of 'propaganda and public enlightenment'.

I THE NAZI PSEUDO-RELIGION

Most spectacular of all the large-scale indoctrination methods which sought to canalize the popular enthusiasm for the new régime were the annual Nazi Party rallies at Nuremberg. Here every device of showmanship was used to mark the celebrations as an evident triumph of the Nazi way of life. Over a million people flocked into the city each year, either as participants or as spectators. Foreign visitors received special attention. The full diplomatic corps was invited. Representatives of the foreign Press and film companies were encouraged to send home full reports on the lavish spectacles and the fervent adulation which the new patriotism and the new ideology were inspiring. The enthusiasm of the people for the parades and torchlight processions and the almost unbearable emotionalism of the ceremonies were all alike impressive.

The rallies, moreover, were designed to be more than mere colourful spectacles or to provide a display of the efficiency of Nazi organization on a large scale. They were the means whereby every branch of the Nazi Party organization could demonstrate its loyalty to the Leader by a series of pseudo-religious ceremonies at which Hitler was accorded the jubilant devotion of his followers.[1]

As Hans Frank, who was later to become Governor General of Poland, recorded,

Hitler's personality dominated the proceedings entirely, for all the processions, rallies, meetings and ceremonies were either led by him or

141

dedicated to him or were the setting for his great speeches. This was his world, in which he moved and had his being and in which everything turned on him. These massive crowds were shouting and rejoicing around him personally. These were his ideas which were here proclaimed, announced and celebrated. These were his organisations who were marching and parading there. His banners and symbols, dedicated and distributed by him, floated in sole glory. The Party rallies became more and more the annual ceremony to celebrate his life's work, created and upheld by him alone, to mark the new foundation of the whole people and race.[2]

In fact, the emphasis and the ceremonies at Nuremberg far transcended a recognition and acknowledgement of Hitler's gifts as a politician. They were indicative of nothing less than the deification of the Leader.

It was Hitler who was celebrated at Nuremberg, not National Socialism as an idea or the Party as an organization, or only insofar as they were Hitler's own creation. No one in Nuremberg thought in 'ideological', 'programmatic' or 'objective-political' terms. The crowd burned with fervour around Hitler, the Saviour, the Creator, the Defender of the German Fatherland. Whatever he said, was right and good; whatever he proclaimed, was destined to happen; howsoever he acted, it was for the best. Hitler, in the hearts of all, was held to be the great deliverer sent from on high to herald the hoped-for deliverance of our nation.[3]

This cult of Hitler demanded faith, and no politician of this century has been more successful than Hitler in both demanding and receiving the worship which is the adjunct of faith. The Hitlerian cult, in fact, became an *ersatz* religion, accompanied by frenzies of enthusiasm. Millions of Germans – and not merely those in the ranks of Hitler's committed supporters – came to worship at the feet of their idol. To some he was the people's deliverer from their country's evil past, the 'unknown soldier' of the Flanders trenches resurrected as a living heroic figure endowed with political statesmanship and oratorical skill. To others he was the future 'Saviour' who would miraculously lead Germany out of the misery of defeat and depression into the promised land.

In the unreal atmosphere in which the German people had

surrounded themselves since 1918, and carried away on a growing wave of Germanic mysticism and mythology, such apocalyptic devotion spread like an epidemic, making it easy for an unscrupulous and fanatical politician to be exalted in a halo of Nordic light and by the incantations to his supposed divinity. Certainly by 1936 many Germans had abandoned their long tradition of sober inquiry and rational discussion and were demonstrating an astonishing readiness to embrace this new idolatry which seemed to be achieving such political miracles.

Probably the man most intoxicated by the emotionalism of the Nuremberg ceremonies was Hitler himself. The rallies undoubtedly contributed to the process of megalomania and self-aggrandizement which led him late in 1937 to declare to a group of propaganda leaders that, after difficult internal struggles, he had liberated himself from his last remaining childhood conceptions of religion. 'I now feel myself as happy as a foal frolicking in the meadows.'[4]

There were two main reasons for Hitler's success. The first was the recognition and skilful exploitation by the Nazis of the already powerful *völkisch* tradition in the German mind. As Dr G. L. Mosse has pointed out:

The *völkisch* ideology cannot be viewed as a transient phenomenon; it was a new religion whose roots, like those of all religions and faiths, not only entered men's subconscience but penetrated deeper and became a whole new way of life ... Hitler only promised to fulfil the concept of life which had permeated much of the nation before he ever entered the scene.[5]

Adolf Hitler, the Nazis claimed, was the embodiment of all that was noblest in Germanic values. He personified all the best in Germany's past and was the dedicated guardian of her future destiny. The racialist and nationalistic elements in the *völkisch* ideology were adroitly dovetailed into Nazi political aims and ambitions. Such biological and natural images and arguments as were current in *völkisch* thinking were exploited for the Party's purposes, while the semi-mystical nature worship of the German Faith Movement, and the visions of such 'prophets' as Lagarde and Wagner, were neatly turned into political channels. The visionary framework of the *völkisch* ideology almost exactly paralleled the concept of Hitler as the 'unifier' of his country destined to bind the whole community to himself in a bond of eternal loyalty. The *völkisch* rejection of such non-Germanic values as those derived from Jerusalem, Athens or Rome was constantly reiterated and re-emphasized by the ideological strategists of the Nazi Party.

The second reason for Hitler's success was his skill in providing a satisfying and convincing explanation for Germany's recent past. In emotional, if non-rational, terms Hitler laid the blame on Germany's enemies – in particular, on the Jews. He exploited, or rather distorted, the whole corpus of religious thought to present, in secular and political terms, the hope for redemption by the purgation of the soul, the need for delivery from the powers of darkness, and the acceptance of the omnipotent power of the deliverer. In their virulent hostility to the Jews the Nazis struck a responsive chord in the minds of many Germans, whose views for two generations had been unceasingly perverted against the alien and despised Jew. For all Germany's evils, political and spiritual, Hitler blamed the Jewish race. He pointed to the failure of every previous attempt, including those of the Churches, to rid Germany of the taint of Judaism. Only the Nazis had fully recognized the danger and had taken prompt steps against it. It was now necessary to complete the work by the total eradication of this mortal disease. The Churches had failed because they were divided in their loyalties. Only those who believed in the person of Adolf Hitler and in his God-given mission to save Germany were fitted to undertake the enormous tasks ahead.

The receptive climate of opinion into which these ideas were sown goes a long way to account for the mass hysteria bordering on frenzy which was whipped up by the Nazis for their new pseudo-religion. Their methods of showmanship were first-rate. Nazi Party meetings rapidly adopted a form calculated to make a profound effect on the participants. Every device of sight and sound was used to stir up a devotional fervour. Meeting-places were emblazoned with the Nazi colours on flags and standards, banners with Nazi slogans festooned the halls, similar posters were lavishly displayed outside. The musical accompaniment of trumpets and trombones evoked memories of martial victories. Monumental architecture gave an impression of enduring strength. When Hitler spoke at Nuremberg he addressed the throng from the top of an enormous embattled wall. He alone, as the charismatic hero, was allowed to ascend to the heights, surrounded by the massed banners and standards of his legions. At his entry at the Nuremberg night rally, the 'hour of dedication', a pyramid of searchlights was switched on to create a baldachino of light over the figure of Germany's deliverer. In the darkness, surrounded by the masses of his followers, the high priest received the adulation of his people.

The ceremony of the dedication of Nazi flags became a religious ritual for the expression of unswerving loyalty to Hitler and his organizations. The endless singing of Nazi campaign songs served the same purpose. The repulsive Horst Wessel song, with its evocation of the early martyrs to the Nazi cause, was designed to glorify the sacrifices of the past. As for the future, the idea of eternal devotion to Nazism was ceaselessly drummed into the ranks of the Hitler Youth by the words of their marching song:

> Our flag is the New Age!
> And leads us into eternity!
> Yes, the flag means more than death!

By every artifice of skilful propaganda, the individual was engulfed in a wave of mass emotionalism which was calculated to seal the whole nation in the cult of Hitler, the Nazi deity.

There was neither the time nor the need to systematize the doctrines of the new pseudo-religion. The Nazi *Weltanschauung* simply adopted from the Churches, especially from the Catholic Church, such precepts and practices as they considered best suited to serve their ends. An *ersatz* theology was built on the Nazi theories of race; the Christian concepts of the creation, the fall of man, redemption, salvation, and the Day of Judgment were all manipulated to fit into Nazi dogma. The Party organization owed much to Hitler's acknowledgement, albeit reluctant, of the Catholic Church's success in the leadership of its people. The hierarchical traditions of the Roman Church exactly matched the *Führerprinzip* which the Nazis hoped to perpetuate. The infallibility of the Pope, in particular, was regarded as a spiritual weapon of the utmost importance, since by its means obedience and discipline were instilled in the ranks of the faithful. The propaganda ministry hoped to achieve the same powers of indoctrination, and of censorship, which had enabled the Catholic Church to exercise its age-old control over the European masses. The Nazi leaders were to perform the same functions in their God-given assignment for the preservation of the 'aryan' race as the Church had exercised by its centrally-controlled Orders. The 'aryan' race was created in the image of God, and its task was therefore seen as part of the *Heilsgeschichte* of the whole world. From Germany the light of the world would shine forth as a city set on a hill, calling the world to salvation. To fulfil the task, a whole corpus of prophets, saints and martyrs to the Nazi cause was to be 'discovered', so that German history could be reshaped in accordance with Nazi ideas. The Jewish race was to play the role of the cosmic force of evil, the destruction of which was the duty and destiny of every German. Thereafter the German race would achieve its own day of salvation; it would perpetuate its own immortality in the thousand-year Reich, and in National Socialism the German people would find tranquillity and spiritual fulfilment.

Close examination of this *ersatz* religion was not encouraged, for, as Professor Schnabel, of the University of Halle commented:

> In a certain sense National Socialism is a religion because it asks its followers not to become convinced of the truth of its doctrines but to believe in it.[6]

Unquestioning obedience and loyalty were the only pre-requisites for the Nazi believer. Indeed, the profession of the Nazi pseudo-religion was the result, not the cause, of personal attachment to Hitler. The oath of allegiance to Hitler, which became one of the main points of resistance in the ranks of the Confessing Church, marked the initiation of the believer into the mysteries of this new paganism. Describing a public ceremony of oath-taking, the Nazi *Westdeutscher Beobachter* commented:

> Yesterday witnessed the profession of the religion of the Blood in all its imposing reality. Yesterday saw the triumphant and decisive begin-

ning of our fight to make National Socialism the only racial religion of the German people. Whoever has sworn his oath of allegiance to Hitler has pledged himself unto death to this sublime idea. There is no more room for doubts and uncertainties, no room for retreat.[7]

The Nazis claimed that this 'religion of the Blood' was patently superior to the sectarianism of the existing Churches, and steadfastly rejected the accusation of atheism. The guiding hand of God was regularly invoked, linked with the name of Adolf Hitler. Himmler publicly declared that atheism would not be tolerated in the ranks of the SS,[8] and in a circular to Party members Hess wrote:

> It is of course obvious that a party member and National Socialist would never describe himself as 'without faith', since the National Socialist ideology presumes a religious attitude; on the other hand, this religious attitude does not presume a Church or denominational connection.[9]

The Nazi leaders themselves, however, were cynical both in their own religious convictions and over the adulation which was so fervently expressed by the people. Hitler and his closest associates were at one in agreeing that their motives for arousing such fanaticism were entirely political. Hitler's uncritical and erratic mind was incapable of a logical formulation of his so-called ideology, and it is difficult to know which of his associates really believed the phrases of eulogy and worship they so readily mouthed. They were probably incapable of devotion in the true sense. But since a hypocritical adulation of Hitler and a ready affirmation of the tenets of the Nazi pseudo-religion were obviously successful in swaying the emotions of the mob and in captivating the minds of the intelligentsia, it was therefore to be encouraged.

So widespread indeed did the worship of Hitler and Nazism become that the component strands were inextricably mixed. The frothy yeast of racialist, historical, *völkisch*, nationalistic and personal elements each contributed to the potent and intoxicating brew, and to the minds of most of the Nazi leaders the mainspring of this idolatry was immaterial. Faith meant loyalty and dedication to Adolf Hitler. The only essential was that the German people should yield themselves to become willing instruments for the furtherance of Hitler's schemes.

It is not surprising that, in their efforts to enlist the German people in the service of the 'inseparable Trinity of State, Movement and *Volk*',[10] the Nazis should adopt the established practices of the Churches. Despite vigorous denials by Hitler, Kerrl and others that Nazism had any intention of creating a cultic ritual, the totalitarian claims of Nazi ideology soon necessitated the invention of 'purely German' liturgical forms which would fulfil man's every need from the cradle to the grave and would leave no room for the out-dated services of the Christian Churches.

In a pamphlet entitled *Entkonfessionalisierung*, published by the Central Publishing House of the Nazi Party, detailed instructions were issued for such ceremonials.

In future a permanent rite will be prescribed for all National Socialist celebrations. Only by fixing certain fundamental features of our programmes shall we gradually succeed in developing forms of celebrations of a liturgical character which shall be valid for centuries. The principal items of a National Socialist celebration are to be: The *Verkündung* (Proclamation), a solemn address of fifteen to twenty minutes in poetical language, followed by the *Bekenntnis* (Confession of Faith) recited by the congregation, and the *Lied Der Verpflichtung* (Hymn of Duty) which, to the accompaniment of the organ, is to be sung in unison by all present. The ceremony is to close with a 'Salute to the Führer' (Sieg Heil) and one verse of each of the National Anthems.[11]

Many of the Nazi rites made use of the Church's terminology for the glorification of Hitler as the embodiment of Nazi ideals. The substitution of nationalistic for Christian symbolism is unmistakable in the following 'creed', which was used at the end of the Nazi ritual of Harvest thanksgiving:

I believe in the land of all the Germans, in a life of service to this land; I believe in the revelation of the Divine creative power and the pure Blood shed in war and peace by the sons of the German National Community, buried in the soil thereby sanctified, risen and living in all for whom it is immolated. I believe in an eternal life on earth of this Blood that was poured out and rose again in all who have recognized the

148

meaning of the sacrifices and are ready to submit to them ... Thus I believe in an eternal God, an eternal Germany, and an eternal life.[12]

In a speech by Robert Ley in February 1937 the process reached its apogee:

Adolf Hitler! We are linked and united with you alone! In this hour we seek to renew our vow to you: we believe on this earth in Adolf Hitler alone. We believe that National Socialism alone is the redemptive faith for our people. We believe that there is a God in Heaven, who has created us, who guides us, who leads us and who visibly blesses us. And we believe that this Almighty God has sent us Adolf Hitler, so that Germany shall have eternal security.[13]

The festivities of the Christian year were likewise transmogrified. On 30 January the Nazi seizure of power was celebrated; in March the Heroes' Memorial Day; on 20 April Hitler's birthday; on 1 May National Labour Day; on 21 June the Day of the Summer Solstice. The Nuremberg rallies in September were the occasion for mass ceremonies on a grand scale. In October the celebration of Harvest Thanksgiving laid stress on the Nazi concept on Blood and Soil; and in place of Christmas the Yule Feast was proclaimed on the Day of the Winter Solstice. Of the whole Nazi year, however, the holiest day was 9 November, the day of commemoration of Hitler's unsuccessful *Putsch* of November 1923. Each year special parades were held in Munich to commemorate the Nazis who were slain in the incident and for the dedication of aspiring novices to the Party who would replace the 'witnesses of blood' who had died for the Nazi cause. Along crowd-filled streets, the élite of German youth marched from the Königsplatz, where the sarcophagi were laid, to the *Feldherrnhalle*. In the Odeonsplatz an enormous stone slab, bearing the swastika surmounted by the German eagle, bore the names of those who 'in true faith in the resurrection of their people fell on this spot'. 'The Blood,' said Hitler, 'which they poured out, is become the altar of baptism for our Reich.' The sacrifice of these 'martyrs' was glorified and extolled in language calculated to excite the onlookers to greater acts of devotion. It was celebrated as a sacrament of the whole German people.

On the steps leading to the *Feldherrnhalle*,
To which today great men come as pilgrims,
The Sacrament of our Struggle was once born.
Through this unique Minster which is called Germany, only those are
    admitted,
Who have expressed their wills in hard deeds.
You are true pilgrims if you esteem the glory of our Nation
Higher than the revelation of all religions!
You feel the sacred atmosphere of the *Feldherrnhalle*:
What are hymns and Mass prayers and the swinging of glittering
    censers
Compared to the rhythm of our muffled drums
When our Führer ascends these steps?
Those that behold him stand with bated breath;
The earth vibrating with our steps is silent;
Noise has withdrawn to the ends of the world.
The Führer stands on high;
The Führer lifts his hand in an eternal salute.
His heart beats as one with that of his people.
Today his ascent is prayer . . .
He ascends and stops, invested with wonder;
He is inflamed by the faith of his comrades.
No priestly consecration ascends with greater power
Than this prayer, silent and hewn in stone,
Of that one man
Whose heart throbs with the heartbeat of a whole nation.
The oath of the *Feldherrnhalle* is the prayer of all of us to our Creator.
Let fire, smoke and death surround us,
We will rejoice if only the flag . . .
Our flag, keeps flying . . .
Touch the steps of the *Feldherrnhalle*,
Lift the flag up higher, the Germans' sublimest symbol,
Steeped in the blood of western battles and proclaiming our faith.
And all our standards joyfully exclaim;
What is death, if thou demandst our lives,
O Germany?[14]

As Dr H. J. Gamm has suggested, the ceremony was designed to
become a sort of passion play, in which the audience would feel
personally identified with the individual victims who had died for

their nation, their devotion rising to ever greater heights as they heard the final proclamation that Providence had sent Hitler to be their leader, to overcome all defeat and humiliation, and to bring Germany into the new Reich.[15]

By similar manipulation and distortion, use was made of the many naturalist and theosophical theories which had been prevalent in Germany for many years. The *völkisch* element cherished by those who sought escape from the problems of modern industrial Germany by invoking the romantic past, the beauty of Germany's landscape, and the splendour of teutonic mythology, provided much of the framework of Nazi ideas. By channelling the energies of the *völkisch* groups, especially of the youth groups, along a definite political line, mainly by stressing their common anti-semitism, the Nazis were able to win them over and gain control.[16] And by encouraging the use of anti-Christian slogans and of ceremonies derived from *völkisch* experience the influence of the Churches was gradually and systematically undermined.

Nevertheless, despite the support of occult and theosophical ideas given by such Nazi leaders as Darré, Rosenberg, Himmler and Ley, the scepticism in the ranks of the Party over the genuineness of their devotion still remained. Those who were primarily interested in the pursuit of power in the Nazi jungle of rivalries could not summon up much enthusiasm for dawn ceremonies to mark the summer solstice. For them the political motive was not obscured by metaphysical or mystical jargon; for their minds the words of Baldur von Schirach were nearer the truth:

It is my purpose neither to re-erect in the forests of Germany heathen altars and introduce youth to any kind of Wotans-cult, nor in any other way to hand over young Germany to the magical arts of any herb-apostles. . . . I promise the German public that the youth of the German Reich, the youth of Adolf Hitler, will fulfil their duty in the spirit of Adolf Hitler, to whom alone their life belongs.[17]

To fire the imagination of the young, however, these teutonic ceremonies and rituals were widely practised. In camps far from the shelter of the pupils' homes, ideological indoctrination could be particularly effective. The instructors, all highly skilled in the necessary techniques, were well aware that their ideology was not to be learned but to be lived. By means of the pulsating rhythms of the marching columns and the united singing of Nazi songs endlessly repeated, each boy and girl was initiated into the collective experience which dissolved their individuality and fused them into unity with their comrades. When they were assembled around the leaping flames of the campfire, it was not difficult to create a sense of danger in the surrounding darkness, to call for unity and comradeship in meeting any challenge to the new Germany, and to evoke a sense of devotion and commitment to Adolf Hitler, the protector and saviour of the Fatherland. Hitler's requirements for German youth were positive and insistent:

My pedagogy is strict. Every weakness must be hammered out. In my new training schools, young people will grow who will shock the world. I want a powerful, masterly, cruel and fearless youth ... They must be able to bear pain. There must be nothing weak or tender about them. The freedom and dignity of the wild beast must shine from their eyes.... That is how I will root out a thousand years of human domestication. Then I will have the pure noble material in front of me; and then I can make something new.[18]

For Schirach this 'something new' presupposed the substitution of a new idealism for the discredited creeds of Christianity. In his *Revolution der Erziehung*, Schirach wrote that 'what we are doing for the unity of Germany takes place not only in the spirit of politics, but also in the spirit of religion'.[19] In the training camps of the Party it was repeatedly impressed upon the students that the three enemies of National Socialism were Judaism, Masonry and Christianity. The Hitler Youth were taught to despise the Christian heritage of their parents and to denigrate the ministers of the Church as traitors to their country. The journals of the Hitler Youth Movement teemed with attacks against church and clergy. Although participation in Church services was not forbidden, from 1937 it was made practically impossible by the regulations which set the time of the compulsory parades to coincide with the hours of the Church services. Church functions were frequently interrupted by rowdy Nazi groups. 20 April, Hitler's birthday, was proclaimed as the day of initiation for the Hitler Youth, to supplant the Churches' confirmation rite which was usually held at Whitsun. 'The poison of Sinai or of Nazareth' was represented as a Jewish feature of the Churches' teaching, and therefore to be rejected in favour of the piety and morality of the German people. The Holy Land, Rosenberg postulated, was no longer somewhere in the East, but wherever German blood defended Germany's holy soil. The worship of nature, particularly of the life-giving power of the sun, was symbolized in the ubiquitous display of the Swastika, the archetype of Nazi emblems. The Nordic inheritance of the German people was to be reinstated after centuries of Christian distortion and error.[20]

Part of the work of the SS, the Nazi élite corps, was, in the words of its leader Heinrich Himmler, 'to spread the knowledge of the Race in the life of our People and to impress it upon the hearts of all, down to the very youngest, as Gospel, our German Gospel'. Officially, Himmler decreed that religion was to be treated as a matter of personal conviction, and, in order to maintain public decorum, he ordered his men to refrain from any attacks on the beliefs of others.[21] But he himself, in whom violent anti-clericalism was combined with a large measure of superstition, ostentatiously left the Church in the summer of 1936, and his example was subsequently followed by other SS members, despite his injunction that such a step was to be taken only from conviction and not merely from a desire to conform.[22] Large numbers of SS men were openly anti-clerical in their views, and the *Schwarze Korps*, Himmler's weekly newspaper, became a vehicle for scurrilous propaganda against the Churches. Furthermore, to foster the idea of the SS as a racially pure corps of shock troops wholly dedicated to the service of the Third Reich, a new marriage service was devised for SS men and a new ceremony for the enrolment of their children in the ranks of the SS dependents.

A newspaper account of one such ceremony described it as follows:

The central point in the ceremonial was represented by the wedding table decorated by two conjoined runic figures: On the table lay a yellow sun disc made of flowers on a blue background; to the left and right stood torch bearers and behind the table a bowl, containing fire, and the pulpit. The choir opened the ceremony with a chorus from 'Lohengrin'.

A representative of the new usage, SS Comrade Elling, gave the dedication – an address which was based upon the song from the Edda about Helgi and Sigrun. The choir chanted both before and after the address. Then the bridal pair were offered bread (representing the germinating force of earth) and salt (the symbol of purity) on silver vessels; finally the pair thus married according to German custom received the wedding rings.[23]

Among Himmler's private papers, photographs were found of the 'baptism' of an SS child, together with a detailed description of the ceremony. The room was decorated with Nazi flags and with a picture of the Tree of Life. In front of the backcloth, branches of young birch trees were placed, flanked by two large candles. In the centre stood an altar on which was placed a framed photograph of Hitler and a copy of *Mein Kampf*. Behind it stood three SS men, the middle one holding a banner. The ritual proceeded thus:

One: musical introduction (string music, no wind instruments) (Grieg's Morning Music).

Two: at the sound of the music, the father, accompanied on his right by his wife and on his left by the Senior SS leader shall bring in the child and lay him on a pillow by the altar.

Three: chorus or speaker: Quotations from Hitler's *Mein Kampf*.

Four: the Celebrant (naturally in SS uniform):

We believe in an almighty God
And in the mission of our German blood
Which grows eternally young on German soil.
We believe in the People who maintain the Blood,
And in the Leader, sent to us by God.
                    (Turning to the parents)
You will dedicate this child to the service of your people.
I ask you what name shall your child have.

Five: Father: We name our son . . .

Six: The Celebrant announces the name of the child and speaks of the obligation of the name.

Seven: The Celebrant to the parents: Will you promise to arouse, cherish and maintain in your child the latent gifts, so that the promise of his name will be turned to reality?

Eight: Parents: We promise to do so.

Nine: Celebrant: Now light the flame, that it may burn as a symbol of our unity.

Ten: The father lights the flame.

Eleven: The parents' friends offer their congratulations and lay their gifts on the table beside the child's burning flame.

Twelve: The Celebrant: Now close the circle around this child, that he may become part of our community.

Thirteen: The SS Leader: We take you now into our community as a member of our body. You will grow up under our protection, and you will bring to your name honour, to your 'clan' pride and to your people inextinguishable fame.

Fourteen: All sing the hymn of loyalty to the SS

Fifteen: The parents leave with the child, with musical accompaniment, while the participants stand to greet him with the Hitler salute.[24]

In the Nazi-run orphanages alternatives were provided for the Christian grace before meals:

> O Führer, my Führer, sent to me by God
> Protect and maintain my life
> Thou who has served Germany in its hour of need
> I thank thee now for my daily bread
> Oh! Stay with me, Oh! Never leave me
> Führer, My Führer, my faith and my light.[25]

And the children were encouraged to sing:

> Silent night! Holy night!
> All is calm, all is bright
> Only the Chancellor steadfast in fight
> Watches o'er Germany by day and by night
> Always caring for us.
>
> Silent night! Holy night!
> All is calm, all is bright
> Adolf Hitler is Germany's wealth
> Brings us greatness, favour and health
> Oh give us Germans all power![26]

A substitute service for Christian burial was also devised, which included the laying of wreaths, the firing of salvoes and the singing of the military song '*Ich hatt'einen Kameraden!*' In the smaller towns and villages these alternative ceremonies were widely ignored, but from time to time, when the death occurred of a younger member of a Nazi organization, a horrifying conflict arose between the parents, the clergy and the local Nazi leaders over possession of the corpse and the responsibility for the burial service.[27]

It is not now possible to obtain statistics of the exact number of people who were baptised, married or buried according to these Nazi rites. Nor is it possible to estimate how widespread the practices were; but the examples quoted give some idea of the use that was made of *völkisch* symbols and rituals to stimulate devotion and a sense of dedication to Nazi ideals and to the person of Hitler. Nevertheless, though the totalitarian ambitions of the Nazi Party were intolerant of the existence of rival centres of loyalty, even for only a portion of German life, there were still members of the Party, even in the upper ranks, who, like Kerrl, clung to a nominal form of the Christianity in which they had been brought up. They believed it possible for the idealism, the self-sacrifice and comradeship which they found in the Nazi Party, to be pursued under the mantle of a German Christianity purged of theological wrangling and dedicated to national and racial purposes – what they called the 'positive Christianity' of practical service and philanthropy.

Such men looked askance at the anti-Christian activities of their fellow Party members, for they were still unable to accept the view that the Church and the Party were irreconcilable and still cherished the hope that the Church would accept the role assigned to it by the Party. In 1936 and 1937, however, the way ahead was still uncertain, and even they were obliged to admit that, if the Church refused to stand beside the Party, and if it continued to indulge in inter-denominational squabbles and in political treachery, then the established position of the Church would have to be discarded, so that National Socialism could become the religion of all Germany.

So far as the common people were concerned, most of them believed that traditional Christianity was compatible with Nazism. They took comfort in the public pronouncements of Hitler on the place of religion in German life, and in the pro-Nazi professions of many of their own Church leaders. With a few notable exceptions, the Bishops, both Catholic and Protestant, were careful not to arouse any conflict in the conscience of their flocks between their Church loyalties and their national obligations. As Professor Gordon Zahn has pointed out:

The intensity of Bismarck's *Kulturkampf* against the [Catholic] Church burdened it with something of an inferiority complex which continued long afterward to manifest itself in a compulsive drive to prove that Catholics *could be* good and loyal Germans, that they *were* good and loyal Germans, that, in fact, their religious formation made it certain that they would be the *best* and *most loyal* Germans of all.[28]

The belief was therefore carefully fostered that the Nazi rituals and ceremonies, and their attempted substitution for Christian doctrines and institutions, were either unknown to Hitler or merely the work of 'enthusiasts'. Not only in the ranks of the 'German Christians' but within the Catholic hierarchy itself the belief was prevalent that, by demonstrating their nationalist fervour, the Christian churches could outbid their rivals for the favours of Adolf Hitler. And the historian today, like the knowledgeable foreign visitor to Germany thirty years ago, can only be astounded at the readiness of vast numbers of German Churchmen to turn a blind eye on the obvious signs of totalitarian encroachment. Guenter Lewy's conclusions are not exaggerated:

The bishops' failure to call a spade a spade, their attempts to trade on the popularity of certain Nazi ideas, their continued admonishments to clergy and faithful not to criticize State and Party certainly were little suited to instil anti-Nazi sentiment in their followers ... In failing to defend not only the liberty of the Church, but human liberty itself ... the bishops had inadvertently doomed the chances of winning the struggle against their oppressors.[29]

II THE STRUGGLE QUICKENS

This new heathenism did not, however, go entirely unchallenged. Those in the Churches, who saw clearly enough where such pernicious doctrines would lead to, undertook a vigorous defence wherever possible. The result was to bring the conflict more openly before the public, and led to a striking deterioration in Church–State relations. In 1936 and 1937, as many observers noted, the high-point of the ideological confrontation between Nazism and Christianity was reached.

In both camps, there were those who regarded the Church struggle as irrevocable. But there were also 'moderates' who wished to prevent, if only for tactical reasons, any sharpening of the tensions. It is possible to see in the events of these years the various measures adopted by the differing groups, whose mutual contradictions, however, were still strong enough to prevent the achievement of any unilateral success. The Church Struggle became more bitter, but it was still not resolved.

Despite Rosenberg's optimistic forecasts of the ultimate triumph of the new paganism by a process of unremitting indoctrination, its chances of success as a permanent substitute for Christianity were problematical. Most of the Nazi leaders were impatient. They were not prepared to wait for years before the new faith effectively replaced the old one in the hearts of the people. In their opinion the crushing of Christian influence should be accelerated. It was not enough just to provide substitute rituals and ideals. The Church's persisting influence was, they were convinced, due to the ubiquitous presence of the clergy. If the clergy were brought to heel the Church would be crippled and the laity would be forced to conform. The Nazi leaders despised the clergy. They assumed that a natural reluctance to lose both position and stipend would quickly prove strong enough to crush clerical opposition, and once that danger had been averted their congregations could soon be taught to appreciate the 'dynamism' of the new era. Recalcitrants who continued to cling to sectarian loyalties could be left to linger on in obscurity, bypassed by the new Nazi order.

But there were wide differences of opinion over the pace at which such action should be put into effect. Some Nazi leaders continued to advocate root-and-branch measures against the clergy. The vicious, often obscene, outbursts of Streicher, the *Gauleiter* of Nuremberg, were matched by the virulence of the anti-clerical attacks of *Das Schwarze Korps*. Under the influence of these extremists, the campaign of vilification against the clergy was intensified in the Nazi Press. Throughout 1936 and 1937 the readers of such papers as the *Völkischer Beobachter* and *Das Schwarze Korps* were regaled with sensational allegations of sexual immorality among the priesthood and among members of the religious orders. Every possible accusation was made in the full glare of Goebbels' publicity. And 'immorality trials', catering for the more salacious tastes of the masses, were staged in the courts and, by ingenious spacing, were made to appear as an unbroken series of clerical offences.

The whole of the controlled Press blazoned the trials in its headlines and fed its readers with lurid details, promising them yet more to come, in the course of which no less than a thousand priests and nuns would be found guilty of immoral conduct.[30] A great hunt was begun for clerical delinquents in a society honeycombed with informers, and offenders who had already been found guilty and punished by their ecclesiastical superiors were again dragged out before the public gaze.[31]

By such means, and by the anti-clerical activities of organized agitators, the established hold of the 'black clergy' would, it was hoped, be broken and the mass of the people be 'conquered' for National Socialism. It was also hoped that public opinion would likewise be turned against the Catholic cause in the matter of the Church Schools, over which the struggle was just then reaching its climax.[32] Among the Bavarian peasantry in particular, these outrageous accusations were calculated to produce so profound an effect that the age-long loyalty of the people to their priests would be broken and the intransigence of the priesthood would thereby be nullified. In fact, the effect was negligible. In the immorality trials the number of proven cases were very few, and the sympathy aroused in the Catholic laity for their clergy served only to intensify their loyalty to their Church.[33]

Other Nazi leaders were of the opinion that more subtle methods of attack would be needed to destroy the power of the Church without arousing unnecessary popular resentment or antipathy. In their view, the anti-clericalism of men like Streicher was more of an embarrassment than a help. Since their prime object was to

complete the separation of Church and State by purely administrative measures, thereby reducing the power of the Church and
with it their influence over the hearts of the people, no steps should
be taken to interfere with Church services or to persecute the clergy
on a nationwide scale. A subservient clergy would be easier to deal
with than a host of martyrs. Hitler himself now gave his support to
these views.

Accordingly, regulations issued by the Party headquarters in
Munich in November 1935, ordered the maintenance of the
strictest reserve towards all Church affairs, though any cases of
political disaffection in the Churches were to be instantly reported.
Orders were given for the gradual dissociation of Party members
from Church activities. In 1936, Party members were forbidden
to take part in uniform in any Church services or activities or to
appear with any similar group, such as the German Faith Movement. On 1 June 1938 Bormann issued a circular forbidding Nazi
Party leaders to hold any Church office even down to the level of
organist, 'because the Party is now faced with enormous tasks
ahead and needs all the energies of its faithful followers'.[34]

The influence of the Church on Party members was likewise
curtailed. Although priests and pastors who were members of the
Party were never officially ordered to resign, as early as 1934 they
had been required to leave the SS, and in 1937 priests and theological students were henceforth banned from becoming members
of the Party. In July 1938 the clergy who were holders of office in
the Party were required to give up their appointments, no matter
how pro-Nazi their sentiments might be, and a very considerable
number of pastors, especially amongst the 'German Christians',
who had eagerly enrolled in the Party or in the ranks of the SA
now found themselves cold-shouldered and ignored.

Within the Church Ministry Kerrl and his associates were
resolutely determined not to allow control of Church policy to
slip from their hands and strove to suppress attempts by other
Nazi organizations and ministries to interfere in Church affairs.
They did their best to put a stop to the unauthorized attacks on the
clergy made by irresponsible local Party elements, being painfully
aware of the effect produced by such attacks on uncommitted

1 Hitler preaching to his earliest supporters in the Sterneckerbräu, about 1920. A painting, entitled 'In the beginning was the word', by Hermann Otto Hoyer

2 A postcard issued in 1933 by the 'German Christians', to stress the supposed Nazi attachment to Church and State. Hitler and Hindenburg in front of the altar of the Potsdam Garrison Church

3 Hitler with Reich Bishop Müller and Abbot Schachleiter, surrounded by party bosses; September 1934

4 Alfred Rosenberg

5 Rudolf Hess and Martin
Bormann going to the polls

6 Reich Bishop Ludwig Müller
on the day of his election at the
National Synod of Wittenberg,
27 September 1933

7 Reich Minister Kerrl,
April 1934

8 Hitler at the baptism of
Goering's child Edda, 1937

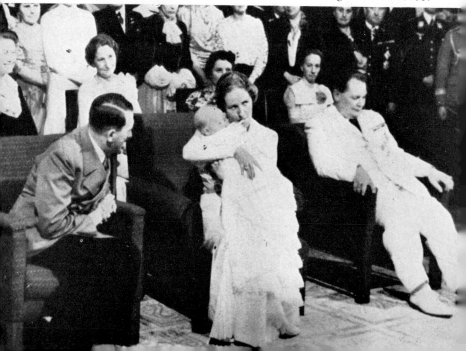

9 A Nazi baptism

10 A Nazi altar

RK 9840 B

Berlin-Charlottenburg, den 1 Juli 1941

Der Vorsitzende
des Geistlichen Vertrauensrats
der Deutschen Evangelischen Kirche

Marchstr. 2

VB 471/41

Abschrift.   Charlottenburg, den 30.Juni 1941

Telegramm

Der Geistliche Vertrauensrat der Deutschen Evangelischen Kirche, erstmalig seit Beginn des Entscheidungskampfes im Osten versammelt, versichert Ihnen, mein Führer, in diesen hinreissend bewegten Stunden aufs neue die unwandelbare Treue und Einsatzbereitschaft der gesamten evangelischen Christenheit des Reiches. Sie haben, mein Führer, die bolschewistische Gefahr im eigenen Lande gebannt und rufen nun unser Volk und die Völker Europas zum entscheidenden Waffengange gegen den Todfeind aller Ordnung und aller abendländisch-christlichen Kultur auf. Das deutsche Volk und mit ihm alle seine christlichen Glieder danken Ihnen für diese Ihre Tat. Dass sich die britische Politik nun auch offen des Bolschewismus als Helfershelfer gegen das Reich bedient macht eindeutig klar, dass es ihr nicht um das Christentum, sondern allein um die Vernichtung des deutschen Volkes geht. Der allmächtige Gott wolle Ihnen und unserem Volk beistehen, dass wir gegen den doppelten Feind den Sieg gewinnen, dem all unser Wollen und Handeln gelten muss.

Die Deutsche Evangelische Kirche gedenkt in dieser Stunde der baltischen evangelischen Märtyrer vom Jahre 1918, sie gedenkt des namenlosen Leids, das der Bolschewismus, wie er es den Völkern seines Machtbereiches zugefügt hat, so allen anderen Nationen bereiten wollte, und sie ist mit allen ihren Gebeten bei Ihnen und bei unseren unvergleichlichen Soldaten, die nun mit so gewaltigen Schlägen daran gehen, den Pestherd zu beseitigen, damit in ganz Europa unter ihrer Führung eine neue Ordnung erstehe und aller inneren Zersetzung, aller Beschmutzung des Heiligsten, aller Schändung der Gewissensfreiheit ein Ende gemacht werde.

Der Geistliche Vertrauensrat der Deutschen Evangelischen Kirche

gez. D.Marahrens   gez. Schultz   gez. D.Hymmen

An den Führer. Führerhauptquartier.

An

27.1.43   1205   L   BV

Telegramm des Deutschen Reiches

27 JAN 1943   RK 1057E

Telegramm aus Berlin P 60/59 N 27/1. 1943

An den
Führer
Führerhauptquartier

Die Deutsche evangelische Kirche gedenkt am 10. Jahrestage der Machtübernahme des Führers in Treue und mit der Bereitschaft, alle Kraft für die Erringung des Sieges einzusetzen. Sie bittet Gott, den Herrn, dass er auch künftig mit seinem Segen über unserem Deutschen Volke walten möge.

Der stellvertretende Leiter der Deutschen evangelischen Kirchenkanzlei und der Geistliche Vertrauensrat.

11 Telegram from the leaders of the Evangelical Church expressing its loyalty to Hitler on the outbreak of the campaign against the Soviet Union, June 1941

12 Telegram of loyalty from the German Evangelical Church on the tenth anniversary of the Nazi take-over of power

13 Hitler's reply to the request of Frau Niemöller for the release of her husband from prison, April 1939

14 Martin
Niemöller

15 Dietrich
Bonhoeffer

opinion, both inside and outside Germany, which they were trying to persuade of the inherent harmony between Nazism and Christianity. They foresaw that the help of the Christian part of the population would still be needed if Hitler's grandiose plans for reshaping the map of Europe were to be fulfilled, and they honestly believed that in time the Church would recognize the greatness of the opportunity to co-operate with Adolf Hitler. Persuasion, they felt, should be tried before persecution, and for that reason Kerrl had decreed that all measures directed against the priests required his approval and intervened to secure reductions in the penalties imposed on priests by the Gestapo.[35]

On the one side, a Party speaker at a school for Party leaders in June 1936 pronounced that

Christianity and Nazism are like fire and water. We must not yet say this openly. Outwardly we must not attack Christianity, we must be far more clever; we are not interfering with denominational matters, but with mathematical exactitude we shall win the victory for ideology. We cannot say this to those who still believe the stupidities they were taught and brought up to believe. But there are times when these things can be said amongst us, sworn comrades.[36]

Simultaneously, however, Kerrl at the Church Ministry was maintaining that Nazi ideology and the Christian religion were identical. And he continued to assert that the 'positive Christianity' of the Nazi Party programme could be made a reality. He too, however, was ready to invoke the powers of the State whenever he believed that counter-attacks by the Churches were being made against his personal authority or against the policies of the Party, and consequently it was not long before the stubborn refusal of the Confessing Church leaders to bow to the authority of the Church commissioners called down upon their heads all the Church Minister's easily aroused wrath and displeasure.

III   THE CHURCHES PROTEST

The situation of the Confessing Church in 1936 was distinctly unhappy. The defection of those who were prepared to collaborate with the Nazis in general and with Kerrl in particular left only a

remnant of 'Dahlemites' (the name given to the followers of
Niemöller) to carry on the work of the Provisional Church
Administration.[37] Hitler's hold over the popular imagination
appeared to be on the increase, and little or no help could be
expected from friends in Ecumenical Church circles abroad.
Nevertheless, the Confessing Church leaders were determined not
to let the process of Nazification to go unopposed. Their public
protest, in the pamphlet already mentioned, *The State Church is
here!*, had evoked a prompt reaction from the Gestapo officials
who had at once been ordered to confiscate all copies, and if
necessary to search the houses of those responsible for it.[38] Undeterred, the Confessing Church leaders in May 1936 composed a
much stronger protest addressed to Hitler personally, an action
later described as both unprecedented and unequalled in the relations of the Evangelical Church and the German State.[39] Politely
but unflinchingly, the memorandum drew Hitler's attention to a
number of crucial points. First, he was asked to state whether the
attempts to 'de-Christianize' Germany were to be regarded as
official policy, in contravention of his previous promises. Secondly,
the Nazi interpretation of 'positive Christianity' was refuted as
theologically unsound. Thirdly, a strong protest was lodged
against the arbitrary police measures which had destroyed the
Church's autonomy. Fourthly, the State was accused of deliberately
interfering with the Church's work by closing the Church schools
and by limitations placed upon the Church in Press, radio and
public education work. In section five the memorandum roundly
declared that

If Christians are pressed to adopt an anti-semitic attitude as part of
the National Socialist ideology, which will incite them to hate the
Jews, then this is against the Christian commandment to love one's
neighbour.

And again:

The Evangelical conscience, which feels itself responsible for people
and government, is hardest of all hit by the fact that in Germany, which
calls itself a law-abiding state, concentration camps can still exist and
the activities of the Gestapo are not subject to any legal scrutiny.

The gravest concern was expressed over the suppression of the Evangelical Church, the perversion of its faith, the abandoning of Evangelical morality, and the nation-wide process of 'de-Christianization'. Could the government tolerate the continuation of such practices?

Lastly the memorandum noted with deep foreboding that the Nation seemed to be setting itself up in the place of God, an act of monstrous human presumptuousness, while Hitler himself, abandoning his previous refutation of personal glorification, had allowed himself to appear not merely as a political leader but as the nation's high priest between God and the people.

It is a measure of the political naivety of the Church leaders that they allowed this memorandum, without previous discussion at any public gathering, to be sent to Hitler himself (through Dr Meissner, the Presidential Secretary), in the expectation that such a private remonstrance would cause Hitler to abandon the policies to which they took exception. The charitable view is probably that, in doing so, they hoped to avoid an open challenge to Hitler's authority and to enable him to take appropriate measures without the discord of public controversy. But such a miscalculation of Hitler's reactions is disconcerting from men who for almost three years had been warning their congregations of the dangers of Nazism and who were well aware of the totalitarian nature of the challenge to the Christian faith. If the members of the Confessing Church could not bring themselves to make a public protest against the crimes of the régime, how much less likely to protest were all those other churchmen who had so readily accepted Nazi 'ideals' and who saw in Hitler the divinely sent leader of the people?

The consequences of the memorandum were disastrous. Hitler ignored it completely. But a copy was smuggled out of the country to Switzerland and there it was published in full. Full reports appeared in most of the foreign press, and the pro-Nazi elements, both inside and without the Evangelical Church, at once accused the Confessing Church of treachery against Hitler and of conspiring with Germany's enemies abroad. The Confessing Church leaders, instead of rallying support for their point of view amongst their lay followers by publishing the memorandum and distributing it throughout their supporting parishes – as the Catholic Church did with its episcopal and papal encyclicals – beat a hasty retreat. They dissociated themselves from the charge of disloyalty to the Nazi régime by disowning their Church House collaborator, Dr Weissler, who had authorized the publication in Switzerland. After the completion of the Olympic Games, Dr Weissler was arrested by the Gestapo and sent to Sachsenhausen Concentration Camp, where a few months later he was brutally done to death.[40]

The leaders of the Confessing Church were now faced with the necessity of choosing between their theological and their national loyalties. To preserve their image as loyal supporters of the State, they had refrained from arousing popular feeling against the Nazi régime by publishing the memorandum in their parishes. But with its appearance in the foreign press they were unable to deny their authorship or to disclaim the document entirely. On 23 August, in an attempt to escape from their embarrassment, they issued, in the form of a pastoral letter, a very much watered-down version of their protest. It contained no reference to the illegality of the concentration camps, to the enormity of the Nazi anti-semitic measures, or to the glorification of Hitler and the nation. Instead, it limited its protests to the attacks against the Evangelical Church and to the irreconcilability of Rosenberg's ideology with Christian doctrine. But their efforts were in vain. The revised document was rejected by the South German Bishops and by Bishop Marahrens of Hanover, on the grounds that its proclamation would prevent 'profitable negotiations' with the Nazi hierarchy though how profitable such negotiations might have been can be seen in the 'agreement' reached a few months later, in November 1936, when the same Bishops declared:

With the Reich Church Commission we wholeheartedly support the Führer in the struggle for the life of the German people against Bolshevism.[41]

The reaction of the Nazis to the pastoral letter of 23 August was surprisingly restrained – possibly because, as a member of the Church Ministry explained to Hitler's adjutant, Hitler had asked

Kerrl to ensure that there should be no controversies over Church affairs while the Olympic games were in progress. To arrest all the pastors who read the letter would probably have resulted in the imprisonment of more than a thousand who sooner or later would have had to be released, thus making the situation as bad as ever. As an alternative, it was suggested that the clergy should be warned not to read the letter, in the hope that the threat of disciplinary measures might prove as effective a deterrent as physical incarceration.[42]

The leaders of the Catholic Church were equally concerned over the trend of events, but their tactics were quite different. Despite their reluctance to jeopardize the possibility of harmonious collaboration with the government and despite their zeal in voicing their patriotic fervour, the Bishops in their pastoral letters and sermons were not slow to express their disquiet over the spread of the 'new heathenism' and the restrictions imposed on Catholic activities. By the end of 1936, after repeated protests by Cardinal Bertram to the Reich Chancellery had all been ignored, an appeal was made for more forceful assistance from Rome. In the Vatican, where the Secretary of State Cardinal Pacelli had had much cause to complain of the treatment of his many diplomatic notes of protest to the German Foreign Ministry, the plea for a stronger protest was accepted by Pope Pius XI, who decided to make his feelings known in a Papal Encyclical. The Encyclical, *Mit Brennender Sorge*, was duly prepared and was secretly smuggled into Germany in March 1937.[43] There, on Palm Sunday, before a single copy had fallen into the hands of the Nazis, it was read from every Catholic pulpit throughout the country.

In the Encyclical, the Pope voiced his growing dismay at the increasing oppression of the Church in Germany. The consistent violations of the Concordat disclosed intrigues which he believed could have no other aim than a war of extermination. Storm-clouds of a destructive religious war were threatening Germany. The Pope called on his followers to uphold their true belief and to resist the idolatrous cult of Race or People, State or Constitution. The perversion of Christian doctrines and of Christian morality must be resisted. The opposition deliberately and systematically fomented between the aims of religion and the aims of the State Youth Movements must be withstood. Both priests and laity were called upon to maintain their loyalty to Christ, His Church, and the primacy of Rome.

Hitler was furious. The Roman Clergy had dared to defy his authority publicly before the whole world. The strength of the opposition which could stage such a coup without the Gestapo's cognizance now stood revealed. The hope of achieving national unity under Nazi leadership was shattered by this treachery of the Catholic Church. On Hitler's direct orders, the Encyclical was treated as a call to battle.[44] All copies were to be seized. Anyone found distributing the Encyclical would be arrested and instantly dismissed from the German Labour Front. Its publication by Church newspapers inside Germany was forbidden. The printers' shops were to be closed and sequestrated. The trials of Catholic clergy for currency offences and alleged immorality were to be resumed forthwith. Plans were to be expedited for the compulsory amalgamation of all Catholic youth groups with the Hitler Youth. The Foreign Ministry was instructed to protest in the strongest terms against the interference in the domestic affairs of Germany, a breach of the restraint agreed upon by the Vatican in the 1933 Concordat. At the Church Ministry, Kerrl embarked on an acrimonious correspondence with Cardinal Bertram, in which he accused the Church of treachery to the State, without attempting to answer the charges made in the Encyclical. Two months later, Hitler was reported to be contemplating still stronger action against the Catholic Church, including a reconsideration of the whole Concordat and a unilateral abrogation of four or five of its most important articles.[45] As a final gesture of contempt, he refused to pay the usual courtesy call on the Vatican during his state visit to Rome in May 1938.

But still there were those who shrank from a radical break with the Catholic Church, arguing that such a move would serve only to confirm the Pope's proclamation of the irreconcilable opposition of Catholicism and Nazism. Despite the unwelcome challenge to Nazi authority contained in the Encyclical, the fact remained that the policies of the Nazi Party in all matters save those of purely ecclesiastical concern were receiving the enthusiastic support of millions of German Catholics. A policy of retaliation might only exacerbate tension. The Encyclical ought therefore to be ignored and the suggestions for revoking the Concordat should be dropped.

No less a person than Rudolf Hess in a speech to Nazi *Gauleiters* in September 1938 argued that:

A religion which has influenced, indeed dominated, the life of a people for two thousand years cannot be destroyed or overcome by external measures – and certainly not through superficial ridicule, or agitation or attacks on God. Such ineptitude and lack of taste could only too easily drive men who would otherwise have supported the new Reich into opposition even in the political field. This cannot be said often enough. . . .

The more we National Socialists avoid religious disputes and stay away from Church ceremonies, and rather earn the loyalty of the people through fulfilling our duties, so men will be drawn more and more to National Socialism. They will recognize that Providence is with us and our work, as a divinely ordained institution, and therefore turn away from the Churches out of internal conviction more and more . . .[46]

The tactic of complete silence, Hess went on, had already proved its value. Only a few people heard the pastoral letters read in the Churches and so long as the Catholics had no opportunity of publishing their views, their influence would be minimal. Most people paid little heed to them, especially in the absence of counter-propaganda from the Nazi side. The churchmen should be told firmly to keep out of politics and rather to give thanks to Hitler for saving them from the menace of Communism.[47]

For reasons of expediency, therefore, the Nazis refrained from a head-on-clash with the Catholic Church relying instead on an intensified attack against all Church activities in order to limit its influence on the German people. The Gestapo were to be given free rein to isolate those of the clergy whose activities could be branded as 'hostile to the State'. One by one, the Church's bastions were to be breached until the possibility of resistance was broken for ever.

7 The Rival Claimants for Body and Soul

'Our generation's path through life must be
National Socialist, and our children must
consequently have but one ideal, and that is
Adolf Hitler.' – MINISTER OF STATE WAGNER,
15 February 1937

The failure of Kerrl's attempt to establish his Ministry of Church Affairs as the controlling force in church policy, and the limited success of Rosenberg's ideological campaign, now left the way open for Himmler and Heydrich to assume the dominant role in the next phase of the Church struggle. In the immediate pre-war years, the efforts of these men were responsible for a rapid extension of administrative restrictions and methods of intimidation, designed to intensify the Nazi persecution of the Churches. In particular, three areas of Church life were to be the Gestapo's especial targets in the Nazi campaign to re-educate the people in the spirit of Adolf Hitler: first the Churches' lay organizations, their press and radio work, and their lines of communication to the general public; second, the educational work of the Churches; and third the activities of the smaller and less significant sects.

I   THE GESTAPO LAYS ITS PLANS

The strategy of this campaign was to be laid down in Gestapo Headquarters in Berlin. Himmler's anti-clericalism was reinforced by the demonic fury of his subordinate Heydrich, who was forever pressing for more violent measures against the Church. Under the direction of these two men, the Gestapo developed a huge network whereby they worked to bring every aspect of German Church life under their influence. A special section, designated IV B, was set up in Gestapo headquarters under the charge of SS-Group Leader Müller, to deal with 'Political Churches, Sects and Jews'. Its task was to collate information about the activities of the Nazis' opponents and to instruct the local units on how to initiate action. Besides Eichmann, whose notorious activities fell within this section, there were three former Catholic priests and one Evangelical pastor, two of whom were Albert Hartl[1] and Friedrich Murawski,[2] who had left the service of the Church to join the ranks of the *Sicherheitspolizei* and whose intimate knowledge of Church life made them invaluable to the Gestapo in suggesting effective measures of repression and intimidation.

Although the Gestapo were nominally under the direction of the Ministry of the Interior, Himmler had, in fact, taken all police power into his own hands. Only in isolated cases was it possible for the decisions of the Gestapo to be reversed by other Ministries – by Kerrl's, for instance – and even less frequently by outside bodies or individuals. Although it is now practically impossible to discover on whose initiative individual acts of terrorism and persecution were carried out, all the evidence indicates that, of the whole Nazi hierarchy, Himmler and Heydrich were by far the most inexorable in their attitude towards the Churches.

In accordance with the Gestapo's plans, therefore, a relentless campaign against the Catholic Church was pursued throughout 1937. The publication of *Mit Brennender Sorge* was, as we have seen, regarded by the Gestapo as a deliberate challenge. To plan their counterblast a conference of church specialists within the Gestapo, under the chairmanship of Hartl, was convened in Berlin in July 1937 to prepare a directive for the intensification of the Gestapo's campaign against the Churches.[3] This interesting document, which has been preserved in its entirety, covered all branches of Church activity and outlined counter-measures to block its development. Its first section, entitled 'Next Objectives in the Campaign Against Denominational Opponents', reviewed the prevailing situation. The Gestapo, it stated, had no hope of success unless they were fully informed on every aspect of the Church's internal administration. The primary requirement therefore was the establishment of an efficient system of contacts (*V-Männer*) who would report back to the Gestapo from within the Church itself. This would provide the Gestapo with a clear picture both of the structure of the Church and of its leading individuals, their strengths and weaknesses, and the possibility of their subversion. The local Gestapo agencies would need to be efficiently organized to supply full information. Thus equipped, the campaign could take shape.

Recognizing the established strength of the Churches, the directive did not recommend a frontal attack, but suggested rather that an appearance of legality should be outwardly maintained. The Concordat was not to be denounced, but its letter and spirit were to be constantly contravened by sporadic but carefully planned incidents. Stronger measures could then be taken against the least defensible portions of the Church's life, i.e., against the smaller sects, which would be denounced as hotbeds of Marxism and the cause of dissension among the people. Against the Catholic Orders, which were regarded as the militant arm of the Catholic Church, energetic steps were called for, to harass and hem them in, and finally to destroy them. Police action was necessary against the lay organizations to enforce administrative regulations and to curb their activities. If individual associations were found to have contravened any of the innumerable regulations, they should be dissolved and their funds confiscated. The publicity agencies of the Church should be restricted, and a close supervision should be kept over all Church publications. Since the pulpit now remained virtually the only means whereby the clergy could inform their parishioners of Church events, a strict and systematic watch should be maintained over the preaching of sermons. The closest scrutiny was necessary of the work of the Jesuits, as the most dangerous of all the Orders by reason of the excellence of their organization, their information network, and the calibre of their members. A means would need to be found to break the courier system operated by the Catholic Church. Contact men should be sent to strategic points abroad especially in Rome and Geneva, to report on the association of German clergy and churchmen with members of the Church elsewhere. Church finances should be examined to ascertain their resources and expenditures and to prevent illegal transfers out of the country. All these measures were to be carried out by the Gestapo's own network of forces. Similar directives were issued for the Evangelical churches:

1. Efforts must be made to penetrate the circles of the Provisional Church Administration and the Lutheran Council with V-men;
2. also to plant V-men in all provincial Churches and in all central offices of the religious societies and agencies in your territory;
3. further to be oriented at all times regarding the incumbents of all the Church offices;
4. to determine the relative strength, as much as possible by statistics, of single groups;
5. to ascertain, by an occasional check of Church attendances, the interest of the population in Church life;
6. to be in possession of a Church directory and to scrutinise the magazine *Junge Kirche*, also official bulletins and the most important Sunday Church paper;
7. to probe the Church-political attitude of the theological faculty in each university, its measure of influence on the other faculties, and the attitude of individual professors;
8. to watch the radio programmes, theatres and films for possible Protestant influence;
9. to be informed regarding all Inner Mission institutions and Church Societies in your area, and to expose, in co-operation with the National Socialist Welfare Agency, unsanitary conditions in hospitals, etc.;
10. to investigate residence halls, student homes, denominational seminaries and Protestant hostels for political attitudes and possible incidents involving paragraph 175 (i.e. sexual irregularities);
11. to observe Church methods of attracting members from the Labour Service, etc.[4]

The results of this conference were soon evident. Almost daily, orders were issued by the Gestapo for the investigation and frequently for the prohibition of one or other of the Church's activities. The campaign for the control of the means of communication was accelerated. Following the suppression of the Catholic daily press in 1935, the Nazis turned their attention to the diocesan weeklies which were the Bishops' chief vehicle of expression. In August 1936 each diocese was ordered to limit itself to one paper only, a mere third of the number previously published. In October, Kerrl forbade the publication of pastoral letters in the weeklies, on the grounds that they were frequently critical of Nazi policies. Under pressure, editors were appointed who, as the price of their continuing existence, were prepared to publish material acceptable to the Party. Those who refused to conform suffered the penalty of having their papers suppressed, as happened in the dioceses of Berlin and Münster. After the outbreak of war, when the denominational press as a whole willingly and patriotically supported the German war effort, its subordination still went on, notably through the refusal to grant adequate paper supplies. Nevertheless, the Catholics did not abandon their ideological counter-offensive. This was maintained in parish bulletins, newsletters, brochures and the book *Studies in the Myth of the Twentieth Century*. In this connection, mention should be made of the Cologne 'Centre for countering anti-Christian propaganda', under the direction of Canon Joseph Teusch, whose *Cathechism Truths* sold seven million copies.[5]

To counter this break in communications and to spread news of Church-political events, the Churches increased their personal contacts and the number of their meetings. In Aschaffenburg, for example, it was noted by the *Sicherheitsdienst* in June 1937 that the number of Catholic meetings was four times greater than in 1933 and that many more people attended. Processions and pilgrimages, such as the Corpus Christi procession were more elaborate than formerly. The number of Catholic organizations and associations was no less than in the years 1930–2, and some of them had a membership of over 1,000. The vitality of the Church was also apparent in a number of new buildings erected or refurnished. In order to circumvent the restrictions on Catholic youth groups, acolyte groups were founded in many parishes.[6] Similarly, in the Evangelical Church 'Evangelical weeks' were organized to bring laymen into contact with the leaders of the Confessing Church and thereby to strengthen their faith. The meetings were frequently prohibited, but even so they served to bring people and clergy more closely together, united in their struggle against increasing restrictions and persecution.

The Nazi response was to wield their weapons of propaganda, police intimidation, economic pressure and personal defamation with increasing vigour. Throughout 1937 and 1938 the Catholic lay organizations, from those catering for the youngest children to the large and powerful Kolping Society and young Men's Society, were one by one forced to close down, and many of them suffered confiscation of their property. As justification of these arbitrary acts, the Gestapo claimed to be acting under the terms of the Presidential decree of 28 February 1933, which had been designed to combat terrorism by the communists. As Guenter Lewy has rightly observed:

It is clear that the Church could not prevail in this fight; the existence of the Concordat perhaps delayed matters but in the long run it could not protect the Catholic organizations against the assaults of a powerful state.[7]

Stringent limitations were also placed on Church processions and pilgrimages. As early as 1935 the Baverian Political Police had ordered that the Corpus Christi day processions, a high-light of Church life throughout the province, were to be carefully controlled lest they should develop into demonstrations against the State. Similar regulations were issued in the following years. In a circular letter addressed to the Churches, Kerrl argued that the celebration of the Eucharist was too holy a rite to be associated with profane gatherings, which should therefore be discontinued. Similarly, while pilgrimages to notable shrines could be continued if they were of long standing and part of the folk life of the community, no new ones were to be instituted, and the efforts of numerous parishes to join together for mass rallies were prohibited.

These limitations were later extended to such activities as church retreats, church camps, and confirmation classes, even to 'hiking' parties under the guidance of the clergy.[8] Permission from the police was obligatory for any activities outside the church walls, lists of participants and the exact programme being required by the police a month in advance. Even church-sponsored courses on domestic science, marriage guidance and baby care were prohibited, since 'the Catholic attitudes to marriage guidance, racial nurture and biological hygiene differ in significant fashion from those of the National Socialist State'.[9]

Orders were made that the names of those who had left the Church were no longer to be published, nor, as was customary, read out from the pulpit. Strict instructions were issued about the flying of church flags; the Nazi colours being obligatory on every state occasion, including Hitler's birthday. Door-to-door selling of Church pamphlets or pictures was forbidden. The erection of wayside crosses was to be banned wherever possible, by reference to the traffic laws. Street collections for the Church or for welfare purposes were prohibited. In Bavaria and Saxony, government subsidies to the Catholic Church were reduced. And, as a measure against the Confessing Church, pastors were required to obtain advance approval for the objects of their collections in case the money might be used to support activities regarded as illegal by the State.

This campaign of attrition was, in fact, only a systematization of a policy already in force in many parts of Germany. It did, however, lead to a steady increase in repression, and many churchmen who had hitherto failed to grasp that isolated incidents might be related, now came to realize that each incident was just part of a comprehensive and concentrated plan. Because of the sporadic nature of the persecution, it is difficult to judge the over-all success of the campaign. The Gestapo was given wide latitude in determining what 'political' acts by the clergy called for police intervention, and insisted on the right to take 'instant' action if the security of the State appeared to be threatened. Local measures by the Gestapo were frequently more severe than the directives allowed, and acts of terrorism and intimidation were glossed over as the only appropriate means of discouraging 'political' opposition.

In fact, the Gestapo were content to play a game of cat and mouse, maintaining their watch over suspected priests, taking notes of sermons, organizing house searches, summoning the clergy for interrogation, confiscating 'hostile' pamphlets or publications, dispersing unwanted meetings, imposing prohibitions on public lecturing, and enforcing expulsions from the parishes.

In relatively few cases did the Gestapo use the full force of repression. With a few important exceptions, imprisonment of the clergy was never of long duration and was intended to act as a deterrent rather than a punishment. More extreme measures were almost invariably used only against individuals whose interpretation of their pastoral duties included some word or act which could be construed as running counter to the State or to the political aims of the Nazi Party. Those who transgressed for supposedly theological reasons were usually treated lightly. Of the 17,000 pastors of the Evangelical Church, the number of those sentenced to lengthy terms of imprisonment was never at any one time more than fifty.[10]

Of the Catholic clergy, one Bishop was expelled from his diocese, and one was sentenced to a short term of imprisonment for complicity in currency smuggling. But even so outspoken a critic of Nazi policy as Bishop Galen was not interfered with, and the number of German Catholic clergy who lost their lives or their freedom through the activities of the Gestapo was very small.[11]

Such restraint, however, was only tactical. As events in Poland after September 1939 were to show, the Nazis had no compunction about launching a campaign of total persecution against the Churches when it suited their political ends. But inside Germany they contented themselves with a curious mixture of radical agitation, bureaucratic regulation and arbitrary repressive measures, all conducted simultaneously, and sometimes running counter to each other.

At best, it was an unequal struggle. The steadfastness of those Churchmen who sought to oppose the mobilized power of a police-state was all the more remarkable because of the small numbers involved. This was not a mass movement of protest but only the isolated and courageous voice of conscience witnessing in a situation totally unexpected and unsought for. Yet it was the witness of these men which prevented the total apostasy of the Church.

II   THE CAMPAIGN IN THE FIELD OF EDUCATION

As part of their attack on the modernistic culture of the Twentieth

Century, the Nazis early proclaimed their aversion to the 'Godless and atheistic' system of education which had been sponsored by the Governments of the Weimar Republic. The dangerous evils of atheism and Marxism, they averred, would be eradicated from Germany by bringing up their Youth in the spirit of the German ethical-religious beliefs which were the true expression of the German *Volk*. One of the first actions taken by Rust, the new Prussian Minister of Education, in February 1933 was to order the introduction of religious instruction into the trade schools and a speedy reduction in the number of 'secular' schools 'in order to prevent the return of heathenism, and with it a regression of German culture by a thousand years'.[12] In his speeches of March 1933 Hitler, with the warm support of his Cabinet colleagues Hugenberg and Papen,[13] gave a definite undertaking that the denominational schools would be maintained and the Reich Concordat of July 1933 expressly affirmed that Catholic denominational schools, theological faculties, and religious instruction would all be continued.

It was not long, however, before the totalitarian nature of Nazi policy in the field of education made itself felt. The first measures were, predictably, directed against prominent opponents of Nazism amongst the University professors, the first victims of the sorry process of exile which was forced upon so many of Germany's most outstanding intellectuals. The student clubs were compulsorily co-ordinated into one Nazi-controlled organization. The *Führerprinzip* was introduced into University administration, with the result that all Rectors were henceforth appointed by the Minister of Education. In the schools, the curricula were altered to include Nazi 'insights'. The Hitler Youth movement was tirelessly promoted. Teachers were coerced into joining the National Socialist ideology, and those of Jewish blood or Jewish origin were dismissed. In a word, 'organized education became the means for the drilling into the bodies and minds of the young a militaristic collective spirit, expressed in terms of a dynamic *völkisch* ideology'.[14]

In the circumstances, and despite specific promises to the contrary, it was inevitable that the theological faculties and Church schools should not long remain untouched by the Nazi policy-makers. After the disillusionment of 1934–35, when the Churches had failed to accept the role allotted to them by the Nazis, their influence over their younger members became a critical issue. As Hess expressed it,

> In the long run the Church question is a question of the young people. This is not only a matter of their education through the Hitler Youth but also by their parents. The less the parents' opposition is aroused on Church matters, the less they will inculcate in their children opposition to the teachings of the Hitler Youth.[15]

In the Nazi view, the Evangelical Church, or rather its leader, Reich Bishop Müller, had acted wisely in merging the Evangelical Youth with the Hitler Youth in December 1933. But the Catholic Youth Organizations still remained, even though circumscribed in their activities, and were ably supported both by the Catholic schools. They were an obvious target for Nazi ambitions.

Once established in power, the Nazis became increasingly critical of the dual system of German education, one system sponsored by the religious authorities and the other by the State. The need for educational reform had, of course, been urged before the rise of Nazism, but the very wide differences which existed between the provinces had merely been strengthened by a policy of devolution during the Weimar Republic. In some provinces, like Prussia and Bavaria, all the schools were denominational; separate facilities were provided for Evangelical and for Catholic children, and the schools were run in accordance with the moral and religious principles of each denomination, but at the State's expense. In other provinces, like Baden and Hesse, the schools were non-denominational, but separate classes in religious instruction were given by the local clergy of the two Churches. Of the senior schools, the majority were non-denominational, but in Bavaria there were both state-supported and private Catholic schools, especially for girls, of whom in 1936 76.7 per cent of the secondary-school pupils were in Catholic schools. Their teachers were trained in denominationally-run training colleges.

Such a diversity of system was highly distasteful to the Nazis, who regarded it as a major hindrance to national unity. As Hitler himself said on 1 May 1937:

There is but one German people, and there can therefore be but one German youth. And there can be but one German Youth Movement, because there is but one way in which German youth can be educated and trained. The handful of people, who perhaps still cherish within themselves the thought that, beginning with the youth, they will be able to divide the German nation again, will be disappointed. This Reich stands, and is building itself up anew, upon its youth. And this Reich will hand over its youth to no one, but will take its education and its formation upon itself.[16]

Or, more succinctly, 'One People – One Leader – One School'.

In view of the provisions of the Concordat, however, as well as the agreements reached with the separate provinces over the provision of religious instruction, it was necessary to proceed with caution, though of the ultimate end there was no doubt. In a directive issued by Bormann to all the Party regions in the first half of 1939, the aim of the Nazi campaign was clearly stated:

The creation of an ideologically objective school system is one of the most important tasks of the Party and the State. In order to achieve this goal, the remains of denominational influence must be completely removed from our German education system wherever it still appears. Not for nothing have the political Catholics, above all, realized the importance of teaching the young and controlling their spiritual growth and character building. Even though the official responsibility for carrying out the necessary measures belongs to the State and its responsible authorities, the Party, of course, and its local branches, is called upon to be the champions of political renewal, to point out circumstances which can no longer be tolerated on political or ideological grounds, and if necessary to bring about their alteration.[17]

Public opinion was first to be prepared by unceasing emphasis upon the disrupting character of the church schools and upon the un-Germanic nature of much of the religious instruction given there.

As Micklem pointed out, 'The rape of the Christian Schools has been carried out systematically but locally and gradually, not by enactments of the Government published in the *Reichsgesetzblatt* but by local authorities'.[18] The stronghold of Catholicism in Bavaria was the scene of the bitterest struggle. As early as the beginning of 1935, parents arriving to enroll their children in denominational schools were subjected to a barrage of propaganda, mixed with threats against their livelihood if they persisted in choosing the church schools in preference to the unifying state schools. A year later, Cardinal Bertram, in his capacity as Chairman of the Fulda Bishops' Conference, addressed a strong protest to Hitler against 'the campaign against the denominational school which is raging throughout southern Germany. . . . An unheard-of terror is being practised in Bavaria, Württemberg and elsewhere. Those who vote for the denominational school are branded as enemies of the State.'[19]

The practice of 'consulting' the parents by the use of local plebiscites resulted in much apparent support for the Nazi measures, but the means whereby the pro-Nazi majorities were obtained were not disclosed. It was enough for the Nazis that the figures justified the closing of the denominational schools and their conversion into 'community schools' (*Gemeinschaftsschulen*). In Munich for example, only 35 per cent of the children were registered for denominational schools in 1936 and 65 per cent for the community schools, exactly reversing the proportions of the previous year. In the following year, when the campaign reached its peak, 95 per cent of the parents followed the Nazi line. The Munich Diocesan Administration had no doubts as to the reasons for this sudden and striking change:

We wish ... to make the following points perfectly clear: the results of the recent school entry were secured by means that were entirely unjust and illegal. The afflicted parents of Munich know this only too well by bitter experience, and it is proved up to the hilt in the episcopal protest, which contains a comprehensive list of incontestible facts. Indescribable terrorism, that contravened every principle of law and justice, made it simply impossible for thousands of parents to exercise their right of entering their children for the Catholic schools. The entire educational organization of the city was organized by the Munich Director of Education to obstruct enrolment for the denominational schools. The whole of the teaching body was officially called upon by the authorities to work for the recruitment of the community schools. All the resources of propaganda at the service of the Party, the daily Press, thousands of handbills, hundreds of public meetings, even the Air Raid Precautions Organization and the official radio broadcasts were employed for the purpose of branding the denominational schools as harmful to the nation and the supporters of these schools as enemies of the State. Workmen, employees and officials were threatened with economic disadvantages and even with the loss of their means of livelihood, in order to induce them to withdraw their children from the Catholic Schools and send them to community schools. Parents in a state of poverty had their allowance from the 'Winter Relief Work' cut down or withdrawn. A special canvassing and checking service was officially organized by the Party, by means of which house-to-house visits were carried out and pressure was brought to bear on mothers and fathers of families to an extent which they were not able to withstand. In contrast to all this, not one word could be said or published in favour of the denominational schools outside the walls of the church, without being at once violently silenced as a disturbance of public order. The police even confiscated a parochial letter circularized by the parish organizations to Catholic parents.[20]

In other parts of the country similar tactics were used, with the same results. In the Saarland, the *Gauleiter* organized a short three-day campaign in which every form of propaganda and intimidation was used, and a 97 per cent response for the community school was achieved. The whole of Württemberg adopted the so-called 'Christian community school'. Parents were assured by Dr Goebbels and others that enrolment in the 'community' schools would ensure that religious instruction was still given 'in harmony with the theistic sentiments of the German people', and the urgent words of the Catholic Bishops appealing to their supporters to remain faithful to their church schools were denounced as evidence of the 'political ambitions' of the hierarchy. It is noteworthy also that these tactics were fully supported by the local provincial governments and educational authorities. The campaign, indeed, was not merely the work of the Party fanatics, but was welcomed, or at any rate not opposed, by those whose constitutional responsibility it was to safeguard the provisions of the Concordat.

The Nazi point of view about these developments was clear enough. SA leader Köglmeier writing in July 1936 stated:

There can be no doubt that our black opponents are trying to attack us with every means. For this purpose, pastoral letters have been a specially useful method lately. It is on the other hand cheerful to note that this influence is rather limited though it should not be minimised.

In the case of the closure of church schools, the measures taken by the Bavarian government against the blacks were right on the target. They will lose thereby a sphere of influence of such importance that they are trying every possible means of preventing the introduction of this law. But this struggle has already been decided in our favour, and all such attempts failed. That such steps may have a bad reaction for a time is understandable and hardly avoidable from the psychological point of view. Our strength and final victory over these opponents is however assured since we have the power of the State behind us. This enables us to go our own way and to take every necessary measure (without letting ourselves be influenced by Jesuitical inventions) to destroy this opponent too. This is in fact the most serious opponent we have, since his organization has existed for 2,000 years. But we will destroy it and all the more easily because we have in the SA the ideological cadre and in our youth the future generation, who have both fully accepted this task and made themselves the warriors of this struggle.[21]

By the end of October 1936 the Bavarian Minister of Education could boast that 'the denominational schools throughout the whole of Bavaria have now been transformed into community schools'.[22] That the initiative for the collective effort came, however, from the Party is apparent from another circular issued in June 1939, in which Bormann wrote:

It is urgently desired that by the end of the year no more denominational schools or monastic or conventual schools should exist. In many cases it should be possible to carry out these orders by the beginning of the second half of the school year 1939. Further, you should take all other possible steps to remove denominational influences from the German educational system. By the end of the year, no educational institutions should exist which are under denominational influence. Particularly, this includes orphanages, foster homes, boarding-houses and hostels. Only in those places where the Church authorities have an overwhelming proportion of the facilities, such as kindergartens, nursing homes, etc. and where the take-over cannot be effected because of the lack of other resources and the necessary personnel within a short time, should the process be stretched out over a longer period.[23]

Accordingly, by the summer of 1939 all the denominational schools in the country had been abolished. A similar fate likewise befell the Church private and boarding schools. Many of these were run by members of the Religious Orders, who were favourite targets for Nazi abuse. Party members were forbidden to send their children to such schools, subsidies towards salaries were withdrawn, and in the summer of 1939 members of the clergy in Bavaria were forbidden to exercise any function in secondary schools other than the teaching of Hebrew or religious instruction. Members of the Religious Orders were dismissed *en masse*, and their schools were either closed or converted into State schools. The churches were forbidden after 1938 to organize holiday camps for the young people.

The Nazi campaign was equally relentless in Austria, where only three months after the *Anschluss* a decree from the Ministry of the Interior in Vienna deprived, by a single stroke of the pen, all Catholic private schools of public recognition and support. By the end of the year the local Nazi educational authorities had ordered the closing of all denominational private schools, training colleges, commercial and industrial schools and boarding schools 'in consideration of the various events which have occurred recently, and bearing in mind the necessity of educating the whole of youth in the National Socialist spirit'.[24]

The closure of the schools and the dismissal of the teachers, especially the nuns, imposed a new and sudden burden on the State school system, which itself was short of qualified teachers. But such practical considerations were overruled in favour of ideological 'necessity'. The Bishops' pastoral letters of protest were either banned or prevented from being published. And when in May 1937 the Bavarian Bishops organized a counter-plebiscite to be held in the Church services, the Gestapo was ordered to list the names of those who took part and to confiscate the results if they were made known outside the Church building.[25]

The most determined onslaught of the whole campaign was directed against the teaching of religious instruction in the State schools. Although leading Nazis such as Dr Goebbels undertook that the Party would unfailingly fulfil its promises of 1933, the necessity of 'de-confessionalizing' the schools was used as an excuse for restricting the attendance of the clergy in the schools and in many cases for replacing Christian teaching with a 'germanified' religion, frequently derived from the tenets of Hauer's German Faith Movement. Rosenberg was not the only Nazi to claim that 'the eternal German People stand higher than all denominations and Churches . . . the fifth symphony of Beethoven is a greater divine revelation than all the books of the Old Testament put together'.[26] Although frequent assurances were made that religious instruction was being given in accordance with 'positive Christianity', it was obvious to the Church authorities that what was actually being taught was, not the Christian gospel, but a hotch-potch of anti-Christian nationalistic ideas.

Once again the familiar methods of blandishments and threats were used to gain acquiescence. While constant promises were made of unbroken continuity of religious instruction, administrative restrictions were simultaneously imposed which effectively rendered them impracticable. In 1939 the school time-tables were altered and religious instruction was placed at the beginning or end of the school day, to be given in the children's free time. In some vocational schools it was made a voluntary subject. Teachers were told that, since religion was a private matter, each should decide for himself whether or not to teach it, and in many schools the lack of 'volunteers' led to the cessation of the classes altogether. Where clergy had previously had the right to enter the schools to give religious instruction, the right was now curtailed, and in some cases abolished. Individual priests were constantly threatened with deprivation of this privilege, and an unguarded word could lead to their inhibition. Those who were also directors of Catholic Youth Groups were automatically excluded on the grounds that teachers of religious instruction were required to support the Hitler Youth both inside and outside the schools.

Finally, on 1 July 1937, the Ministry of Education, acting in accordance with Party policy, decreed that priests should no longer be permitted to conduct courses of religious instruction which in future would be in the hands of laymen. A long-established practice was thus brought to an end, and the Gestapo was ordered to watch for signs of protests, especially in rural areas. In 1939 religious instruction in vocational and continuation schools was limited to half an hour a week, and soon afterwards it was abolished entirely. In the same year, orders were given that no more church services were to be held within the school buildings, as at the opening or closing of the school year, nor were the pupils during school hours to be allowed to attend services in the churches. In Württemberg and Saxony the Ministry of Education tried to introduce an inter-denominational form of religious instruction, which omitted the Old Testament – a flagrant violation of the provisions of the Concordat as well as of the wishes of both Churches. In other areas the number of periods allotted to religious instruction was reduced to two a week, and in March 1940 'for reasons of war' they were abolished altogether in all the high schools except those in Bavaria.

Considerable economic and social pressure was brought to bear on parents and on teachers to accept these regulations. Children were encouraged to report on any misconduct by the priests during religious instruction periods. The lay teachers were subjected to professional pressure from the National Socialist Teachers' League to use the periods of religious instruction for the purpose of inculcating doctrines helpful to Nazism. In face of this subordination of religious education to political demands the many protests of the Bishops were unavailing.

The syllabus for religious education was increasingly altered to eliminate the Jewish background, particularly by the rigorous excision of passages from the Old Testament.[27] In December 1937 Hebrew was dropped from the curriculum of the high schools. In the teaching of the Gospels Jesus was presented as a Germanic hero, and long debates were held over whether He had in fact been a member of the Jewish race. According to one Nazi version, He could not have been a Jew because there are no Jewish carpenters anywhere in the world. Had He been born a Jew, He would have behaved like one; but His actions were truly Nordic, and His teachings were in accordance with Nordic, not with Jewish, blood. The Nordic races had embraced Christianity, and the affinity therefore proved that Christ must have been of Nordic stock. Christianity indeed should be proud of being one of the greatest anti-Jewish movements of all time.

Hitler's own view was similar:

It is the tragedy of the Germanic world that no German 'Heiland' (Saviour) was born among us; that our organic, spiritual evolution was suddenly violently interrupted; that Jesus was judaized, distorted, falsified, and an alien Asiatic spirit was forced upon us. That is a crime we must repair.[28]

In 1938 the National Socialist Teachers' League instigated the celebration of a non-Christian school Christmas. The custom of saying morning prayers or grace before meals was discouraged or discontinued. The customary services held at the beginning of the new school year, which had been specifically recommended in 1933, were later prohibited. Material for religious education was withheld. Pictures of Christ or the saints were replaced by Nazi symbols. Avowed Christian teachers were ostracized, and the Nazi press kept up a continual agitation against religious instruction in the classrooms. By November 1938, the situation was such that Rosenberg could declare with approbation:

The curriculum of all categories in our schools has already been so far reformed in an anti-Christian and anti-Jewish spirit that the generation which is growing up will be protected from the black swindle.[29]

And a few months later, in June 1939, the Munich School Inspector, Herr Bauer, publicly announced that

Religious instruction must disappear from the schools. We make our demand: instruction in the German faith by German teachers in German schools! The man who is tied to the dogmas of the Church need look for nothing from us in the future.[30]

To take the place of the denominational schools, new 'model Schools' were planned, to be run under the direct sponsorship of the Party or one of its affiliates. The plans were prepared in 1936, and in January 1938 the building of ten new Adolf Hitler schools was announced. These were intended for the élite of German youth, from whom the Nazi organizations would cull the boys and girls who showed the greatest devotion to the Nazi creed. The schools were to be located near to the Reich frontiers or in strongly Catholic areas where regard for the Concordat was a hindrance to the propagation of Nazi ideology in the State schools. Being under Party control and not bound by the normal regulations of the Ministry of Education, these schools were under no obligation to provide religious instruction. In fact, the curriculum was concentrated on the inculcation of unconditional acceptance of the Nazi creed, the incompatibility of which with Christian doctrines would be impressed on the pupils on every possible occasion.

The Nazi tactics were eminently successful. Only in a few isolated instances did their plans meet with resistance. Such of the clergy who objected to the increasing limitations on their work in the schools were deprived of the right to teach, and in most cases the threat of such deprivation was enough to silence further complaints.

It was small wonder that the *Neue Zuricher Zeitung*, commenting on the situation in Germany in February 1937, could claim that

The same methods which Germany used to break the military clauses of the Versailles Treaty are already being used to get around the school clauses of the Concordat. One step after another is taken which creates a certain atmosphere, so that in the end a proclamation of the *fait accompli* is doing nothing more than call matters by their proper name.[31]

There were, however, two factors which militated against the complete success of the campaign. In the first place, even though active resistance was virtually impossible, passive resistance continued. In the rural areas particularly, the position of the pastor in the Church schools was too firmly established to be easily destroyed. And in the many villages where the priest was active and enjoyed a greater following than the local Nazi leader, the Party's edicts were often circumvented. In Oldenburg a storm of public protest followed an order by the Minister of Education in November

1936 for the removal of the crucifixes from the walls of the school-rooms. Despite a public meeting arranged by the local *Gauleiter* to explain the reason for the order, so strong was the opposition that the crucifixes were hurriedly rehung. In rural Bavaria a similar attempt to replace the crucifixes with pictures of Adolf Hitler met with such bitter hostility from the women of the villages, that even the Party organizers recoiled. To placate the people whose indignation had been so strongly aroused, the Nazi hierarchy promptly disavowed the actions of their underlings, safe in the knowledge that though the influence of Catholicism might not be overcome by such pin-pricks, they held within their power more effective measures to bring about its eventual downfall.

Secondly, most of the teachers responsible for religious instruction continued to believe that their loyalties to Church and State could be combined. Indeed they questioned, if unavailingly, the wisdom of those Nazis who wished to see religious instruction abolished in favour of political indoctrination. Many teachers, even those who were ardent supporters of the régime, still believed that religious instruction was an integral part of education, holding that the moulding of character must go hand in hand with the impart-ing of knowledge, and that in this process religious instruction played an essential and indispensable part. Kerrl himself went so far as to say that religious instruction would not be limited in the schools because the doctrines of Christianity were in no way contrary to Nazism. The 'German Christians' were not slow to prepare their own courses in religious instruction based on 'German Christian' ideas, with the heroic searcher after God, 'Jesus of Nazareth' as the perfect example. In one area of Thuringia, emphasis on the anti-semitic aspect of religious instruction was encouraged by the recommendation of the *Stürmer* as suitable classroom material.[32]

Great stress was laid on the character-forming influence of obedience and loyalty to God, People and Führer. In practice, as the many cases reported to the Church authorities served to prove, frequently the cult of the Führer completely supplanted the Christian faith. As a young girl in a confirmation class in Welsau wrote,

In our religious knowledge period we have to speak about our Führer and must learn poems about him. We do not need any poems or sayings about Paul or John.[33]

The uncertainty of the official Nazi attitude is revealed by an incident which occurred in November 1938. A junior member of the German Embassy in Paris was shot by an exiled Jew, and in revenge the notorious 'Crystal Night' attack was made upon all Jewish persons and property throughout Germany. In Bayreuth the leader of the National Socialist Teachers' League, *Gauleiter* Wächtler, taking advantage of the wave of anti-Jewish feeling, issued a circular calling on all teachers to abandon the teaching of religion in view of the criminal actions of world Jewry against the new Germany, and urging them to sign the following document:

As a result of the infamous assassination in Paris, I cannot bring myself any longer to extol in my teaching the national figures of a people which thrives exclusively on hatred of Germany. I declare myself, therefore, unable to impart religious instruction . . . November 1938.

(signed.............................)[34]

Such an outcry ensued, however, especially from the teachers who were endeavouring to use the religious instruction periods to advance the claims of 'positive Christianity', and so obviously was the move a breach in the Party's professed neutrality in denominational affairs, that on orders from Berlin the document was hastily withdrawn on the following day.

Throughout 1938 and 1939, the differences between the 'moderates' and the 'radicals' became increasingly more marked. A running battle developed between Kerrl and his Nazi colleagues Rosenberg and Bormann, whose violent divergence of views was due to both ideological and personal conflict.

Martin Bormann, whose anti-clericalism increased as he rose in Hitler's favour, was the most outspoken. Writing to Rosenberg in in February 1940, he stated bluntly:

Christianity and National Socialism are phenomena which originated from entirely different basic causes. Fundamentally both differ so strongly that it would not be possible to conduct a Christian teaching which would be completely compatible with the point of view of the National Socialist ideology, just as the communities of Christian faith would never be able to stand by the ideology of National Socialism in its entirety. The issuing of National Socialist directives for the teaching of religious classes would ... be based on a synthesis of National Socialist and Christianity; which I find impossible.[35]

In a word, no accommodation, he believed, could be reached that would prove satisfactory to both Church and Party. The churches could not be conquered by a compromise between National Socialism and Christian teaching, but only by a new ideology; this it would be Rosenberg's duty to supply. The attempt at a synthesis between National Socialism and Christianity would only choke and cripple the German soul, which it was the aim of National Socialism to liberate.

He admitted, however, the danger of abolishing religious instruction in the schools without replacing it with something more suitable for the moral education of youth. A short directive on National Socialist ideals should therefore be prepared, to take the place of the shorter Catechism. In the meantime, religious instruction should be continued until such time as a more fertile and productive educational work would replace it.[36]

An example of what this would entail was to be seen in Württemberg. The Premier and Minister of Education, *SA Obergruppenführer* Mergenthaler had already sought before the outbreak of the war to 'clean up' the religious instruction syllabus, and in May 1940 he forbade the schools to offer religious instruction during the normal school hours. Instead he sought to institute a course of 'ideological instruction', using the excuse that some pupils no longer belonged to any Church, but required some form of communal and moral indoctrination. In order to find enough pupils for such activities, enormous pressure was brought on both children and parents to abandon denominational instruction in favour of the Minister's new scheme. Strenuous protests from the Church authorities to Berlin only met with the answer that education was a provincial matter and nothing could be done. On the other hand, in a private minute on the file, one of Lammers' assistants in the *Reichkanzlei* noted:

To choose Württemberg as a field of experiment would seem to be particularly unsuitable, since it has the most active evangelical church life, an awake populace and a forceful bishop. Just here should caution and reflection be uppermost. The case of the school in Maulbrons shows that the action of the Württemberg Minister of Education lacks the necessary legal and cultural preparation. One has the feeling that a better handling by the State authorities could easily have led to a peaceful solution. Instead of that the Minister of Education has now caused a situation in which the processes of law will be used against the province of Württemberg. This can only cause trouble and anxiety in the population, which ought best to be avoided in war-time. The Reich Minister of Education has for years answered none of our letters about conditions in Württemberg.

To which the Reich Education Minister, Rust, replied

Given the nature of these two opponents – Wurm and Mergenthaler – trouble could not be avoided. The Church was just as much to blame as the State. The Führer's Deputy believes that concessions over the Church question in Württemberg are not possible.[37]

With the outbreak of war and its attendant strains, Hitler was loath to stir up unnecessary domestic disputes over matters which he regarded as of secondary importance. As Hess reported to Goering in April 1940, religious instruction should be left as it was. Any attempt to provide a synthesis between Nazism and the rival Christian doctrines was patently impossible, and in any case would not eliminate denominational conflicts. The Party was accordingly directed to steer clear of the denominational frictions that would almost certainly result from an attempt to impose a single pattern of religious instruction throughout the country. So long as religious instruction was given in the schools, it should be made the responsibility of the Churches, and teachers should be warned not to attempt a synthesis of their own. Among the general population, Hess believed, the situation with regard to religious instruction was relatively satisfactory. Trouble arose only through the efforts of some of the bishops to stir up opposition by inflam-

matory sermons, or through the wholly unsuccessful efforts of
the Evangelical Church officers, backed by Kerrl, to re-organize
their affairs at a time when most of the members were serving in
the Army. No concession should be made in response to protests
from the Catholic Church in the matter of religious instruction,
since any concession would most certainly be regarded as a victory
over the Party and the State. When the war was over there would
be plenty of time to consider the future of religious instruction as
part of the education of National Socialist youth; then the problem
could be solved without the interference of the Churches. Rosenberg indeed had already received instructions to draw up plans for
this future time.[38]

The campaign against religious instruction in the schools was
closely paralleled by measures against the theological faculties and
colleges, the teachers and professors of which were regarded as the
leaders and chief participants in the Church opposition. As early as
1933 certain well-known opponents of Nazism were dismissed
from their professorships in theology and philosophy including
Paul Tillich, Martin Buber, K. L. Schmidt, Ernst Fuchs and Otto
Piper. In 1935 Karl Barth was forced to leave Bonn for his native
Switzerland. In March 1936 the Gestapo in Bavaria was ordered to
report any signs of hostility to the régime among theology teachers
in Catholic seminaries. In the *Schwarze Korps* and other organs of
the radical Nazi press theologians were under constant attack as
useless drones or agents of political reaction. Courses of theological
training which the Confessing Church attempted to establish were
declared illegal in 1937 and were finally dissolved by the Gestapo
in 1941.[39] In 1938 repressive measures were intensified. Scholarships
in theology were reserved for students approved for their Nazi
sympathies. The agitation for the separation of Church and State
was used as an excuse for withdrawing financial support from the
Catholic seminaries and from the faculties within the universities.
When separation was completed, it was reckoned, the training of
the priesthood would thus be left solely in the hands of the
Churches, and the State-supported theological faculties and the
established colleges of philosophy and theology could be systematically and finally demolished.

In carrying out these measures, the Government and the Party agencies worked in close association. They were agreed that the terms of the Concordat would have to be borne in mind;[40] but, according to a memorandum prepared in the Gestapo headquarters and in January 1939 sent to the Ministry of Education in Berlin, there were certain loopholes whereby its terms could be evaded.[41] First, any theological faculty known to be a centre of resistance to Nazism could be closed – as for instance the Jesuit-run college in Innsbruck.[42] Secondly, in any dioceses where two or more theological institutions existed, all but one could be closed down, since the Concordat did not cover a multiplicity of such establishments. Thirdly, the number of professorships could be drastically reduced, since the professorial staff of most of the German colleges was larger than the official Roman establishment laid down. These measures, it was confidently believed, would force the Churches to rely on their own independent seminaries, and would open the way for the complete suppression of State-supported religious institutions.

With these proposals the Party Headquarters concurred, and Bormann himself expressed very similar views in a letter to the Minister of Education written in the same month.[43] Certain institutions, he suggested, not mentioned in the Concordat – the one at Munich, for instance, and a few others – should be suppressed without further ado; so also should the theological faculties in Austria, at Salzburg and Graz – which were consequently closed by the Gestapo early in 1939. Where there were reduced enrolments of students, some professorships could be abolished, though this intention was not to be made known either to the Churches or by public announcement.

I would appreciate it very much [Bormann wrote] if professorial chairs thus vacated could then be turned over to the newly created fields of inquiry of recent years, such as racial research, archaeological studies, etc.[44]

To this suggestion an official of the Ministry of Education responded by pointing out the danger that the Church might attempt to provide alternative facilities where the students would no longer be subject to the pro-Nazi influence prevailing in the State Universities, though the Gestapo, he was confident, would be able to prevent the establishment of new seminaries. The time was ripe, he believed, for a final solution, whereby the community would be spared further disruptive struggles.[45] There were, nevertheless, certain practical difficulties which had to be faced. The loyalty of the Evangelical pastorate to its Prussian tradition, coupled with its outstanding record of war service, made it tactically impracticable to launch an immediate campaign to reduce the number of Protestant ordinands. As for the Catholics, a method of reducing the number of ordinands would be to rescind the privilege of exemption from conscription which had been written into the Concordat. It was believed that large numbers of Catholic youths entered the seminaries only to escape from their national duty. Other measures should be considered as soon as the time appeared propitious, especially against the Catholics and particularly after the final abrogation of the provisions of the Concordat.[46]

In April 1939, a new scheme for the reduction of the theological faculties throughout Greater Germany was drawn up by the Ministry of Education, and sent, not to the Ministry of Church Affairs, but to the Party offices from which in due course Bormann wrote to the Minister of Education informing him of the Party's acceptance.[47] The Catholic training college at Braunsburg was to be merged with the Catholic faculty at the University of Breslau; the Evangelical faculties of Rostock and Greifswald were to be merged with that of Kiel. The theological faculty of Berlin would be closed in the near future. In Bavaria there was no necessity for five state philosophical–theological faculties in the universities. The colleges at Passau, Regensburg and Bamberg should be dissolved because of their extremely strong denominational opposition to National Socialism. The theological faculty of Göttingen would be moved to Giessen; Leipzig's was to merge with Halle and Münster's with Bonn. A considerable number of professorial chairs would thus become vacant, but they should not be filled. The resources made available by the closures should be transferred to new areas of knowledge.

Similar ideas were suggested in a letter to the Minister of Education from Professor Walther Schultze, the Reich University Teachers' leader (*Reichsdozentenführer*). He divided the Evangelical theological faculties into three groups: in group A he placed Berlin, Vienna, Jena and Giessen, which were favourable to National Socialism; in Group B, Bonn, Breslau, Königsberg and Kiel, where the attitude of the faculties was indeterminate; and in group C, Tübingen, Erlangen, Leipzig, Halle, Marburg, Heidelberg, Göttingen, Greifswald, Rostock and Münster, which were close to the Confessing Church. As three-quarters of the theological students were enrolled in group C institutions, the anti-Nazi sentiments which might be expected in the next generation of pastors was apparent. Steps should therefore be taken to limit this source of potential political opposition by reducing their numbers from ten to four or five.[48]

With the outbreak of war a few months later, however, Bormann was obliged to modify his ideas. In a second letter to Rust he intimated that the plans would of necessity have to be postponed, though in the meantime, and in order to facilitate their later completion, no new theological professors should be appointed and no replacements should be made of men called up for army service. The exigencies of war necessitated this slowing-down in the policy of closures, though not its abandonment.[49] The Ministry of Education estimated that, even with an increase in the number of entrants after the war, four or five Evangelical faculties of theology would be enough to accommodate them, and following the post-war boom even that small number could be further reduced.[50]

This close supervision of the theological faculties was unquestionably due to Nazi convictions that they were the seed-bed of the Church's future leaders, and hence of likely champions of resistance to Nazi totalitarianism. The statistics of enrolments in the theological faculties were closely watched, and it is undeniable that the impact of Nazism upon the recruitment for the ministry of the Churches was severe. By 1939 only 2 per cent of the university student body was enrolled in theological studies, as compared with 6 per cent in 1933. The student enrolment in Berlin, which had been about 1,000 in 1933, fell to 472 in 1937 and to 20 in 1940

With the continuation of the war the situation rapidly deteriorated, and it soon became clear that if the trend continued the position of the Churches would be imperilled.[51] The close co-operation between the Ministry of Education, Gestapo Headquarters and the Party Chancellery was particularly ominous, for policies were planned without consultation with the Church Ministry which was frequently informed of important decisions only after they had already been reached. The restrictions and limitations were not perhaps as bold as some of the more radical anti-clericalists would have liked, but the Nazi policy-makers were confident that they would be effective in achieving their ends without arousing any large-scale opposition by the Church population.

III   THE PERSECUTION OF THE SECTS

Despite all this repression the Nazis, with incredible disregard for reality, still continued to claim that the Party stood by its support of 'positive Christianity'. Officially, there was no Church struggle; the measures that had been taken were, they maintained, designed solely to prevent the Churches from interfering in politics. As late as 1938 the *Schwarze Korps* was still boasting that

One need only count up all the forms of religious associations previously established here, and one cannot find a single example of the suppression or destruction of any of them by the National Socialist State . . .

It is nothing but a sign of ill-will if the obvious desire of the National Socialist State for complete loyalty and tolerance in Church and religious matters is disputed . . .

Up to now there has never been any hindrance by State or Party measures of the religious activities of the Churches in National Socialist Germany, so long as they were of a religious and not of a political character. Every German has the free opportunity for religious participation.[52]

The facts are otherwise. It was against the weakest and least popular of the religious groups – that is to say the free sects – whose interest and participation in German political affairs had never been more than peripheral, that the Nazis, believing them to be most easily dispensable, directed their earliest and most relentless attacks.

Unlike the two main Churches with their strongly entrenched positions, the sects had little legal standing and received no state subsidies from Church taxes. Since many of them were derived from non-German sources, from whom they received financial support, they were early suspected by the Nazis of treasonable activities, despite the tiny percentage of the population that they represented. Since they played little part in Germany's leading circles, they had few friends at court, and the measures taken against them aroused no feelings of political or popular opposition.

Foremost amongst the opponents of Nazism were the Jehovah's Witnesses, of whom a higher proportion (97 per cent) suffered some form of persecution than any of the other churches.[53] No less than a third of the whole following were to lose their lives as a result of their refusal to conform or compromise. In contrast to the compliance of the larger churches, the Jehovah's Witnesses maintained their doctrinal opposition to the point of fanaticism. Such opposition was all too rare. Already on 13 April 1933 their members were prohibited in Bavaria, on 26 April in Thuringia, on 15 May in Baden, and on 24 June in Prussia. Their pamphlets issued in protest against the national government were seized and confiscated. It was reported that the Witnesses had been instructed not to take part in the November plebiscite, and whether or not the report was true, in December Heydrich ordered that anyone found propagating the views of this illegal society was to be taken into protective custody.

The Witnesses, however, refused to be cowed, strengthened no doubt by the plans drawn up at an international conference at Basle promising intensified propaganda on behalf of the sect in Germany. In April 1935 the Gestapo seized the property of the Witnesses' publishing company in Magdeburg, and a few months later the Bavarian Political Police were ordered to intensify their campaign against individual members of the sect. But the Nazi persecution of the Witnesses was not simply due to their refusal to co-operate loyally with the Nazi State, to join any Nazi organizations, or even their refusal to be conscripted for military service. Rather it stemmed from the Nazi belief that this tiny sect presented a real political danger. In the first place, the international connections of the Witnesses and their reliance on Old Testament apocalyptic prophecies were together taken as 'proof' of their being disciples of the Jew Karl Marx and 'pacemakers of world Bolshevism'.[54] But even more significantly, in the Witnesses' 'petit bourgeois' milieu, their messianic message, their fanaticism and readiness to make ultimate sacrifices, and their skilful manipulation of propaganda, the Nazis believed they saw a new form of their own Party organization. Since the Nazis could not credit the reality of the Witnesses' so-called theological beliefs, they believed that these must be only a subtle disguise for much more dangerous political purposes, designed to repeat their own astonishing success in achieving total control of the country within a matter of years.[55]

The particularly ruthless persecution of the Witnesses began within weeks of the Nazis' assumption of power.

The danger to the State from these Jehovah's Witnesses is not to be underestimated, since the members of this sect on the grounds of their unbelievably strong fanaticism are completely hostile to the law and order of the State. Not only do they refuse to use the German greeting [Hitler salute], to participate in any National Socialist or State functions and to do military service, but they put out propaganda against joining the army, and attempt, despite prohibition, to distribute their publications.[56]

When short periods of protective custody failed to deter the Witnesses, orders were issued that persistent offenders should be sent to concentration camps, though in the case of families both parents were not to be arrested at the same time, since the State could not be burdened with the care of the children.[57] The Witnesses, still undeterred, continued their activities as best they could. When their supporters abroad broadcast the details of their widespread persecution in Germany, the Nazis redoubled their efforts against an intransigence which they feared might infect the public mind. Extended periods of incarceration were ordered by the courts. After 1937, whole families were imprisoned and the children were placed in State homes; when the wife of an official embraced the faith, her conversion became actionable as grounds for divorce. Those who had served a term of imprisonment found re-employment on release difficult or impossible to secure. As a condition for release some were called on to sign an undertaking to have no further association with the Sect on pain of continued incarceration.[58] By 1938, 700 members had been taken into protective custody for refusing to comply with such an undertaking.

The resistance of the Witnesses was centred chiefly against any form of collaboration with the Nazis and against service in the army. Basing their case on biblical commandment, they refused to take up arms even against the nation's enemies. In a society where the rights of private conscience had long since been stamped out, such a breach of discipline could not go unpunished and it was no surprise when a special law was passed in August 1938 laying down that refusal or incitement to refuse to serve in the armed forces was to be punishable by death, or in lesser cases by imprisonment or protective custody. Since such refusal was an article of belief for Jehovah's Witnesses, they were thus all practically brought under sentence of death.[59] Many in fact paid the penalty; others were sentenced to enforced service with the troops, while others were consigned to lunatic asylums, and large numbers were transported to Dachau.

The unflinching determination of the Jehovah's Witnesses in face of hopeless odds eventually made an impression even on the Nazi mind. No less a person than Himmler himself, in a letter to Kaltenbrunner in September 1944, when the German armies were everywhere in retreat, expressed admiration for the Witnesses, who, he suggested, once victory had been won, would be a useful group to settle in the vast plains of Russia where they would act as a barrier to Russian ambitions beyond the fringes of the German empire. If they converted the local population, so much the better, since their pacifism would prevent them from taking up arms against the Nazis, and their hatred of both Roman Catholics and Jews would ensure their non-collaboration with those enemies of the German Reich. Moreover, they were sober, abstemious and hard-working people who kept their word; they were excellent farmers, and, with their minds set on eternity, they were not ambitious for worldly goods. Like the Mennonites wrote Himmler, the dedicated Witnesses had characteristics which were to be envied.[60]

The sincerity of Himmler's words is questionable, but even if it were genuine, it was in no way reflected in the behaviour of his SS troops who guarded the concentration camps.

No other sect displayed anything like the same determination in face of the full force of Gestapo terrorism. Indeed, many of the smaller groups, aware of their impotence, attempted to purchase their independence by warm professions of support for the political aims of the new Germany.[61] But their compliance availed them nothing. The most dangerous organization was Freemasonry, which to the Nazi mind ranked with Judaism and Christianity as their chief opponents. In the Nazi view, Freemasonry, with its international power and influence, presented a very real threat to the political ascendancy of the Party. They refused to credit that German Freemasons were just as patriotic as any other section of the German community, and assumed that any such protestations were merely a cloak to disguise secret and subversive activities. Freemasonry, moreover, could not be dismissed as just an unwelcome part of 'petit-bourgeois' life, for its world-wide influence was uniting the middle classes much as Marxism was attempting to capture the allegiance of the workers. Also the place of the Jews in the upper leadership of World Freemasonry was, the Nazis believed, of special significance. Jewish influence coupled with the secrecy that is an essential part of Masonry, was enough to convince the Party that, no matter how earnestly the Masons might proclaim their loyalty, they were covertly working to undermine the essential purity of the German race.

From 1933 onwards, a relentless campaign was launched against the German lodges, which were declared to be superfluous and undesirable. Freemasons were prohibited from holding office in the Party, and even former members were dismissed if their past association came to light.

Many of the lodges, which were mainly concerned with humanitarian activities, were dissolved, either voluntarily or under duress. By 1935 the Gestapo was able to report that even the longest established, such as the Grand Master Lodge of the Three Globes, the Grand Prussian Lodge of Friendship and the Grand Lodge of Freemasons of Germany, were all on the point of dissolution, and in some cases Masonic property was seized and sequestrated. When the membership lists were finally secured and examined, however, such violent measures were found to be needless, for the society, which the Nazis had assumed to be on the scale of a world conspiracy, enjoyed but a pathetically small following in Germany and constituted no danger at all to Nazi supremacy.

Most of the other small sects were similarly suspected of endangering the cohesion of the German People's community. They were accused of having connections with foreign agencies through which the influence of world Jewry and Communism might infiltrate, and as such they were proclaimed deserving of eradication – a fate which most of them were, in fact, destined to suffer.[62]

Some of the larger sects, such as the Methodists, the Baptists, the Seventh Day Adventists and the Old Catholics, were numerically sufficiently important for the Nazis to play one against the other and so to demonstrate the disunity prevailing among them. For example, the Methodist Bishop Melle was permitted to attend the conference of the World Council of Churches at Oxford in July 1937 expressly in order to counter the efforts of the Confessing Church to obtain a declaration against the persecution of Christianity in Germany. Some of these larger groups were in fact left unmolested, and some were even rewarded; but the majority of them were eventually dissolved and their property was sequestrated by the State. Most of the dissolutions were effected in 1937, but it was not until 1941 that Heydrich ordered final steps to be taken by the local police forces against all astrologists, occultists, spiritualists, fortune-tellers, homeopaths, anthroposophists, theosophists, and any other group of persons who, by occult or secret practices, were suspected of perverting the spiritual health of the German people.[63] The Christian Scientists also were particularly suspected both because of their views on the practice of medicine, which were not in harmony with Nazi ideas, and because of alleged Jewish and Masonic influence at their international headquarters in Boston.

In March 1939 Party members were forbidden to belong to the movement and in 1941 it was finally dissolved.

The thoroughness with which the activities of all these groups were watched and probed by the Gestapo, and the ruthlessness with which they were eventually stamped out, were a measure of the Nazis' determination to tolerate the existence of no organization that might lay claim to loyalties which rivalled their own. That the same forceful measures were not applied to the larger denominations was only because their hour of challenge had not yet come.

8 Collaboration or Intimidation?

> We have captured all the positions
> And on the heights we have planted
> The banners of our revolution.
> You had imagined that that was all that we
>   wanted
> We want more
> We want *all*
> Your hearts are our goal,
> It is your souls we want.
> —ANONYMOUS NAZI VERSE, 1939[1]

I THE NAZI RIVALRIES UNRESOLVED

By 1937 the Nazi campaign to restrict and limit the influence of
the Church appeared to be well on the way to success. Dr Goebbels'
propaganda machine controlled all the means of communication
and was geared to the unremitting dissemination of Nazi views
and doctrines. The ideas of Rosenberg and the *völkisch* groups were
expressed in semi-pagan ceremonies and were taught in the Party
schools. The Hitler Youth had captured the allegiance of most of
the young people and had jeopardized the future of the Churches'
educational work. Streicher was pouring out anti-semitic and
anti-clerical propaganda unchecked by any sense of truth or
justice. The Education Minister Rust had undermined the position
of the Church schools and had transformed the universities into
Nazi-dominated institutions. Himmler was using the power of the
police to suppress all signs of opposition; the processes of the law
were perverted to serve Nazi ends; and all resistance from opposing
Church movements was being suppressed by Kerrl. In short, as the
Vicar-General of the Catholic Diocese of Berlin wrote thirty years
later, the situation as it appeared at the time could briefly be
summarized thus:

Hitler himself was the author of the anti-Christian policy. But he had no need to complain about the lack of collaborators. In the Gestapo there was ready at hand a central command for the practical persecution and terrorization of religion. But Goebbels in the Propaganda Ministry, even Kerrl in the Church Ministry and Party offices such as those of Bormann and Rosenberg were all fanatically united in the attempt to root out the Christian faith from German hearts.[2]

That was the broad picture; but in actual fact the situation was considerably more complicated. Within the Nazi leadership itself personal rivalries and differing views on tactics were causing considerable dissension over the future of the Nazi relations with the Churches. Among Himmler's papers an interesting analysis was found of the various Nazi views, which, though not dated, appears to have been written about this time. The author, who is identified only as a Catholic who was formerly a well-known politician, expressed the view that the Church struggle had reached its pitch of intensity solely because of the fanaticism displayed on both sides; more moderate men, in his opinion, feared a repetition of Bismarck's *Kulturkampf*.

The moderate shrewd wing of the National Socialists, which thinks only in terms of a *realpolitik* approach, is symbolised by the name of Hess. The quiet never-rowdy Deputy of the Führer is a more powerful factor in the Third Reich than most people at home or abroad allow . . . He puts the brake on the radicalism of the Party members. He believes in a policy of building bridges with Catholicism. And he enjoys Hitler's complete confidence. The second pillar of a policy of reconciliation is the clever *Gauleiter* of the Saarland and the Palatinate. Bürckel carries weight far beyond his position as the expert on the Catholic problem, on which he feels justified to speak because of his experience in the Saar. Even Goebbels, the spiritual head of the 'Old Fighters' and the 'Socialists' . . . is not uninfluenced by his Catholic Rhineland background.[3]

Goering and Ley, the author believed, could likewise be relied on to adopt a moderate attitude that would effectively curb the extremer policy of Rosenberg and Schirach. Hitler's own view was still undecided, but he had definitely shown his desire for a political solution that would settle the matter of Church and State along practical rather than ideological lines. There was also – though the analysis does not mention it – the position take up by

Kerrl and others like him, who still hoped to reconcile Nazism and Christianity by the exercise of closer co-operation and better understanding.

These differing points of view were manifold, but they should perhaps not be over-emphasized. All the Nazi hierarchy believed in totalitarian control. All could at one time display fanatical extremism and at another urge a policy of moderation. Clashes of personality frequently determined the attitude to be adopted by individual leaders, and their concern for personal power within the Nazi jungle was often more compelling than consistency in their attitude towards the Churches.

As the Minister most immediately responsible, Kerrl in his speeches throughout 1937 and 1938 set himself the task of convincing his Party colleagues and the mass of Churchmen that a reconciliation could be achieved between State and Church. He still hoped both to convince Hitler that the Churches could play a positive role in the Third Reich, and to reduce the influence of Rosenberg and his followers, whom he not surprisingly feared and dreaded. With all his energies he set out to demonstrate to the more radical Nazis that National Socialism was a religious movement and that Nazi ideology and the Christian religion were complementary. The National Socialist, he declared,

not only full recognizes his obligations to God and the Divine order but lives them. The true National Socialist was he who knew God's commands in his conscience and his blood. Thus the State itself is the living form of the national community – faith in God expressed in experience.[4]

To orthodox members of the Churches Kerrl was equally concerned to prove that the teachings of Christ in no way ran counter to the doctrines of National Socialism. Indeed, he maintained,

Christ did not teach us to fight against the National Socialist doctrine of the Race. Rather He waged an unprecedented warfare against Judaism, which for that reason slew Him on the Cross.[5]

The State, he pointed out, had given enormous subsidies to the Churches. How then could the State be described as anti-Christian or anti-religious? It was only by the political manoeuvres of some ambitious Churchmen that the spirit of dissension had been kept alive. Had the Churches confined themselves to their religion and not ventured to meddle in politics, there would have been no trouble. In Germany the State must rule under a single leader, and the people must follow in obedience and discipline. The National Socialist State had no intention of founding a State Church to add yet another doctrine to those already causing dissension, for National Socialism itself was the new Christianity, brought up to date and reincarnated in the purity of the German soul.

National Socialism is the fulfilment of the will of God which is demonstrated to us in our blood ... Christianity is not dependent upon the Apostles' Creed ... The true Christianity is represented in the Party, and the German people are now called by the Party and especially by the Führer to a real Christianity ... It is not the Church which has demonstrated that Faith which could move mountains. But the Führer has. He is the herald of a new revelation.[6]

The closeness of these views to those of the Thuringian wing of the 'German Christians' is obvious. The Confessing Church justifiably rejected such a hotchpotch of heretical ideas, well knowing that adoption of Kerrl's doctrines would open the floodgates to a religion of Blood and Soil. And even among the 'neutral' clergy the realization was growing that the chasm between Rosenberg's mythology and the orthodoxy of the Christian Churches was rapidly becoming unbridgeable.

Furthermore, churchmen of all shades of opinion were increasingly alarmed by the divergence between Kerrl's professions of tolerance and sympathy and the open acts of persecution by the Gestapo which he instigated, or at least tacitly accepted. Which, they wondered, represented the true Nazi attitude? In public, widely contradictory statements were made, some supporting, some castigating the Churches. Were these some sort of a trap, or did they indeed reflect conflicts in Nazi Church policy? The ordinary Churchman had no means of knowing.

Few were in a position to realize that Kerrl was himself so caught up in a network of feuds and quarrels with his Nazi rivals that over and over again he was being baulked in his efforts to make his Ministry a success. Despite his attempts to convince the clergy that his sole aim was to resolve their divisions so that all could stand united behind Hitler in the gigantic task of creating the new Germany, he was destined only to lose the confidence of them all.

With the inability of the Reich Church Commissioners to find a compromise policy that would satisfy both the demands of the Confessing Church and the radical aims of the 'German Christians', their work grew increasingly sterile, and on 12 February 1937 they finally resigned their commission on the grounds that:

The confidence of the pastors and the parishes in the purposes of the Church Ministry and in the possibilities of collaboration with the Church Commissioners cannot be maintained if their work of reconciliation is damaged by an unrestricted campaign against the Christian faith from outside.[7]

On the following day Kerrl summoned a meeting of the Chairmen of the Provincial Church Commissions and threatened them with severe measures if his wishes were not carried out. He denounced the Reich Church Commissioners for their failure to realize the dimension of their task, and for their abortive attempts to patch up Church quarrels instead of initiating a reformation in the new Germany. The task of the Church, he reminded them, was to carry out the will of God. If the Church Commissioners were unable to fulfil that task, then he personally would be obliged to take over the leadership of the Church's administration. Elections were out of the question because of the prevailing disunity among their members. Forcible steps would have to be taken against the pastors who worked against the State and the Party, and the 'Aryan' paragraph must finally be introduced into the Church, so that no Jews could continue to hold a pastoral charge or office. All the necessary ordinances thereto were already being printed.[8]

Two days later, however, there was a sudden reversal of policy. Hitler himself intervened to overrule Kerrl by announcing a free election for the establishment of a new constituent General Synod to produce a new constitution for the whole Evangelical Church.

Since the Reich Church Commission has not succeeded in bringing about unity between the several groups in the German Evangelical

Church, the Church shall now give itself a new constitution and with it a new structure in full freedom by its own determination. I hereby empower the Reich Minister for Church Affairs to prepare an election for a General Synod for this purpose and to take all necessary measures thereto.

Berchtesgaden   signed
15 February 1937   The Führer and Reich Chancellor
                                         Adolf Hitler[9]

The reasons for this sudden change are still uncertain; nor is it clear what Hitler hoped to achieve by his unexpected move. Presumably he wished to dissociate himself and the Party from the comprehensive control of Church affairs which Kerrl appeared anxious to assume. Possibly, in view of the pronounced reaction to Kerrl's speech, Hitler was unwilling to stir up further conflict that might redound abroad to Germany's discredit. It was all the more remarkable that Hitler's decree called for the free expression of views, which Kerrl had so recently declared to be impossible.

Such an open disavowal of the Church Minister weakened Kerrl's position still further, both within the ranks of the Church and in the Nazi Party.[10] Many waverers were emboldened to take fresh heart, and, according to one witness, speculation ran wild over why Kerrl's threats were not to be carried out. Was the Confessing Church too strong for the Nazis to control? Would Kerrl be dismissed?

In short, a fresh breeze blew through the Third Reich, and the feeling of grateful relief that ran through the Confessing Church members was comparable to the reaction that must have greeted Moses' announcement to the children of Israel that Pharaoh had promised to let them depart from Egypt. But it was Kerrl who was Pharaoh and Hitler who was Moses. The Führer's prestige actually rose, because it was he who had countermanded Kerrl's orders by decreeing the new synodical election.[11]

To restore his own self-confidence, Kerrl absented himself from his office for long periods and began work on a full-scale book expounding his concepts of the relationship between Christianity and Nazism and their inseparable nature – material from which his speeches, quoted above, were largely drawn. Meanwhile, the Confessing Church set to work to rally its members for the coming election campaign. In a remarkable open letter to Kerrl published at the end of February, Dibelius expressed the views of his followers and friends in unusually forthright terms.[12] The Christian faith, he averred, was based on the historical personality of Jesus Christ, the crucified and resurrected. It was not subject to new revelations or interpretations according to political expediency. Any attempt to make it so constituted an invasion of the Church's autonomy by the State.

Let the Church regulate its own affairs in true freedom and independence. If that happens the Church struggle would be over in three months.[13]

Unfortunately there was no possibility of such freedom and independence, since a free election was inconceivable in Nazi Germany. The hasty promise of Hitler's decree was proving an embarrassment to the Party, and Kerrl was not slow to take advantage of it in an attempt to regain lost ground. He issued an order that, until the elections were held, he would assume control of the Church's administration by means of the executive members of a financial department appointed to take responsibility for all non-theological matters.[14]

This plan, as might be expected, was received with vehement protests from the Confessing Church and by a prompt counterattack in the form of a pamphlet entitled 'Regarding a Church Election: What every man must know!' In the weeks that followed, a flood of speeches, sermons, discussions and protests burst forth with a violence that demonstrated afresh the hopeless disunity of the churches, and also served to show that large sections of German opinion were not prepared to be deprived of the right to express their individual views. The vigorous participation of so many laymen led the Nazis to postpone the promised election first until after Easter and later for another six months. In June Kerrl prohibited the use of churches for electioneering purposes or for any public gathering in preparation for the election – an unpopular move which did nothing to bring the controversy to an end.

At this juncture Nazi policy changed again. Kerrl's efforts to persuade the churches to unite had failed; Hitler's hopes for the churches' voluntary support of the Nazi state were clearly doomed; and a policy of vigorous repression was therefore now decreed. The reason for the change undoubtedly lay in Kerrl's determination to vindicate his position. On taking office, he had promised Hitler that within two years he would have the Churches under control. The time was very nearly up, and the opportunity of proving that he was master in his own house might not occur again. Therefore, a frontal attack against the Confessing Church was now put in hand, with all the power of the Gestapo openly used to compel submission. In June 1937 Dibelius was placed on trial for breaches of the Conspiracy Law in his open letter of February. A meeting of the Reich Brethren Council in a Berlin Church was interrupted by the Gestapo on 23 June and eight of its members were arrested.[15] In the succeeding days 48 prominent Confessing Churchmen were taken into custody, culminating, on Hitler's personal order, in the detention on 1 July of Dr Martin Niemöller, the chief target of the Nazis' attack and their most outspoken opponent in the Confessing Church.

Niemöller's nominal offence was that he had read from the pulpit the names of those who had declared their intention to leave the Church, a contravention of the prohibition of such publication decreed by Kerrl on 20 March. The news of Niemöller's arrest caused a tremendous stir both inside and outside Germany, a stir which continued unabated throughout the months before his trial. Nevertheless, Kerrl and his associates, undeterred by such a demonstration of what they considered 'political disloyalty', continued to press ahead with their measures of repression.

Niemöller's arrest was followed by the detention of many other pastors who had ignored Kerrl's decree forbidding the collection of money for purposes not approved by his Ministry. By November 1937 over 700 pastors had been arrested, including Paul Schneider, the pastor of a country parish in the southern Rhineland. Schneider's offence was his refusal to leave his parish after the Gestapo had ordered him to do so. In November 1937 he was sent to Buchenwald concentration camp, and there he died eighteen months later, the first of the German Evangelical pastorate to lose his life as a result of Nazi persecution.

Other less drastic measures were also instituted to curb the resistance of the Confessing Church. Some pastors were forbidden to preach or lecture; some were ejected from their parishes; some were deprived of their stipends. Kerrl publicly threatened to reduce the subsidies paid to the Church unless these 'disloyal elements' repented. In July all pastors were forbidden to teach religious instruction in State schools. Orders were issued banning the Confessing Church's private seminaries and forbidding the payment of stipends to pastors who had taken their ordination examinations at such seminaries.[16] All theological students were obliged to become members of one or other of the Nazi affiliated associations. The programme of the German Student Christian Movement was severely cut down. One of the main Evangelical publishing houses was seized and its property was confiscated. In Munich, the demolition of one of the largest Protestant churches was ordered in the name of 'urban renewal'.

These measures inevitably raised grave doubts of the sincerity of the Nazi assurance of February 1937, especially among the radical wing of the Confessing Church, which was already sceptical about the promised free elections. To counter the prevailing suspicions, a Nazi monthly bulletin for September 1937 proclaimed:

> The doubts which have been expressed whether the Church elections will take place, must be sharply attacked. There can be no suspicion of doubt about the Führer's word. We must leave it to him to find the suitable time for such elections, and remember that he has a lot more things to think of than the demands of impatient pastors.
>
> It is not surprising to find the Church reaction so strong in Dahlem, which is the resort of the upper-class relics of feudalism who seek refuge in the Church where they can complain because others are treated better than are 'their ladyships'.[17]

On 23 November 1937 Kerrl announced that, because of the disturbed state of the Evangelical Church, the long-promised elections would be postponed until an unspecified date – a bitter blow to all who had hoped for a new era in the Church's relations with the State. On 10 December new orders appeared for the administration of the Church, by means of which Kerrl hoped to gain a more effective hold over the separate provincial churches and thereby to mould them into a single unit under his control. In January 1938 he also put forward a tentative suggestion that the disciplinary control of pastors should be taken out of the hands of the provincial bishops and transferred to the central church office, which was under the control of one of his own supporters, the 'German Christian' Dr Werner. By this means measures could be strengthened against the pastors of the Confessing Church who in his opinion were receiving undue sympathy from the South German bishops, and the bishops would no longer be able to thwart the endeavours of the 'German Christian' pastors within their dioceses.[18]

Another scheme, put forward by Dr Werner in April 1938 as a gesture of gratitude to Hitler for the successful *Anschluss* with Austria, was to call on all pastors to take a personal oath of loyalty to Hitler in the same way as army officers were required to do. The majority of pastors subscribed,[19] but a small handful from the Confessing Church refused to do so, regardless of the consequences. In the event, their courageous stand went unpunished, for, as gradually became known, the scheme was unwelcome to the Nazi Party leaders themselves. On 13 June Bormann issued a circular to all the *Gauleiters* stating that the oath of loyalty had been proposed without the Führer's consent, and that it was therefore to be treated merely as an internal church matter. No pastor was to be disciplined for refusing to take it.[20]

Despite all Kerrl's efforts, however, the Evangelical Churches were no nearer to unity with the State than they had been before his Ministry was instituted. Indeed his measures served only to bind the Churchmen more closely together. The Confessing Church organized widespread services of intercession for all those – including Pastor Niemöller – who had been persecuted for their steadfastness, a form of service which proved to be a most effective means of informing loyal churchmen of the plight of their fellow-campaigners, for, since it was placed in a liturgical setting, the Gestapo were powerless to prevent it.

Nor did the tactics of Kerrl and Muhs win the public support for which they had hoped. Aided by the propaganda efforts of

Goebbels, Kerrl attempted to turn the trial of Dibelius in August 1937 into a public arraignment of the old reactionary factions, which, he averred, were using ecclesiastical office as a cover for politically subversive moves against the State. He hoped that in the verdict the will of the people would be demonstrated; but unfortunately for his schemes, the judges refused to bow to his pressure and acquitted Dibelius. As Dibelius himself later commented, it was the only occasion in the history of the Nazi State in which the wishes of a Nazi Minister of the Reich were publicly rejected by the judges of the courts. Kerrl immediately applied to have Dibelius sent to a concentration camp, but his application was rejected by the Minister of Justice.

Still undeterred, Kerrl and Goebbels then concentrated their efforts on the even more important trial of Niemöller, which finally came before the courts in February 1938. Instructions had been given that all cases concerning church matters were to be so carefully prepared that an acquittal was impossible.[21] Seven months had been spent in preparing the prosecution's case. A public campaign of defamation was conducted by the Propaganda Ministry, in which Niemöller was accused, among other things, of being a traitor to his country on the grounds of the almost unanimous support accorded to him by the foreign press.[22] Despite all the Ministry's efforts, however, the judges on 2 March returned a verdict of not guilty on the major charges and declared that Niemöller's minor infringements of the law had been fully expiated by the period of incarceration which he had already suffered.[23]

But Hitler was not to be defied. On his immediate orders Niemöller was re-arrested and placed in protective custody, first in the concentration camp at Sachsenhausen and later at Dachau. Despite urgent representations from a host of Niemöller's friends, including a number of high-ranking officers in the Navy, Hitler refused to consider his release.[24] But the political consequences of Hitler's decision proved costly. The arbitrary nature of Niemöller's second incarceration and the flagrant disregard for the law which it evinced were a potent demonstration, especially to foreign observers, of the scant respect paid by the Nazis to the practice of the German legal system and to the established position of the Lutheran Church.²⁵ For the next eight years, Niemöller was regarded as the symbol of the Church's martyrdom, and his name was daily remembered in church services throughout Germany and abroad.

Regardless of events, however, the Ministry of Church Affairs laboured on with its plans. In 1938 State Secretary Muhs suggested another plan for the pacification of the Evangelical Church, to stress the necessity of removing the danger of political involvement from the Church.²⁶

The State has only a welfare role towards the Evangelical Church. Part of the task is to protect the Church from the danger which constantly recurs throughout history of its getting involved in politics.

For the same reason, Muhs opposed the separation of Church and State, which might well lead to the creation of Free Churches, beyond the State's control and receiving financial, political and cultural support from World Protestantism.

Muhs based his case on the need for the Evangelical Church to continue its historic role as the spiritual arm of the State providing ideological education for the people in accordance with the prevailing political leadership. The responsibility lay on the spiritual leaders to cast away old ideas and to embrace the new era introduced by Nazism.

The support of the authorities will naturally be given only to those members among the spiritual leaders who carry out the Church's task in fundamental agreement with the National Socialist ideology ... Their chief task is the education and influencing of the clergy, and through them of the parishes, in the spirit of a church closely tied to State and people ...

Conclusion. It must be realized that all these measures are only temporary. The Church's thinking and feeling have been rooted in tradition for centuries, and are so deeply anchored in the people's souls that only a slow planned progression will succeed ... There is need therefore to avoid any measures which by violence or unplanned attacks might disturb the quiet development which is in line with the educational measures of the Party, the Hitler Youth, the SA, the Labour Front etc. The main value of these measures is that they will prevent the

Church from becoming the refuge of politically unreliable elements. A fundamental clarification of the relationship between Party and Christianity must follow sooner or later. Only after that can concrete plans be laid for the future form of a Church in the Third Reich.

All these plans by Kerrl and his supporters were watched with increasing scepticism by the other Nazi leaders. His ineptitude in handling the pastors, and his futile attempts to mobilize the Evangelical Church behind the Nazi Party were regarded with increasing contempt. Neither Rosenberg nor Bormann was prepared to accept Kerrl's so-called theoretical arguments, which, they suspected, he was using merely to bolster up his own political position. In May 1938 Hess predicted that all Kerrl's efforts to weld the Church into unity by disciplinary measures would end in failure, and that any attempt to use the power of the State to heal doctrinal differences would inevitably result in the State's being called upon to support one doctrine against another – an intolerable situation which conflicted with the declared policy of the Nazi Party. For these reasons he refused to subscribe to Kerrl's proposed plans.[27] Himmler, in a letter to Goering in July 1938, wrote:

I am afraid that the Church Minister is pursuing his pernicious policy of forcibly bringing into being a 'German Christian' national church. We of course, particularly in the next few weeks, want to avoid any possible trouble.[28]

Rosenberg likewise rejected Kerrl's plans. In November 1938 he complained to Hitler that Kerrl was trying to attach one group of Evangelical Churchmen to the Nazi State and were thereby involving the Party in theological disputes which could only be detrimental to the State. He argued that, since religious differences had led to religious wars throughout the centuries, the Nazi Party would be well advised to steer clear of any association with Biblical tradition. It would do nothing but harm, he argued,

if the National Socialist State were not only to supervise the Church's organization and the handling of its financial matters but also to attempt under the form of a National Socialist Church Ministry, to bring about a legally-established order along the lines of the private views of the

214

Reich Minister for Church Affairs on the possibility of the fusion of National Socialism and the New Testament.[29]

Hitler fully agreed: he too was determined not to accept Kerrl's suggestions for closer links between State and Church, in which he could see no political advantage. He curtly recommended Kerrl to confine himself to keeping the rival factions in order and to prevent political opposition from taking root among them.

He did not, however, disavow Kerrl entirely, for, with his usual shrewd political sense, he realized the dangers inherent in a root and branch attack on all the Churches simultaneously. From the evidence available it would appear that he was still undecided between a declared policy of reconstruction in Church–State relations and a more cautious approach which would allow the Churches to continue as before but would strangle their activities by restriction and decree.

In the Foreign Ministry records the following note appears, dated September 1937:

The Führer, in agreement with Reich Minister Kerrl, intends in the near future to settle the matter of Church and State as a whole. This settlement is to take place in the form of a fundamental speech in the Reichstag by the Führer – for historical reasons presumably scheduled for Reformation Day [31 October]. The Führer is said to have stated that in its effect this speech would greatly eclipse Luther's ninety-five Theses and would complete the work of the Reformation in the German spirit.

The Churches would remain incorporated bodies under public law; they would, however, lose their rights to taxes, without prejudice to the right to collect voluntary contributions. In the future there would be no question of the State's officially carrying any burdens whatsoever for the Church.

On the day of the speech planned by the Führer, the Vatican is to be given the note in which the Concordat will be described as outdated by the course of developments.[30]

In the event, the speech was never made, and no such note was delivered to the Vatican. A year later, in September 1938, at the height of the Sudetenland crisis, Rosenberg made a remarkably frank but (for him) moderate announcement to a Nazi gathering at Nuremberg, which, on account of the political excitement at the time, passed almost unnoticed. In his speech he outlined the change that had taken place in Hitler's views on the conduct of the Church campaign;

We must remember that the international position of the Catholic Church calls for very careful tactics on our part towards that Church. Every attack upon the Church affects international relations and can intensify the difficulties of a position which is already serious enough. That the Catholic Church and the Confessing Church in their present form must disappear from the life of our people is my full conviction, and I believe I am entitled to say that this is also our Führer's view. But when various groups representing the so-called German *Weltanschauung* think it fit in their public statements to exhibit a wild radicalism, I am compelled to tell these gentlemen that, in so doing they not only injure the prestige of the Reich Government, but also foster martyrdom among the believers. We have already gone far ahead in permeating the German Youth with the National Socialist philosophy of life. Whatever still functions of the Catholic Youth movement is nothing more than various fractional groups which will be absorbed in the course of time. The Hitler Youth organization is an absorbent sponge which nothing can withstand. Furthermore, the development of our teaching scheme in schools of all categories is of such an anti-Christian-Jewish type that the growing generations will be forewarned against the black-coat swindle. You should also remember that even in the Catholic Church there are sincere Germans working as priests who are utterly devoted to the National Socialist philosophy. With their help we shall occupy the last – and, I admit, extremely strong – positions of the Church . . . We do not want to make the same mistake as Bismarck made, since our opponent is shrewd and works with means which we can only overcome with better weapons. [31]

In practice, the situation regarding the legal obligations of the Concordat was much more definite. As an official of the Foreign Ministry commented a few months later:

Secretly we regard the Reich Concordat and the Länder Concordats as out of date. Many of their provisions are fundamentally opposed to the basic principles of National Socialism, such as the provisions concerning schooling and youth education . . . Thus we no longer regard the Reich Concordat and the Länder Concordats as a legal norm in domestic policy. Therefore, in our relations with organs of the Catholic Church we also avoid all reference to provisions under the Concordats or discussions of alleged violations of the Concordats. Some provisions are, however, observed by us and we also demand that the Catholic Church should do the same. But an explicit declaration on our attitude to the Concordats has not yet been given to the Vatican.[32]

In fact, however, the Nazi intentions continued to remain secret. No open declaration of opposition to the entrenched position of the Church was made, but in private, Bormann, writing to the Armed Forces Supreme Command Headquarters on 28 January 1939, expressed the view that most of the clergy could only be regarded as potential political enemies of the Reich:

A great portion of the ministers of both Churches stand, in accordance with the attitude of those Churches, in concealed or open opposition to National Socialism and the State led by it. In this respect the situation has changed from the time before or during the World War, when the Churches were in a more positive relationship with the State. Today, however, should a crisis arise for the National Socialist State, the Churches and the ministers would pass from concealed to open opposition. They would not in time of crisis help or support this State, but would at best leave it to its own fate.[33]

From this assessment of the situation Bormann drew the conclusion that any closer connection between the State and the Church was to be strongly deprecated. The impossibility of marshalling the doctrinally-divided Churches behind the Nazi State was matched only by the incompatibility of their ideological aims. The State's principle of freedom of faith and conscience necessitated the maintenance of a rigidly neutral attitude in all denominational affairs, and the Government could therefore not be accused of being anti-Church or anti-Christian. On the other hand, such neutrality left the field clear for the dissemination of the Nazi Party's own philosophy, which was to be uniformly undertaken in all organizations and teaching institutions from the Armed Forces to the Hitler Youth. In this way, the spiritual integrity of the German people could be maintained and purified, free from the dividing and subversive influence of the Christian Churches.

In his secret annual report of the *Sicherheitshauptamt* for 1938,

Heydrich expressed an equally pejorative view of the attitude of the clergy towards the Nazi State.

At the beginning of 1938 the political Churches concentrated their activities on the mobilization of their forces . . . With the help of their international connections they still hoped to see the collapse of the National Socialist Reich. . . . These hopes were re-awakened at the end of August when the foreign political situation began to be more critical. Immediately, the Church forces saw in the foreign crisis the possibility of an eventual destruction of the National Socialist power, which gave them hope for a revival of their own positions . . . They attempted to spread uncertainty and nervousness amongst the people and to weaken the dynamic of the Third Reich. This treacherous attitude of the German Church circles in a time of foreign political crisis united them with the international subversive activities of world Catholicism, world Protestantism and the supranational sects.[34]

He further cited the hostility constantly displayed by the Vatican, the negative attitude of the Bishops towards the *Anschluss* as typified by the conduct of Bishop Sproll of Württemberg, the attempt to make the Catholic Eucharistic Congress in Budapest a demonstration of united opposition to Germany, and the continued accusations of Nazi Godlessness and of the Nazi destruction of church life made by church leaders in their pastoral letters.

In the spring of 1938, Heydrich recalled, the Fulda Bishops' Conference had announced its intention of conducting a full-scale campaign against the State in the 'propositions on the Church political situation'. The Bishops at the time of the Sudetenland crisis took advantage of the situation to bring pressure on the government by threatening to call the people to active resistance. Their use of pastoral letters to stir up trouble had, however, proved unavailing, for the political events of the spring and summer had exercised a far greater effect on the Catholic faithful than the agitatory attempts of the Church hierarchy.[35]

But these views were never made public, nor did they find any place in the official policy of the Nazi Government. In public, Hitler could still call for the Churches' support of the régime and could still lay the charge of ingratitude against those doubters amongst the clergy who refused to accept his leadership. It was still felt politically advantageous to claim, both at home and abroad, that the State was anxious to support the Church. In his speech to the Reichstag on 30 January 1939, Hitler asserted:

1. In Germany no one so far has been persecuted because of his religious attitude, nor will he be in the future.
2. The National Socialist State since the 30th of January 1933 has through its public taxation contributions put the following sums of money at the disposal of both Churches: in the financial year 1933, 130 million Reichsmarks; in 1934, 170 million; in 1935, 250 million; in 1936, 320 million; in 1937, 400 million; and in 1938, 500 million Reichsmarks. In addition, there were 85 million Reichsmarks from subsidies from the provinces and 7 million from the local authorities. As well as this, the Churches were the largest land owners after the State. The value of their agricultural and forest lands was well over 10 billion Reichsmarks. The income alone was estimated at over 300 million. There were also numerous gifts, legacies and the results of church collections. And the Church in the Nazi State receives favourable tax concessions.

   It is therefore – to put it bluntly – a disgrace when . . . foreign politicians dare to talk about the supposed hostility towards the Church practised by the National Socialist State . . .
3. The National Socialist State has neither closed a church nor prevented a church service, still less tried to influence the form of any church liturgy. It has not sought to alter the teachings of the creeds of any denomination. In the National Socialist State, everyone can be saved in his own fashion.[36]

And then, as if to show the claws within the velvet glove, he continued:

The National Socialist State will ruthlessly bring to their senses any priests, who, instead of serving God, think it their mission to vilify our present Reich, its institutions, or its leaders. The destruction of this State will not be tolerated from anyone . . . We will protect the German priest who is the servant of God, we will wipe out the priest who is a political enemy of the German Reich.[37]

II THE RESPONSE OF THE CHURCH

With the arrest of Niemöller, the Confessing Church lost much of its confidence in eventual victory. Disillusionment spread gradually among even the staunchest Churchmen, and a readiness to compromise was slowly growing. 'By the middle of the summer of 1938', the head of the Gestapo shrewdly noted in his annual report, 'the situation in the Churches was characterized by weariness with the struggle, by uncertainty of purpose and by lack of courage.'[38] After five years of unceasing stress, endurance was running out, helped by the success of Hitler's foreign policy during 1938, which was raising Nazi popularity to new and alarming heights. The annexation of Austria was achieved swiftly and successfully in March, and was welcomed by no less a person than the Cardinal Archbishop of Vienna, Cardinal Innitzer, in the name of the Austrian bishops, with a declaration of sympathy and support for the new Nazi régime.

The Austrian bishops are convinced that the danger of an all-devastating, atheistic Bolshevism was averted by the actions of the National Socialist movement. They therefore welcome these measures for the future and bestow their blessing on them, and would instruct the faithful in this sense.

On the day of the plebiscite it will be an obvious national duty for the bishops to confess themselves as Germans in the German Reich. They expect, therefore, that all faithful Christians should know what they owe to their *Volk*.[39]

An equally fervent declaration was signed by the Austrian Evangelical leaders.[40] And the propaganda campaign against Czechoslovakia which shortly afterwards was launched on behalf of the 'persecuted' Sudetenlanders made a further instant appeal to the nationalistic emotions of the German people. Faithful churchmen found themselves more and more isolated in a position of increasing doubt and uncertainty.

With the development of the Sudeten crisis, there was a small group of the Confessing Church leaders who foresaw with terrible clarity the danger of war which the Nazi policies were creating. To warn their followers, they circulated to their supporting parishes a service of intercession (*Fürbitteliturgie*) to be held in the Churches on 30 September, in which war was described as a punishment and the forgiveness of Almighty God was besought for the personal and national sins of His people.[41] Then on 28 September the Munich Conference was announced, and in the altered circumstances the service was withdrawn; but a copy of the proposed intercession, which had been circulated privately, fell into Himmler's hands and was published a month later in the *Schwarze Korps* which branded it as a deliberate stab-in-the-back for Hitler's policies in Germany's hour of danger, and as final and irrefutable proof of the disloyalty of the Confessing Church – a view which was shared by the whole Nazi hierarchy, including Bormann:

This liturgy of intercession is a piece of high treason and proves that the Churches have only been waiting until the National Socialist State found itself, at least in their opinion, in a moment of uneasiness, to take up the fight against the State with their whole psychologically influential means. In my opinion this fact deserves special attention because this liturgy of intercession clearly demonstrates the extraordinarily successful manner in which these churches try to exercise their spiritual influence over individuals.[42]

The man most discomfited by this disclosure was Kerrl. The alleged 'treachery' of the Confessing Church was now openly revealed and his whole strategy on which he had worked since his installation as Church Minister, was completely destroyed by this demonstration that the Evangelical Churches were as disunited in their attitude to the Nazi State as they had ever been. Moreover, the revelation of the 'betrayal' made, without his knowledge, by his bitter rivals in the SS, revealed his lamentable failure to exercise control within the sphere of which he was the nominal head. On 9 November he complained bitterly to Lammers:

My thankless task is continually made extremely difficult because of the interference by all sorts of agencies in the sphere of my responsibilities. My public statements are thus brought in doubt and lose their value.

I will have to report to the Führer that I am no longer in the position to fulfil my responsibilities with success, if *this* interference does not stop. There must remain no doubt that I alone am authorised to be the representative of the Führer for Church affairs.[43]

In a desperate effort to assert his authority, Kerrl summoned the

Lutheran provincial bishops to his Ministry and, after a six-hours'
session, coerced them into issuing a declaration dissociating themselves from the action of the Confessing Church.

We hereby declare that the Circular published by the 'Provisional
Church Administration' on 27 September 1938 regarding the holding
of services, containing a 'Liturgy of Intercession' because of the approaching danger of war, is repudiated by us on religious and patriotic grounds,
and has been refused in our churches. We condemn the attitude made
public here most strongly and dissociate ourselves entirely from those
persons responsible for this publication.[44]

At the same meeting, Kerrl also laid before the bishops a new set
of regulations for the administration of the Church which would
ensure a stricter control over disaffected priests. Immediate suspension from their offices, including the cessation of their stipends,
was ordered for the authors of the liturgy, and a few days later
Kerrl wrote to Heydrich:

Now is the time for an annihilating blow against the treacherous
organization of the radical Confessing movement [*Bekenntnisfront*].
The whole German people is united in their prejudice against these
traitors. Also for the first time the bishops (including the moderate
Confessing movement Bishops) have denounced the Provisional Church
Leadership, so that severe measures against the Confessing movement
could not be ascribed to anti-Christian hostilities, as on previous occasions.[45]

In his anger Kerrl also suggested that the provisional Church
leadership and the provincial Brethren Councils should be forcibly
dissolved; but Hitler, possibly recalling the outcry which had
arisen over Niemöller's arrest, refused to sanction such steps merely
to save Kerrl's face.

The majority of Evangelical churchmen were deeply shocked by
the implications of the whole affair. Their sympathies had been
wholly with the Sudetenlanders, and now, in fear of being mis-
judged by their fellow countrymen, they hastily dissociated themselves from the Confessing Church. Their reaction was further
quickened when Karl Barth, in an open letter to his Czech friend,
Joseph Hromadka, declared that every Czech soldier who took

up arms against Nazism could be counted as a soldier of the Church of Jesus Christ. Even Barth's staunchest supporters were horrified by his words. But the damage was done. Under a barrage of accusations and vilification, the Confessing Church members grew more and more confused between their political and their theological loyalties. Their resolution weakened and their morale sank to its lowest ebb.

By November 1938 when, under the leadership of Goebbels, the notorious 'Crystal Night' attack was launched against the Jewish community, their discomfiture was painfully apparent. Despite the burning of 177 synagogues and the arrest of 20,000 Jews, the Church leaders, both Catholic and Evangelical, turned a blind eye. Exhausted and demoralized by their previous efforts, they fell silent even in the face of such monstrous outrages.[46] The only voice raised in dissent was that of Fr Lichtenberg, the Catholic Provost of Berlin, who on the following day led his congregation in prayer for the persecuted non-Aryans among the German community. His action immediately made him a marked man, and destined him to suffer imprisonment and finally death for his courageous act. None the less, his example was promptly followed by the Evangelical Pastor Grüber, who established an office in Berlin where Christian Jews could receive advice and assistance in escaping from the country, until he himself was arrested in December 1940.[47] It was left to Karl Barth to point the final warning, that 'the burning of the synagogues is only the first step to treating the churches in the same way. The abolition of the *Old* Testament from the school curriculum has laid the axe to the roots of the Church which is founded upon the *New*'.[48]

Meanwhile, in the ranks of the Catholic Church, there was a similar sense of pessimism and weariness with the whole interminable struggle. Though the protection of the Concordat still left the outward semblance of autonomy, the Catholic hierarchy were painfully aware of their loss of support among the laity and of the increasing respect evinced for the apparently invincible progress of Nazism. The protests contained in the pastoral letters of the Catholic bishops against the abolition of church schools, against the severity of restrictions imposed upon the Churches' organizations and the Church press, and against the frequent police measures taken against individuals, did little but show that the Church was losing ground.

Particularly shocking to loyal Catholics was the treatment meted out to Bishop Sproll of Rottenburg in Württemberg. In sermons and public speeches he had many times expressed his opposition to the Nazi régime, and at the time of the plebiscite approving the *Anschluss* with Austria he had refused to vote. In retaliation a Nazi-organized demonstration in July 1938 stormed and ransacked his episcopal residence,[49] and, despite the protests of his fellow bishops, he was banished from his diocese until the end of the war on the grounds that his presence was a 'permanent menace to the public peace'.[50] In reply to a protest from Cardinal Bertram, Kerrl wrote:

> The German Reich cannot permit a German bishop of the Roman Catholic Church to go unpunished in that he set such a provocative example by deliberately refusing to carry out his duties as a citizen. Since the Holy See has refused to agree to the repeated suggestions that Bishop Sproll should be persuaded to give up his bishopric, although his behaviour has been such as to make his further activity there impossible, I have ordered that, in the interests of peace and order in Church and State, Bishop Sproll should be forbidden to reside in Württemberg any longer. I regret that the Bishop's conduct has forced this action upon me and believe that I am supported by Your Eminence and the whole German episcopate in trusting that the same thing will not happen again.[51]

Sproll was, in fact, the only German bishop to be so maltreated, but the example was not encouraging.

Equally discouraging was the series of events which transpired in Austria during its first year under Nazi rule. Following the enthusiastic welcome to the new régime given by the Austrian Catholic bishops, their optimism quickly turned to disillusionment and dismay. Hitler was no more impressed by their subservience than he had been with the German Catholic bishops' willingness to sign the Concordat of 1933. In the new Greater German Reich, the Austrian Catholics were of little political significance, and in July 1938, less than four months after the

Anschluss, Hitler decided to revoke the Austrian Concordat and to deprive the Church of any legal status.

> Since Austria is no longer an independent state after its reunification with the German Reich and has lost its position in international law, the Austrian Concordat is extinguished on its own account. The reunification does *not* have the result of extending the German Concordat which is composed purely for the conditions of Germany proper [*Alt-Reich*] and therefore can find no appropriate application in the different circumstances of Austria. The result is that at the present time Austria finds itself without a Concordat.[52]

Nazi policy was flexible and was always determined by tactical necessity. The Reich Commissar in Vienna, *Gauleiter* Bürckel, was accordingly given a free hand to implement as many of the Nazi regulations as would wipe out Church resistance in the individual dioceses, which simply meant the rapid institution of prohibitions to bring the country into line with the situation in Germany proper.

In the summer of 1938 the Austrian Catholic educational institutions were subjected to the same stringent measures as had already been imposed in Germany. The theological faculties of Salzburg, Graz and Innsbruck were closed. 'In view of the necessity of educating the whole youth in the spirit of National Socialism', private schools were banned, hostels, kindergartens and orphanages were forced to shut down, and 'National' schools replaced church schools. [53] Youth activities were severely curtailed. Pastoral care in the hospitals and other welfare institutions was restricted. Catholic organizations, such as the large *Volksbund der Katholiken Oesterreichs*, were dissolved and their property was confiscated. The Catholic publishing houses were closed. In May 1938 sixty Austrian Roman Catholic priests were arrested on charges of immoral conduct. A year later a law was passed abolishing the compulsory church tax and making all contributions voluntary; this, it was alleged, was to save the national exchequer 25–30 million Reich Marks, though the Churches' budgets were still to be approved by the State; there was no intention of introducing complete separation.[54] The Austrian marriage laws were altered by the introduction of civil marriage and new procedures for

I

divorce. A full-scale anti-clerical campaign was launched in the press, and new recruits to the Austrian Hitler Youth were sedulously instructed in Nazi doctrines. Some idea of the sort of teaching to which Austria was subjected can be gained from the following series of notes prepared for a propaganda speech.

1. Christianity is a religion for slaves and idiots, for 'The last shall be first and the first last' . . . 'Blessed are the poor in spirit'. 2. Christianity equals Communism. 3. According to Christianity, negroes and Germans are equal. 4. The Church is international. 5. The New Testament is a Jewish fraud of four Evangelists, for the doctrine is exactly copied from the Indian doctrine of a jishnu Christa. 6. The Church always works by violence and terror. Where is the love of one's neighbour and the love of one's enemies? It was not Charles the Great but the Catholic Church that through him massacred the Saxons. 7. Before Christianity German culture was at a high level which was destroyed only by Christianity . . . While the Romans had merely the hoe, the Germans were already using the plough. 8. In the Crusades German blood was shed uselessly. . . . 9. Christianity has always been alien and hostile to the German people and their unification. 10. The Bible is the continuation of the Talmud, which is a purely Jewish composition. Especially the Old Testament. 11. The Germans of Transylvania are Protestants exiled by Maria Theresa. 12. Joseph II and his successor were murdered by the Catholic Church. Poison in the heart. 13. All that is contrary to Christianity, even if it be of another race (Napoleon and Prince Eugene), is good. 14. Because the Catholic Church was very strong in 1648 the Austrians were again subdued. . . . 15. That constituted the most cruel counter-reformation, since in Austria 90 per cent were Protestants. 16. There is no such thing as a Christian culture. 17. Christianity is always undesired and is everywhere introduced by force. 18. Christianity corrupted the Germans because it introduced the ideas of adultery and theft hitherto unknown. 19. Evil passes; good abides. The Catholic Church will come to an end. 20. Christianity is a substitute Judaism; the Jews contrived it; its centre is in Rome. 21. Jesus was a Jew. 22. Contradictions in the genealogy of Christ as given in the Gospels. 23. Proof that Christ was not God; 'Woman, what have I to do with thee?' 24. How Christ dies (whimpering on the Cross) and how Planetta died ('Heil Hitler! Heil Germany!'). 25. The fourth commandment is simply a Jewish bargain (*do ut des*). 26. The Ten Commandments are the depository of the lowest human instincts. 27. A universal Messianic idea could only be found in

an inferior people; a pure race has no need of a Redeemer. 28. Nero did right in his persecution: he eradicated the Jewish spirit (Christianity). 29. The cult of the saints is ridiculous. When any one had his palm greased or was preeminently filthy he was pronounced a saint. 30. The Virgin Mary. The Immaculate Conception. 31. Miracles are proof of divinity. But Christianity says they need not be believed. 32. The Papacy is a swindle. The Pope claims to be God's representative on earth, but after Peter there was no Pope for 150 years. The Popes were always men of the baser sort. 'Only' Alexander vi, for example. 33. The Papacy of John. 34. Christianity is simply the mask of Judaism. 35. Galileo had to repudiate his discoveries under pressure of force, because it is written in the Bible. 'The sun goes round the earth'. 36. Christianity has always hindered the development of science, medicine, etc. 37. The sale of indulgences. 38. The *ius primae noctis*. Since the feudal lords were mostly ecclesiastics it was applied by them. 39. Ignatius Loyola was of Hebrew origin. 40. With the Jesuits all personality is suppressed. They become the blind instruments of the Pope. 41. The Catholic Church provoked the Thirty Years' War. 42. The strength of the Church and its inability to promote peace during the World War. Reason: destruction of German culture. 43. The Catholic Church opposes the national move-ment of the German people. 44. At present no more churches are being built; there is no one who wishes to do so (moral decadence of Christi-anity). Stadiums are being built instead (Berlin, Nürnberg). 45. The new eternal centre of the world is Nürnberg. Rome is waning. 46. If Germany no longer supports the Catholic Church, it is finished. 47. Destiny stands above God. 48. For us Germans the inactivity of eternal life is foolishness. 49. The 'infallibility' of the Pope? 50. Predestination, rites of the Church, the divine Trinity, original sin, etc. – what bosh![55]

In August 1938 detachments of the Party were ordered to make a survey of all the buildings, houses and hostels in the possession of 'the Churches, church organizations, Jews or politically implicated individuals', and local Party representatives were instructed to inform headquarters of the buildings needed for 'the local detach-ment of the Party, its affiliates or associated organizations, or for rest homes'.[56] Many Church properties, including the famous monastery of St Lamprecht, were confiscated by Party functionaries even before the outbreak of war. And in October, when the Austrian bishops in desperation were finally driven to protest, the Nazis provoked a riot in the main square outside St Stephen's

Cathedral in Vienna, culminating on the following day in the looting and burning of Cardinal Innitzer's palace.

These violent moves shocked the Austrian population to the core, coming as they did at a time when many people were striving to reconcile their long-established Catholicism with their new-found enthusiasm for Nazism. In fact, of course, there was nothing new in any of these repressive measures, all of which had already been applied on the other side of the border. Only the illusion died hard. From the Nazis' point of view, the one novelty in their Austrian Church policy lay in the decision to leave the organization of anti-clerical measures in the hands of the Reich Commissar, Bürckel, and to exclude the Ministry of Church affairs in Berlin from jurisdiction over the Austrian Church. There can be little doubt that this decision was not due to the improvised character of the Nazi administration of Austria, but stemmed simply from the determination of the Party leaders, particularly Bormann, to do everything possible to undermine Kerrl's influence and competency: by leaving Austrian Church affairs in the charge of local officials who were responsible only to the Party, the Ministry of Church Affairs was neatly circumvented and ignored.

Kerrl, not surprisingly, objected strongly. He complained directly to Hitler protesting against the decisions taken without his knowledge or approval, but Hitler refused to support him. And so the long series of Kerrl's political humiliations went on. But so far as the Churches were concerned, Kerrl or no Kerrl, the restrictions and persecutions continued, ruthlessly and inescapably.

In these disturbing circumstances, many leading churchmen were reluctantly obliged to conclude that collaboration with the Nazis was the only practical policy open to them to save the remnants of church life. In their anxiety not to be branded as opponents of Germany's national progress, and since they were largely in sympathy with much of Hitler's foreign policy, the Catholic bishops marked the return of the Sudetenland to Germany and the safeguarding of peace at Munich with a surprisingly cordial telegram to Hitler:

The great deed of safeguarding international peace moves the German episcopate, acting in the name of Catholics of all the German dioceses, respectfully to tender their congratulations and thanks and to order a festive peal of bells on Sunday.

In the name of the Cardinals of
Germany, Archbishop Cardinal Bertram.[57]

The bells were indeed rung and services of thanksgiving were held, for the 'rescue' of so many people of German nationality, most of them Catholics, was not unreasonably held to be a cause for rejoicing. Six months later, immediately after his election to the Papacy in March 1939, Pope Pius XII, with his long familiarity with Germany and in the hope of maintaining the improved atmosphere, sent a friendly letter of greetings to Hitler.[58] Even the seizure of Czechoslovakia, which followed a few days later, aroused no opposition. It was reported from the Vatican that, despite strong French pressure, the Pope had refused to protest against the 'historic processes in which, from the political point of view, the Church is not interested'.[59]

In April 1939 Hitler's fiftieth birthday was similarly celebrated by special services and prayers throughout the country by the ringing of church bells, and by a telegram of greetings from Cardinal Bertram. The Church press marked the occasion by praising the achievements of Hitler in the renewal of German life, and in return by order of Goebbels' Propaganda Ministry, the attacks on the Pope and the Vatican in the secular press were temporarily suspended.

In the Evangelical Churches, the 'German Christians', backed up by Kerrl, also saw fit to issue a declaration of support for Hitler who 'had brought Germany out of slavery and depression into a time of freedom and glorious greatness'.[60] The Thuringian Evangelical Church had in February taken the first step towards abetting the Nazi campaign against the German Jews by a decree forbidding the admission of Jews to their Church. In April 1939 the *National Church Union of German Christians* issued the notorious 'Godesberg Declaration' which called for the full expurgation of Jewry from the Church.

The central questions of the religious differences of opinion are as follows:

(a) What is the relation between politics and religion and between the national socialist ideology and the Christian faith?

We give the answer to this question:

National Socialism attacks any claim to political power in the Churches, and makes the native [*artgemässe*] national socialist ideology prerequisite for all. In doing this it is carrying on Martin Luther's work in the ideological–political field and helps us thereby to a true understanding of the Christian faith in its religious aspects.

(b) What is the relation between Judaism and Christianity? Is Christianity derived from Judaism and has therefore become its continuation and completion, or does Christianity stand in opposition to Judaism?

We answer:

Christianity is in irreconcilable opposition to Judaism.

(c) Is Christianity by its nature above the states and above the nations?

We answer:

A supranational or international church of a roman catholic or a world-protestant type is a political denial of the nature of Christianity. The true Christian faith can only develop within the given orders of creation.[61]

A month later the provincial churches of the 'German Christian' movement announced their intention of establishing a special institution 'for the research and removal of Jewish influences on the Church life of the German people', to be set up in Eisenach under the direction of Professor Walter Grundmann.[62] Their anti-semitic publications were, however, so obviously designed to demonstrate the loyalty of the 'German Christians' to the Nazi State that Rosenberg refused either to recognize or to support this initiative.

In this atmosphere of doubt and uncertainty, the Churches took no action as the diplomatic situation in Europe grew heavy with crisis throughout the summer of 1939. In general, churchmen were inclined to believe the Nazi reports of Polish mistreatment of Germans in the Polish corridor and upper Silesia, including the 'cruel fate' of German pastors allegedly expelled from Polish cities. Their isolation from churchmen of other nations, and their unwillingness to make any move that might endanger their own church organization inevitably obliged them to accept the Nazi point of view.[63] The whole sorry process of accommodation and compromise that had gone on since 1933 now reached its logical conclusion when, in face of Hitler's attack on Poland in September 1939, the Churches stood dumb and confused, unable to raise a voice of protest, spiritless and without initiative. The Nazis' war of attrition had at last triumphantly achieved its miserable objective.

9 The Uneasy Armistice

'The best soldier is a pious soldier.' –
ADOLF HITLER

I

The outbreak of war brought about a change in Nazi Church policy. The preoccupation of the authorities in mobilizing the German people behind the war effort necessitated the abandonment of policies likely to lead to internal strife or tension, and, since Church matters were considered of minor importance in comparison with the large issues now at stake, a truce was called in the Church conflict. Hitler himself, fully alive to the need for national unity, commanded that 'no further action should be taken against the Evangelical and Catholic Churches for the duration of the war',[1] and ten months later he ordered the suspension of all non-essential measures that might lead to a worsening of relations between the Churches and the State and Party.[2]

The Nazis had to reckon with the fact that, despite all Rosenberg's efforts, only 5 per cent of the population registered themselves in the 1939 census as no longer connected with the Christian Churches: 3.5 per cent declared themselves to be 'God believers' (*gottgläubig*) and another 1.5 per cent atheists. The remaining 95 per cent of the eighty million people of the greater German Reich were still registered as members of the Catholic or Evangelical Churches, and even the majority of the three million Nazi Party members still paid the Church taxes and registered themselves as Christians. The united support of all these millions of German

Christians was needed for the war effort if Hitler's plans for Germany were to be fulfilled. According to Goering, it was Hitler's view that

If religious belief is a help, it can only be an advantage, and any disturbances in this connection could conceivably affect the soldier's inward strength. The main concern now was that every German should do his duty and that every soldier should, if need be, go to his death bravely.[3]

Furthermore, it was fully appreciated that measures against the Churches might cause dissension at home, and that, if the news of such steps reached the outside world, it might create an impression of disunity within Germany. Even Goebbels, with his notorious record of anticlericalism, switched to the view that there should be a complete cessation of activities against the Church, being now convinced, as frequent entries in his diary show, that the church question would be best left in abeyance until the war was over.[4]

The mood of the German people was also not to be discounted. As Dr Stewart Herman observed,

The keenly felt catastrophe of another World War, following so closely on the heels of the last, had the effect of sobering the German people and placing them under spiritual pressures which gradually evoked a hunger for the substantial bread of a real religion rather than the inadequate cake of political ideology. The Party was as prompt as the Church to recognize the fact and to try to satisfy it.[5]

The Party agencies, especially the Ministry of Propaganda, brought considerable pressure to bear on the Churches to declare their whole-hearted support of the war effort, and even threatened reprisals against church newspapers that did not devote themselves to that end. On 7 September the Gestapo prohibited all church meetings for the next few weeks, lest the congregations should be influenced by defeatist ideas similar to those spread abroad by the authors of the *Fürbitteliturgie* a year earlier, though commemoration services for Germans living in Poland who had suffered persecution for their nationality were approved and even encouraged.[6]

Most churchmen, like the rest of their fellow-countrymen, were torn between loyalty to their country and a desire for peace. The clergy, while recognizing that war was no longer a cause for popular enthusiasm but could only be regarded as a national disaster, were anxious not to appear as what Bismarck called the 'enemies of the Reich' by displaying less fervour for the war effort than other members of the community. And it is not improbable that they also cherished the hope that the Nazis might reward their co-operation by easing the persecution of the institutional life of their churches. Such considerations certainly dominated their public attitude in the first months of hostilities. On 2 September the German Evangelical Church proclaimed:

Since yesterday our German people have been called on to fight for the land of their fathers in order that German blood may be reunified with German blood. The German Evangelical Church stands in true fellowship with the fate of the German people. The Church has added to the weapons of steel her own invincible weapons from the Word of God: the assurance of faith that our people and each individual is in God's hand, and the power of prayer which strengthens us in days of good and evil. So we unite in this hour with our people in intercession for our Führer and Reich, for all the armed forces, and for all who do their duty for the fatherland.[7]

A few days later the Catholic bishops likewise called upon their following to support the war effort:

In this decisive hour we encourage and admonish our Catholic soldiers, in obedience to the Führer, to do their duty and to be ready to sacrifice their whole existence. We appeal to the faithful to join in ardent prayer that God's providence may lead this war to blessed success for Fatherland and people.[8]

There was no denunciation by any of the German churches against the invasion of Poland nor against the methods employed in the *Blitzkrieg* which brought victory so swiftly to the German armies. Indeed, at the Harvest Festival at the end of September, Bishop Marahrens of Hanover gave thanks not only for the agricultural harvest but for

another no less rich harvest with which we have been blessed. The fight on the Polish battlefields is ended, as we can proudly read in the reports from the front. Our German brothers and sisters in Poland have been delivered from all horrors and pressures of body and soul from which they have suffered so much. We thank God that He has granted our armies a quick victory.[9]

At the suggestion of the Ministry of Church Affairs, church bells throughout the country were rung for a week in celebration, and pastors and priests flocked in to volunteer as chaplains for the victorious armed forces.

Despite the evidence of Nazi atrocities against Catholic priests and laymen in Poland, details of which were not only known to those engaged in the Polish campaign but were broadcast by the Vatican Radio, the German Catholic bishops still continued their support of the war effort and still urged their congregations to 'fulfil their duty to Führer, *Volk* and Fatherland'. The German aggressions of 1940 and 1941 similarly called forth patriotic exhortations to show that the Church

assents to the just war, especially one designed for the safeguarding of state and people, that she prays for a victorious termination of the present war in a peace beneficial for Germany and Europe and rouses the faithful to fulfil their civil and military virtues.[10]

Regardless, however, of these signs of ready compliance and in face even of Hitler's express commands, a nucleus of the Nazi hierarchy, anxious not to let slip the opportunities offered by the circumstances of war, steadily continued their campaign to cripple the Churches while they were in no position to defend themselves. At the very time when the Church leaders were urging their followers to give their undivided support to the war effort, the Gestapo was scheming to undermine their influence by measures that could be justified by the exigencies of war without appearing to be aimed specifically against the Churches.

In a lengthy report submitted to Hitler in October 1939, Heydrich weighed up the position and outlined ways and means of exploiting it.[11] The majority of Church people were, he believed, loyally collaborating in the war effort, though a few well-known agitators among the pastors needed to be dealt with. The dissolution of the Churches' lay organizations had restricted the influence of the clergy; the Church schools had been abolished; religious instruction was reduced to a minimum; Church influence in film and radio had been eliminated; and the number of ordinands was falling rapidly. Moreover, the Church lacked united leadership. After the failure of their attempt to arouse opposition at the time of the Sudetenland crisis, churchmen were now keeping very quiet. The news of the Nazi–Soviet Pact had caused them some uncertainty, but whereas certain leading Catholics had expressed the hope that the pact might open the way for the evangelization of Russia, those who were opposed to the Nazi State had seen it as the beginning of the end for the Church in Europe unless England and France were able to overthrow the Reich.[12]

Heydrich did not attach much importance to the declarations of support made by the Church leaders. Indeed, he believed that most of them would probably practise some sort of passive resistance and would quietly sabotage the work of the Führer and Reich. But the clergy's influence over the civilians and dependents of men in the armed forces could be particularly dangerous, if it adopted a defeatist tone and laid stress on war as a punishment. Even if the Church leaders appeared to collaborate, their aim would be only to win concessions for themselves. And within the Evangelical Churches, with their overseas connection with World Protestantism and their regular contacts with Churches abroad, certain elements were known to favour a stand against the war. The Oxford Group too, with its stress on moral rearmament, needed watching because of its intimate connection with Englishmen of high standing.

Heydrich therefore suggested that anyone who was found guilty of sabotage, attempted subversion of the people or open resistance should, regardless of rank, be consigned to a concentration camp. In no circumstances should the Church be allowed to regain its former power; nor should pre-war measures against church organizations, religious societies or church schools be revoked. Should a hostile move be taken by any of the remaining organizations, they should be dissolved forthwith. Foreign travel should be forbidden to all members of religious orders and officials of religious sects. The state subsidies to the Churches should be scaled down and the Churches themselves should be more heavily taxed. Members of the armed forces should be under no compulsion to take part in church services. Denominational meetings, pilgrimages and other gatherings should be prohibited on grounds of transportation difficulties. Church welfare organizations, such as kindergartens, should be placed under Nazi direction and supervision, and other denominational organizations should be prohibited. The supply of newsprint to Church newspapers should be drastically reduced by rationing.

These measures, Heydrich believed, could be carried out quickly and without arousing opposition, and would prevent inter-denominational squabbles from sapping the strength of the rest of the German people, as they had done in the first World War. Blind support from the Church leaders could not be expected because of the very nature of their doctrines and international obligations. But the measures suggested offered a means of inducing church people to co-operate in Germany's hour of need and of crippling the political activity of the clergy.

Hitler presumably agreed, for, following the success of the German armies in Poland, and under the plea of war-time defence measures, new moves against the Churches were instigated which went much further than the exigencies of the war necessitated. In the main no resistance was encountered, and the Nazis' belief that churchmen could be persuaded to accept any sacrifices for the sake of the war effort was seen to be fully justified. Many Catholic Churches were closed down on the grounds that they were dangerously far from the air-raid shelters. Church bells, regardless of their historical or artistic value, were removed and melted down, leaving only the smallest to summon the faithful. By late 1939 the last of the Church publishing facilities were reduced almost to extinction. Many journals were obliged to dissolve because of lack of funds, and those that remained were directed to make no mention of political affairs but to concentrate exclusively on the certainty of victory. Religious journals were forbidden to advertise for subscriptions amongst the members of the armed forces, whose religious care was the concern solely of the appointed chaplains.[13] Efforts were made to sever connection between the local priest and his parishioners in the forces, and on 1 December 1939 the

Bavarian Gestapo forbade the sending of circular letters from home parishes, on the grounds of possible 'espionage'. Strict regulations were laid down as to the role of the chaplains, and any priest who joined the army in a role other than that of chaplain was forbidden to exercise his priestly office for the duration of the war. Goering as head of the *Luftwaffe*, went even further and refused to admit any chaplains at all within the ranks of the Air Force. In August 1940, arrangements for memorial services for those who had fallen in battle were taken out of the hands of the Churches and transferred to the charge of the *Gauleiters*.

In the following October, all pastors were required to sign a form promising not to hold services before 10 o'clock on the morning following an air-raid, or to ring their single remaining church bell until after 1.00 pm. And a month later, in a move directed against the Confessing Church, the Gestapo, in agreement with Hess and the Ministry of Labour, ordered that all ordinands, curates and assistant pastors who had been trained or ordained at any of the illegal theological colleges of the Confessing Church, and whose behaviour was held to exercise a disturbing influence on the population, should be considered as unemployed and allocated to some 'useful' employment.[14]

In the schools priests were forbidden to act as substitutes for laymen called up in the army. More theological institutions and universities were closed. Children evacuated from the large cities and placed in Nazi-run boarding institutions in the country were dissuaded from saying their prayers or from attending the local churches. A nation-wide card index was compiled by the Gestapo to facilitate action against the Jesuits.[15] In September 1940 the Ministry of Labour ordered that no more novices were to be allowed to join the religious orders.[16] A month later the Ministry of the Interior issued a new regulation forbidding the Churches to refuse burial in their churchyards for nonbelievers, since 'the churchyard regardless of its ownership, is a public institution available for any citizen as his last resting-place'.[17] Nor were the Churches allowed to charge a different scale of fees for believers and non-believers, or to refuse the tolling of bells at the funerals of those who had severed their connection with the Church.

Church holidays, such as Ascension Day or Corpus Christi, were ordered to be postponed to the Sunday following the festival, in order that a day's work should not be lost; but this injunction was largely ignored, many rural people simply stating that Ascension Day had always been a holiday and the crops still came up.[18]

Finally, Bormann, having expressed surprise to the Reich Finance Minister that the Churches had not been asked to contribute a much larger proportion of their wealth to the war-effort,[19] demanded that the Finance Ministry should cease to pay 24.5 million marks from the traditional Prussian state subsidies to the Evangelical Church and 9 million to the Catholic Church.[20]

News of this continued persecution of the churches quickly became known abroad, especially in Switzerland, the USA and Rome. The Vatican, particularly, already shocked by the Nazi treatment of the Catholic Church in Poland, received the news with deep foreboding. Pope Pius XII, as we have seen, had begun his reign with friendly overtures to the Nazi régime. But the failure of his last-minute attempts to preserve the peace, even at the expense of Polish territorial concessions, was a bitter disillusionment, that was still further increased by the news of the Nazi–Soviet Pact, which was as unpalatable as it was unwelcome. This alliance between the two revolutionary powers most hostile to the Church's interests, and the consequent *Blitzkrieg* destruction of Catholic Poland, were grievous blows. The relations between the Holy See and Berlin sank to a very low ebb.

In the first encyclical of his reign, *Summi Pontificatus*, issued on 20 October 1939, Pope Pius expressed sympathy and sorrow for all the people who had been drawn into the tragic abyss of war, but made no reference to German aggression. In reply to those who maintain that the Pope failed in his duty to denounce Nazi crimes and atrocities because of a certain sympathy for Hitler's authoritarian régime, it must be stressed that the Nazi hierarchy in Berlin never regarded the Pope as an ally. Indeed, the Gestapo was quick to declare the encyclical as an expression of hostility. In a letter to Hitler dated 10 November Müller, the head of the *Reichssicherheitshauptamt*'s section B IV (Political Churches), commented:

The Encyclical is directed explicitly against Germany, both in the ideological field and as regards the German–Polish confrontation. Its dangerous nature both for the internal and external scene needs no further mention.[21]

It was expected that the encyclical would be read from the pulpits throughout Germany on 5 November, but in fact it was read only in a few isolated cases – no doubt because of the heightened feeling of nationalist euphoria after the victory of Poland, in which German Catholics fully shared. The Gestapo, desirous that this welcome forebearance should not be jeopardized, resolved to act with caution.

I have given instructions, in line with previous regulations, that the reading of the Encyclical in the Churches is not to be prevented, but that all other forms of circulation, in particular in pamphlet form, are to be forbidden. The Reich Ministry for Public Enlightenment and Propaganda has prohibited any discussion of the Encyclical in the press, including the Church press.[22]

In the German Foreign Ministry, the change in the Vatican's attitude did not pass unnoticed. Despite the Pope's failure to condemn Germany's aggression in Poland, and despite his even more extraordinary letter of congratulation to Hitler of November 1939 after the Führer's escape from an alleged assassination attempt in Munich, the German Foreign Ministry refused to believe that the Pope was sympathetic to the Nazi cause. On the contrary, as was pointed out on 8 January 1940 by Woermann, the Under Secretary of State,

Several statements by the present Pope, such as the Encyclical *Summi Pontificatus* and his last Christmas address, are incompatible with the endeavours to reach an understanding. . . . On the Polish question, the Vatican has repeatedly taken Poland's side, as for example in the above mentioned Encyclical, in the solemn reception by the Pope on 30 September of the Polish colony led by Cardinal Hlond, and in a provocative address by Cardinal Hlond, who was allowed to use the Vatican radio for his purpose.[23]

It is therefore not surprising that neither Ribbentrop nor his officials were prepared to tolerate papal interference on such matters as the German treatment of Poland. The lack of success of the numerous protests submitted by the Nuncio was in fact due far more to the hostility of the Nazi authorities than to the alleged reluctance of Pope Pius XII to speak out.

Nevertheless, the Foreign Ministry had no wish for further unfriendly pronouncements from the Vatican, and considered that, for the duration of the war, it would be desirable not to embark on measures that would alienate the German Catholics from supporting the war effort.

It does not seem possible to change the basic problems within the scope of the Concordats, especially that of youth education, by reaching an understanding with the Vatican through negotiations for a new Concordat. Moreover, when the time is ripe, the upshot will probably be that we shall break off the Concordat and regulate the legal position of the Catholic Church in Germany ourselves. But, as long as the war continues, the time is not ripe for such a move.

It seems possible to achieve a certain degree of compromise, at least for the duration of the war; for us this appears desirable for reasons of foreign policy.[24]

This opinion was endorsed by Weizsäcker, the State Secretary, in a letter addressed to the German Ambassador to the Vatican on 25 January 1940:

I think we all agree that no general settlement can be reached at the present time. . . . The only thing to do at the moment is probably to avoid creating new points of friction and gradually to improve relations by attending to certain individual complaints. Naturally this must apply to both parties.[25]

Two months later, therefore, in March 1940, Ribbentrop visited Rome and made a special point of seeking an audience with the Pope. His purpose was two-fold: to attempt to prevent any open declaration by the Vatican against Nazi Germany, and to ensure that the Pope's influence was used to strengthen the nationalist – and hence the pro-Nazi – sympathies, of the German Catholics. With these ends in view, he informed the Pope that Hitler was still anxious to reach a settlement with the Catholic Church over outstanding questions:

The Führer was of the opinion that a basic settlement between National Socialism and the Catholic Church was quite possible. There was, however, no point in trying to settle the relations between these two by raising separate questions of one kind or another or by provisional agreements. Rather, they must eventually reach a comprehensive and, so to speak, secular settlement of their relations; this would then form a lasting basis for harmonious co-operation between them. However, the time had not yet arrived for such a settlement.[26]

Hitler, Ribbentrop claimed, was too engrossed in the war-time struggle for victory to devote his full attention to the problem, but as a prerequisite it would be necessary

that the Catholic clergy in Germany should abandon any kind of political activity and limit themselves solely to the cure of souls, the only activity that was in the clergy's province. The recognition of the necessity of such a radical separation, however, could not yet be considered to be the dominant view of Catholic clergymen in Germany . . . The Catholic clergy must be imbued with the realization that with National Socialism an entirely new form of political and national life had appeared in the world . . . In the opinion of the Führer, what mattered for the time being was to maintain the existing truce and, if possible, to expand it. In this respect Germany had made very considerable preliminary concessions. The Führer had quashed no less than 7,000 indictments of Catholic clergymen. Also, it should not be forgotten that the National Socialist State was spending one billion Reichsmarks annually on the Catholic Church; no other state could boast of such an achievement.[27]

The sincerity of Ribbentrop's attitude can, however, be measured by his refusal to listen to the carefully-prepared dossier of Papal complaints, particularly those relating to Poland. When Cardinal Maglione asked for permission to send to Warsaw a representative of the Nunciature in Berlin, Ribbentrop coldly replied that the General Government was still under military rule and that the admission of diplomatic representatives into Warsaw was not possible.

Attempts by the Papal Nuncio to intercede on humanitarian grounds for the safety of Catholic priests imprisoned in concentration camps, and for hostages held by the Germans in several of the occupied countries as well as for individual Catholic bishops and priests, were likewise rejected.[28] In July 1940, Weizsäcker informed the Nuncio that the Nunciatures in Brussels and

Amsterdam were to be closed.[29] Pressure was brought to bear by the Foreign Ministry on the Nuncio for the nomination of a German to fill a vacant bishopric in the former territory of Czechoslovakia, and the increasingly frequent complaints to the Foreign Ministry made by the Nuncio over the seizure of Church properties in the vast areas now controlled by Germany were politely but inexorably countered by promises of investigation, most of which came to nothing.[30]

The dilemma of the Papacy was a cruel one. Pius XII still entertained hopes of a compromise peace, and any criticism of Germany would, he believed, serve only to destroy the Vatican's potentiality as a diplomatic medium for the negotiation of peace. Moreover, any such pronouncement would inevitably be used as propaganda by Germany's enemies, who were eager to enlist the Papacy as an ally. On the other hand, information on German atrocities in Poland and elsewhere was rapidly accumulating. The Western Allies were not alone in demanding some form of moral protest, and the neutral countries, especially the USA, were openly complaining that, by failing to denounce German brutalities, the Pope was guilty of pro-Nazi sympathies. In the next three months the dilemma grew still more acute, following the invasion of Denmark and Norway, the onslaught against the Low Countries and France, the French humiliation and enforced armistice, and the egregious entry of Italy into the war. After one final abortive attempt at the end of June 1940 to initiate peace negotiations, Papal diplomacy fell silent.

Of the 'harmonious co-operation' of which Ribbentrop had spoken to the Pope there was no sign in the instructions issued by Heydrich in April 1940, to the commanders of the SD units as to the future treatment of the Catholic Church hierarchy. Heydrich ordered the maintenance of the strictest control. The degree of surveillance to be imposed on the Catholic bishops both over their private lives and over their official activities, was unprecedented even by Nazi standards.

1. All material suggesting that the bishops are using the Nuncio's courier service to maintain contact with the Vatican is to be carefully collected and sent to headquarters.

2. Trustworthy contact men are to be found who can determine the identity of the episcopal and Vatican couriers.

3. All internal conflicts between the Bishops and the Nuncio, among the Bishops themselves or their collaborators or their inferior clergy, as well as all personal weaknesses of the representatives of the Church hierarchy, are to be noted and reported. Reliable contact men must be found in every diocesan office.

4. The Bishops' quinquennial reports, especially those issued since 1933, are if possible to be obtained. In any action [i.e. police raids] particular note should be taken of this point.

5. Lists of candidates for Bishoprics should be obtained.

6. The minutes of Diocesan synods should always be sent here [i.e. to the *Reichssicherheitshauptamt*] by the quickest means.

7. The particular responsibilities entrusted to each Bishop at the Fulda Bishops' Conference are to be discovered. Each local SD detachment should remember to pay attention to the national scope of those activities for which Bishop in its area is responsible. The SD detachment in Mainz has thus particular responsibility for information about the national activities relating to Catholic Youth Work. The SD detachment in Berlin has the most important task of collecting information about Catholic Press services. The SD detachment in Karlsruhe has likewise to concern itself with information on Catholic charitable works.

8. Inside each diocese exact knowledge must be obtained about the persons responsible for each department of the diocesan office.

9. The greatest importance should be placed on information on the diocesan offices, especially on the bishop's own staff.

10. Besides this, of course, in any actions [i.e. police raids] attention should be paid to the diocesan archives and the bishop's secret files.

11. Each detachment should pay attention to the Deans, as the eyes and ears of the Bishops. Their annual reports to the Bishops are of the utmost value as a source of information.

12. A widespread network of informants should be set up among the lower clergy, so that, if contact men or other agents are removed, replacements can be found and a complete and thorough information service can be maintained.

Since these opponents are of such importance, I wish the inspectors of the Security Police and the SD to pay particular attention in their inspections to this area and the questions raised above.[31]

Confiscation and sequestration of church property were always an effective means of attacking the Churches' position. As early as 1937 Himmler had made plans for the expropriation of church properties, with a view to using them for Nazi purposes.[32] In that year he had instigated SS moves to take possession of the historical Cathedral of Quedlinburg, the burial place of the 'Germanic hero' Henry the Lion, for use in ceremonies of a Germanic and non-Christian nature. In 1939 he founded a special society, known as the Reich Society for Popular Welfare and Aid to Settlers (*Reichsverein für Volkspflege und Siedlerhilfe*), with the express purpose of taking over the Churches' institutions in the welfare field and transferring them to Nazi control. In conjunction with the government authorities and the Gestapo, the first steps to this end were taken in the Rhineland in January 1939, when Church organizations owning or controlling charitable institutions were compelled to dismiss their executives and to appoint the Reich Society as trustees. Thereafter the property so acquired could be transferred to other use as the Party decided – to the Army for instance, or to Nazi welfare or other organizations. Between January and June 1939, under the direction of SS Group Leader Hildebrandt, some 20 Church institutions were thus dealt with, including a Catholic retreat house which was turned into a Nazi maternity home, and a monastery which was converted to a political training school. By April 1940 it was reported that in Wiesbaden alone property worth 30 million Reichsmarks had been seized from the Catholic Church and transferred to the German State.[33]

This wholesale seizure of Church property was made easier by the support given to the project both by Himmler and by the *Reichssicherheitshauptamt*. Himmler regarded the sequestrations as an effective device in the campaign against the 'dead hand' of the Churches, which, he sourly noted, still possessed large land holdings to the value of at least 60 milliard marks.

It must be explicitly stated that this new organization had a purely political purpose, namely the destruction of the complete property holdings of the Churches which had been purloined over the centuries and their return to the possession of the German Reich.[34]

No sooner had the rump state of Czechoslovakia been seized by the Nazis than Himmler's emissaries, in the name of the Reich Society for Popular Welfare, were dispatched to the newly won territories to evaluate all Church property and all property owned by Jews. Since both the Christian Churches and the Jews could, in Himmler's opinion, be charged with enmity to the State, their goods could be justifiably seized. Should legal difficulties arise, he suggested, a compulsory trusteeship could be established in accordance with the new regulations for land reform. It was a cunning and plausible piece of trickery, but in the event it came to nothing, for Hitler's decision of September 1939 halted measures against the Churches and brought Himmler's plans to a temporary stand-still.

A significant development in the early war years was the further weakening of Kerrl's authority. After his discomfiture at the hands of the SS over the affair of the *Fürbitteliturgie* in October 1938, Kerrl complained to Lammers of further usurpation of his office. Bürckel, the Reich Commissar in Austria, had, he asserted, been conducting negotiations with the Austrian Catholic Bishops behind his back, and Bishop Berning had deliberately circumvented his authority by petitioning the Reich Chancellery direct. All his efforts to strengthen control over the Evangelical Church had, he complained, been constantly sabotaged by the refusal of Hess and the Party Chancellery to approve his suggestions.[35]

Throughout 1939 Hitler refused to see Kerrl and returned no answer to a lengthy letter which Kerrl addressed to him requesting permission to present a memorandum dedicated 'to the Führer on his 50th birthday'.[36] This memorandum outlined Kerrl's policy for the reconciliation of Nazism and Christianity by means of a clearly defined differentiation between ideology and religion whereby the State and the Church would each be allotted its proper sphere of activity. Though Hitler never replied, Kerrl still persisted with his plans. In late 1939 he prepared yet another memorandum on 'the tasks and purposes of National Socialist leadership of the People in the religious question', in which he defended his view that the German people should have a German church, not under the control of a self-seeking priesthood, but as part of the beneficent provisions of the National Socialist State.

Only thus, he claimed, could Luther's call for the separation of politics and religion at last be brought to reality.[37]

Writing in September to Dr Stapel, one of his 'German Christian' friends, Kerrl stated that for fifteen years he had been working on a book setting out the scientific basis of National Socialism, the boundaries of reason and ideology, and the need for the Christian religion ascertainable through the power of faith. Unfortunately, he complained, he had not received the co-operation from his Party colleagues that he deserved, some of whom were campaigning not only against the political elements of Christianity but against any participation by Party members in any Christian denomination.[38]

His book, from which long passages were read to his staff, was intended to be a counter-attack against Rosenberg's *Myth*. Kerrl's hope was by this book to convince Hitler to issue appropriate commands to his Party henchmen to alter their policy in accordance with Kerrl's wishes. But Kerrl was neither able to persuade, nor even to see Hitler face to face, despite his faithful services as one of Hitler's earliest followers. Nor was his ambition to hold the rank of *Reichsleiter* satisfied, for the opposition of his rivals to such an appointment was far too strong.

From the fiasco of the experiment with the Reich Church Commissioners, Kerrl drew the conclusion that a full-scale revision of the Evangelical Church's structures was needed to ensure that a unified Evangelical Church would become a powerful support for the National Socialist movement. For that purpose he had prepared plans for a new constitution for the German Evangelical Church, which unfortunately had had to be abandoned with the outbreak of war.

A few months later, despite Hitler's injunction, a new and sweeping proposal, backed by Kerrl, was put forward by Dr Engelke, a leading 'German Christian' and the deputy of Reich Bishop Müller.

Suggestion

To the Führer and Reich Chancellor Adolf Hitler:

The Evangelical Church transfers itself to you with all its possessions, lands, buildings and institutions.

It thereby desires to prove that it wishes to be considered as nothing apart from the State, but rather feels itself bound up with the prosperity and fate of the State. It would bring to an end the unfortunate processes of the past by which the church became a separate state within the State, and often became a power opposed to the State.

The Church makes this transfer at the present time because it desires to show its deep gratitude that you have brought our German people from the depths and weakness to the height of power and world-importance, that you have placed our economy on a new basis, which has not only done away with the unemployment that destroys men's souls, but will solve all social problems. Above all, you have wakened the physical and spiritual powers of achievement of our people and unified them so that this wonderful Great-Germany was made possible by means of this war and victory.

The Church makes this transfer in the unshakeable confidence that the state needs positive Christianity, according to your manifold assurances that the powers which come from the Christian belief may be productive of internal uplift that the undoubted religious need of the largest portion of our people may have a further right of spiritual comfort. . . .

In our position as Evangelical Christians we have internal freedom to place our Church, our teachings, and ourselves under strict examination to learn from history and from the present, and in particular to exclude every influence of Jewish thinking on Christianity.

God granted the German people a reformation in the person of Martin Luther, which was of great importance not only for the German people, but for many others, especially the Nordic peoples.

We are of the firm opinion that God has given a new task to people in your person, to overcome finally all opposition of state, our people and church, and to solve the problem of the schism in the church.

Just as we are certain that every attempt at religious compulsion would bring about new schisms, so are we certain that the deep thankfulness for Great Germany which God has given us through you will make all true Germans willing to forego their old prejudices. . . .

Our constituency waits with longing for the word which will solve the Church problem. Out of deepest gratitude to you for giving us the Great-Germany of today, out of fervent love for our people, we beg you to grant unity for at least the evangelical part of the church in our nation.

Schwerin, 10.6.40[39]

This was simply an attempt to restore the situation of 1918. Adolf Hitler, like Kaiser Wilhelm II, was to be elevated to the supreme headship of the German Evangelical Church, and was to assume the position of *Summus Episcopus*. It was, commented Rosenberg, an 'eleventh-hour attempt to salvage the complete bankruptcy of the Evangelical Church by transferring it to the National Socialist State'.[40] The fact that Kerrl and his supporters could in all seriousness make such a preposterous offer reveals how far they had lost touch with the realities of Nazi Church policies.

Hitler refused to sanction these plans, and Kerrl's opponents in the Nazi hierarchy seized on the opportunity to discredit him yet further. As we have already seen, after the outbreak of war Heydrich pressed for an increase of police control over church activities; Goebbels attempted to impose regulations on the issuing of denominational leaflets and tracts; and the local *Gauleiters* instigated measures which Kerrl regarded as encroaching on his authority. But these vindictive actions were mere pinpricks in comparison with the perpetual running feud between Kerrl on the one hand and Rosenberg and Bormann on the other.

Rosenberg's animosity was undoubtedly increased by the check on his own activities brought about by the signing of the Nazi–Soviet Pact. Years of propaganda against the perils of the Bolshevik menace were suddenly sacrificed for reasons of state, and the press was now instructed to celebrate the traditional friendship of the German and Russian peoples as though the anti-Communist campaign had all been a misunderstanding and the Bolsheviks were the most loyal of Russians.[41] In his discomfiture, Rosenberg made a desperate attempt to win back some of his authority by preparing a plan to bring under his control all the ideological and propaganda activities both of the Party and of the State.

War is a struggle for the soul and character of the people. The Party dare not let *this* opportunity for leadership slip out of its hands. Reports from the regions indicate that the churches are rebuilding their strength, not for the direction of souls but for their confusion. On our side we have only such minor figures as Kerrl and Rust. What we need is to bring the unity of the National Socialist ideology for Party and State under one authority, to prevent any divisions in the ranks. . . . Our task would be to train selected officers to understand the historical importance of our struggle, and to place them in the barracks and camps in order to secure the leadership in the war for the soul and character of the people. . . .

The ideological dispute looks like being stepped up by the circumstances of the war. The Church presses are working hard to produce tracts, sermons and collections of psalms, which are pouring out to the front-line troops and in which the Churches are in effect preaching sermons which amount to deliberate sabotage.[42]

In Rosenberg's view, Kerrl was completely unsuited to be left in charge of the counter-attack. Commenting to Hess on Kerrl's letter to Dr Stapel mentioned above, which by some means had fallen into his hands, Rosenberg accused Kerrl of damaging the Party by his inability to comprehend the force of the National Socialist faith or its influence on the people. Despite Hitler's interdict, Kerrl was still trying to coerce the different factions to unite in a single State Church; such a policy must be checked.[43] Only by the granting of complete authority to himself, as the Deputy of the Führer for such matters, could the unity of National Socialist ideology be safeguarded.[44]

Rosenberg's plan was submitted to the various ministries, but there, not surprisingly, it met with considerable opposition especially from those who resented his attempt to re-establish his position at their expense.[45] At a meeting held on 9 February 1940, under the chairmanship of Lammers at which Goebbels, Kerrl, Rust, Rosenberg, Ley, Weizsäcker and Heydrich were all present, a lengthy discussion took place, but little agreement was reached. Kerrl refused to approve the plan unless Church matters were removed from Rosenberg's jurisdiction, and he vigorously defended his own opinion that the support of the Churches should be encouraged rather than suppressed.[46] Rosenberg, he contended, was known to the people as an exponent of anti-clerical, anti-Christian views, and his proposed appointment could only result in serious disturbances which in war-time should be avoided at all costs.

Kerrl's views were supported by Ribbentrop and the Foreign Ministry, where antipathy to Rosenberg was deeply entrenched, but the Party Chancellery, and in particular Bormann, whose influence in matters concerned with the Churches grew steadily during the war years, were all in favour of Rosenberg's plan. Whereas Hess, Bormann's nominal superior had thrown his influence mainly on the side of compromise, Bormann, as we have seen, consistently adopted a more intransigent line. After Hess's flight to Scotland in May 1941, Bormann was promoted to become 'Leader of the Party Chancellery' and, later, Hitler's secretary. From then on, he, almost alone amongst the Nazi satraps, was in daily contact with Hitler at the Führer's war-time headquarters, and the evidence shows that he used his increased authority to urge further acts of persecution against the Churches. Under his direction, new discriminatory measures were taken against the clergy, as well as new administrative limitations of church activities and new acts of spoliation of church property. Against such formidable opposition, Kerrl had little hope of success. In May 1940 he wrote to Lammers:

Unfortunately I can only presume that objections to the principles on which I have been operating are due to personal antagonism. Although I repeatedly tried at the beginning of the war to arrange a meeting with the Führer's deputy [Hess], this was refused in so forceful a manner that I felt myself obliged to make a verbal report to the Führer. But since this interview has not yet been granted to me, the conflict still remains.[47]

In turn, Bormann complained that Kerrl's obstinacy was getting out of hand, and threatened to seek Hitler's decision himself. 'How the Führer will decide I have little doubt.'[48]

Both Rosenberg and Bormann were undoubtedly strengthened by the assurance that their attitude was shared by Hitler himself. On 19 January 1940 Rosenberg noted in his diary that:

The Führer said it had been his great mistake to try to establish a unified Evangelical Church as a counterweight against the Romans. He had previously had certain impressions which he had brought from his Austrian background, where the Protestants had been a national Church. ...

The Christian-Jewish pestilence is now reaching its end. It is truly horrifying to think that there could be a religion which professed

251

literally to eat its God at the communion table. Furthermore 'good works' were only 'effective' when one was in the 'condition of grace'. But the Church decided that too. ...

I remarked that soon one man would be able to carry out a new Reformation, but not Hanns Kerrl – a remark that caused general laughter.[49]

And Hess in a letter to Goering in the following April, very succinctly stated that

The Führer has not only abandoned the originally much-prized plan of creating a Reich Church, but he now opposes it absolutely.[50]

Kerrl's plans were thus finally repudiated, and with their repudiation came an increasing diminution of his authority. On 4 October 1940 Lammers informed Kerrl that his quarrel with the Nazi leaders in the occupied territories had been decided against him.

Dear Party Comrade Kerrl:

At my last audience with the Führer, he expressed the wish that you should practice the greatest reserve with regards to church-political questions in the occupied territories and in those areas incorporated or annexed into the Reich since 1938, in which the Reich Concordat does not apply (Austria, Memel, Sudetenland, the Protectorate of Bohemia and Moravia, Danzig–West Prussia, the Warthegau, the General Government of Poland, Eupen and Malmedy). Where possible, the direction in Church–political matters should be left to the Reich Governors or to those who are politically responsible for those areas. If you think your intervention is necessary, please obtain the Führer's decision through me.[51]

A month later Bormann categorically stated that in Hitler's view the fragmentation of the churches would facilitate the ideological struggle against Christianity:

The Führer, who, as you know, no longer wants an Evangelical Reich Church, yesterday again decided that Reich Minister Kerrl should restrict his activity to Germany proper [*Alt-Reich*]. In no circumstances should he make decisions about church affairs in the new territories. Otherwise the *Gauleiters* of Austria and of the Warthegau etc. would not be in a position to avail themselves of the possibilities for ideological work which are offered in areas where the Concordat does not apply. With these areas outside the Concordat's terms, Reich Minister Kerrl should have nothing more to do.[52]

Kerrl's waning authority was thus restricted to Germany proper, and even there he was bedevilled by the inroads of the SS, the Propaganda Ministry and various other ministries who, on the plea of war-time necessity, claimed increasing jurisdiction over church affairs. Against such opponents Kerrl was powerless. In a last bid to regain some of his lost authority, he addressed a memorandum to Lammers urging that, since he had been unable to discuss his Ministry's affairs with Hitler since the end of 1937, important issues which needed Hitler's decisions should be held in abeyance for the duration of the war. Since 1938, he reminded Lammers, the Church Ministry had followed a completely neutral line, neither for nor against the Churches.[53]

But his pleas availed him nothing. He was not consulted over the plans initiated early in 1941 which led to the wholesale confiscation of the monasteries[54] and in despair he sent his last letter to Lammers in August 1941:

My job is becoming increasingly unbearable since I am not given any opportunity to prevent even those acts which are most damaging to the Reich. If it were possible for me to speak to the Führer personally, I would ask him, in the interests of the Reich and of National Socialism, to give me finally those powers without which my office must be ineffectual.[55]

His wish was not granted. Dispirited and utterly disillusioned, he died on 12 December 1941 at the age of 54 an exhausted and embittered man. In his obituary notice the *Völkischer Beobachter* praised him for his services in the early days of the Party's struggle, but passed over his tenure of the Church Ministry in silence. And Hitler, on hearing the news of his death, remarked to his entourage:

Kerrl, with the noblest of intentions, wanted to attempt a synthesis between National Socialism and Christianity. I do not believe this is possible, and I see the obstacle in Christianity itself. . . .
Pure Christianity – the Christianity of the catacombs – is concerned with translating the Christian doctrine into fact. It leads simply to the annihilation of mankind. It is merely wholehearted Bolshevism, under a tinsel of metaphysics.[56]

10 The Hammer and the Anvil

1941-45

'We are at this moment not a hammer but an
anvil. The anvil which is hard and tough
lasts longer than the hammer.' – BISHOP
GALEN, 20 July 1941

In the first half of 1941 the Nazis launched a series of new offences
against the countries of eastern Europe, which involved yet more
millions in the terror and miseries of war. In April German troops
marched into Yugoslavia and Greece, and on 22 June the full
weight of the army was hurled in an unprovoked attack against the
Soviet Union. To arouse popular enthusiasm for these campaigns,
floods of propaganda poured out on the home front calling for
more and greater sacrifices. Churchmen, who, like everyone else,
found that guns were now to be substituted for butter, were faced
with increasing difficulties in the conduct of their church services.
Coal rationing limited the heating of the churches; supplies of
paper were reduced; electricity was curtailed, and the indifferent
quality of the only candles available proved them to be but a poor
substitute; limitations on public transportation hindered worship-
pers from reaching their churches; and when bombing raids
began on the German cities the churches and church institutions
suffered their full share.

Local churchmen still did their best to continue some sort of
regular church life. But the Nazis' determination to impose totalitarian control over every aspect of life, including that of the
churches, led them in self-defence to make a three-fold stand, first,
against the confiscation of church property, especially of the

monastic orders, and the elimination of non-parochial institutions;
secondly, against the racial persecution of the Jews; and, thirdly,
against the undermining of Christian principles and the attempted
substitution of Nazi ideology for Christian ethics. It was on these
three counts that the struggle between Church and State was
centred during the remaining years of the war.

I THE ATTACK ON CHURCH INSTITUTIONS

From the beginning of 1941 such new and stringent measures were
taken against the churches by the Nazi authorities that more
damage, it was said, was done 'physically and morally by the land
raids of the Gestapo than by the air raids of the RAF'.[1]

The number of expropriated church properties rose rapidly. In
a secret circular addressed to the *Gauleiters* on 20 March, Bormann
wrote:

Many valuable church properties have had to be sequestred lately,
especially in Austria; according to reports from the *Gauleiters* to the
Führer, these sequestrations were frequently caused by offences against
ordinances relating to the war economy (e.g. hoarding of food-stuffs of
various kinds, textiles, leather goods, etc.). In other cases they were
caused by offences against the law relating to malicious attacks against
the State [*Heimtückegesetz*], and in others because of prohibited possession of firearms. Obviously, *no compensation is to be paid to the Churches
for sequestrations made because of the above-mentioned reasons. . . .*[2]

The reasons given for the seizures were the need for auxiliary
hospitals or resettlement centres for refugees and evacuated
children, or, alternatively, acts of hostility to the State perpetrated by members of the religious orders, particularly the Jesuits.
If an individual member of a monastic community was adjudged
guilty of an offence, it was seized upon as a pretext for the closure
of the whole institution. In actual fact, the Churches' properties
were expropriated solely for the Nazis' own ends, each of the
Nazi leaders making a bid for what he considered their most
appropriate use. Dr Ley in June 1940 argued in favour of using
monasteries as homes for the Aged[3] or for the *Kraft durch Freude*.[4]
In April 1941 Bormann suggested that Church orphanages should

be taken over for the housing of evacuees, a move to which Hitler agreed.[5] In a circular issued from Hitler's headquarters in May 1941, Bormann decreed that

the Nazi State and movement cannot permit children to be brought up in denominational kindergartens according to Church principles, or along the lines of denominational divisions. Today this question can be finally cleaned up by withdrawing permission from the organizers of Church-sponsored institutions for children. In justification, the special role of the Party in this area should be stressed.[6]

The requisite orders were accordingly issued, and by 31 July all Church kindergartens had been seized by the Gestapo and transferred to the sponsorship of the Nazi Welfare organization.

The requisitioning of monastic properties had first been adumbrated by Himmler, in December 1939, when, in his capacity as Reich Commissar for the Strengthening of the German People's Community (*Reichskommissar für die Festigung deutschen Volkstums*), he had ordered the *Volksdeutsche Mittelstelle* in Berlin to take over 'suitable accommodation which could be used for the housing of returning *Volksdeutsche*'.[7] When, eleven months later, Cardinal Bertram protested that the decree had been used to requisition entire monasteries and convents and to evacuate their inhabitants, his protest was ignored. In January 1941 Himmler ordered the complete evacuation of all such Church properties without compensation.[8] War-time necessity, the Cardinal was informed, was a sufficient justification for the measure, and the question of compensation, could be settled after the end of the war.[9] In December 1940 the *Gauleiter* of Alsace ordered all Church organizations to be dissolved and their property confiscated.[10] In Innsbruck, *Gauleiter* Hofer coerced the Premonstratensian Order into 'selling' their monastery at Wilten to the provincial government of Tyrol. In Silesia no less than 60 monasteries and church institutions were seized. In Luxembourg, 400 priests were expelled on Hitler's personal orders; all the institutions run by members of Catholic Orders were confiscated and their inhabitants were transported across the border into the diocese of Trier; all hospitals in the territory were declared secular institutions. In Lorraine, the Warthegau, Lower Austria and South Germany where the measures were particularly severe, the Church authorities estimated that by the beginning of May no less than 130 monasteries and Church institutions had been confiscated.

This was only the beginning. A letter from the Party head-quarters for Mainfranken on 24 April 1941 informed the local Party organizers that:

By order of the *Gauleiter*, I request from you an immediate report on the situation of all monasteries and convents in your area. A short description of each building should include its size, its place in the countryside, and its activities or participation in agricultural work. Very important is an account of the transportation facilties, since the rural setting of many monasteries makes them very suitable for the needs of the *Kraft durch Freude* (Hotels, Rest houses, holiday and sports resorts). Furthermore your report should include the view of the County Party leader on the future use of these buildings. Since the matter is being treated as very urgent on the national level, I am asking for an *immediate reply by return of post, in an express and registered letter*.[11]

The German bishops and the Roman Curia itself immediately launched a protest. For some time past the Papal Nuncio had almost monthly complained either verbally, by letter, or with a Verbal Note to State Secretary Weizsäcker about similar sequestrations, some of them involving considerable properties. In May 1941 he again protested against the abruptness with which the confiscations had been carried out without prior warning either to himself or to the Church authorities. Weizsäcker's reply was a curt statement to the effect that the war-time need for housing was so great that further requisitions could be expected.[12] Rome could draw only one conclusion. In a letter to the German Embassy dated January 1942, the Curia protested that because of

the increasing difficulties put in the way of the religious Orders and Congregations in the spiritual, cultural and social field, and above all the suppression of abbeys, monasteries, convents, and religious houses in such great numbers, one is led to infer a deliberate intention of rendering impossible the very existence of the Orders and Congregations in Germany.[13]

In June 1941 Cardinal Bertram again bitterly complained that, 'at a time when the whole German people were united in a decisive

struggle for the future of our country', the rights of Catholics were
disregarded and overridden throughout the land. In the regions of
Trier, Kassel, Saxony, Thuringia, Cologne, Aachen, and Silesia, he
stated, church kindergartens had been expropriated, such Catholic
insignia as crucifixes and religious paintings had been removed,
and teachers and nuns had been expelled. Catholic parents, he
averred, were alarmed by these events, which contravened the
provisions of the Concordat and served to strengthen the impression 'that a systematic campaign for the destruction of all that was
Christian was now in process'.[14]

Despite the Nazis' oft-repeated desire not to exacerbate tension
between Church and State, restrictions on Church work continued
to multiply. On 1 June 1941, the Church press was totally suppressed for the duration of the war in contrast to the press of the
German Faith Movement and the anti-clerical pamphlets of the
Ludendorff Publishing House, which continued to be published
though on a reduced scale.[15] In April, new regulations for the
pastoral care of patients in hospitals were promulgated, whereby
priests were prohibited from entering the hospitals unless specifically requested by patients and with the approval of the medical
authorities,[16] and Church welfare agencies were replaced by the
National Socialist Welfare organization and the Winter Aid Programme. In the same month religious education in Saxony was
abolished altogether; the Ministry of Education in Berlin prohibited the use of prayers at school assemblies; and the gradual
removal of crucifixes and religious paintings from every school
was ordered by the Bavarian Ministry of Education.[17]

On Bormann's instructions, every pastor who resigned his
office and, preferably withdrew from the Church, was to be
offered a government job; and Hitler himself ordered that any
Jesuits serving in the Army were to be declared unfit for service
and released.[18] Anti-clerical propaganda was stepped up in an
attempt to alienate the sympathy of the laity from their clerical
leaders, and anti-church literature denigrating the sacraments was
handed out free of charge. On 12 June the *Gauleiter* of Baden,
Robert Wagner, announced to an enthusiastic audience of Party
followers in the Festival Hall in Karlsruhe that

when our foreign foes lie at our feet, then we will tackle the foes at home; there are still some running around the country in purple and ermine.[19]

On 4 June all *Gauleiters*, provincial governments and police head-quarters, were ordered by Heydrich to take final and immediate action against such remaining small sects as the astrologists, occultists, spiritualists, Christian Scientists and their associated organizations.[20] Protective custody was decreed for everyone engaged in such practices, with relegation to the concentration camps for the more dangerous individuals; the organizations were then finally to be dissolved and all the material relevant to their activities was to be confiscated.

To justify his actions, Heydrich declared that

today, when we are building the nation of our Führer, we have no more tolerance for such dark spirits and jesters. Everyone now has to do his duty with all his energy. We stand at the point of danger for our people, and we need healthy spiritual forces in all our people. ... We cannot understand why German men should still be playing with theories of the world which are opposed to national thought and to National Socialism. We must help such people to overcome this fanaticism and put themselves at the disposition of the State.

There is no doubt that the Gestapo was taking advantage of the favourable climate of opinion following Germany's victories in the Balkans to eliminate the small sects, especially those of non-German origin, such as Christian Science or the Salvation Army which were suspected of having ties with outside and rival powers.[21] The political significance of these lesser sects was practically nil, but a totalitarian state can tolerate no form of rivalry.

It is significant that these repressive measures were initiated not by the Ministry of Church Affairs but by the Party agencies. Proof – if any be needed – that the whole campaign was aimed, not merely against the Churches' institutional life, but against Christianity itself is provided in the secret circular addressed to the *Gauleiters* by Bormann on 9 June. The importance of this document as indicating the attitude of mind of the newly-appointed leader of the Party Chancellery cannot be doubted. It begins with the blunt statement that 'National Socialism and Christianity are irreconcilable',[22] and goes on to pronounce the replacement of the outdated and mythical dogmas of Christianity by the 'scientific' views of Nazism. Christianity, it states, was derived from the Jews, ignored the laws of race and biology, split its adherents into factious denominations, and had preyed upon German political leaders for far too long. The situation under Nazism was quite different.

For the first time in German history, the Führer consciously and completely has the leadership of the people in his own hand. With the Party, its components and attached affiliates, the Führer has created for himself, and thereby for the German Reich leadership, an instrument which makes him independent of the Church. ... Never again must influence in the leadership of the people be yielded to the Churches. This (influence) must be broken completely and finally.

To eliminate the power of the Churches, every attempt to strengthen their internal structure must be opposed. Far from supporting such movements as the 'German Christians', 'the interest of the Reich lies not in conquering but in preserving and strengthening ecclesiastical particularism'.

This declaration was not altogether welcomed by the Party. Some members of the hierarchy felt that its appearance was inopportune, while others maintained that the Party programme was in favour of 'positive Christianity' and could not believe the time was ripe for any encouragement of the anti-clericalism of those who were still regarded as 'hot-heads'. Under pressure, Bormann was constrained to admit that an explicitly anti-Christian crusade was bound to meet with opposition within the Party ranks, a view which Hitler, persuaded by the volume of protests addressed to him, eventually concurred. A few days later the circular, as a statement of official policy, was therefore withdrawn. The more precipitous members of the Party, Hitler pronounced, must restrain their activities until the war was won, for the inevitable reaction on the part of the Churches was certain to cause disunity at a time when it was essential for the whole nation to unite in the campaign against the Soviet Union which was launched on 22 June 1941.

II THE FAILURE OF BROTHERLY LOVE TOWARDS THE JEWS

The rapid succession of victories on the eastern front was celebrated
with jubilation by the whole German people. Only a few individuals foresaw the disastrous consequences that a total Nazi
victory would bring, not only upon the Christian Churches, but
upon the whole moral life of the country. Most churchmen were
content to accept the commonly-held view that Germany had
been drawn into war by foreign conspiracies, that she was fighting
a defensive action, and that the acts of persecution of which they
had personal knowledge were but isolated incidents and not the
deliberate policy of their Nazi masters. The brutalities and atrocities inflicted on the occupied countries were explained away as
the regrettable penalties of war. And the repressive power of the
Gestapo, even though it daily became more menacing and more
widespread, was excused as a war-time necessity. In the circumstances, therefore, it is not surprising that the most terrible outrage
of the whole Nazi era – the attempted extermination of the Jews,
with all its attendant horrors of mass murders and gas-chambers –
was not loudly and urgently denounced by the Churches. At a
time of unprecedented challenge to the moral courage and conscience of the German people, all save a handful of German churchmen continued to turn a blind eye on events, retreated into
apathetic indifference, and even manifested a sort of sympathetic
acquiescence. The resolute protests which, as some critics maintain,
might have in part at least mitigated these awful atrocities, were
never made. The Christian principle of the sanctity of human life
was upheld by only a tiny minority, and their voices were too
few and too faint to be either representative or effective.[23]

The increasingly manifest discrimination against the Jews, both
by word and in practice, implicated the German Churches at one
of their weakest and most vulnerable points. Large sections of
both clerical and lay opinion held anti-semitic sentiments, and
little or no remonstrance, save by the followers of Pastor Niemöller,
had been made to earlier Nazi racialist measures – to the Nuremberg laws, for instance, or to the application of the 'aryan' clause
for all government appointees. The burning of the synagogues on

the 'Kristallnacht' of November 1938 had revealed beyond a shadow of doubt the nature of the Nazis' intentions against such members of the Jewish race as had not already fled from the Nazi terror to come. On that occasion, at least 20,000 Jews were placed in concentration camps, where some hundreds died of maltreatment; another 17,000 were transported to Poland, while a collective fine of 1 billion Marks was imposed on the remaining Jewish community.[24] With the outbreak of war, the Jews were held responsible for kindling hostility by means of their international connections, and of instigating Poland, England, the Soviet Union and finally the United States 'to launch their infamous and unprovoked aggression' against Germany. Reports of the disappearance of Jewish individuals and of atrocities in the concentration camps daily increased and spread, particularly after the first wholesale clearance of Jews from the city of Stettin in the biting winter of 1940. The efforts of Pastor Grüber's aid committee to assist the helpless victims by medical aid and by caring for abandoned Jewish children, were promptly stopped by the Gestapo. In December 1940, the house 'an der Stechbahn' in Berlin, where the aid committee had its headquarters was closed, and Dr Grüber was arrested. A few weeks later his collaborator, Dr Sylten, was taken to Dachau, where he was later put to death. Individual illegal efforts to procure identity cards, rations, and work permits enabled a few of the victims to be saved, and a few others were hidden in remote vicarages in distant parts of the country; but any organized endeavour to alleviate the plight of the Jews was impossible.

In September 1941 the discrimination against Jewry was brought to a head by the edict that every Jew over the age of six was to wear the yellow star of David on the left breast whenever he appeared in public. Despite the efforts of certain priests to encourage their congregations to be especially solicitous to the 'non-aryan' Christians in their parishes, the fear of yet further dark measures grew steadily deeper. It was realized beyond all doubt on 15 October when the forcible transportation began of the whole Jewish population to unknown destinations in the East.

At this point the leaders of the Christian churches at last woke to

the fact that they had been silent for too long. At last they realized
that Christianity and Judaism could no longer be regarded as
opposing movements but were one in their needs and their adver-
sity. Only the 'German Christians' stood firm in their acceptance
of the Nazi view of the role of the Jews. In a declaration issued at
the end of 1941 the 'German Christian' Church leaders affirmed
that

The German National Socialist Leadership has irrefutably proved by
numerous documents that this war in its world-wide dimensions has
been hatched by the Jews. It has therefore taken internal and external
decisions and measures against Jewry which are indispensable for the
safeguarding of German life.

As members of the community of the German nation the undersigned
German Evangelical Provincial Churches and their Presidents are in the
front line of this historic defensive affair, which *inter alia* necessitated the
Reich Police regulations of marking the Jews as the born enemies of the
world and the Reich. Dr Martin Luther, too, after bitter experience,
demanded the strictest measures against the Jews and their expulsion
from German territories.

From the crucifixion of Christ to our own day the Jews have com-
batted Christianity and abused or falsified it in pursuance of their selfish
goals. By Christian baptism nothing is changed in the racial peculiarities
of a Jew, nor in his national characteristics or his biological being. The
German Evangelical Church has to preserve and support the religious
life of fellow Germans. Christians of Jewish race have no room and no
right in it.

The ... German Evangelical Churches and their Presidents have
therefore annulled each and all intercourse with Jewish Christians. They
are determined not to tolerate any influence of the Jewish mind on
German religious and ecclesiastical life.[25]

The Confessing Church was silent until 1943, when its position
was so fraught with doubts and anxieties on this matter that a
group of laymen were constrained to address the Evangelical
Bishop of Bavaria as follows:

... The Church must never weary of confessing before all the Jews, as
did the first apostles after Golgatha: 'unto you first, God, having raised
up his Son Jesus, sent him to bless you, in turning away everyone of

you from his iniquities' (*Acts* 3: 26). The Church can only make this belief credible to Israel if she simultaneously accepts those Jews who have 'fallen amongst murderers'.

Particularly she must resist those tendencies towards Christian anti-semitism in the parishes themselves, which excused the non-Christian world's treatment of the Jews and the passivity of the Church in this matter by talking of the 'well-earned' curse over Israel. They forget the warning of the Apostle to us Gentiles: 'Be not proud, but fear: for if God spared not the natural branches, take heed lest he also spare not thee' (*Romans* 11: 20).

The Church must witness before the State to the significance of the saving grace of Israel. She must ardently withstand every attempt to 'settle' the Jewish question by some artificial political formula, i.e. to destroy the Jews. This is an attempt to attack the God of the First Commandment. The Church must confess that she as the true Israel is bound indissolubly with the Jews, both in the knowledge of sin and the promise of salvation. She can no longer attempt to save herself by avoiding the attacks made on the Jews. She must rather witness to the fact that along with Israel it is the Church and her Master Jesus Christ who are being assaulted . . .[26]

This courageous statement was, however, robbed of much of its effect by the fact that it was sent anonymously. When the Bishop asked for at least two signatures to be appended to the document, not a single volunteer was forthcoming. Nevertheless, a copy went also to Bishop Wurm of Württemberg, who showed himself to be made of sterner stuff and who was prepared to risk the reprisals of the Gestapo. Although Wurm, like Niemöller, had previously shared many of the nationalist prejudices against Jews and foreigners, and although he had in 1938 publicly accepted the necessity of racialist laws, he now acknowledged where the call of the Gospel lay.

On 12 March 1943 he wrote to the Church Ministry in the following terms:

The measures taken against the Jews, in particular, so far as they do not take place in the scope of the laws at present in force, have for a long time been depressing many circles in our nation, particularly the Christian ones. In the present difficult circumstances, the question auto-matically arises in many minds whether our nation has not made itself guilty of bereaving men of their homes, their occupations and their lives without the sentence of a civil or military court.

In view of a possible political exploitation of a public protest by the enemy countries, the Christian Churches have exercised great restraint in this respect. They cannot, however, possibly be silent when lately even Jews living in mixed marriage with Christian Germans, some even being themselves members of Christian Churches, have been torn from their homes and occupations to be transported to the East. By this means, marriages which were contracted in Church are broken and the children by these marriages are heavily penalized. . . .[27]

In two further letters written in July and December 1943 to various members of the Government and later secretly circulated throughout the parishes, Bishop Wurm continued his protests in the name of the Church and of humanity.

. . . in the name of God and of the German Reich, we here express the further plea that the responsible leadership of the Reich should abandon the persecution and destruction of many men and women who have been struck down while in German hands without legal conviction. Already those non-aryans who were under German control have been to a great extent removed. Now, in the light of certain individual cases, fears have been expressed for the so-called privileged non-aryans who have remained unharmed up to now, lest they be treated in the same way. In particular we must raise forceful protest against any measures which threaten the sanctity of marriage in legally immune families or their children. Such purposes like the extermination measures already taken against the other non-aryans, stand in the strongest possible opposition to the commandments of God and destroy the foundation of all our Western thought and life, in particular our fundamental belief in the God-given right to human existence and human dignity.[28]

In this tragic chapter of German history, the role of the Catholic Church, as Guenter Lewy has made abundantly clear, was, with only a few individual exceptions, similarly irresolute and hesitant. Although well substantiated rumours of the Nazis' policy of extermination were circulating among the general public in the winter of 1941, the Catholic Bishops limited their intervention to letters of protest on behalf of 'non-aryan' Catholics or of Jews married to Catholics. They protested in November against a proposal that Jews should be compulsorily divorced, on the grounds that the Catholic sacrament of marriage could not thus be arbitrarily dissolved. But the protest lost much of its force by a rider inserted by Cardinal Bertram, one of the signatories, to the effect that his words were not prompted by any 'lack of love for the German nationality, or of feeling for national dignity, or of underestimation of the harmful Jewish influences upon German culture and national interests'.[29]

Confronted with government measures of unprecedented ferocity, and with a people almost wholly persuaded of the iniquities of the Jews, the German Catholic leaders made but little effort to arouse their congregations against the enormity of the atrocities perpetrated by their political leaders. The vague general statements which emanated from the pulpits on the need for love to all mankind were insufficient to deter their people from participating in the ensuing mass slaughter, and were totally disregarded by the Nazis.

If they failed to speak up for the Jews facing the ... gas chambers, one of the main reasons was the widespread indifference of the German population. In France, Belgium and Holland, declarations of solidarity and help for the Jews were almost universally regarded as signs of patriotism. In Germany, on the other hand, the bishops in so acting would have incurred new charges of being un-German and in league with Germany's mortal enemy. Their own followers would probably have failed to understand and approve such sympathy for the Jews, whom the Church for many long years had branded as a harmful factor in German life.[30]

It was not until 1943 that the necessity of abandoning their long silence was at last realized by the Churches. In October of that year the Prussian synod of the Confessing Church addressed a pastoral letter to all their congregations setting out the obligations of the Fifth Commandment:

The State is not entrusted with the power to take away life, except in the case of criminals or war-time enemies ... Terms like 'eradication', 'liquidation', or 'unfit to live' are not known in the law of God [*göttliche Ordnung*]. The murdering of men solely because they are members of a foreign race, or because they are old, or mentally ill, or the relatives of a criminal, cannot be considered as carrying out the authority entrusted to the State by God.[31]

The declaration hardly ventured forward towards a new understanding of the relations between Christians and Jews, and made no call for repentance for what had been done to those 'who had fallen among thieves'. But it at least recognized the ethical demands of the situation, though unhappily it came ten years too late.

III   THE NAZI CHALLENGE TO THE CHURCH ON EUTHANASIA

The majority of the population thus accepted the persecution of the Jews with indifference, and the terrible implication that other groups might likewise be marked for similar treatment apparently passed them by unnoticed. Against the Nazis' secret practice of euthanasia, which was gradually becoming known, and the public propaganda in favour of sexual promiscuity, regrettably few Churchmen raised their voices; and, indeed, few seemed to understand that such practices presented a fundamental challenge to Christian thought and doctrine.

According to a witness at the Nuremberg Trials, Hitler as early as 1935 had announced his intention

if war comes, to take up the euthanasia question and to implement it. Such a problem could be dealt with more smoothly and easily in war time, since any open resistance which was to be expected from the Churches would not count for as much amongst the general effects of the war as otherwise.[32]

In fact, no sooner had the war begun than Hitler decreed that

Reichsleiter Bouhler and Dr Brandt are to be given the responsibility of enlarging the authority of certain doctors, to be designated by name, who should perform the operation of euthanasia on persons whose condition, according to human judgment, is held to be incurable after most careful diagnosis of their state of health.[33]

Hitler refused, however, to legalize euthanasia, or to make the Ministry of the Interior responsible for the operations, which in the course of the next five years were to take away the lives of approximately one hundred thousand people.[34]

The first step in preparation for this mass extermination of unwanted persons was to recruit a Reich Working Party for Hospitals and Rehabilitation Centres (*Reichsarbeitsgemeinschaft Heil-und Pflegeanstalten*) of about 50 functionaries, including lawyers, doctors and university professors, to be responsible for the smooth working of the operation. They were instructed that the action was not to be limited to individual cases, but should cover any category of 'unworthy' persons, beginning with the inmates of lunatic asylums and afterwards to be extended to senile and tubercular patients.

As the second stage, the inmates of the lunatic asylums were registered with the Reich Working Party. Questionnaires were submitted to the directors of all such institutions, and were then 'evaluated' in Berlin until a target figure was achieved of some 70,000 people whose lives were considered to be a drag on the community.

Orders were then issued for the patients thus selected to be transferred to Nazi-run institutions, under the pretext of rationalizing their care under war-time circumstances. The transfer of the patients was undertaken by the 'General Welfare Transport Society' (*Gemeinnützigen Transportgesellschaft G.m.b.H.*), operated by the SS. The actual practice of euthanasia was organized by the 'General Welfare Foundation for Institutional Care' (*Gemeinnützige Stiftung für Anstaltspflege*), which held funds sufficient to build gas-chambers and crematoria in six institutions in Hadamar near Limburg, Grafeneck in Württemberg, Brandenburg on the Havel, Bernburg in Anhalt, Hartheim near Linz and Sonnenstein in Saxony. The whole operation was declared to be 'top secret', and all persons involved were threatened with severe penalties if any knowledge of it became known.

From the beginning of 1940, regular transports of buses brought the hapless patients to these six institutions, where they were speedily put to death, mostly by gas but sometimes by the injection of drugs.[35] A few days later the relatives of the victims were informed that death had occurred from natural causes. Because of the danger of infection, the corpses were cremated, but urns containing the ashes were handed over to the relatives if requested.

Frequently the so-called cause of death was palpably false, and the numbers of reported deaths soon became so large as to cause alarm not only among the relatives and the inhabitants of the towns and villages where the institutions were situated, but even among the patients themselves. Terrible scenes of anguish followed. Rumours began to spread throughout the country that as soon as the mental hospitals had been 'cleaned up', the old-age homes would be next on the list. And it was reported to Berlin that even soldiers at the front were afraid that, if they were incurably wounded, they too would be treated as 'unworthy of life'.

The Churches in Germany had long had a tradition of caring for epileptics and the mentally-ill, in institutions which were among the earliest and best developed of their kind. Accordingly the Church authorities' fears were early aroused by the growing reports of these appalling atrocities. Even before the war, as part of the campaign against Church organizations, the Nazis had attempted to enforce the transfer of mentally-ill patients from Church-run asylums to institutions controlled by the State. The Churches had then resisted strongly, and it was therefore unlikely that they would be prepared to acquiesce in any programme of euthanasia. Nevertheless, in 1940 and 1941 pressure was again brought to bear on them for the transfer of their patients. The dilemma of the bishops was acute. If the Nazi commands were not obeyed, the Churches' institutions were in danger of being forcibly taken over, which would undoubtedly cost the patients their lives. The refusal of the director of the institution at Kückenmühle, near Stettin, to 'co-operate' in this way had had just such a result in July 1940. As it became evident that the policy of euthanasia was not only being permitted, but was being actively pursued on the orders of Hitler himself, the possibility of resistance became increasingly more difficult and more dangerous.

In these terrible circumstances, both Cardinal Bertram and Bishop Wurm determined to make strongly-worded personal protests to the highest authorities. On 11 August 1940, Cardinal Bertram wrote to Lammers stressing the grave anxiety which was growing among the people over the activities of certain government officials who were alleged to be practising euthanasia and conducting experiments on the mentally sick.[36] In July Bishop Wurm wrote to the Minister of the Interior, Frick, that Christians could not condone the practice of euthanasia.

... we understand well that certain circles in the Party, whose voice is primarily to be heard in the *Schwarze Korps*, want to get rid not only of the churches, but of Christianity entirely because it is a barrier to such measures. ... But in fact right up to the present the Führer and the Party have publicly taken their stand on the basis of positive Christianity, which regards as self-evident the merciful and humane handling of suffering fellow men.[37]

In August Archbishop Gröber of Freiburg also wrote to Lammers calling for an immediate end to the practice of euthanasia, which, he said, was causing alarm among the people already distressed by the sacrifices of war.[38] Similar representations were likewise made by Cardinal Faulhaber, the bishops of the provinces of Cologne and Paderborn, and the Bishop of Limburg,[39] and in March 1941 Bishop Preysing of Berlin preached a sermon against the whole concept of euthanasia:

No justification and no excuse can be found for taking away the life of the weak or the ill for any sort of economic or eugenic reasons. ... With the same determination as she has protected the institution of marriage ... the church will protect the right of every individual to live.[40]

The most courageous intervention of all was made by Pastor Braune, the Director of the Evangelical Hoffnungstal Institution, who, after collecting all the available evidence, visited no fewer than four ministries in Berlin in July 1940 to lodge the strongest and most urgent protests against the measures in hand.[41] At the Reich Chancellery he was threatened with severe penalties for interfering in a matter designated as 'top secret'; but at the Ministry of Justice he was received in person by the Minister, Gürtner, who expressed astonishment and dismay that such inhumane measures could be perpetrated in Germany without his knowledge. The only result of Pastor Braune's brave efforts, however, was that he was arrested in August 1940 and imprisoned for ten weeks, on Heydrich's orders, for 'sabotaging the measures of the Party and

State'. On the same grounds, Pastor Ernst Wilm, who delivered a lecture on the same subject to a group of colleagues in Westphalia in the winter of 1940–1, was imprisoned in Dachau until the end of the war.

These protests by leading churchmen were in some way reinforced by doubts expressed by some of the officials of the Ministry of Justice itself. Since no law on euthanasia had been promulgated, and since the measures taken had been kept secret, all sorts of inflammatory rumours were spreading throughout the population, though they themselves were in no doubt as to the truth of the matter. Confidence in the doctors and directors of the six designated institutions was fading rapidly, and one official of the Ministry of Justice described them as nothing less than 'institutions for liquidation' (*Liquidationsanstalten*).[42] Even Himmler himself began to doubt the wisdom of the operation. Writing to his subordinate Brack in December 1940, he said:

I hear that there is considerable disturbance about the hospital at Grafeneck. People recognize the grey buses of the SS and believe that they know what is going on when they see the chimney of the crematorium burning continuously. What is happening there should be a secret, but it is no longer so; so the worst suspicions have been aroused. In my view it will be necessary to end this use of the institution and at the same time to institute some propaganda in a clever and capable way of showing films about mental or hereditary illnesses in that region. I would like you to submit a report on how this difficult problem has been solved.[43]

The whole matter came to a head in 1941 when Bishop Galen of Münster publicly denounced the euthanasia programme in a sermon preached on 3 August. The response of the population was immediate and bitter – so much so that Hitler was forced to take note and on 28 August ordered that the operation was to be halted. Thereafter, the utmost secrecy was maintained over the whole affair. Extermination centres, it was decided, were to be established only in remote areas where few Germans were settled and where there was little likelihood of interference by meddling priests – in Poland, for instance, which was considered especially suitable. Notifications of death would no longer be sent to relatives, and the personnel involved in the work were to be sworn to the utmost secrecy and held in complete isolation.

So the work went on, and in 1943 the practice of euthanasia was extended to include orphan children who had been evacuated from the large towns as a precaution against air raids. The unhappy children were sent to concentration camps, where their official guardians were powerless to protect them, and there they were put to death in the gas chambers, along with the incurably sick.

The intentions of the Nazis in the execution of the euthanasia programme were unquestionably ideological in character. Although some of those involved may have believed that euthanasia of the mentally-ill was ethically justified – a view which they advanced in their own defence at the post-war trials – the primary intention of the chief perpetrators was palpably otherwise. The extermination of useless lives relieved the country of the burden of housing and feeding those who could no longer care for themselves, and at the same time provided invaluable information on the most effective methods for exterminating others who were considered unworthy of life, such as the gypsies, the Jews, and the inmates of concentration camps. There is ample evidence that the techniques of the gas-chambers and the equipment of the crematoria first used in the euthanasia operation were later used at the extermination camps at Auschwitz and Treblinka, where they were put to use on a much larger scale during the subsequent years of terror and annihilation.

IV   THE CONFLICT OVER RACIAL EUGENICS

More widely known among churchmen, although unfortunately not fully understood, were the Nazis' deliberate attempts to undermine Christian ethical values, in regard to sexual morality. Motives both of policy and of race-culture led the régime to attack and vilify Christian customs with a view to replacing them with policies consistent with Nazi ideology. As early as 1933 the Reich Sterilization Law had been enacted. Since it contravened basic Catholic doctrine, the Vatican had been quick to lodge an indignant protest. In 1936, under Himmler's auspices, an institution had been established known as *Lebensborn* (Fount of Life).

Lebensborn has to foster fecundity among the SS, to protect all mothers of good (i.e. racially pure) blood, as well as to care for them and to look after pregnant mothers and children of good blood. From this endeavour there will arise an élite youth of equal worth both spiritually and physically, the nobility of the future.[44]

This experiment in race-culture was partially due to a fear that Germany's enemies might become numerically superior and so prevent her expansion in search of '*Lebensraum*'. The rank and file of the SS were encouraged to enter into promiscuous or even adulterous relationships for selective breeding, provided that such breeding was 'racially pure'. The stigma of illegitimacy was to be removed from the child, and the unmarried mother was given comfort and attention in country welfare homes, many of them plundered from the Jews or opponents of Nazism. After their convalescence, the mothers were given further encouragement to become pregnant again as soon as possible. By 1945 *Lebensborn* had established eight mothers' and three children's homes in Germany proper, and had taken charge of 11,000 births, of which between 50 and 80 per cent were illegitimate.

After the Polish campaign of 1939 Himmler issued the following order to the SS and the police:

28 October 1939
In every war the nation suffers a haemorrhage of its best blood. Many military victories have turned out to be a disastrous defeat for the nation because of the loss of its energies and its blood. The worst feature is not the unfortunately necessary death in battle of its best men, however regrettable that may be. Much worse is the lack of children, who cannot be produced by the living during the war or by the dead after it.

The old proverb that a man can die happy only if he has sons and children must ring especially true for the SS in this war. A man can die happy if he knows that his family [*Sippe*], and everything that he and his forefathers have striven for, will be carried on in his children. The greatest gift the widow of a soldier killed in battle can have is a child of a man whom she has loved. It must therefore be an important task for German wives and girls of good blood to become the mothers of children by fathers who were sent to the front, of whom only fate knows whether they will return home or will die for Germany. This task will not be undertaken in any light-hearted way, but with a sense of deep responsibility and with a call of duty higher than the otherwise perhaps necessary bourgeois laws and habits and than the marriage bond itself.

For those men and women to whose duty it is to remain on the home front there is the holy responsibility to become again the fathers and mothers of children.

We should never forget that the victory of the sword and the bloodshed of our soldiers would be meaningless if it were not followed by the victory of the cradle and the consequent settlement of the newly-acquired territories.

In the last war many a soldier, from a sense of responsibility and not wanting to leave his wife, if she had another child, in difficulties and need after his death, decided not to have any more children during the war. No SS man need any longer have these thoughts and cares. They are removed by the following regulations:

1. All legitimate and illegitimate children of good blood whose fathers were killed in the war will be brought under the sponsorship of specially chose representatives of the *Reichsführer SS*, responsible to me personally. We will undertake to look after the human cares of these mothers and their material necessities, and will be responsible for the upbringing of these children until they are grown up, so that no mother or widow need have anxiety about her future.
2. During the war the SS will be responsible for protecting these mothers and children, whether legitimate or illegitimate, from any immediate dangers or difficulty. After the war, if the fathers return, the SS will grant suitable financial help for the re-establishment of the family.

SS men and mothers of the children for whom Germany is waiting, who are so resolute in your faith in the Führer and in your desire for the eternal life of our blood and our people; you who know how to fight for Germany and to die for her; prove to us that you are ready for Germany's sake to give life to the following generation.[45]

This incitement to promiscuity was made known only to the SS and the police. But much wider publicity was given to a letter addressed 'to an unmarried mother' and signed by no less a person than the Führer's Deputy, Hess, which was published throughout the country in the *Völkischer Beobachter* on Christmas Day 1939. In this letter Hess declared that, in times of special danger for the *Volk*, measures must be taken over and beyond the normal laws of society. When young and racially pure men were taken off to the battle-field leaving children to carry on their blood in future generations, or when girls of equally pure blood bore children but for some reason were unable to marry, then 'care must be taken to preserve this valuable natural wealth. Objections which might be raised in normal times must be waived.'

Especially during a war the *Volk* cannot afford not to preserve and increase to the greatest possible extent its racially valuable inheritance. Higher than any principles devised by man, higher than any conventions ... and higher than any prejudices, are the welfare of the community and the life of the *Volk*.

The highest duty which a woman can do for the community is to contribute to the continuation of the nation through racially healthy children.[46]

With this aim of recouping Germany's population losses in mind, Himmler, while on an inspection tour of SS units in occupied Poland, remarked that many of the Polish children appeared to be of the Nordic type. They were promptly declared to be clearly of Germanic origin, and therefore fit for 'Germanization'. *Lebensborn* accordingly set up an adoptions department which arranged for these and other children in the occupied territories, provided that they were held to be 'racially pure', to be taken away from their parents, 'adopted', and compulsorily Germanized by suitable German couples in the Reich. The same policy was also carried out by *Lebensborn* in the case of the illegitimate children of the German occupation forces, of which there were some 50,000 in France and over 6,000 in Norway. The Norwegian children were held to be of a special worth, because the 'output' of Nordic women folk was much valued by the Nazi racial theorists. No less than eight *Lebensborn* homes were established in Norway with the official approval of the German Chief of Police in Norway, Rediess, who, in a booklet significantly entitled 'SS for Greater Germany: with Sword and Cradle', pronounced: 'it means something for future generations if there are 20 or 30 divisions more to defend the space our comrades conquered'.[47] In a similar vein, *Gauleiter* Giessler, addressing a large gathering of female students at the University of Munich, advised them not to 'hang around' the University during the war but rather 'to present the Führer with a child'. Unhappily, only a few of his audience grasped the ethical implications expressed in his exhortation, and still fewer followed the example of Sophie Scholl, one of his listeners, who resolved to resist to the death the spread of so pernicious a doctrine.

Churchmen who were sympathetic to Nazi imperialist goals continued to avert their eyes from the possible consequences of these racialist theories, failing – or refusing – to see that they were all a part of a plan to establish a 'Master Race', in which the SS would form an elite while the rest would be merely obedient workers and those considered 'unworthy of life' would be exterminated. As one SS leader stated:

The choice of the new class of leaders will be carried out by the SS – positively, through the National Political Educational establishments (Napola) as a beginning, and then through the *Ordensburgen* as the true universities for the future National Socialist aristocracy, along with some political training; negatively through the eradication of racially and biologically less valuable elements and the radical elimination of all incorrigible political opponents who basically refuse to accept the ideological basis of the National Socialist State and its significant institutions.[48]

Such evidence as is available suggests that, if this monstrous plan had been known among churchmen, they would have refused to believe it.

V   BISHOP GALEN'S CHALLENGE

Torn between their patriotic desire to show devotion to the Fatherland and their wish to preserve the Church's institutions, most churchmen lapsed into passive acceptance of the Nazi conduct of the war, concerning themselves primarily with the bare essentials of life, with shortages of food and fuel and with the dangers and horrors of air-raids. This lack of enthusiasm for the war-effort was much deplored by the Nazi authorities.[49] But as the war dragged on and the possibility of total defeat became apparent, this same submissiveness was the main reason why churchmen failed to make any effort towards organizing opposition to the régime and to hastening the end of hostilities.

An instance of this passivity was shown at the meeting of the German Catholic Bishops held at Fulda at the end of June 1941. The Nazis had hoped that the Catholic Church would demonstrate its patriotism by issuing a pastoral letter calling for a crusade to liberate the Russian people from atheist bolshevism. Instead, the bishops made no reference to the military situation, and concerned themselves only with the dangers facing loyal churchmen and with the limitations and restrictions placed on the Church's activities.[50]

Much more to the Nazis' liking was a telegram sent to Hitler by the German Evangelical Churches' executive, thanking the Führer for his inspiring call 'to take up arms against the deadly enemy of all stability (*Ordnung*) and of our Christian western culture'. 'Since British policy', said the telegram, 'now aligns itself as an ally of Bolshevism against the Reich, this is an ultimate sign that it is not concerned about Christianity but only with the annihilation of the German nation.'[51]

Despite such expressions of gratitude and co-operation, however, there was still no readiness on the part of the Nazis to reciprocate by granting the Churches any concessions. The fear persisted, said Bormann in one of his circulars to the *Gauleiters* in May 1941, that the Churches would attempt to strengthen their position by making a virtue out of their patriotism, and by pointing to the numerous clerics who were decorated for bravery on the battle-field.[52] The Churches, he thought, might also attempt to show that Christianity, not Nazism, was the cause for which the war was being fought. Such attempts would best be overcome by ignoring them entirely.

This uneasy truce was of short duration. Early in July 1941, very heavy bombing raids took place on Münster, the see city of Bishop Galen. On Saturday, 12 July, *Gauleiter* Meyer of Westphalia ordered the Gestapo to confiscate two Jesuit monasteries in the city and the house of the Mission Sisters of the Immaculate Conception, and to expel the members from the province. Within a week six further institutions were confiscated, and all the property, movable and immovable, was transferred to the Westphalia *Gauleitung* for use by the victims of the air raids. It is not clear whether Meyer was carrying out orders or whether he was acting on his own initiative, perhaps with the idea of showing himself at least as anti-clerical as his colleagues elsewhere. In any case, such confiscations had previously proved an effective means of attacking the Church without arousing the outcry which would certainly have followed an attack on the bishops themselves. In order to teach Bishop Galen a lesson, Meyer in the previous year had tried to obtain cancellation of the official endowments to the diocese, but Hitler had refused to agree. In January 1941 Meyer tried again. On his orders, a pastoral letter issued by the Bishop was confiscated, and two of the Cathedral Canons, close colleagues of the Bishop, were expelled from the diocese. Now, he believed, the moment had come for another and more powerful blow to the authority of the Bishop and the 'political Catholics' who stood behind him.

Bishop Galen, however, refused to countenance the confiscations without complaint. He addressed telegrams of bitter protest to various ministries in Berlin; he enlisted the help of his numerous friends in high places; and he preached two outspoken sermons on 10 and 17 July denouncing the iniquitous proceedings of the Gestapo, which he described as 'an inner enemy', and calling on his congregations to become as hard as stone and as unbreakable as the anvil, which would last longer than the hammer. His words were greeted with enthusiasm and unqualified approval.

In a subsequent letter to Lammers, Galen, claiming to speak for the whole of Westphalia, both as a descendant of the old aristocracy, and as a Bishop, strongly attacked the unwillingness of the Reich authorities to put a stop to the arbitrary expropriations of the Gestapo.

Similar protests, if less strongly worded and less widely publicized, flowed into the Reich Chancellery from other parts of the country. But still the confiscations went on. In Württemberg four Evangelical theological seminaries were seized and turned into hostels run by the SS. Two properties of the Archdiocese of Cologne were taken over. The Bishop of Trier complained that on 7 July the Gestapo had confiscated his seminary in Trier 'by verbal notice to the Vicar-General and without giving any reasons'. In the same city St Matthew's Abbey was forcibly seized, despite physical resistance by the local population. The monastery of Ottbergen was expropriated, despite protests from the Bishop of Hildesheim, and the Franciscan Monastery at Bochum received similar treatment. The Papal Nuncio himself made representations to the Foreign Ministry about the confiscations of monasteries in Aachen, Dresden and Vienna.[53]

In the midst of the stresses and strains of the Russian campaign, Hitler was particularly anxious that the mood of the people should not be unsettled by such extraneous problems. On receiving reports of Galen's sermons, he directed Bormann to investigate the charges made by the Bishop and to instruct the *Gauleiters* to halt all further expropriations.

The Führer has ordered that confiscation of church or monastic property is to be suspended immediately until further notice. Independent measures by the *Gauleiters* are not to be permitted under any circumstances, even if special circumstances in individual cases would seem to warrant the expropriation of church or monastic property on the basis of legal regulations. If a *Gauleiter* believes these preconditions are fulfilled in special cases, he should prepare a report which can be submitted to the Führer by me.[54]

Several of the *Gauleiters*, in view of this directive, felt called upon to justify their previous actions.[55] Meyer informed Lammers on 1 August that the seizure of the Jesuit houses in Münster had been necessary because of the Jesuits' notorious hostility to the Nazi state, and because the inmates of the Abbey of Gerleve had been found guilty of 'pacifist activity and destructive criticism'; the monks, moreover, had been guilty of hoarding rotting grain. The monasteries, Meyer pointed out, were to be used for the housing of bombed-out families and evacuees, and it had therefore been necessary to transfer the properties to the Nazi Welfare organization, in whose hands lay responsibility for the care of the homeless. Meyer also wrote to Bormann complaining that Bishop Galen's sermons were a 'deliberate provocation of the population'.

I would like to ask you, Reich Leader, to be good enough to obtain a decision from the Führer whether he would allow further measures to be taken, which are already planned. The preconditions for the interventions for the police already exist. My object is to overcome the severe shortage of accommodation and to provide school classrooms, since the schools were also badly bombed. . . . I am sure such future measures would be carried out without difficulty after some time has elapsed and if the Party can undertake to prepare the ground for them with propaganda.[56]

Within a week the situation became still more critical. Although Bishop Galen could not have known of Hitler's latest decree, he continued to press his uncompromising opposition, strengthened by alarming reports from the directors of the Diocesan mental hospitals that orders had been received for the transfer of mentally-ill patients, orders, which, in the circumstances, could mean only one thing – that the patients were destined to die by euthanasia. On 3 August Bishop Galen again preached in St Lambert's church. This time he delivered a powerful attack against the murder of innocent persons and the disregard of the sanctity of human life. Nor did he limit himself to generalities. He spoke in detail of the whole euthanasia programme – the secret transportation of patients to unknown destinations, the consequent announcement of their death, the deliberate flouting of Catholic doctrine through cremation, and the deception of the relatives by means of false death certificates. He stressed the justifiable fears felt by badly-wounded soldiers, the sick and the senile, if their future were to depend upon their 'productive capacity'.

So eloquent were Galen's words and so apposite his timing that the fame of his sermons reached far beyond the crowded congregations that flocked to hear him. Copies were mimeographed and distributed throughout the country, often by hand and at great personal risk; they were smuggled to the soldiers at the front and even found their way to occupied territories. Within a matter of days all hope was gone of suppressing this act of so-called treason, which in Berlin was described as 'the strongest attack against the German political leadership for decades'.[57] The matter was adjudged by the Nazis to be not merely a question of the justification of euthanasia but a challenge to their whole political control over the nation, since it was not a mild protest addressed to an insignificant number of people, but a nation-wide blast which, despite the censorship, had been read with avidity by thousands.

In the Nazi hierarchy, feelings ran high. On 13 August Bormann uncompromisingly declared that Galen deserved the death sentence. *Gauleiter* Meyer in Münster maintained that the Bishop should be imprisoned and anyone who spread his statements should be placed in a concentration camp. If proceedings were not immediately taken against the Bishop, he declared everyone would believe that his accusations were correct; the worst fears of the German people at home would be confirmed, and by their correspondence with their men in the army, they would weaken the morale and the fighting capacity of the troops. Moreover, Meyer contended, since the Bishop would undoubtedly have taken steps to circulate his sermons abroad, they would be used by the English as a most powerful piece of anti-Nazi propaganda. He further posed the question of whether Galen's accusations might be the advance guard of a planned attack by the Catholic Church, and suggested that the Pope might be induced to take disciplinary action. Since any such measures, however, were unlikely to be prompt or effective, and since in any case it was inconsistent with the dignity of the Nazi State to ask help from the Papacy, he was strongly of the opinion that only the imprisonment or expulsion of the Bishop would serve to show how 'political Catholicism' would be dealt with. This, he suggested, might best be done following the announcement of some major victory.[58]

In Berlin, one of Goebbels' staff, Party Comrade Tiessler, roundly declared that the Bishop should be hanged. The Church Ministry suggested that the State subsidies paid in lieu of endowments should be suspended. The Gestapo ordered all copies of the sermons to be confiscated, and imposed continuous surveillance of the Bishop's postal and telephone communications. Goebbels' propaganda machine was tireless in its charges and counter-charges, and Hitler ordered Bormann to investigate the whole question and to report back. Since Hitler was not prepared to abandon the secrecy surrounding the euthanasia action, the Bishop's accusations could not be answered directly. But failure to act might encourage the other Bishops to speak out, and their opposition might infect the Protestants. At the same time, as Tiessler noted, police measures against the Bishop were of doubtful value, since they would inevitably cause him to be regarded as a martyr and the other Bishops would be obliged to take up his cause. In Tiessler's view the best course would be to inform the population of the euthanasia measures, although, he was obliged to admit, the time was hardly ripe for such an action.[59]

Goebbels held that the whole of Münster and Westphalia would be lost to the Nazis if so popular a figure as Bishop Galen were to be treated with the severity he deserved. He thought the time inauspicious for a major clash with the Church, and adhered to his oft-repeated view that the church question should at all costs be postponed until the war was won, when it would be comparatively easy to confiscate the Churches' material possessions, to break their resistance, and to rid themselves of the Bishop of Münster. In the meantime, nothing should be done.

Hitler, Bormann noted on 13 August, was undecided on the issue, but a month later Lammers informed the Church Ministry that the Führer had decided not to proceed against Galen for the moment.[60] Indeed Hitler's only public reference to the Bishop's words was a rather sinister warning in a speech delivered in a Munich beer-cellar on 8 November 1941, to his 'first and most loyal comrades':

... should anyone here really be hoping to break our unity, it does not matter where he comes from or to which camp he belongs, then I will – and you know my methods – keep my eye on him for a while.

This is just a time of probation. But then comes the moment when I will attack like lightning and remove the danger as quickly as possible. And then no disguise will protect him, not even the disguise of religion.[61]

Seven months later, in one of his rambling discourses at the supper table, he said:

I am quite sure that a man like Bishop von Galen knows full well that I shall extract retribution to the last farthing. And, if he does not succeed in getting himself transferred in the meanwhile to the Collegium Germanicum in Rome, he may rest assured that in the balancing of our accounts, no t will remain uncrossed, no i undotted![62]

The significance of Bishop Galen's challenge should neither be exaggerated nor minimized. It is possible that if other equally courageous individuals had raised their voices against the crimes of the Nazis, the terrorist régime might at least have been modified. But such suppositions over-simplify the issue. The reason for Bishop Galen's success lay in the fact that he spoke for a public which was already aroused and which instantly responded. It was because strong feelings of outrage already existed over the liquidation of the mentally infirm that the Nazis dared not take action against the protesting church leaders. With the public behind them, the Bishops were in a position to make their challenge felt. It was otherwise, alas, in other matters. As Guenter Lewy points out:

The large majority of the very people who had been outraged when their sons and daughters, brothers and sisters had been put to death, failed to react in the same manner when their Jewish neighbours were deported and eventually killed in the very gas chambers designed and first tried out in the euthanasia programme.[63]

Nevertheless, the effect of the protests cannot be denied. Hitler's order of 28 August, which interrupted the euthanasia programme, saved countless lives.[64] His previous decree putting an end to the confiscation of church property also gave some respite to the persecution of the churches. Above all, the effect of the protests showed that, even with all the means of terrorism at his command, even at the height of his military successes and regardless of popular feeling, Hitler was forced to abandon his policy of murder and extermination in the face of the full weight of mobilized public opinion. The far-reaching effect of Bishop Galen's challenge on the Nazi leadership cannot be assessed here. But the conclusion can be drawn that the Church's responsibility to uphold the worth of every individual in the sight of God and to be the guardian of the sanctity of human life, was here, in part at least, successfully defended and upheld.

VI THE FINAL SETTLEMENT POSTPONED

After the summer of 1941 the Churches' struggle within the borders of Germany proper lost some of its heat. The Nazis were anxious to avoid a repetition of the Bishops' outburst, and the Church leaders were caught in a cleft stick between their desire to support Germany in her hour of need and their revulsion against the Nazi-inspired bestialities that were leading the population to moral catastrophe.[65] Hitler held to his belief that the church question could be disposed of after the war, and that the 'hot-heads' in the Party were to blame for the wide approval of Galen's protests.[66] He now decreed that the persecution of the church in all its forms was to stop, so that the whole nation could be rallied in a supreme effort to win the war.[67] Eighteen months later, in 1943, Bormann addressed a secret circular to Party Leaders stressing the need for the strictest discipline on church matters. 'Every petty policy of pin-pricks must be halted,'[68] he declared; every article of the decree putting a stop to the confiscation of Church property must be upheld; and no pressure was to be brought to bear on individuals to withdraw from the Churches.

The NSDAP should commit itself to working heart and soul for positive ends in the people's community (*Volksgemeinschaft*).... All matters which are not essential for the conduct of the war, or which tend to cause differences and divisions in the people's community, should be dropped. This particularly applies to political–denominational affairs, which must not now be touched.[69]

Nevertheless, the Churches' loyal collaboration never earned them the slightest consideration from Hitler. Among the many monologues recorded in his *Table Talk* there are frequent pejorative references to Christianity and the Churches, reflecting both his prejudices against the clergy and his shrewd awareness of the tenacity with which the ordinary people were prepared to cling on to their religious organizations.

... It is not opportune to hurl ourselves now into a struggle with the

Churches. The best thing is to let Christianity die a natural death.
A slow death has something comforting about it. The dogma of
Christianity gets worn away before the advances of science . . .

A movement like ours must not let itself be drawn into metaphysical
digressions. It must stick to the spirit of exact science. It is not the Party's
function to be a counterfeit for religion. . . . If at this moment we were
to eliminate the religions by force, the people would unanimously
beseech us for a new form of worship. You can imagine our *Gauleiters*
giving up their pranks to play at being saints! As for our Minister of
Religion, according to his own co-religionists, God himself would
turn away from his family![70]

Hitler's determination in due course to avenge himself against
the Churches was likewise left in no doubt:

The evil that is gnawing at our vitals is our priests of both denominations. I cannot at present give them the answer they have been asking
for, but it will cost them nothing to wait. It is all written down in my
big book. The time will come when I shall settle my accounts with
them and I shall go straight to the point . . . I shall not let myself be
hampered by juridical scruples. Only necessity has legal force. In less
than ten years from now, things will have quite another look, I can
promise them.[71]

His decision to postpone a settlement of church affairs was welcomed by many of the Nazi leaders, notably by Goebbels, who was
preoccupied with the task of mobilizing the population for total
war and who spoke disparagingly of those who continued to
instigate individual acts of persecution against the Churches. In
March 1942 he noted in his diary:

I have been trying hard to keep all these elements of conflict out of
my *Gau*, and now these trouble-makers and anarchists (*Krachmacher und
Radikalinskis*) are causing me this stupid trouble right here in the capital.
The Church question should, if possible, remain untouched during the
war, however much these parsons prove to be recalcitrant in this or that
area. After the war we shall have plenty of possibilities of bringing them
to see sense.[72]

In September 1941, the Gestapo were informed that restraint on
Church matters was to be rigorously observed. At a conference of the
Gestapo's 'church specialists' – whose activities were remarkably

successful in keeping Heydrich informed of events within the Church hierarchies[73] – *SS-Sturmbannführer* Hartl ordered:

1. The avoidance of all major operations and measures against the Churches and their institutions.
2. The cancellation of further measures against monasteries, including disguised measures in this matter.
3. In individual cases action may be taken but the Reich Security Head Office is to be informed. Particularly important cases must be left for the Führer's decision.
4. The main thing is to see that the Church does not win back any of its former positions. We must limit ourselves to seeing that we maintain positions already captured.
5. The main stress should be put on intelligence work. Any material of significance which might be of future importance is to be collected carefully. The Führer's instructions are that captured documents etc. are to be photocopied, since ordinary copies are not adequate for the preparation of decisive steps. The network of agents is to be carefully maintained and extended by recruiting new contact men. Particular attention should be paid to the connections between the Church circles and government offices.[74]

Hartl closed his address with the words:

Each of us must go to work wholeheartedly and with true fanaticism. Even if mistakes are made here and there in this work, this should not depress us, since mistakes are made everywhere. The main thing is to demonstrate our decisiveness, determination and effective initiative against these opponents.[75]

An indication of how this 'effective initiative' was to operate was given in secret instructions issued a few months later to the Gestapo in Aachen:

It must once again be repeated that the network of contact men for church affairs is not adequate enough. The contact men are almost exclusively Catholic priests, who do not have the opportunity of getting details from the diocesan offices. It is not good enough for us to learn about important decisions only after they are announced in the general pastoral letters of the German bishops. We must know beforehand about such intended steps ... We must also succeed in obtaining exact information about the secret meetings of the bishops' conferences.

This is certainly becoming more and more difficult, since the bishops themselves are more and more careful. But there is no castle so secure that a secret entrance to it cannot be found.[76]

In October Heydrich informed the SS commanders and police chiefs of the SD that

Our fundamental ideological attitude to denominational opponents has been clearly and unambiguously laid down. The practical regulations for guarding against actions of denominational groups hostile to the state must, however, be guided by tactics of expediency.[77]

He therefore ordered all measures likely to lead to opposition among the people to be stopped, and confiscation of church property was to be restricted to Poland and Slovenia. To prevent the Churches from forming any mistaken ideas, however, individual cases of suspected subversion should be punished by transfer to a concentration camp. The intelligence network was to be perfected, so that all evidence of the Churches' hostility would be ready to hand for the eventual day of reckoning.

Another factor which undoubtedly contributed to the amelioration of the Church's position was the assassination of Heydrich in May 1942. Heydrich's hatred of the Churches, especially of the Catholic Church, bordered on the pathological. He was obsessed with the idea that the Churches, led by the Vatican, were conspiring to destroy Germany. Blinded by an apostate's hatred, his evaluation of the Church situation was always so biased and his suggestions so radical, that even Hitler, perhaps for tactical reasons, was obliged to restrain his subordinate.[78] Heydrich's death, according to one witness, liberated the Christian churches from their most active enemy.[79] His apparatus of 'church specialists' within the Gestapo and his network of informers and agents was broken up and discharged. His successor, Kaltenbrunner, was an Austrian of quite another colour, who believed that the Gestapo could be employed more profitably than by persecuting the Churches – a view in which, however, he was strongly opposed by Martin Bormann.

In March 1942 Catholic priests in many parts of the country read from their pulpits a letter alleged to have been written by a popular

Air Force pilot Colonel Mölders shortly before his death in action. The consolations of the Church, the Colonel wrote, were an untold comfort to him in hours of peril and many of his comrades, in the face of imminent danger, had ceased their former ridicule of the Church. As soon as the letter became known, the Gestapo promptly intervened. A number of persons, including some priests, were sent to concentration camps, and a reward of 100,000 marks was offered for information leading to the author of the letter, which the Nazis claimed to be a forgery.[80] In vain Cardinal Bertram protested that Colonel Mölders' only intention was to show the Christian faith as a source of strength to the faithful in the execution of their duty to the Fatherland. The Gestapo, he claimed, by their arbitrary actions, were providing further evidence of the

limitless attacks of certain small but influential circles in Germany against Christianity and the Church, who claim to find a conflict, even an irreconcilable conflict between Christianity and the German way of life, which leads them, among other things, to describe the priests and the faithful as enemies of the Reich.[81]

But the appetite of the anti-clericals was insatiable. In August 1942 further instructions from Bormann went out to the Party offices that correspondence with any branch of the Churches, particularly complaints about anti-clerical activities, was to be dealt with only at Party headquarters. In March 1943, an official of Rosenberg's staff declared that the truce with the Churches could no longer be allowed to continue, since it enabled the priests to influence the people against the war effort. Instead, he recommended the establishment of an 'executive Committee to establish training centres for ideological shock troops and for the provision of suitable "fighting material" (*Kampfschriften*)'.[82] The monthly reports submitted to the SD by local Party officials noted with increasing frequency that the attitude of the Catholic part of the population was still unsatisfactory, and other Party officials continued to call for more radical measures against signs of 'political Catholicism'.[83] It is impossible now to establish how far these opinions were shared by the Nazi hierarchy at this stage of the war, but they were unquestionably reflected in the actions taken by the Nazis following the abortive *Putsch* of 20 July 1944. 'Tools of the Church', 'Clerically-dominated opposition groups', and agents of 'political Catholicism', were held by the Nazis to be among the mainsprings of the *Putsch* and were believed to be hand in glove with intractable elements of the aristocracy and traitors to the Fatherland.

On these grounds the members of the 'Kreisau Circle', under the leadership of Count Helmuth von Moltke, were arraigned before the Nazi people's court (*Volksgerichthof*) under its notorious president Roland Freisler. This tiny group, which met at intervals at Moltke's estate of Kreisau in Silesia, was comprised of men with deeply held Christian convictions, whose opposition to the Nazi régime was primarily based on moral aversion. Their concern was less with the practical details of ridding the nation of Hitler than with the fundamental problems that would confront Germany when the Nazi era was over. Although it was never proved that any of this circle of high-minded men were actually engaged in the plot of 20 July, the fact that they had discussed matters that were 'the exclusive concern of the Führer' was sufficient to ensure their condemnation to death. Freisler, in one of his speeches to the Court, stated that

Count Moltke, Christianity and we National Socialists have one thing in common, and one thing only: we claim the whole man.[84]

The Gestapo made every effort to prove that Father Alfred Delp, SJ, and Pastor Eugen Gerstenmaier, the clerical members of the Kreisau Circle, had used their connections with church circles to involve others in the plot. One of the accusations against the conspirators, Count Stauffenberg, Count Yorck, Count Schwerin and Count Fritz-Dietlof Schulenburg, was that they had had a long discussion, some three or four weeks before the *coup*, on the need to make Christianity the most important spiritual force of the future.[85] Father Delp, who held an important post on the staff of the Jesuit journal *Stimmen der Zeit*, was accused of trying to persuade other Jesuits in Bavaria to accept his 'defeatist' views. Gerstenmaier was known to have been in contact with Bishop Wurm in Stuttgart, and others were in touch with Cardinal

Faulhaber, Bishop Preysing and the Bishops of Fulda and Salzburg. Although the Gestapo were aware that such information was insufficient to warrant the arrest of members of the episcopate, there can be no doubt that the treatment of Father Delp at the trial and his condemnation to death on 11 January 1945, were designed to intimidate the whole Catholic Church. Before his execution on 2 February 1945, Father Delp wrote:

The actual reason for my sentence is that I am and remain a Jesuit. It was not possible to establish any connection with the event of 20 July. Neither was the charge of a tie to Stauffenberg upheld. Other sentences demanded by the prosecutor in cases actually involving knowledge of the affair of 20 July, were much less severe and less biased. The air was filled with hatred and animosity.

The basic tenet is that a Jesuit is *a priori* an enemy and an adversary of the Reich. . . . This was not a trial: it was simply a functioning of the will to annihilate.[86]

The same hatred and animosity pursued Pastor Dietrich Bonhoeffer, who was held to be so dangerous a character that in 1942 he was arrested and held for two and a half years without trial. His name was included on a secret list of enemies of Nazism who were not to be allowed to escape with their lives, even if the whole Nazi state should collapse. Only a few days before the end of the war he was put to death in Flossenbürg concentration camp.

Alfred Delp and Dietrich Bonhoeffer had both adjudged the nature of Nazism from the viewpoint of their Christian faith, which led them into opposition to the régime and resulted in their deaths. Their fate and that of the many other churchmen who were executed after 20 July 1944 is a standing proof of the implacable enmity of the Nazis towards the churches. There can be no doubt that, had Hitler won the war, the same fate would have been meted out to countless other churchmen of every rank and denomination. There would have been no trials; it would simply have been 'a functioning of the will to annihilate'.

11 The Final Settlement

> 'Let us gather together and fervently pray
> for a speedy deliverance from Nazi evil.
> Let us pray that God may give us strength to
> remain faithful to His Word. Let us pray
> that He may give us courage to endure all
> the sufferings in the hours of trial and distress
> that lie ahead of us. Let us pray that we may
> be granted a cheerful spirit to fight the evil,
> so that we may gain Salvation and the ful-
> filment of His Promises. Oh Lord deliver us
> from the evil'. – From a secretly circulated
> Austrian leaflet, Christmas 1941

When the German military campaigns began in the years 1939, 1940 and 1941, no plans had been prepared beforehand on the manner in which the Churches were to be treated in the conquered countries. As in other aspects of their policy, the Nazi attitude to the Churches was dictated partly by racial theories, partly by military and political exigencies, and partly by the continuing rivalries within the Nazi hierarchy, whereby each of Hitler's henchmen strove to hold as much of the conquered areas as he could grasp and as much of the larger spoils as he could seize. In general, Nazi church policy in the occupied areas reflected, on a larger scale and in more extreme measure, the same mixture of fanaticism, contradictions and inconsistencies as had been seen in Germany proper.

At the outset, the *ad hoc* arrangements adopted in the occupied countries left room for a wide divergence in the treatment of the Churches. Broadly speaking, one group within the Nazi hierarchy advocated a flexible policy of persuasion and gradual assimilation, while another pressed for repression and persecution. As the war progressed, and as the more extreme anti-clerical members of the Party organization rose in Hitler's favour, the first group became discredited and Hitler increasingly inclined towards the plans for forcible suppression which Himmler, Bormann and their associates tried out in certain of the eastern territories. Undeterred by opposition from their colleagues or by the reasons which had held them in check within the borders of Germany proper, Himmler and Bormann began to put into operation the measures which were to constitute the Nazis' 'final settlement' of Church–State relations. In the Warthegau, the model Nazi region that had been carved out of conquered Polish territory, the apotheosis of Nazi Church policy can be seen. The draconian measures introduced there can leave little doubt of what would have happened elsewhere had Hitler been able to carry out his frequently repeated threat 'after the war, to deal decisively with the Churches'.[1]

In this process of 'final settlement' three stages are discernible: first, the eradication of the Churches' resistance; second, the elimination of any outside interference, including that of the Vatican; and third, the establishment of a new era in Church–State relations, in which the Churches would be subordinated to the German 'New Order', the priests stripped of their privileges, and Christianity left to suffer what Hitler called 'a natural death'.

I THE ERADICATION OF THE CHURCHES' RESISTANCE

As exponents of the more moderate group, Goering, Ribbentrop, and – surprisingly – Rosenberg argued that the conquered peoples should be persuaded into becoming willing collaborators with Germany in the 'New Order'. The new régime, they believed, should set itself to coin some form of popular support, after which the agricultural and industrial resources of the occupied territories could, for the foreseeable future, be exploited without the use of military force or political repression. Failing such willing co-operation, they argued, many fighting units would be tied down which might more profitably be used elsewhere, and the eventual establishment of willingly-accepted German civilian control would be infinitely more difficult.

They therefore urged the expediency of granting to the local populations concerned some concessions on matters of church policy. Some degree of freedom of worship should be allowed, provided that it involved no political activity. Rosenberg, in his capacity as Minister for the Occupied Eastern Territories, went so far as to propose a 'toleration edict' for the satellite areas of the Ukraine, the Caucasus, and the Baltic territories, which would be part of the 'liberation' of the Russian people from the yoke of Bolshevism.[2]

A similar policy was proposed for the countries of western and northern Europe, whose peoples, it was thought, could without undue difficulty be persuaded of the advantages of collaboration with their Nazi conquerors. Eugen Gerstenmaier, then an official of the Reich Evangelical Church's Foreign Relations Department,[3] was dispatched to Norway a few days after the German invasion to assure the Norwegian Primate Bishop Berggrav that the Norwegian Church would be untouched during the German occupation, and that the position of the Primate himself would be respected if he would urge his countrymen not to resist the *de facto* occupation. It all sounded persuasive enough, but there is little doubt that the move was a deliberate attempt to discredit the Bishop in the eyes of his fellow-countrymen.[4]

By the use of such honeyed words, it was hoped that the possibility of resistance by the Churches in the occupied territories would be removed, and an extensive propaganda campaign among the clergy urged them to act as collaborators with their invaders and to undermine the authority of such 'reactionary' bishops as showed political and theological 'disloyalty' to the new régime.[5]

In the so-called Germanic areas like Norway and Holland, churchmen were advised to adapt their dogmas to true Germanic philosophy by purging the Church of its Jewish traits. The Nazis urged that the Church's mission was to spread the 'Aryan' gospel in the building of the new world 'from the Urals to the Atlantic',[6] and called upon all Christian people to join in the 'noble work' of defending the basic values of Christianity in the Nazi-led 'crusade against atheistic Bolshevism'.[7]

These tactics were willingly espoused by such of the Nazi military governors who had no wish to make their occupation task more difficult by a needless campaign against the Churches. In France and Belgium, the Germans were well aware of wide differences of opinion among churchmen on how far the Church

should go in collaboration with the new authorities. It was therefore deemed more advantageous to sow seeds of doubt in the
Churches themselves than to unite Church opposition by arbitrary
acts of persecution. Some of the Nazi rulers were even opposed to
any overt oppression of the Churches, and it is a sign of the disunity
prevailing amongst the Nazi hierarchy on church questions that in
Holland *Reichsstatthalter* Seyss-Inquart proudly boasted in a public
speech that 'We have no martyrs here'.[8]

The more militant group of Nazi leaders, believing that these
tactics of assimilation and persuasion were entirely misguided,
argued that the Churches' opposition should be smashed, not
cajoled. Goebbels considered Rosenberg to be 'completely at sea
as far as organization is concerned, besides having rather childish
ideas'.[9] Himmler did his best to circumvent Ribbentrop's influence
in the occupied areas and to gain a free hand for the SS. Hitler
poured scorn on an idea proposed to him by Papen in July 1941,
that the time had come for the 're-Christianization of Russia',
declaring such a suggestion for missionary activity to be
'completely out of the question'.

If one did it at all, one should permit all the Christian denominations
to enter Russia 'in order that they club each other to death with their
crucifixes'.[10]

And again:

Methods of persuasion of a moral order are not an effective weapon
against those who despise the truth – when we have to do with priests,
for example, of a Church who know that everything about it is based
on lies and who live by it.[11]

In any case, Hitler's racial ideas about the Slavs of eastern Europe,
which dominated his thinking, ruled out the possibility of any
concessions in that region. Heydrich too believed the Churches
in the occupied territories to be among the chief enemies of the
new Germany, and consistently opposed any suggestion that the
Church question was not a vital issue to the future of Nazism.
Similarly, Bormann and Frank, the Nazi governor of central
Poland, the so-called 'Government-General', increasingly came to

regard 'black Catholicism' as a treacherous and evil force that would have to be rooted out if the ideas of the 'New Order' were to prevail.[12]

In the opinion of all these men the Churches could be expected automatically to become the centres of political resistance to the Nazi occupation. Military as well as political and ideological considerations dictated the need for eradication of all forms of opposition and the imposition of totalitarian control. No clear line could be drawn between political and theological opposition, since Christian and national resistance was one and the same thing. They considered the attempts to cajole the Churches of western and northern Europe to be lamentable failures, since, with a few insignificant exceptions, the clergy had been conspicuous only by their silence on the subject of relations with the new Germany. As for the 'sly foxes' at the Vatican, they were just biding their time until they could again strike Germany as treacherously as they had done with the Encyclical of 1937. And the readiness of the Archbishops of Canterbury and York to lend their support to the Bolsheviks of the Soviet Union 'proved' that the Protestant Churches were equally hostile to the 'New Order'.

In the areas of Europe where the full force of Nazi violence was unleashed, the Churches were therefore destined to suffer drastically. In Poland, for example, Hitler refused to consider any suggestion that the country might be treated as a political ally or satellite, and ordered the mobilization of every Nazi agency to carry out the Nazi racial theories *in toto*. The Poles were to be treated as inferior beings, which, the Nazis declared, their overwhelming defeat by the German army had in fact shown them to be.

Immediately after the military victory of September 1939, Himmler, in his capacity as Reich Commissar for the Strengthening of the German People's Community (*Reichskommisar für die Festigung deutscher Volkstums*) laid claim to the new 'fief' of Poland and promptly instigated measures to consolidate the power of the SS within it. By the forcible suppression of all national institutions, by the 'Germanization' (*Germanisierung*) of cultural associations, and by the reduction of the population to the status of slave labour for the German Reich, any sort of resistance would be rendered impossible. In the western half of the territory, mass expulsion of the inhabitants took place to make room for German settlers. Simultaneously, the first systematic executions of members of the Polish intelligentsia and ruling classes were carried out, to 'eradicate the damaging influence of those elements of the population who are hostile to the life of the people and who constitute a danger for the Reich and the German *Volksgemeinschaft*'.[13]

From the first the Catholic Church was one of the main targets of this policy of annihilation. The SS was given a free hand in a reign of terror against both clergy and laity, as a demonstration that any institution or individual who might become a focal point of national resistance would be destroyed. The clergy, as always, were the chief suspects. Lists were drawn up of Catholics who were 'especially hostile to Germany' and who, as such, deserved summary treatment. In November 1939 it was reported from the Polish town of Bromberg (Bydgoszcz) that the 'eradication of Polish priests was planned, preceded only by the prior extermination of the Jews',[14] allegedly as a 'reprisal' for Polish treatment of the German population. In West Prussia, out of 690 parish priests, at least two-thirds were arrested, and the remainder escaped only by fleeing from their parishes. After a month's imprisonment, no less than 214 of these priests were executed, including the whole cathedral chapter of Pelplin. Of the remainder, most were expelled from the western territories into the newly created 'Government-General', with the result that by the end of 1940 only twenty priests were left in their parishes – about three per cent of the number of parish priests in the pre-war period.

The much smaller Evangelical Churches in Poland were treated with equal ferocity[15]. In 1939 their members totalled about 600,000, over half of whom were German-speaking. Some 20,000 were Calvinists, most of them living in the Wilna (Vilnius) area of north-east Poland, where they fell victims to the Soviet invasion. From previously prepared lists, members of the clergy were arrested immediately following the German occupation, and virtually the whole of the Evangelical clergy in the Teschen (Cieszyn) area of Silesia were consigned to the concentration camps of Mauthausen, Buchenwald, Dachau and Oranienburg, their places being taken by Germans who conducted their services in German only. Among those who succumbed in the concentration camps were the Reverend Karol Kulisz, the director of the largest Evangelical charitable institution, who died in Buchenwald in November 1939, and Professor Edmund Bursche, of the Evangelical Faculty of Theology in the University of Warsaw, who died while working in the stone quarries of Mauthausen.[16]

In most of the occupied countries, only the fear of widespread public revolt deterred the Nazis from launching a general onslaught against the whole body of the clergy, particularly against the upper ranks of the hierarchy. The bishops generally escaped imprisonment, but the treatment meted out to a few notable exceptions, especially in Poland and Czechoslovakia, was indicative of the probable fate which awaited the hierarchy when Nazi control was finally established. The Czech Orthodox Bishop Gorazd was executed. Four bishops, Kozal of Wladislavia, Fulman and his suffragan Goral of Lublin, and Picquet of Clermont-Ferrand, were exiled to concentration camps in Germany. The Bishop of Plock, Nowowiejski, and his suffragan, Wetmanski, both died of their sufferings while imprisoned in Poland. The seventy-nine-year-old Bishop of the Polish Evangelical Church, Juliusz Bursche, was sent into exile in Berlin where he was held in solitary confinement until his death several months later. Other leaders of the Churches, some of whom had rashly expressed enthusiasm for Germany's success,[17] were placed under arrest or isolated from their clergy and parishioners.[18]

The lesser clergy fared likewise. In Czechoslovakia, for instance, it was reported that

At the outbreak of war, 487 Catholic priests were among the thousands of Czech patriots arrested and sent to concentration camps as hostages. Venerable high ecclesiastical dignitaries were dragged to concentration camps in Germany. It was a common sight on the roads near the concentration camps to see a priest dressed in rags, exhausted, pulling a cart, and behind him a youth in SA uniform, whip in hand.[19]

The Gestapo was instructed to use every means to brand the clergy as criminals.

The German authorities endeavoured to humiliate and ridicule the priests in the eyes of the population. They hoped to obtain this objective by forcing the priests to perform hard labour in public places – in the streets, on roads and bridges. ... In many towns in the Province of Poznania and Pomerania, priests were compelled to witness the mass executions of their countrymen and then to dig graves for the dead and bury them.[20]

In 1941 it was reported:

As a general principle all priests and Jews in concentration camps are assigned to the so-called penal platoons, which have to do the worst work and are subjected to the worst treatment, so that they provide the largest percentage of deaths. News comes continually of priests who have died, or caskets containing their ashes arrive. Of some four hundred priests and eighty seminary students from Poland imprisoned at the Oranienburg camp, eighty died in the course of the first five months of 1940. During the same period, of some hundred and sixty priests belonging mostly to the dioceses of Poznan (Posen) and Gniezno (Gnesen), thirty-five died at Mauthausen and Gusen.[21]

The Gestapo's agents were everywhere active, sometimes in the guise of possible converts, sometimes in the confessionals, where under the seal of Confession they attempted to trap the priests into unguarded statements. Hundreds of clergymen were arraigned before Nazi courts of summary jurisdiction and many were sentenced to death for the most trivial offences or upon the slightest pretext. Yet Heydrich was still not satisfied. In April 1941 he complained to the Ministry of Justice that the law courts were being too lenient in their treatment of offenders, and insisted upon more repressive measures.[22] The many protests registered by the church leaders against these atrocities were all rejected.

To separate the priests and pastors from their parishioners, any trumped up charge was sufficient for the Nazis to consign the clergy to the concentration camps, whither they were transported in filthy and overcrowded cattle-trucks.[23] According to a recent careful collation of the available evidence, no fewer than 2,771 priests were imprisoned at Dachau alone,[24] of whom at least 1,000 were estimated to have died in the camp from hunger, disease, or ill-treatment between 1942 and 1945. According to one source, no less than 4,000 Catholic priests were put to death during the same years, either as 'political saboteurs' or, after incarceration in the concentration camps, by hanging, starvation, mishandling, lack of medical aid, or as the victims of medical experiments, including euthanasia.[25] Students at the theological seminaries were for the most part deported to Germany as forced labourers. Yet these victims were no more than the vanguard of the noble army of martyrs. The laity too were likewise condemned to suffer for their beliefs, and many thousands were done to death at the hands of the Nazis. The anti-clerical and anti-Slav atrocities perpetrated by the Nazis during their campaigns in Poland and Russia were the culmination of diabolical prejudice run mad, the terrible consequence of Himmler's boast to Frau von Weizsäcker that 'We shall not rest until we have rooted out Christianity'.[26]

As in Germany itself the persecution of the Churches in the occupied countries was not confined to Church members, but was rapidly extended to include their buildings, their institutions, and every other aspect of church life. All the measures that in Germany had been instituted since 1933 to wipe out the Churches' resistance were immediately applied in Poland, the Soviet Union, and elsewhere. Ruthless measures were taken to seize church property, to dissolve lay associations, to remove the legal privileges of the churches, to inhibit the educational work of the denominations, and to maintain a minute surveillance of all church activities. Monks and nuns were expelled from the monasteries, and their charitable work in hospitals and schools was brought to an end. Church buildings in all the occupied countries were closed down, profaned, looted or destroyed. Such Church services as still took place were constantly spied upon; the fear of denunciation was ever present; priests were forbidden to perform marriages between Germans and other nationals; services in the vernacular were prohibited in some areas; the church press was censored or suppressed; and pastoral letters were forbidden to be read in the parishes. Nazi censorship suppressed hymns in supplication for liberation from the hands of the enemy. Some passages from the Bible were forbidden to be read in public, and strong objections were raised to the preaching of such doctrines as the equality of all men before

God, the universal character of the Christian church, and the Judaic origin of the Gospel. Church schools were closed, and the state schools were ordered 'to bring education into line with the present circumstances'. Church organizations were dissolved or compulsorily *'gleichgeschaltet'*. Seminaries and theological faculties were shut down on the grounds that they were 'breeding-grounds for hatred of Germany',[27] and State subsidies to the Churches were stopped. The protests of the Papal Nuncio and of the bishops were invariably ignored. As Cardinal Bertram noted in December 1942:

> Even if we present our complaints to the so-called *Reichssichersheits-hauptamt*, there is rarely any reply; and when there is, it is negative.[28]

According to a report submitted to Cardinal Hlond, the Polish Primate, as early as 29 November 1939:

> The Germans openly declare in their speeches that they are masters of the occupied land, and that the Poles are their slaves. . . . The church is entering the catacombs. . . . The Polish language is forbidden in sacred functions. A prayer for Hitler [sic] has been introduced and made obligatory. . . . The Gestapo is the master of the Church. . . .[29]

A second report, submitted to the Pope in April 1940 and fore-shadowing the measures that were introduced to eliminate the churches' resistance, concluded with the words:

> Everything has been deliberately planned with the aim of completely destroying the Church in its entirety in one of the most religious countries in the whole world. . . . After so many centuries passed in the service of the Church, Poland witnesses the establishment in its midst of a paganism so godless, so immoral, atrocious and inhuman, that it could only be accepted by morbid-minded individuals who have lost all human dignity and are blinded by hatred of the cross of Christ.[30]

II THE ELIMINATION OF FOREIGN INTERFERENCE

The Nazi determination to impose totalitarian control over every aspect of life in German-occupied Europe left no loophole for possible intervention by outside bodies such as the Vatican. Hitler anticipated no danger from the Protestants, who, in his view, were so rent with factional disputes, both at home and abroad, as to be negligible.

Once only in my life have I been stupid enough to try to unite some twenty different sects under one head; and God, to whom be thanks, endowed my twenty Protestant Bishops with such stupidity that I was saved from my own folly.[31]

The Catholic Church, however, was more dangerous an adversary. The Vatican, the Nazis believed, never intended to observe the terms of the Concordat save as a means of preserving its age-long position of power and influence.

The Catholic Church strives always to seek advantage where we are weakest, by demanding the application to the whole Reich of those of the various Concordats which conform most closely to its aspirations.[32]

This would now have to be changed. In July 1942 Hitler announced that only 'military reasons connected with the war' had deterred him from severing diplomatic relations with the Vatican and from abrogating the Reich Concordat. But

Once the war is over we will put a swift end to the Concordat. It will give me the greatest personal pleasure to point out to the Church all those occasions on which it has broken the terms of it. . . .[33]

With the repudiation of the Concordat, the Catholic Church would no longer be able to depend upon the backing of Rome or of the State subsidies paid to it.

Once we cease handing out milliards of marks a year to the Church, our damned parsons will very quickly change their tune, and instead of having the impudence to revile us and attack us in the most shameful manner, will very soon be eating out of our hands. We can make this clerical gang go the way we want, quite easily – and at far less cost than at present.[34]

The danger of outside interference would then finally be removed.

It will be the duty of the *Reichsstatthalter* after the war to make it quite clear that he will deal with the Church in exactly the same way as he deals with any other national association, and that he will not tolerate the intervention of any foreign influence. The Papal Nuncio can then return happily to Rome, we shall be saved the expense of an embassy at the Vatican, and the only people who will weep a tear over the jobs that have been lost will be the Foreign Ministry.[35]

In the Wilhelmstrasse itself, however, the hope was still being entertained that Nazi church policy could be continued on ortho-dox lines. Indeed, as mentioned above, Ribbentrop and the German Foreign Ministry were still trying to maintain German–Vatican relations on a normal course, at least for the duration of the war and as late as January 1943 Ribbentrop instructed the Ambassador at the Vatican to make representations that

Nothing has happened in Germany during the war that could be construed as deliberate German action aimed at aggravating our relations with the Vatican.[36]

There were a number of cogent reasons why the Foreign Ministry wished to prevent an open clash with the Papal authorities. In the first place, Vatican support of Germany's enemies would undoubtedly strengthen the anti-Nazi alliance and would probably affect the opinion of neutral countries, such as those of Latin America. Secondly, outright opposition by the Pope would arouse conflict of conscience within the minds of Catholics both in Germany and in the occupied territories, and would thereby endanger the unity of national endeavour in the waging of the war. Thirdly, the Foreign Ministry was anxious to obtain recognition by foreign states, including the Vatican, of Germany's recent conquests and of their incorporation into the Third Reich, and such recognition could only be achieved by regularizing the situation and hence rendering innocuous the efforts of the governments-in-exile to nurture the hope that Catholicism would become a centre of resistance to German rule.[37] Finally, Ribbentrop, in his efforts to uphold the authority of the Foreign Ministry and to prevent other Ministries or Party agencies from encroaching on his preserves, was desperately anxious that the conduct of all relations with the Vatican should be channelled through the Foreign Ministry alone. It was with these aims in view that he had undertaken to visit the Pope in March 1940 and had exerted his influence against the suggestion that the Concordat should be abrogated, a move which would inevitably have caused a breach with the Vatican.

But the Foreign Ministry had to contend with formidable opposition from Rosenberg, from the Party headquarters under Bormann, and from the *Reichssicherheitshauptamt* under Himmler, all of whom exercised sufficient power to thwart most of the Foreign Ministry's placatory moves both political and humanitarian. Moreover, the measures taken in the occupied countries were so contrary to the Foreign Ministry's professions of goodwill that its officials found themselves in the unhappy position of being the recipients of outraged protests from the Papal Nuncio and other Church dignitaries which they were quite unable to remedy. We have already seen how the treatment of the Catholics in Poland in 1939, including the Nazis' refusal to allow the Primate to return to his own country, had led to a rapid cooling of relations between Germany and the Vatican.[38] And, when in November of the same year, the Nuncio demanded satisfaction for his repeated complaints, the Director of the Political Department of the Foreign Ministry, Under Secretary Woermann, could only reply that

I could not recommend him to approach high-ranking German personalities because they would perhaps not listen to him as quietly as I had done and would at once object that, as Nuncio, he had no right to speak of such things.[39]

For the same reason, Ribbentrop in March 1940 was obliged to decline to discuss with the Pope the Vatican's carefully prepared dossier of complaints dealing with the state of the Catholic Church in Poland.

During 1940, despite all Ribbentrop's efforts, the position of the Foreign Ministry was further weakened by pressure from the Party authorities. The Reich Concordat was declared to be invalid in the conquered areas; the German-speaking Lutheran communities were forbidden to look for help from their parent churches in Germany proper; the Vatican representatives were not allowed to enter Poland, and the existing Nunciatures in Amsterdam and Brussels, were closed. In October Kerrl's authority over Church affairs in the occupied territories was repudiated, and Church policy was transferred to the hands of the local Nazi party officials.

Both the Foreign Ministry and the Ministry of Church Affairs were thus deprived of much of their former influence over Church policy. They realized that the arbitrary measures of the local *Gauleiters* could lead only to a heightening of tension with the Papacy and to unco-ordinated and perhaps conflicting policies throughout the German-controlled parts of Europe. But the Nazi extremists dismissed all their arguments as irrelevancies, advanced merely to bolster the waning authority of Ribbentrop and his staff, and the Foreign Ministry itself had reluctantly to admit the claims of political and military necessity.

Our measures against the Catholic clergy in Poland [Woermann noted in January 1940] are actually unavoidable because leading members of the Catholic clergy as well as all other leading personalities of former Poland must be eliminated.[40]

On 27 July 1940 Ribbentrop instructed the German Ambassador to the Holy See to notify the Vatican authorities that the episcopal sees in the Protectorate of Bohemia and Moravia and in Poland must in future be conferred on German priests or at least on priests of German origin.[41] A year later, after the invasion of Russia, the Nazis extended their demands to cover appointments in all territories where the Concordat was not in effect and to include such lesser ranks in the hierarchy as Apostolic Administrators and other substitute bishops.[42] The Vatican indignantly refused, stating that such limitations to its freedom of selection had not been made even to governments 'which by their favourable treatment of the Church have earned for themselves particular merits'.[43]

This disagreement over church appointments was but one of many points of dispute with the Holy See. The distress of the Pope at the failure of his mediatory attempts in 1939 was increased by the mounting number of reports of suffering inflicted on his people by Nazi tyranny and by the further military invasions launched by the Nazis in 1940 and 1941, to which the Pope refused to signify his support or to call upon Catholics to join in a Nazi-led 'crusade against atheistic Bolshevism'. The failure of the Pope's efforts to secure any satisfaction from protests submitted by the Papal Nuncio, and his awareness of the humiliations to which his people were being subjected, necessarily caused him increasing alarm. On 1 June 1941 he wrote to Bishop Preysing in Berlin:

The tension between Church and Party in Germany is so obvious that a Memorandum written in a calm but frank tone by the Bishops to the competent authorities could cause no surprise. It is above all the need to think of the loyalty of faithful Catholics which justifies such a step or something like it, for they must be made aware that in these difficult days the hierarchy is doing everything it can to prepare for an amelioration of affairs and to defend the rights of the Church by appropriate and worthy means.[44]

Nevertheless the Pope was not sanguine of success. Writing again to Bishop Preysing in September 1941 he said:

Your suggestion that the Holy See might undertake representations to the Reich government through the German Embassy in order to strengthen the hands of the Bishops has already been anticipated not once but frequently in recent years. But in fact with so little success that up to now not a single answer to these letters has been received. At the same time care will be taken here not to neglect any opportunity, even if it offers only the hope of a slight result, to urge the cause of the German Catholics either in writing or verbally.[45]

Despite the bleak prospect of obtaining satisfaction, the Vatican continued to despatch the Nuncio to the Foreign Ministry with complaints and inquiries.[46] Msgr Orsenigo made persistent representations on a vast number of matters and returned to raise again and again the questions on which the Vatican had received equivocal replies. So frequent did his interventions become that the German Foreign Ministry at last politely intimated that his complaints should be limited only to matters of larger importance.[47] Nevertheless the Nuncio still persisted, doggedly determined not to be deterred from carrying out his responsibilities so far as the increasingly narrow limits imposed by the German authorities allowed. On instructions from the Vatican he protested vehemently against the ill-treatment, expulsion and imprisonment of bishops, priests and nuns in the occupied territories, especially in Poland, and against their transportation to Oranienburg, Buchenwald and Dachau in Germany.[48] He requested a personal interview with Himmler to plead for improved conditions; but the request was refused. He asked permission to visit the priests imprisoned in Sachsenhausen concentration camp; but this too was rejected, though he was allowed to make a single visit to a prisoner-of-war camp where some French priests were interned. He complained of discrimination against Polish priests in Dachau who were forbidden to say Mass though imprisoned German priests were allowed to do so. The Vatican also protested strongly against the regulations under which Polish workers transported to Germany as slave labour were allowed to attend Mass only once a month – a prohibition which, it was feared, might be extended to other Catholics and become a permanent measure when the war was over. The Nuncio conducted lengthy and heated arguments over the reorganization of vacant sees and the appointment of incumbents whom the Nazis, in defiance of the Vatican's rights, wished to install. He continually besought permission to visit areas where church conditions were gravest; he pleaded for the release of Dutch Catholics imprisoned in Buchenwald as hostages for Germans held in the Dutch East Indies; he strove to obtain permission for priests who had been imprisoned and were banned from returning to their parishes to be allowed to emigrate overseas; and he tirelessly returned to the question of church properties which had been closed or confiscated even after Hitler's decree of July 1941 ordering such seizures to stop.[49] But his endeavours were almost all in vain. Only a few minor concessions were granted.

Nor were his interventions concerned only with ecclesiastical matters. He made repeated inquiries about other victims of German atrocities, including the 33,000 Slovenes who were ejected from their homes in 1941, the Jews expelled from France and Lemberg, and the hostages held in Belgium, Serbia and France in retaliation for attacks on the German occupation forces.[50] He made frequent pleas for clemency on behalf of individuals who had been condemned to death by German military tribunals, particularly in

Belgium, and, on instructions from the Curia, he interceded on behalf of relatives of members of the former diplomatic corps at the Vatican. Particularly notable were his efforts on behalf of the seventeen professors of Lemberg (Lvov) University who, as was later reported, were 'liquidated' in 1942,[51] and on behalf of Provost Lichtenberg of Berlin, who died on his way to Dachau from the privations suffered in imprisonment.[52] The Nuncio also sought to gain permission for the Vatican to send aid to the starving children in Greece and to the hundreds of refugees in Yugoslavia, and for typhoid vaccine for the sick and suffering Polish population. The German authorities were implacable on every count; nor would they consent even to make use of the Vatican's information service to exchange lists of prisoners-of-war between the combatant states. In fact, with one or two minor exceptions, all the Nuncio's attempts to mitigate the sufferings inflicted on these helpless victims were repudiated by one or other of the Nazi agencies. So far from co-operating with the Nuncio and the Curia in their efforts to secure peace, the Nazis' obvious intention, as expressed in a draft telegram prepared for Ribbentrop in October 1942, was simply that 'relations between the German Embassy and the Vatican should be handled in a dilatory manner'.[53]

Of all the Vatican's representations the most forceful and the most repeated concerned the scandalous treatment of the Catholic Church in the Warthegau region, the details of which are discussed below. For both personal and political reasons, some members of the Foreign Ministry, including State Secretary Weizsäcker,[54] were ready to consider these protests with sympathy, but their views were thwarted by the high-handed measures of the local *Gauleiter*, Greiser. In vain Weizsäcker wrote to Greiser in January 1942, urging that

the request of the Nuncio to expand his jurisdiction to cover the Warthegau does imply a certain recognition by the Curia of the incorporation of the territory of the Warthegau [into the Reich proper]. For this reason we are concerned on grounds of general foreign political interest to support the Nuncio's request ... I entirely agree with you that our Church policy in the Warthegau should not in any way be endangered by the approval of this suggestion, which is required in the interests of our foreign policy. But I do not believe this would follow from any recognition in principle of the Nuncio's jurisdiction in the Warthegau. The competent German authorities will doubtless find ways and means at their disposal to protect the interests of the Reich against any unwarranted interference from outside.[55]

These arguments were curtly dismissed by Hitler, as yet another attempt by the Foreign Ministry to assert its own authority; in his *Table Talk* he derided their efforts with the words:

Unfortunately, the Wilhelmstrasse, with its usual greed for fresh fields of authority, has allowed itself to be imposed upon by the Papal legate.[56]

In accordance with the Nazi doctrine of *Führerprinzip*, the Nazi *Gauleiters* were encouraged to establish themselves in their own 'fiefs' as conquerors of the occupied territories. The affairs of the churches, it was held, should be their responsibility, unhampered by diplomatic interference or by limitations and legal quibbles imposed by the Concordat. In May 1942, in a dispute between Ribbentrop and Rosenberg over their respective rights to deal with the Vatican in matters concerning the Catholic Church in lands formerly held by the Soviet Union, Hitler decided in favour of Rosenberg. And two months later Hitler declared with evident satisfaction:

As regards future relations between State and Church, it is very satisfactory from our point of view that in nearly half the Reich negotiations can now be conducted by the appropriate *Reichsstatthalter*, unfettered by the clauses of the Concordat. . . . For this means that in each district the *Gauleiter* can, according to the degree of emancipation acquired by the population of his *Gau*, lead the people forward step by step in the sense that we desire.[57]

It was in accordance with this view and in order to put an end to the importunities of the Vatican, that at the beginning of June of the same year Hitler decided that henceforth the Nuncio in Berlin was to be denied jurisdiction over any of the German-held areas beyond Germany proper.[58]

1. The Fuhrer wishes that relations with the Catholic Church should

not be handled or maintained in a uniform manner for the whole Reich.

2. Germany will maintain relations with the Vatican only for the old Reich, i.e. for that part of the Reich for which the Concordat of 1933 has been signed.
3. Although the Concordat is outdated at many points, the Führer considers it to be officially in force.
4. Having informed the German Government that it could not recognize any political territorial changes for the duration of the war, the Vatican automatically severed official connections with the territories incorporated or occupied after September 1939. The Führer wishes, however, the same relationship to be established for the former Austria and other territories incorporated before September 1939.
5. In these territories the following are held to be responsible: On the German side, the regular representatives of the Reich, i.e., for instance, the Reich Protector, Governor, Reich Commissioner, *Reichsstatthalter*; on the side of the Church, the local representatives of the Church, for instance Cardinals, Bishops etc.

In these territories therefore no diplomatic or political links with the Vatican will be permitted; it follows that, for the rest, the Foreign Ministry is to retain exclusive connections with the Vatican.[59]

On 25 June Weizsäcker informed the Nuncio of this decision, adding that 'No further consideration will be taken of proposals or requests concerning territories which do not belong to Germany proper [*Alt-Reich*], and that he should confine his activities solely to matters concerning the pre-1938 Germany'.[60]

The decision was a blow to the Vatican. It was a blow also to Ribbentrop and Kerrl, for it signified Hitler's approval of the assumption of power by the Party authorities and the exclusion of their ministries from any influence over church policy in the conquered areas.[61] Ribbentrop and his officials, while desperately anxious to retain as much control over relations with the Vatican as they could, were equally anxious not to appear too sympathetic to protests submitted by the Holy See. Indeed in May 1942 Ribbentrop made the silly boast that

Up to now my Ministry has obeyed the Führer's wishes, and I am following the example of the Republic of Venice which, over the space of a life-time, made a special collection of unanswered notes from the Vatican.[62]

The futility of the situation became increasingly apparent in the subsequent months. While pretending that German–Vatican relations had not deteriorated, Ribbentrop was at the same time refusing to allow his officials to accept the Vatican's protests about conditions in the Warthegau. Finally, when he found himself unable to defeat his rivals in the Nazi hierarchy, Ribbentrop turned his rancour upon the Holy See, and even threatened to take measures against the Catholic Church 'should the Vatican . . . threaten to undertake or carry out a political or propaganda campaign against Germany'.[63]

The Pope refused to be blackmailed. In October 1942 and again in March 1943 two further protests, couched in stronger and sterner terms, were sent to the German representatives.[64] Again they fell on deaf ears, and the Pope was at last reluctantly forced to the realization that nothing could be achieved by this method of 'non-diplomacy'. A month later, writing to Bishop Preysing, he noted sadly:

. . . As you know, most severely hit of all is the Catholic Church in the Warthegau. We feel greatly the limitless sufferings of the faithful there, all the more since every attempt to negotiate for them with the government authorities has met with the most peremptory refusals . . .[65]

The more moderate-minded in the Nazi echelons of power, who had believed that a 'correct' policy towards the Vatican would reap substantial benefits for Germany, thus saw their hopes torn to shreds by the anti-Papism of Hitler and his closest advisors. Ideological considerations superimposed on hatred of the influence exerted by the centuries-old Roman Curia, dictated the Nazis' aversion to the Vatican. There could be little room for doubt that the Nazi aim was to exclude the Holy See entirely from German-held territory, so that the last remnants of the power of 'black Catholicism' could be wiped out. The same policy was not yet possible in Germany proper, but its final implementation was obviously only a matter of time.

III THE MODEL NAZI REGION AND THE NEW ERA IN CHURCH–
STATE RELATIONS

On 8 October 1939, Hitler issued a decree instituting the further
partition of Poland and restoring to Germany proper the two
regions of West Prussia–Danzig and the neighbouring province of
Posnania, or the Wartheland, which was officially known as the
Reichsgau Wartheland, or, more commonly, the Warthegau. This
area, which in 1939 had a population of four and a half million
people, had prior to 1914 belonged to Germany, and during the
inter-war period had been colonized by the Poles. This process of
history was now to be reversed, and the whole area was to be
're-Germanized' and incorporated into the territory of the Fatherland. The man chosen by Hitler to carry out the reorganization
was a former inhabitant of Danzig called Arthur Greiser, who by
1939 had risen to become President of the Nazi-controlled Senate
in Danzig and an *Obergruppenführer* (Lt.-General) in the SS.
Probably because of his connection with Himmler, Greiser was on
26 October appointed to the dual post of *Gauleiter* and *Reichsstatthalter*, thereby combining the policies of both Party and State
in the Warthegau under his unified control. As his deputy in
charge of civil administration, Greiser chose August Jäger, whose
baleful influence in the early years of the Church Struggle has been
noted earlier in this book.

Greiser's ambition was to make the Wartheland a model Nazi
Gau. In a speech later in celebration of the completion of two years
of office, he proclaimed:

... Here in the virgin territory of the German East, we are all offered
the chance of the new reconstruction of the State, which will reflect
the principles of National Socialism in all aspects of public life, or at
least will come nearest to it. As a result we have the exhilarating feeling
that the work of reconstruction which has been laid on our shoulders
is today providing the start of a reform for the whole Reich that will
be implemented later.[66]

Greiser's object was to introduce 'the norms of our revolutionary and ideological principles' and thus to fashion in his region 'a
Gau in the Greater German Reich which is free from all traditional

bureaucratic restrictions'. The Warthegau was to become 'the training ground for the Nazi ideology' and the 'model for the whole Party'.

Such a concept demanded both a clean sweep and total control. Despite the terms of Hitler's original decree which implied the application of German law to the newly-conquered territory, Greiser preferred to regard his fief as an area in which all previous legal statutes had been annulled (*rechtsfreien Raum*). The task of reconstruction demanded that

the ruling power in its boldness and readiness to take the initiative needs not only a secure knitting together of all the technical and special responsibilities in the hands of the supreme authority, but also a strictly centralized direction in the leadership of all areas of public life.[67]

The reasons for the Party's choice of the Warthegau 'as the virgin territory' in which to put their ideologies into practice are understandable. The rapid overrunning of the area had destroyed the Polish administration. The decision to 're-Germanify' the territory led to a radical alteration in the character of the population, with the expulsion of the Poles and the Jews and the re-introduction of Germans, some of them brought 'home to the Reich' from the Baltic States of Estonia, Latvia and Lithuania, and others 're-settled' from Germany itself. The inhabitants, most of whom were thus prepared for new conditions and new laws, were to be exposed to direct rule by the Nazi Party 'bosses'. The traditional supervision by government ministries would be replaced by policies of the Party's own devising, the time now being considered ripe for an advance towards the remodelling of society. Old institutions could thus be discarded without difficulty and Hitler's plan could be set in hand to

plant a seed of Nordic blood wherever the population stands in need of regeneration. . . . As regards the Germanization of the Eastern territories, we shall not succeed except by the application of the most severe measures. Nevertheless I am convinced that these territories will bear a profound Germanic imprint after fifty years of National Socialist history.[68]

To carry out these plans, the Nazi officials at Party headquarters and the *Reichssicherheitshauptamt* demanded a free hand for their work and no interference by the bureaucrats in Berlin. From the outset it was accepted that the Churches in the occupied territories would be included in the traditional institutions which would need to be radically altered. Immediately after the completion of the military campaign of 1939 Himmler showed his authority in the Warthegau by promulgating measures for the extermination or expulsion of most of the Polish clergy, justifying his action by the claim that more than enough priests were left to cater for the spiritual needs of the population. In December of the same year Bormann instructed Lammers to demand that the 'provisions of the Concordats and the regulations in force in Germany proper [*Alt-Reich*] should not be introduced into the newly-conquered lands'.[69] Heydrich announced that 'security measures' necessitated the exclusion of all the regular ministerial officials; and Greiser's dual role of *Gauleiter* and *Reichsstatthalter* enabled him to ignore the regular channels of government administration and to receive orders directly from Bormann or Himmler.[70]

These autocratic moves aroused great resentment in several of the Ministries in Berlin, whose hopes had been raised of regaining in the newly-won territories some of their dwindling influence. In March 1940, Kerrl complained bitterly to Frick that his responsibilities in the Warthegau had been usurped by Greiser in matters concerning the financial affairs of the Churches. 'This', Kerrl averred, 'goes far beyond his authority.'[71] But the Ministries were powerless against the Party authorities. In vain they protested that such transfer of authority had not been sanctioned by Hitler, and that anomalies must arise if different regulations were to be enacted in different parts of the Reich. Their protests led only to prolonged wranglings between Ministerial and Party Offices, which dragged on fruitlessly until after the invasion of Russia, when more pressing matters took precedence and Ministerial opposition was at last abandoned as useless. There is little doubt, however, that Kerrl's unsuccessful efforts to assert his jurisdiction were the cause of Hitler's final repudiation of his authority over any of the annexed territories.

The initiative for church policy in the new *Gaus* henceforward

313

came directly from the Nazi Party chancellery in Munich. In June 1940 a draft decree for the judicial status of religious organizations in the newly formed *Gau* of Danzig–West Prussia was forwarded by Bormann to Rosenberg.[72] Here for the first time the separation of Church and State was proclaimed as official Nazi policy, in accordance with Bormann's plans first expressed to the Supreme Command of the Armed Forces and later repeated in his circular of June 1941.[73]

In recent years the Party has had to announce again and again its rejection of the plan of establishing a State Church, or of a closer connection between the State and the Church. The Party has repudiated these plans with all its force for the following reasons. In the first place, it would not be compatible with the doctrinal demands of National Socialism to unite the State with the Churches as the external forms of the religious communities, which do not have as their whole-hearted objectives the implementation of National Socialist principles. In the second place, considerations of a political character oppose such an outward unity.

Bormann's determination to have his own way in the treatment of Church questions in the newly-incorporated territories, both in the East and in the West, can be further inferred from two secret circulars issued to the *Gauleiters* in September 1941 and May 1942. Local Party authorities were ordered not to deal with any complaints from the representatives of the Churches, but to forward them to Party headquarters, so that

a unified regulation of Church policy in these areas can be achieved. This is valid also as regards the approval of official subsidies for the Churches and the appointments to the highest Church offices. . . . In denominational affairs in the new areas I stress once again that my viewpoint must be obtained in good time for all important and fundamental questions.[74]

Greiser and Jäger were in complete agreement with these regulations. In Greiser's view, the policy advocated by the Ministries in Berlin that existing German laws should apply in the newly-conquered territories was entirely inappropriate. The Churches had, in his opinion, now ceased to be legally established pillars of the German community, and it was only a matter of time before their centuries-old influence was completely swept away. In the Warthegau, where the fortunes of war had already removed their legal status, there could be no question of restoring to the remnants of the Churches a status which was now out-of-date. Instead, the opportunity should be seized to 'implement a new legal status more in accordance with the Nazi ideology'.[75]

In a letter to Kerrl written in February 1940, Greiser outlined the basis of his policy:

> With regard to the regulation of Church life, I take the fundamental position, which I would like you to note, that neither the German Reich nor the *Reichsgau* Wartheland is to be considered the legal successor of the former Polish state. . . . It has been left to me, in conjunction with the Ministry of the Interior, to decide which legal system – the former Polish, the German, or a specially devised one for the Warthegau – will be adopted for the reorganization of these matters.
>
> As part of my basic policy, I do not propose to allow the incorporation or reorganization of Church life in the Warthegau along lines which are applicable in Germany proper. Rather I propose to recognize the former churches only as religious societies and associations under definite and limited conditions.[76]

Without more ado, Greiser and his henchmen accordingly set about preparing their own plans for the control of the Warthegau Churches, which in the following winter, according to Bormann, were presented to Hitler and received his approval.[77]

The Nazi extremists anticipated little opposition. The Roman Catholic clergy, being mainly Poles, had already been decimated by the SS, and vast numbers of the Polish laity had been driven into exile. Even the appointment of a German-speaking bishop to take over responsibility in the orphaned diocese of Posen (Poznan), was vetoed by Heydrich on the grounds that

> the revival of episcopal functions in the territory . . . had been deliberately and purposely repudiated through the expulsion of the Church hierarchy.[78]

Possible interventions by the Vatican could, it was reckoned, be countered by accusations that the Curia had shown hostility by allowing Cardinal Hlond to use the Vatican radio for anti-German propaganda, by refusing to recognize Germany's conquests, and by the continued presence of a Polish Ambassador at the Vatican. The Nuncio was not allowed to establish contact with Church officials still in the Warthegau; the right of the Vatican to be consulted about the appointments of new Church administrators was brusquely denied;[79] and organizational connections between the Churches of the Warthegau and those of Germany proper were refused recognition. Even the obviously pro-German sympathies of the German-speaking portion of the Evangelical Church, which had prided itself on remaining loyal throughout the twenty years of Polish rule and which regarded the Nazi conquest of Poland as a 'liberation', failed to earn them the slightest respect.

Greiser was equally adamant against interference from any of the Ministries in Berlin, particularly from the Minister of Church Affairs, whose authority, he declared 'did not exist for him'.[80] He suspected Kerrl of scheming to unite the local Evangelical Church with the mother Church of Prussia, which was, of course, subject to Kerrl's authority, and early in February 1940, he addressed a sharply-worded rebuke to Kerrl as follows:

I must hereby inform you that I am not at all prepared to tolerate a repudiation of my political aims by the German Evangelical Church. The decision as to whether the Evangelical Church in my *Gau* shall be united with the Evangelical Church in Germany ... will never be taken behind my back, but solely and only in consultation with me. ... The timing of such a settlement [*Bereinigung*] will be determined, however, exclusively by me in Posen, taking into account all other political aims. It will not be determined behind my back by the church authorities, apparently with the approval of your subordinates in Germany proper.[81]

Hitler's two decisions, to deprive Kerrl of control in the Warthegau and to repudiate the Papal Nuncio's jurisdiction in the area, immensely strengthened Greiser's hand. Confident of support in the highest quarters, he had no fear of further interference by the bureaucrats, whose minds he considered capable of dealing only with points of law and precedents set by tradition.

His intentions were formulated in thirteen points, which were

first made known verbally to Church leaders in the summer of
1940.[82] It is probable that the original draft of these points had been
composed at Party headquarters, for a specialist in Church Affairs
on Greiser's staff, Pastor Dudzus, declared in an interview with the
Evangelical Church leaders in July 1940 that the plans could be
taken as the Führer's instructions for the 'clarification' of the
relationship between Church and State in the 'youngest and most
difficult *Gau*'.

According to Dudzus, the Churches were to be recognized, not
as official bodies, but only as religious associations which would be
accorded the legal status of juridical persons under private law.
Only societies approved by the *Reichsstatthalter* would be sanctioned, and their rights and properties would be determined by
him. No official church taxes would be levied, and the associations
would exist solely from contributions from their members. Under
point four 'no connections with groups outside the *Gau* would be
allowed. There was to be no legal, financial or official connection
with the Reich Church.' The Catholic Church in the Warthegau
would be made independent of Rome. Under point five only
adults who signed a written declaration could become members
of an association, and children were excluded until they reached
adulthood; anyone entering the Warthegau from Germany
proper would not be assumed to be a member until he had signed
the official declaration. Point six banned all subsidiary organizations and youth groups. Under point seven, Germans and Poles
were forbidden to worship together in the same church, the religious associations being now strictly divided according to nationality. Under point eight, the schools were forbidden to hold
confirmation classes, as religious instruction was to be divorced
from secular education; nor were the churches allowed to undertake welfare work. The property of the Churches was limited to
their Church buildings. Point twelve decreed the dissolution of all
monasteries and nunneries, 'since these did not fit in with German
morality and its population policy'. The final point forbade priests
from outside the Warthegau to minister in the region; priests
who were granted official Nazi approval must hold some other
profession and would not be permitted to minister full-time to

their congregations.[83] The Polish Catholic theological faculty of the University of Posen would be closed, and only very limited facilities for the training of priests would be sanctioned.

The Evangelical Church was greatly disturbed by these reported plans. To make the position clear, the *Gauleiter* granted an interview to their leaders in Posen in September 1940 and announced that the special treatment of the Churches in the Warthegau was due to the 'emergency situation' and to the fact that 'here the National Socialist State is being constructed. The idea behind the National Socialist State demands a separation of State and Church and therefore the Church must take the form of a private association.'[84]

The illusions entertained by the Evangelical Church since September 1939 were now completely at an end. In October 1940 the Superintendent of the Posen Evangelical Church, Dr Blau, wrote indignantly to Greiser:

> I am still today shocked ... by the statement that the idea of the National Socialist state demands the separation of Church and State. ... Such words have never been expressed in the last seven years by any official spokesman to representatives of any Evangelical Church. ... This will affect the German people deeply. ... It means the separation of the Church from the people, and the expulsion of the Churches' ministry from the life of the people.[85]

When no satisfactory answer was received, Dr Blau addressed a lengthy letter to Hitler, which was passed on to Bormann, who replied on 30 April 1941 in unmistakable terms.

> In the opinion of the Church authorities, *Gauleiter* Greiser justifies his measures on the grounds of the intended separation of Church and State. However, he also demands that the State should have far-reaching rights to influence and supervise religious associations. This, the Church claims, contradicts the basis of separation of Church and State as it has been implemented in France and the United States. All that needs to be said here is that our National Socialist principles for the separation of Church and State are not the same as those of the democracies. ... For your information, I can tell you that *Gauleiter* Greiser issued the regulations, against which Herr Blau complains, with the approval of the Führer.[86]

The decision to abrogate the legal status of the Churches proved to be only a preliminary measure. Although Greiser declared that such a change need have no effect on the 'spiritual' work of the Churches, further measures to curtail their activities were soon forthcoming. In March 1940, without prior consultation with the Church Ministry or with the German Evangelical Church, Greiser instituted a strict control over the finances of the Churches, including the collections taken at Church services, the property of the Churches, the subsidies paid by official bodies, and the contributions from endowments.[87] On 23 September all charitable institutions and welfare organizations were placed under the control of the *Reichsstatthalter* – a measure which led to the confiscation of many Church properties in addition to those already seized on the grounds that they had formerly belonged to Polish citizens, and the National Socialist Welfare Organization (NSV) was empowered to take over Church hostels and institutions for its own use. In a lecture delivered at Kiel in 1942 Greiser declared

If we have taken away the property of the Polish Church, this is not to punish faithful Catholics, but rather because economic resources for the political struggle against the German people were derived from this property. That is why there are no more monasteries and no more church properties left in the *Reichsgau* Wartheland. They have all been confiscated.[88]

In 1941 the measures were extended. In May Greiser refused to recognize the authority of the Evangelical Church leaders or of the former Catholic Diocesan officials, and forbade the presentation of complaints and protests from Polish Church authorities or Polish priests. After May no parish was allowed to hold members of both Polish and German nationalities. Polish priests were forbidden to minister to German congregations, and vice-versa; churches which had belonged to Polish adherents before the war were treated as Polish, and those in the charge of a German minister were obliged to display a notice stating 'Poles forbidden'.[89] In August new regulations for confirmation classes were issued: only German children between the ages of ten and eighteen were permitted to attend; the hours of instruction were limited to between three o'clock and five o'clock on weekdays; the classes were restricted to officially approved religious groups and could be held only in the Church buildings; and the police were to be informed beforehand of the time and place of the classes and the names of the teachers. A month later all religious instruction was banned in the schools. House-to-house missionary work by lay-men or lay preachers was prohibited, and all such activity was confined to Church buildings, not including the rectories.

The culmination of these moves came on 13 September 1941 when Greiser, by virtue of his 'vested authority', issued his 'Ordinance on religious associations and societies in the *Reichsgau* Warthe-land',[90] which he described as 'a milestone on the way to our goal of removing all connections with the Church'.[91] The ordinance which expunged the legal provisions of former years, set out in legal form the notorious thirteen points. According to Bormann, its publication had been delayed because of lengthy discussions with the authorities concerned, but it now brought 'the developments first undertaken in Austria a much greater step nearer to completion'.[92]

The *Gauleiter* declared that henceforth four religious associa-tions would be recognized as juridical persons under private law:

1. The Posen Evangelical Church of German nationality in the Warthe-land.
2. The Litzmannstadt Evangelical Church of German nationality in the Wartheland.
3. The Evangelical–Lutheran Church of German nationality in the Western Wartheland.
4. The Roman Catholic Church of German nationality in the Reichsgau Wartheland.

These four entities would replace the erstwhile legally-established bodies of the Evangelical and Roman Catholic Churches, though the *Gauleiter* reserved the right to grant legal status to other religious associations as he thought fit. The right of individual parishes to be considered as legal entities was withdrawn. There was no provision for a Polish Church of any sort, an omission that clearly foreshadowed the eventual abolition of Polish Church life in its entirety.[93]

Each of the religious associations were required to produce a constitution to be submitted for the *Gauleiter*'s approval. Without his permission no person could hold a post of responsibility in any of the Churches – a provision (obviously directed against the Poles) which covered, not only the customary procedure of submitting the names of new appointees to the government authorities, but also the members of the Church hierarchy already ordained and in office.

Paragraphs six to fifteen of the ordinance laid down new regulations concerning membership in the Churches. Only adult residents of the Warthegau were declared to be eligible. The procedure for admission was a declaration, either verbal or in writing, made to the local government officials. The Church's ceremonies of baptism, confirmation and Holy Communion were without legal status. The children of Church members were to be allowed full membership only upon the reaching of age of twenty-one and after making a signed declaration of intent.

Within a few days of the promulgation of these regulations, and without waiting to see the result of their impact upon the population, Greiser pressed forward with further measures. All German government officials posted to the Warthegau who were not considered as residents of the area, were required to sign a statement of their intention to withdraw from the Church.[94] In January 1942 all school-teachers were declared automatically excluded from the Churches; in May the same regulation was extended to members of the Nazi Party and its affiliated associations, who were further required to promise not to rejoin the Church even if they were posted back to Germany proper – a move intended to show that those in official positions were voluntarily leading the way towards 'liberating' themselves from any connection with the Churches.[95]

On 3 October 1941 a new ordinance by the *Reichsstatthalter* confiscated without compensation all Church-owned cemeteries, which were henceforward to be placed under the control of the local authorities; Poles would no longer be buried in the same cemeteries as Germans.[96] In the following March the holding of Church services on Good Friday was prohibited, on the grounds that

M

the Party also has its Good Friday – 9 November 1923; it also has its martyrs – those who died for the Movement; it also possesses its altar – the *Felderrnhalle* in Munich.[97]

But on this matter the churchmen refused to be coerced. So many gathered outside their locked Churches on Good Friday morning that the Gestapo was obliged to withdraw its prohibition, and in the following years the services were allowed to proceed without intervention.

The many protests registered by churchmen against these baleful measures were totally ignored by Greiser,[98] and the Church leaders had now to consider not only how to safeguard their legal existence, but how to secure continuation of their pastoral ministry. Some believed that the whole ordinance should be rejected as an unwarrantable interference in the affairs of a community which owed its loyalty, not to the State, but to God, and that anything less than total rejection would be a betrayal of the Church's divine ministry. Others counselled a policy of caution, in the hope of winning some concessions whereby they might at least be allowed to continue their pastoral functions, and perhaps in the hope that influential voices within Germany, or even from Rome itself, might eventually bring about the disavowal of the *Gauleiter*. They even considered the advisability of a direct appeal to Hitler, drawing his attention to the similarity of the new measures to the anti-Christian campaign launched by the Bolshevik authorities after the seizure of the Baltic lands in 1940.[99] But their deliberations and their hopes were all quickly extinguished by a laconic note issued on 6 November intimating that

The Führer approves the ordinance of 13 September issued by *Reichsstatthalter* Greiser.[100]

A few days later, the church authorities were informed accordingly.[101]

The Nazis' confidence in a German victory over the Soviet Union was probably the reason for their preparations to remove all possible opponents from the German Eastern territories. On 6 October 1941 the Gestapo ordered the systematic arrest of nearly all the few remaining Polish priests still in their parishes. No less than four hundred and eighty priests were taken to three 'transit camps' in Konstantynow, Posen and Lad, for transportation in cattle-trucks to Dachau as 'human freight,' though since large numbers of them were already in retirement, their arrest could in no way be attributed to political moves against the occupying power.[102] In the diocese of Kattowitz (Kattowice), if a priest 'due' for arrest could not be found, an innocent substitute was taken in his place in order to maintain the quota set by SS headquarters.[103] At least ninety priests from the diocese of Kulm (Chelm) lost their lives in the concentration camps of Stutthof, Grenzdorf, Auschwitz (Oswiecim), Sachsenhausen and Dachau. In the diocese of Plock, where both the bishop and his suffragan died in captivity in 1941, a large number of priests were taken to the concentration camp of Soldau (Dzialdovo), where at least fifty are known to have died.[104] By 1942 there were no fewer than 1,773 Polish priests in Dachau where they formed by far the largest single group of prisoners.[105]

According to a German Catholic priest, the arrests of the Polish priests in the Warthegau in October 1941 were the result of a directive entitled 'Action for the Destruction of the Catholic Church in the *Reichsgau* Wartheland'.

On these two days, all the Polish priests were arrested in one fell swoop [*schlagartig*] and taken to a concentration camp, with the exception only of those who were considered by the *Landräten* and *Kreisleitern* [administrative officials appointed by the Nazi Party] to be definitely indispensable. The *Landräten* were advised to retain two priests in each county for the pastoral care of the Polish population, if this seemed necessary to the *Landrat*. The majority of these officers took advantage of this concession, though several declared that Polish priests were no longer necessary at all.[106]

The 3,200,000 Poles resident in the Warthegau were now deprived even of the meagre ministry which had been left to them by the Nazis after the first wave of persecutions in 1939. On average, each county in the Warthegau was allowed only one Polish church and at most two Polish priests.[107] Greiser's decision to permit the continuance of a German Catholic Church meant that there were relatively more churches for the religious needs of

German Catholics, even though they represented only ten per cent of the total Catholic population – a concession undoubtedly designed to stress the superiority of the 'Master Race'. The Catholic diocese of Posen had before the war possessed 441 churches; of these only thirty were left open for the use of Poles and fifteen for Germans. In the city of Posen itself, only three of its 30 churches were permitted to continue, two for Poles and one for Germans.[108] Thirteen churches were locked up and abandoned, six served as warehouses, and four others, including the cathedral, were used as furniture store-houses. According to figures recorded in a German Foreign Ministry document, of the 681 regular and 147 monastic priests in the diocese of Posen, no less than 451 were imprisoned or sent to concentration camps, 120 were expelled to the territory of the Government-General in Central Poland, 74 were shot or died in concentration camps, 32 were refused permission to carry out their ministry, 24 fled abroad, and 12 were missing. Only 34 of the original 828 were left to minister to their Polish parishioners and 17 to the Germans.[109] In May 1942 the Papal Nuncio, in a bitter note to the Foreign Ministry, pointed out that in the portion of the Archdiocese of Gnesen which lay in the Warthegau, only about 16 of approximately 220 parishes had incumbents, while in the county of Dietfurt

the two remaining Catholic priests have been forbidden to hold services for over a year on the order of the *Kreisleiter* . . . in Mogilno county with about 30 parishes no religious services have been held for a long time, nor are the Holy Sacraments administered there. . . . In Jaretschi county, with about 32 Catholic parishes, there is no Catholic priest and no Catholic service.[110]

The agonized protests against these conditions registered by the Papal Nuncio, by Cardinal Bertram and by the Evangelical Church bodies to the authorities in Berlin reveal a tragic picture of the martyrdom of the Church.[111] A combination of anti-Polish, anti-Catholic, and anti-clerical prejudice dominated the actions of the *Gauleiter* and his staff. And Hitler's decision to allow the *Gauleiters* a free hand in the ideological 're-education' of their territories, placed the territories wholly in the hands of the Nazi extremists without possibility of appeal. In August 1943 the German Catholic bishops in their annual pastoral letter stigmatized the increasing persecution of the Church as intolerable and the conditions in the Warthegau as approximating to 'an almost complete suppression of Christian religion'.[112] With growing apprehension they expressed fear that conditions there were, as many Party representatives had exultantly proclaimed, the 'prelude for the future status of the Church in Germany itself'.

The most forceful of all the protests was made in March 1943 by Cardinal Maglione, Papal Secretary of State, in a twenty-eight-page letter addressed to the German Government, in which he castigated the 'grave and systematic difficulties which are being put in the way of the free profession of the Catholic faith and the practice of the Catholic religion'.[113] Six bishops, he declared, had resided in the area in August 1939; now there was only one, and he was interned in his own residence. More than 2,000 priests had exercised their ministry in the Warthegau before the war; they were now reduced to a mere handful. Not even the nuns were able to continue their charitable work without molestation; a special concentration camp had been established for them at Bojanowo, where towards the middle of 1941 about 400 sisters were interned and employed on manual labour.[114] All Catholic schools had been suppressed, and the theological seminaries of Gnesen, Posen, Litzmannstadt (Lodz), and Wladislavia (Leslau) were closed. Church services, were limited by the Gestapo to set hours – on Sundays and feast days from 8 to 11 am and on week-days from 8 to 9 am; only on Saturdays were the laity allowed to attend. Confirmation classes and confessions for the young were permitted only on Wednesdays from 2 to 4 pm, and for adults on Saturdays from 2 to 6 pm. The members of one parish were forbidden to attend the services of another. The use of the Polish language was prohibited in church services, even for the Sacrament of Penance, and priests were forbidden to perform the marriage service for Polish men under the age of twenty-eight and for Polish women under twenty-five. Catholic lay organizations had been disbanded and the press services abolished. The spoliation of church properties was carried out with a wilful destructiveness designed to eradicate the spiritual heritage built up over a thousand years.[115]

In 1945, Pope Pius XII himself described the final stages of the Nazi persecution of the Churches:

The struggle against the Church did, in fact, become even more bitter: there was the dissolution of Catholic organizations; the gradual suppression of the flourishing Catholic schools, both public and private; the enforced weaning of youth from family and Church; the pressure brought to bear on the conscience of citizens, and especially of civil servants; the systematic defamation, by means of a clever, closely organized propaganda, of the Church, the faithful, the Church's institutions, teaching and history; the closing, dissolution, confiscation of religious houses and other ecclesiastical institutions; the complete suppression of the Catholic press and publishing houses.[116]

In short, the Pope declared, the 'satanic spectre' of National Socialism was in reality 'the arrogant apostasy from Jesus Christ, the denial of His doctrine and of His work of redemption, the cult of violence, the idolatry of race and blood, the overthrow of human liberty and dignity'.[117]

This terrible chapter of Nazi despotism was brought to an end only by Germany's total military defeat, when Greiser and his deputy Jäger were handed over to the Polish authorities and hanged for their crimes. But Greiser and Jäger were only the most conspicuous evil-doers in a policy of racial oppression which had been fully supported by practically every grade of the Nazi Party. As Professor Stasiewski has rightly stressed,

If the war had been carried to a successful conclusion, the Nazi dictatorship would not have introduced a compulsory separation of Church and State, but rather the dissolution of all religious communities, in order to achieve the victory of its 'ideology' throughout the areas under its control. Nazi Church policy in the Warthegau for this reason deserves the close attention of scholars in the field of contemporary history. For the state of affairs already implemented there, to a large extent, was in no way merely a separation of Church and State, for which there are many other examples; rather, this was an attempt to destroy Christianity by the agents of a state which sought to set itself up as autonomous. The struggle was in truth a campaign for the souls of faithful men and women, on whose allegiance Nazism made totalitarian claims.[118]

The sufferings of Christians in the years of Nazi persecution were the toll exacted by an overweening tyranny convinced of its own superiority and determined to have its own way. The danger still exists, in the possibility that men may again attempt to create neopagan idolatries out of secular ideologies, disguising their aims under a cloak of nationalism and imposing their will by force of arms. The Nazi attempt to break the resistance of the Churches failed, but it did so only with the collapse of its military forces; and the record of its reign of terror stands as a horrifying warning not only to the Christian world, but to mankind as a whole.

Conclusion

The persecution of the churches was the outcome of two of the most significant aspects of the Nazi system, its political nihilism and its ideological fanaticism. The Nazis' ambition to destroy the existing order of society went hand in hand with their determination to propagate a new German racial *Weltanschauung*. Their attack on the traditions and institutions which had moulded the German character for a thousand years was part and parcel of their attempt to impose their will upon the whole of German life. Their schemes went much further than the earlier nineteenth-century attempts to separate Church and State. By trying to prevent the Churches from exercising any influence over national affairs, and by attempting to drive them into obscurity to die out as unlamented relics of the past, the Nazi campaign exhibited a more menacing trend of the twentieth century. Here for the first time the totalitarian concept of a *Volksgemeinschaft*, dominated by a single ideology and dedicated to the will of a single political *Führer*, was proclaimed as the 'destiny' predicted by history. The Nazi claims for the supremacy of an all-embracing racial ideal were based on an appeal to mass instincts, and recognized the expediency of political ambition as the only morality. Their determination to remould society in the crucible of Hitler's ambitions was nothing less than an attempt to create a new 'Age of Absolutism'.

The Nazis' antagonism towards the Churches arose from their intolerance of any compromise with a system of belief that spanned the centuries and embraced all men under a doctrine of equality before God. Though Hitler's political shrewdness and sense of political tactics induced him from time to time to moderate the radical measures which his paranoid followers advocated, there can be no doubt of his innate antipathy to Christianity and to the Christian Churches. Christianity, he believed, was a 'hoax', and

328

'gangrene' which must be cut out before it infected the new growth of Nazi racialism; Germans had too long been held in bondage by the alien beliefs of a Jewish-derived faith and by the political conspiracy of Roman Catholic prelates. To the clergy he ascribed only the lowest motives of money-grubbing and political opportunism, and to the laity a befuddled obscurantism, from which he conceived it to be the Nazi duty to rescue them.

Hitler was neither alone nor original in holding such opinions. Indeed, his views, spiced with tendentious prejudice, were derived from the accepted clichés which had been current in Europe for decades, even for centuries. The Nazi campaign against the Churches was part of a wider process in which the banner of anti-clericalism was raised from one end of Europe to the other as a justification for violent repression carried out in the name of progress. In Germany itself the Nazis evoked the anti-Papist traditions of Bismarck's *Kulturkampf* to brand Catholics as *Reichsfeinde*, and resistance to totalitarianism was countered by claims that they were completing the task of eradicating 'political Catholicism' from the life of the nation.

The Nazis' campaign would never have achieved the success it did if the estrangement of millions from the faith of the Church had not already revealed a fatal weakening of Christianity. It was a sign of the grave sickness in the so-called Christian west that an ugly rash of emotional slogans, whipped up by dogmatic intolerance, was able to inflame the baser passions of men in the service of a primitive *Volksegoismus*. The Nazi radicals were motivated not only by a political desire for total control, but by an ideological fanaticism that believed it possible to create an *ersatz* religion of blood and soil. Their determination to root out the influence of the Church from the hearts of their countrymen by every device of slander and innuendo at their command was strengthened by the conviction that the appeal of the Christian faith was doomed to extinction.

Their attempt to find a secular substitute for Christianity was but the latest of many similar efforts in the past. The plans of the radical Nazis owed much – albeit unconsciously – to the iconoclasm and perversion of some of the French Revolutionary

M*   329 zealots, whose plans for the 'de-Christianization' of France, even Robespierre had finally dismissed as 'philosophical masquerades'. The efforts of the Nazi extremists had been foreshadowed by these earlier abortive attempts to create a new political faith, with its 'credo in the Declaration of the Rights of Man, its priesthood in the lawgivers, its baptismal ceremonies in the civic oaths administered at "altars of the Patrie", its symbols in the cockade, the tricolour and cap of liberty, its hymns, processions and calendar'.[1] The French Revolution was the first movement in modern times to attempt 'to replace Catholicism, with its supernatural frame of reference, by a secular religion of humanity, which, in various forms, runs through the subsequent history of Europe'.[2]

Nazi racial ideology also held out an eschatological promise of a new age to come. In return, it demanded the absolute allegiance of every citizen, refusing to concede that any area of life lay outside the scope of its *Weltanschauung*. If its rivalry with the Churches had at first been obscured by an unwillingness to launch a new *Kulturkampf*, the ultimate incompatibility was succinctly expressed by Bormann: 'National Socialism and Christianity are irreconcilable'.

Even so, there were many Nazis who did not succumb to such ideological extremism. A very considerable proportion of Party members saw the Church struggle solely in terms of politics. They continued to support adherence to the 'positive Christianity' of the Party programme and welcomed the Concordat of 1933. The subordination rather than the suppression of the Churches was their aim, and they subscribed to Napoleon's dictum that 'A religion is necessary for the people. This religion must be in the hands of the government. Fifty émigré bishops in the pay of England lead the French clergy today. We must destroy their influence. The authority of the Pope is necessary for that.'[3] In the view of these moderates, Rosenberg's fantastic imaginings of a new Nordic revelation would be powerless to destroy the people's age-long adherence to Catholicism or the engrafted Germanic traditions of Lutheranism; only the validity of Nazism as a political movement would be able to overwhelm the timid 'pietism' of Churchmen.

Christianity, they believed, was fast becoming so irrelevant to modern man that it was no longer a significant issue; it could be left as a solace to those who hankered after the benefits of 'the next world' or who lacked the courage to identify themselves with the ambitious designs of the 'Thousand Year Reich'.

The collapse of Nazism in 1945 left unsettled the question of which of these two strategies would have prevailed had a German military victory established Nazi rule throughout Europe. It is possible that motives of political expediency might have led to the adoption of a less savage treatment of the Churches. But there is evidence to show that the often-proclaimed determination to wipe out Christianity altogether would have been extended beyond the Warthegau to the other areas of German-held territory, and would have ended in the persecution of Christians by the same methods as had so effectively 'dealt with' the Jews. If the imagination falters at such a horrendous '*Endlösung*', who can doubt that the perpetrators of Auschwitz, Treblinka, Lidice and Oradour would have hesitated to repeat their experiments?

The reasons for the Church's failure to avert the moral and political catastrophe which Nazism brought upon Germany and the world are complex and still not wholly resolved. How was it possible that the Church should willingly have abetted such a totalitarian régime? How could so many reputable and responsible churchmen have lent their support, even if only passively, to the perpetration of such crimes as genocide? What fever seized so many millions of German Christians, both Evangelical and Catholic, in those few short years of Nazi tyranny? And what has been the legacy of the Nazi persecution upon the Churches themselves?

This study has tried to show that the unprecedented challenge of the Nazi State exposed churchmen to new and unforeseen dangers, which were to reveal both disastrous weaknesses and unexpected heroism. The Church was unprepared and totally unsuited to cope with the situation. Neither the hierarchy nor the laity had the courage or the means to mobilize the Church against the embattled might of Nazism, and thereby to jeopardize the very existence of their own institutions. The warning voices, first heard

331

at the Barmen Synod of 1934, went largely unheeded. Too late the leaders of the German Evangelical Church, meeting in the ruined city of Stuttgart in October 1945, lamented:

... we know ourselves to be one with our people in a great company of suffering and in a great solidarity of guilt. With great pain do we say: Through us endless suffering has been brought to many people and countries ... We accuse ourselves for not witnessing more courageously, for not praying more faithfully, for not believing more joyously, and for not loving more ardently.[4]

Their call for the spiritual renewal in the Church through a desire 'to cleanse themselves from influences alien to the faith and to set themselves in order' implied an acceptance of their own shortcomings during the years of Nazi misrule and a determination to start afresh. But how far this hope has been fulfilled is still a debatable point.

Since 1945 many reasons have been advanced for the failure of the German churches during the Nazi era. It has often been argued that the German people were not aware of what was happening in their own country, at a time when all the means of communication were controlled by the Government, and ignorance was consequently widespread. In times of national emergency, the security of the State is paramount and open protests cannot be tolerated; how then could the Germans have known? What is not certain, however, is whether the Germans would have done anything had they been fully aware of the situation. The question raised by Pastor Maas of the Heidelberg Confessing Church is significant: 'Was not what we *did* see and hear quite enough?'

Another, and possibly more valid, defence is that resistance is impossible in a highly organized police State, where the full power of the authorities is mobilized to crush any incipient sign of dissent. Yet there were churchmen – albeit very few – who had the courage to refuse submission to the Nazis' demands. Their steadfastness was unavailing; but who can say that their sacrifice was in vain? While Pastor Niemöller was awaiting trial in a Berlin prison, he was visited by the prison chaplain, who asked him in

Conclusion

astonishment: 'But Brother! What brings *you* here? Why are you in prison?' To which Niemöller replied, 'And, Brother, why are you *not* in prison?'

When the war was over, many Germans argued that the German catastrophe was only part of a wider downfall of civilization throughout the whole of Europe. Nationalism, racialism, propaganda, violence, tyranny and lawlessness, they pointed out, were not peculiarly German features; the crimes of the Nazi period were only the end-product of a process in which many other peoples and factors played a part. Other apologists took refuge in strange doctrines of demonic forces which, as Stewart Herman has noted, endowed 'Hitler personally with all sorts of mysterious attributes ... The professors seem to be particularly guilty of spinning gauzy webs of rationalization around Hitler to explain the impotence of the common people which, as a matter of plain fact, was due to their susceptibility to mass hypnotism and their refusal to acknowledge personal responsibility'.[5]

Even in the less disturbed circumstances of the post-war-era, many churchmen have still tried to evade the searching question of the Church's failure against Nazi atheistic oppression. Some Germans postulate that the expulsion of so many millions of their fellow-countrymen from their homes since 1945 constitutes a grievance which precludes any unilateral acknowledgement of German guilt. Others see in the political divisions that have split Europe into two armed camps since the war a new challenge in Church–State relations which overrides the unpleasant problems of the past, and call for a united stand against the 'alien' ideology of Communism. In this atmosphere of convenient amnesia, the prophetic words of Pastor Asmussen are easily overlooked:

How we wish we knew nothing of all this and could start anew. But the world grants us no rest: she screams at us with questions of guilt, and whether we will or no we must answer. We must answer our own nation, and we must answer the whole world. One can well understand when no one dares attempt an answer. For that reason it is necessary for the Church to step into the breach ... The Church is to blame, the Church of both denominations (i.e. Evangelical and Roman Catholic). Our guilt stretches far into the past ... The citizen is guilty ... The

333

Party is guilty . . . All this demands justice . . . Therefore, we dare not resist the arm of justice especially as we did not resist injustice.[6]

These words have lost none of their appositeness in the twenty years since they were spoken. Indeed, subsequent events have increased rather than removed the need for the Christian churches to learn and profit from their failures in the Nazi struggle. Unhappily, many German churchmen have misunderstood the call of Karl Barth and other foreigners for a frank appraisal of their shortcomings during the Nazi era, such self-examination proving beyond their capacity in the circumstances. Yet Barth's appeal was made not in a spirit of recrimination but from the conviction that the German Church struggle had a significance far beyond its national boundaries, and one that could shed light on the path of the Christian Churches in every part of the world.

The main lessons of the German Church struggle have not yet been fully learnt. The temptations and difficulties which beset the Churches in 1933 are still prevalent and in some places paramount. Theologically speaking, the problem of how the Church can confront its community with the need for taking up arms against injustice and violence has never been solved. The dichotomy of Lutheran teaching, which appears to draw a line between political affairs on the one hand and the search for the Kingdom of God on the other, has long influenced churchmen of all denominations. But as Guenter Lewy has observed:

The Church's hold upon the faithful in many situations is too precarious to risk an open clash with a state trampling upon human dignity and freedom. The situation is worsened when, as in Nazi Germany, the bishops and clergy are themselves infected with an alien creed. Whenever either of these manifestations is present, many seemingly good reasons can be brought forth to defend the Church's political quietism and her surrender to Caesar.[7]

Nevertheless, four factors may be held chiefly responsible for the Churches' meagre resistance to Nazi oppression. First was the ingrained tradition of pietism. The tendency of many Christians to limit their religious loyalties to the narrow goal of personal redemption has undoubtedly led to sincere and devout lives and

334

has inspired the successive waves of missionary movements. But their failure to carry their Christian principles into political life has opened the way for a dangerous subjectivism, which drew from its Reformation background the belief that 'politics do not concern the Church', and an almost Manichaean conviction that the affairs of political and social life are irredeemable. The danger of such a retreat into the sacristy was recognized and deplored by the authors of the Barmen declaration:

> We reject the false doctrine, as though there were areas of our life in which we would not belong to Jesus Christ, but to other Lords – areas in which we would not need justification and sanctification through him.

Secondly, there was the characteristic German readiness to accept the existing political order without criticism and to exact obedience to established authority. The illusions entertained by churchmen about their Nazi rulers, even after the horrifying consequences of the Röhm *Putsch*, the Crystal Night and the overrunning of their neighbouring countries, can be explained – if not explained away – by the traditional acceptance that 'the powers that be are ordained of God'. The German Church was not equipped with a theology adequate to sustain any critical attack upon the actions of its political rulers, and for that reason, even at the end of the Nazi era there was no more than what Professor Wolf has called a 'reluctant resistance'.

Some German churchmen shook themselves free from these old loyalties and, even during the Weimar Republic, threw in their lot with the Nazis in their call for a renewal of the nation and a revival of its spiritual life. The sudden rise to prominence of the 'German Christians' owed much to a well-timed sense of political opportunism, but their so-called Christian principles were wholly superficial and their fallacies were quickly exposed. By rejecting theological study in favour of 'positive' Christianity, many of its adherents produced nothing more than thinly-disguised apologies for their political ambitions, clothed in the garments of Christian righteousness. Their claims of divine authority for unorthodox views, and their ready adoption of precepts and practices freed, they claimed, from dogma and sectarianism, rapidly led them into nationalist and racial heresies which differed little, if at all, from the pagan mythologies of Rosenberg.

Finally there was the Churches' basically conservative outlook, which led them to accept without question the claim of Nazism to be the only alternative to communism. For decades the Churches had looked askance at any hint of radical political reform; and in their distrust of left-wing tendencies they had carried with them the bulk of their middle-class supporters. The Socialists' challenge to the Churches' authority, with its implied threat to Church property and the rejection of Church doctrine, their espousal of the cause of the poor and oppressed, their refusal to accept the current concept of a static society so beloved of the Church, and their adoption of the revolutionary tactics that had once been the hallmark of the Church itself – all these blinded churchmen to the possibility that left-wing programmes for social and political reform might be a vehicle for God's redemptive activity.

No such prophylactics had been taken against the challenge of the 'radical right', which advocated authoritarian principles, proclaimed itself fervent in its devotion to Christianity – especially as opposed to Judaism – promised to maintain the economic and social status-quo, attacked anti-national and disloyal elements who refused to identify *Kirche, Staat und Volk*, re-emphasized the fellowship of all its supporters, and exalted faith as a cardinal virtue. All these elements were sufficient to lessen the doubts engendered by the emotionalism of Hitler and the brutality of some of his supporters. The appeal of a *Volkskirche* which renounced the pluralism of the Weimar Republic and offered the vision of a united people, with Church and State working hand in hand to renew the nation's strength, acted as a screen that hid the evil consequences of Nazi ambitions. The illusion that a political system which rejected the rationalistic ideas of the nineteenth century would automatically foster the supernatural claims of Christian orthodoxy was abandoned grudgingly and far too late. And, as a corollary, the Churches' willingness to defend the nation's actions, even those which stood condemned by the generality of mankind, revealed how far the heresy of a nationalist pseudo-religion had succeeded in bringing about this contemporary *trahison des clercs*.

The significance of the German Church struggle, however, lies deeper than the obvious dangers of a narrow individualism, a submissive allegiance to the State, a pursuit of pseudo-Christian doctrines, or a doctrinaire anti-communism. The real outcome of the struggle is only now emerging in a reawakening of the Church, not merely in the two Germanies of today, but throughout the Christian world. The theological influence of Dietrich Bonhoeffer stands foremost in the post-war world. The courageousness of Martin Niemöller shines like a torch to guide lesser men in the complexities of political affairs. Realization of the fate of the Jews at German hands has brought to the Church a sense of shame for its deeply-entrenched anti-semitism, and a new awareness of Christianity's indissoluble bond with the Chosen People of Israel. German participation in the oecumenical movement arises from a renewed realization of the unity which binds together Christians of every nation, colour and race. The revitalization of the role of the laity, as seen in the work of the *Kirchentag* and the Evangelical Academies, has awakened men to the fact that political and social responsibility is laid upon them as a Christian duty, and calls for vigilance and dedication. Above all, there is the realization that totalitarianism, with its ultimate nihilism and disregard of human life, can be combated only by the rejection of its pseudo-religious appeal to national self-glorification and personal submission.

'Who can deny', wrote Bonhoeffer, 'that in obedience, duty and calling, we Germans have again and again excelled in bravery and self-sacrifice? But the German has preserved his freedom – what nation has talked so passionately of freedom as we have, from Luther to the idealists? – by seeking deliverance from his own will through service to the community ... Only now are we Germans learning to discover the meaning of free responsibility. It depends upon a God who demands bold action as the free response of faith, and who promises forgiveness and consolation to the man who becomes a sinner in the process.'[8]

During the last 35 years, the German Church has passed through a period of much temptation and great suffering. Yet it has, if fitfully and inadequately, never ceased in its attempts to bring the

337

reconciling word of Christ's teaching to the world. It found in
Dietrich Bonhoeffer a martyr whose life and example have become a watchword throughout the world. The courage and energy
of Martin Niemöller in the face of political persecution have
redeemed some of the vacillating compromises of weaker men.
The influence and stature of such theologians as Karl Barth and
Rudolf Bultmann reach far beyond their own generation. They
and a host of others have laboured indomitably to make Christian
truth known in its fullness. Four hundred and fifty years after
Luther's challenge to the authorities of his day, the German Church
is again alive to the crises of the times. If the era of Nazi persecution
has revealed that man is still ready to worship the false gods of
nationalism and expediency, it also produced men whose readiness
to suffer for their faith saved the Church from total apostasy
during that most tragic and fateful chapter of German history.

Appendix 1: Principles of the religious movement of 'German Christians', issued in June 1932

(*Printed in K. Kupisch, Quellen zur Geschichte des deutschen Protestantismus 1871–1945 (Göttingen 1960) pp. 251–3*)

1. These principles shall show all faithful German men and women the ways and means of attaining a reorganization of the Church. These principles shall not be, or become, a substitute for a confession of faith, nor shall they undermine the fundamental creeds of the Evangelical Church. They are a confession of life.

2. We fight for the integration of the 29 Churches comprised within the 'German Evangelical Church Association' into one Evangelical Reich Church and we march under the motto and object:

> Outwards one and strong in spirit,
> Rallied round Jesus and his works,
> Inside rich and polymorphic,
> Every Christian to his call and ways.
>   (Adapted from Geibel)

3. The description 'German Christians' does not mean an ecclesiastical political party in the conventional interpretation of the term. It addresses itself to all Evangelical Christians of the German race. Parliamentarianism has had its day, in the Church as well. Ecclesiastical political parties have not the religious credentials of representing the church-nation, and stand in the way of our high aim of becoming one church-nation. We want a vigorous national church which is the expression of all forces of faith in our nation.

4. We stand on the ground of positive Christianity. We profess an

affirmative faith in Christ, fitting our race and being in accordance with the German Lutheran mind and heroic piety.

5. We want to bring the reawakened German sense of life to bear in our Church and to fill our Church with vitality. In the fateful struggle for German liberty, and the German future, the Church has turned out to be too weak in its leadership. Up to now the Church has not summoned the faithful to a determined fight against ungodly Marxism and against the Centre Party, but has concluded a concordat with the political parties of these powers. We want our Church to fight in the front-line in the decisive battle of our nation for life or death. She must not stand aside or even dissociate herself from the champions of liberation.

6. We demand a revision of the political clauses of our Church treaty and a fight against unreligious and unpatriotic Marxism and its Christian–Socialist train-bearers of all shades. We miss in the present treaty the venturing confidence in God and in the mission of the Church. The way to the Kingdom of Heaven is through struggles, the cross and sacrifice, not through a false peace.

7. We see in race, nationality and nation, orders of life given and entrusted to us by God, to care for the preservation of which is for us God's law. For these reasons, racial miscegenation has to be opposed. On the strength of its experience, the German Foreign Mission has been admonishing the German nation for a long time: 'Keep your race pure!' and has told us that faith in Christ does not destroy but heightens and sanctifies the race.

8. We see in a soundly conceived Home Mission a living Christianity of action which, however, from our point of view has its roots, not in mere compassion, but in obedience to the will of God and in gratitude for Christ's death on the cross. Mere compassion is 'charity' and leads to presumption, paired with a bad conscience, and effeminates a nation. We know something about Christian obligation and charity toward the helpless, but we also demand the protection of the nation from the unfit and the inferior. The Home Mission must not in any case contribute to the degeneration of our nation. In addition, it must keep aloof from economic adventures and must not become a shopkeeper.

9. We see a great danger to our nationality in the Jewish Mission. It promises to allow foreign blood into our nation. It has no right to exist side by side with the Foreign Mission. We object to the Jewish mission in Germany so long as the Jews have the citizenship and so long as

there is the danger of racial mixture and bastardization. The Holy Scriptures tell us also something about holy wrath and self-denying love. Marriages between Jews and Germans particularly must be prohibited.

10. We want an Evangelical Church, having its roots in the nation and we reject the spirit of Christian cosmopolitanism. We want to overcome by faith in our national mission as ordered by God the ruinous phenomena arising out of this spirit, such as pacifism, internationalism, freemasonry etc. Membership of an Evangelical clergyman in a Masonic lodge is not permissible.

These ten points of the religious movement of 'German Christians' are an appeal for us to unite and they form in outline the direction of a future Evangelical Reich Church, which, by preserving peace among the denominations, will develop the forces of our reforming creed for the benefit of the German nation.

Appendix 2: A Radio Broadcast by General Superintendent O. Dibelius

(Reprinted from Reichsanzeiger, Nr. 8, 6 April 1933)

EVANGELICAL APPEAL TO AMERICA

General Superintendent D. Dibelius and Methodist Bishop D. Dr Ruelsen spoke in a German short wave transmission.

In a talk, transmitted by the German short wave station to America on Tuesday evening, General Superintendent Dr Dibelius, of Berlin, addressed himself to the American public to take a stand against the atrocity propaganda, and to inform Christians across the ocean of the true situation in Germany. The introductory words were spoken by the Senior Bishop of the Episcopal Methodist Church, Dr Ruelsen, who has been staying in Germany for several days and who after audiences with Reich Ministers Dr. Neurath and Dr. Goebbels has thoroughly acquainted himself with the conditions in Germany. A Methodist statement on the situation was wired to England and America under the direction of D. Ruelsen on 30 March. It ran as follows:

The undersigned leaders of the Methodist Church in Germany enter a strong protest against the public meetings and the press reports in America and England about alleged prosecutions of Jews and atrocities by the National movement in Germany. They see in this the attempt to revive the dreadful atrocity propaganda of the World War from which the psyche of the nations has scarcely freed itself. Under these conditions the endeavours for an understanding between the nations must be most heavily endangered. Apart from few slips by individual and irresponsible persons, against whom the new government has

342

immediately taken the strongest measures, peace and order have never been endangered. Our Church has always been leading in all endeavours to restore true peace among the nations. The German Methodists, who are represented in all provinces of the German Reich, therefore send an urgent appeal to entire world-wide Methodism for reasons of truth and justice to help combat the pernicious activities of this lying propaganda against Germany.

The two clergymen had the opportunity of informing themselves by personal inspection of the treatment of political prisoners. At the outset of his statement General Superintendent Dr Dibelius pointed out the difference between the 1918 and the present revolutions in Germany. The revolution of 1918 was a violent revolution. Bloodshed and atrocities of all kinds were the order of the day. The new revolution is of a quite different nature. It has been brought about by the lawful decision of the German people. Reich Chancellor Adolf Hitler has taken over, as he always announced, in a strictly legal way. As its first great task the new government has set about saving Germany from Bolshevism. We Germans know better than any other nation what Bolshevism is like. We Germans watch at closest range how Bolshevism in Russia destroys churches, disintegrates families, annihilates property and renders men the outlawed slaves of a ferocious and despotic government. During the winter of 1918–19 we experienced in Munich for a short time the terrorist rule of Bolshevism. In Thuringia we had the communist revolt of Max Hölz. The old governments hoped to be able to bring the German communists up to national *loyalty* by restraining their organization and their newspapers to the least possible extent. Experience has shown that this method failed. The Bolshevist propaganda prepared a new revolution. With increasing uneasiness we waited for the decisive battle between western civilization and Bolshevism, which had to be fought on German soil. Now it has come in a way different from what we thought possible. It was won without street riots and without bloodshed. By drastic measures the new government eliminated the communist agitators and their confederates from public life. This met with astonishingly little resistance. There were, of course, some excesses particularly during the first days. That cannot be otherwise in a country with 65 million people. But the persistent admonition of the government to keep absolute discipline had its effects very quickly. The picture of public life in Germany has remained a picture of order and discipline. All communist leaders have been imprisoned. For how long they will stay in prison – this will not be decided until complete stabilization will have returned to Germany and the other countries. For the time being these drastic steps had the effect that there is no danger of excesses – neither on the part of the Communists nor on the part of the National Socialists. We paid a visit to the communist leaders in prison. They told us in agreement with each other that they were treated quite correctly. Not one word in the hair-raising reports on the cruel and bloody treatment of Communists in Germany is true. On the basis of such false reports world Jewry has started an agitation against Germany in several countries. To break this boycott the German National Socialists in turn have initiated a boycott movement against Jewry in Germany. For the present this boycott has been restricted to one single day: it went off in absolute peace and order. There was only one sanguinary incident in Kiel. In Berlin and throughout the Reich nothing of the kind happened. The boycott has been suspended until further notice. The government wants to wait and see what happens in these days out in the world. This is accompanied by a government measure to remove Jews from the public administration, particularly from judicial offices. The Jews form less than one per cent of Germany's total population. The conditions and relations here are to be brought back to their former level. The Christian Church stands for gallantry and charity. She has the strong wish that the hour may come soon in which restraint and order in the state will leave room for charity and justice. This will depend on whether out in the world agitation against Germany will stop or not.

For this reason I ask, as a servant of my Church that Christian friends in America cordially and pressingly should use their influences that no further false reports about Germany should be diffused or believed.

In conclusion Dr Dibelius addressed the audience in a few German words. He said: 'Today, the German Reich is firmly united as never before in our history. In millions of German hearts there is the ardent wish that the German name may again stand pure and spotless before the whole world. Revolutionary times, even if experienced in discipline and ethical eagerness, are hard times. Don't aggravate these hard times for the German people by believing sensational reports!

Have confidence! Again: Have confidence!

You will live to see the time when that which is now happening in Germany will lead to an end for which everybody who loves and honours the German character can be grateful! And that it will not only be in the interest of Germany, but to the advantage of the entire world!'

Appendix 3: The 10 Principles of the religious movement of 'German Christians'

(*Printed in K. D. Schmidt, Die Bekenntnisse des Jahres 1933 (Göttingen 1937) pp. 144–5*)

MEMORANDUM OF REICHSLEITER HOSSENFELDER TO PRESIDENT D. KAPLER ON THE OCCASION OF THE CONFERENCE IN LOCCUM, MAY 1933.

1. We want an *'Evangelical Reich Church of Lutheran Character'* incorporating the Reformed congregations whose *individuality* will be guaranteed.

2. We do *not* want a *State Church* and also not a Church as a state within the state, but an Evangelical Reich Church which acknowledges the National Socialist state out of belief and preaches the gospel in the Third Reich.

3. The Evangelical Reich Church is the Church of the German Christians, i.e. the Christians of Aryan race. In this respect she is also linked with the German Christians in foreign countries. Preaching the gospel among people of a foreign race is the concern of Foreign Missions.

4. This Church must neither be the focus of reaction nor a democratic–parliamentary debating forum.

5. The Evangelical Reich Church will be sustained by the confidence of the nation and will be led by the Reich Bishop.

6. The Evangelical Reich Church is to be divided into not more than ten Church provinces with a Provincial Bishop at the head of each.

345

7. The Reich Bishop is to be *Lutheran* according to the predominantly Lutheran majority in the national church. He is to be assisted by a Reich Curate of the Reformed Church.

8. The Reich Bishop will have his official residence in Luther's town of Wittenberg. The Castle Church is his cathedral church.

9. The whole Evangelical Congregation shall decide on the Reich Church as defined by the above principles and on the person of the Reich Bishop in a preliminary election on 31 October 1933. Entitled to vote are all members of the Evangelical Congregation under the terms of the national suffrage. Excluded from the suffrage are Christians of non-Aryan descent.

10. According to the above principles the Reich Bishop will carry out the further completion of the Evangelical Reich Church.

Appendix 4: Pressure upon individuals to withdraw from the Church

A: (from the files of the Reich Leader of the SS)

1. Archdiocesan Office, Freiburg in Breisgau   25 November 1942

TO THE ARMED FORCES HIGH COMMAND

For many years so many men from the Waffen-SS have withdrawn from the Church in our diocese that it is impossible to escape the conclusion that a systematic movement is being organized in favour of leaving the Church, which is endangering every Christian commitment in the ranks. Such announcements of the decision to withdraw from the Church from the ranks of the Waffen-SS have lately reached us in an increasing number from field-stations. Last year there were 24, this year there have been so far 27, who have declared their determination to leave the Church, while such declarations from the other armed forces units are scarcely noticeable.

In Radolfzell since 1937 there has been a barracks of the Waffen-SS which holds about 1000 men, formerly the III Germania Regt.; in 1940 it became the garrison of the SS Infantry Training Battalion I, and since the beginning of 1941 an SS-NCO Training School. About a third of the unit used to belong to the Catholic Church, but nothing was ever known about any participation by the Catholic members of this barracks in the church services of Radolfzell, which is to a great degree Catholic. Participation in uniform is apparently strictly forbidden, and leaving the camp in civilian clothing is only possible in exceptional cases. Now the Catholic Parish office informed us that the following declaration of intentions to leave the Church have been received from the members of this barracks: 1937, 4; 1938 and 1939, 3 each; 1940, 67, of which 31 were in February, 13 in April; 1941, 56 of which 16 were in April, 26 in August; 1942 up to now 129; groups of such declarations being made in March, April, July and August.

These collective declarations of intention to withdraw from the Church, which have increased so strikingly in the last few years, have regularly followed the end of an ideological training course.

In this situation it is hardly to be wondered at if faithful people, both Catholic and Protestant, are more and more convinced that the Christian faith is in danger amongst the Waffen-SS and even that men are being finally forced to withdraw from their Church. We may remark here that a priest of our archdiocese, Schneider from Beuggen, who carried out his duty in warning one of his flock, whose son had put his name down for the SS, of the danger for the faith, because of this was taken off to concentration camp at Dachau, where he has been for the last two years.

On 28 January 1942 SS-man Franz Waldmann from Spessart near Karlsruhe also declared his decision to leave the Catholic Church, very much against the will of his parents. Waldmann was killed in battle on 8 October 1942 in Finland. A report on the circumstances in which he was persuaded to leave the Church is given in the enclosure which is a thoroughly reliable account given by his parents and attested by the priest. The kind of direct pressure, which has been here applied, can hardly be an isolated example.

We request the Armed Forces High Command to take steps to ensure that similar attacks on the freedom of conscience of members of the Waffen-SS should be prevented.

The Vicar General, Frösch

COPY

Spessart, 10 November 1942
RE: The leaving of the Church by Franz Waldmann

After his call-up, Franz Waldmann was asked if he would volunteer for the Waffen-SS. Without knowing the ideological attitudes of these troops, he agreed. His father also, who had served as an enthusiastic soldier in the 109th Imperial Baden Bodyguard Regiment, gave his permission because he regarded the Waffen-SS as a kind of Guards regiment.

After a short period of training, Franz was posted to the prison camp Mauthausen, in Perg County, Austria, as a guard. Here began the pressure urging him to withdraw from the Church. According to his account, given to his mother, 30 of his comrades refused to accede to this pressure. Then began a period of sorrows, which young men are hardly able to withstand. At every roll-call, and especially at every instruction period, the order was given: Whoever has not yet left the Church, three paces forward! No opportunity was neglected to pour scorn on these people. Franz defended himself by saying, what matters here is not my religion, but how I do my duties. One after the other of his comrades succumbed to this pressure, so that by October of last year Franz stood alone. At this time one of Franz's friends wrote to his father, saying that Franz could not hold out for long. Franz was also tired of the struggle. He knew however how much it would grieve his parents and therefore on 7 October he wrote his father the following letter:

I am writing to you today about an affair of our faith. Today I have served for 16 months in the Waffen-SS. . . . Then I needed your signature and only received it with the promise that I would remain in the Church. Today I am now with a unit which holds an entirely opposite opinion on this matter. The Reich Leader demands for every SS man only one faith, and that is faith in Germany.

My NCO today advised me to make up my mind, since any promotion for me is otherwise impossible . . . There is no other decision possible for me. Because I know very well how much this will affect Mother, I have written to you, Father, at work. My reputation, so long as I was a civilian, was definitely not a bad one, and as long as I have been in uniform, no one has anything against me. But now I have a request from you, Father, and that is your answer.

This letter must presumably have been submitted to his superior officer, because at the same time he wrote a second letter not through Army Post Office channels in which he openly described his distress. This letter was destroyed by his father.

The father arrived with this letter at the Vicarage and sorrowfully asked for the advice of his priest. Together they worked out an answer and the father wrote it in such a way that it could and should be read by the superior officer, as indeed was to be feared.

He made these points:

1. No one can force you to deny your faith, not even your superior officer, since the highest gift which the Führer has given to the German people is freedom of conscience. Nor have I any legal right to influence you, since you are now 21 years old.
2. All our ancestors were true Catholic churchmen and loyal Germans.
3. My brother was killed in the Great War. You can therefore believe in

Germany and in God, there is no conflict here. The Führer teaches to respect our ancestors.

4. My Company commander always said, the best soldier is the pious Christian soldier.

5. Today we are fighting against Bolshevists, whom the Führer rightly described as beasts. The Russians were deprived of their religion and so have been driven to bestiality.

6. You may pray, the Führer prays too, and in all of his great speeches asks for prayers.

7. Behave as your conscience dictates, but I want to have a son of whom I can be proud and who is not a coward.

Franz's parents learnt of his decision to withdraw from the Church through their parish office.

Shortly afterwards Franz was posted to another unit and was sent to Dahlherta near Fulda. Here he met comrades who had remained loyal to the Church. Apparently therefore these pressures were applied according to the inclinations of the local commander. Here his parents visited him around the feast of St Peter and St Paul. His father was particularly struck by the depressed state of his son. He was no longer the happy and exuberant youngster of earlier days, and no friendly laughter greeted his parents. Franz told his mother sorrowfully the whole sad story. 'Day after day I was pressed to abandon my faith. You will never go far in this unit, even if you are a good soldier. I didn't capitulate when they promised me that after the war I could be free to be what I was before.' Very pregnantly he said: 'I will never forget what I had to go through on my 21st birthday, even if I live to be a hundred.' His promise: 'Inwardly I have remained what I used to be, and when I am home again I will put it all to rights.' This was his parents' consolation when they left. And the memory of this promise was the only consolation when they received the news on 29 October that he had been killed in battle in Finland.

2. To the Archdiocesan Office   Field Headquarters
   Freiburg i. Br.
   Herrenstrasse 35.

The Reich Leader of the SS has received from the Armed Forces High Command the letter of 25 November 1942 concerning the withdrawal from the Church of members of the Waffen-SS.

This letter interested the Reich Leader of the SS very much. After investigating these cases, the conclusion has been reached that these withdrawals from the Church are in no way due to any form of pressure on consciences.

The only reason for them must be that the faithful men are appalled by the particularly bad conditions in the Archdiocese of Freiburg.

HEIL HITLER
signed
(signature illegible)
SS-Colonel and Staff Officer
of the Personal Staff of the Reich
Leader of the SS.

[Marginal annotation: Dictated by the Reich Leader]

B: (*from Alexander Hohenstein, Wartheländisches Tagebuch 1941–2 (Munich 1963) pp. 189–91.*)

Wednesday, 29 October 1941

Frau Werner announced *Ortsgruppenleiter* Puffmann and *Organisationsleiter* Gerberin. The gentlemen appeared in Party uniform with full decorations. After a short greeting Puffmann produced a folder from his brief-case, opened it up and laid in front of me a printed form in the style of an official communication.

'Mr Mayor, please be good enough to read this and then sign it.' I read it once, and then read it a second time, and could not believe my eyes. What the paper contained was so shocking that the sentences danced in front of my eyes. Even now when it is all over, I cannot yet recollect the words clearly. Their intent however very well. And I will never again forget them as long as I live.

At the top was written: 'Declaration'. And this declaration was described in the text as being voluntarily subscribed to. It ran somewhat as follows:

'I am well aware of the orders of the *Gauleiter* concerning the regulation of church life in the *Reichsgau* Wartheland. I acknowledge that, according to this order, I have to declare myself as having left the Church which I belonged to in Germany proper [*Alt-Reich*] and have to describe myself henceforward as a "god-believer" ...'

So far this was all compulsory. But I was enraged by what followed:

'I promise not to take up membership in one of the two Churches of the Wartheland. I promise never again to resume membership in my former church, should I be transferred back to Germany proper.'

'Must I really sign this?'

'No one obliges you to do so. It is left up to your free decision.'

'And if I do not now sign it?'

'Then you will have to draw the consequences for yourself.'

'What kind of consequences could these be?'

'If you do not sign, you thereby demonstrate that you are not in tune with the ideology of the Party and that you disavow the National Socialist thinking and purpose. That could have the result that your suitability for public office in the Warthegau or at all would be brought into question, that . . .'

'That I would either then be obliged to retire or would be dismissed with shame and ignominy. Is that what you mean, Herr Puffmann?'

'I would not have expressed it that way.'

'Which does not mean, that you do not think so.'

'We do not have the right to force you. Just keep the form with you and consider your attitude. In three days' time I have to send in the signed forms and at the same time report any failures to sign. By that time I must have your decision.'

It was a direct blackmail. I was threatened with the loss of my post. If that happened, it would mean the end of my career as an official and the loss of all my well-earned rights. It is a question of my living, and that of my family. The alternative would be clear to a blind bat.

I considered the matter for a long time, my head in my hands, disgusted by the political blackmail, ashamed of my better self. I was so agitated that my hand shook.

The two party officials watched my every expression attentively, though Gerberin had not yet said anything. They obviously enjoyed the opportunity of demonstrating their importance to me, of bringing me into a situation of embarrassment, and of putting pressure on me. These were enjoyable minutes for them, but cost me nerve-wracking efforts at self-control. But I must not let my true feelings be recognized.

I did not need to hand over the piece of paper to the *Ortsgruppenleiter*. He quickly took it from my desk. It was almost as if he was afraid I might change my mind.

And that is what one calls freedom of conscience, freedom for the individual. A life of freedom and dignity. . . .

Appendix 5: The Twenty-Eight Theses of the Saxon National Church for the Internal strengthening of the German Evangelical Church

(Printed in Kirkliches Jahrbuch 1933–44 (Gütersloh 1948), pp. 30–2)

CHURCH AND STATE

The Theses 1 to 5 are to be read in conjunction with Paragraph 24 (2) of the programme of the NSDAP, since the Party and therewith the State represent the viewpoint of positive Christianity.

1. The German Evangelical Church exists within the State. She cannot lead a secondary role besides the State as certain factors hostile to Christianity would wish it to be. She cannot remain in a neutral position vis-a-vis the State, as those circles would prefer which meet the National Socialist State with suspicion. She cannot be a Church above the State which corresponds to the Roman Catholic attitude. Neither can she be a Church below the state. Only as a Church within the State can she be a National Church. Thus Luther's original theories about the State and Church can become a reality.

2. The Lutheran Church for the sake of its close relationship to the people cannot assume a hostile attitude vis-a-vis the National Socialist State. As the people's Church she must have full confidence in the State. The leaders of the Church can be only persons who possess the confidence of the leadership of the State. The State grants the Church full and free action because both State and Church belong to the two great forces of order in a nation. Their relationship is based on confidence not on legalistic agreements.

3. The National Church commits itself to the doctrines of blood and race because our people share a common blood and a common existence.

Therefore, a member of the National Church can only be such a person who, according to the law of the State, is also a peoples' comrade (*Volksgenosse*). An official of the National Church can only be such a person, who according to the law of the State, is fit to be a civil servant. (The so-called Aryan paragraph.)

4. The National Church does not intend to exclude Christians of another race from the Word and the Sacraments, nor from the great family of Christian believers. The Christian of another race is not a Christian of lesser rank, but a Christian of a different kind. Thus the National Church takes seriously the assertion that the Christian Church does not yet live in the perfection of divine eternity, but is bound to those natural laws which God has given to this life.

5. Since the German National Church esteems race as a law of God's creation, she also recognizes the demand that the race should be kept pure and healthy as God's command. She regards marriage between members of different races as an offence against God's will.

PROCLAMATION OF THE CHURCH

6. God demands the whole of man. The aim of the proclamation of the Church is to put man under the will of God.

7. As the Church of Jesus Christ she has the special task to proclaim the Gospel of Jesus Christ to the German people whom God has created as Germans.

8. The gospel of Jesus Christ means that God is our master and father, that this God has revealed himself through Jesus Christ, and that we the people will find the road to the Father through Jesus Christ alone. The church is bound to this proclamation.

9. God places man into the orders of life: family, nation and state. Therefore, the National Church recognizes the totalitarian claims of the National Socialist State namely, God's call to family, people and State.

THE FOUNDATIONS OF THE CHURCH

10. The foundations of the Church remain the Bible and the creeds. The Bible contains the gospel of Christ, the creeds testify to the gospel of Christ.

11. The decisive revelation of God is Jesus Christ. The deed of the

revelation is the New Testament. Therefore, it has for all proclamations of the Church a norm-giving significance.

12. The Old Testament does not possess the same value. The specifically Jewish national morality and national religion is superceded. The Old Testament remains important because it hands down the history and the downfall of a nation that despite the revelation of God continuously separated itself from God. The believing (*gottgebundenen*) prophets gave a sign not just to their peoples but to us all: The attitude of a nation toward God is decisive for its destiny in history.

13. We recognize, therefore, in the Old Testament the apostasy of the Jews from God and therein their sin. This sin becomes evident in the crucifixion of Jesus. From thereon God's curse lies as a burden upon this nation until today. We recognize however in the Old Testament the first rays of God's love, which was finally revealed in Jesus Christ. Because of this perception the National Church cannot abandon the Old Testament.

14. The content of the Christian proclamation is shown in the Augsburg confession and the remaining documented confessions of the German reformation. Through these confessions we are united in the faith of our fathers. A church without a confession would be the equivalent of a state without constitution and law.

15. The proclamation and creeds of the Church are always ties to a certain period of time and the questions raised then. Certain questions to which the creeds of our fathers answer do not exist for us any more. Other questions, however, are faced by us today to which the creed of our fathers cannot answer. The National Church therefore takes pains to find a confessional answer from the creeds of our fathers to meet the question of our time: No retreat to the faith of the ancestors, but forward in the faith of our ancestors!

THE ROAD OF THE CHURCH

16. The National Church turns against liberalism. Liberalism loosens the faith in Jesus Christ because it sees only a human being in Him. It knows Jesus only as a prophet of high morality or of heroic personality. It puts a human rationale above God. Jesus Christ, to us, is the son of God, his appearance is the miracle of the history of mankind.

17. The National Church turns just as strongly against a new

Orthodoxy. This Orthodoxy through its dogmatic rigidity bars the struggling and searching human being from the road to Christ and prevents a living proclamation of the gospel.

18. The National Church turns also against those experiments which try to replace the Christian faith with a religion based on racial experiences. All religions in their search and questions about God are different according to the race. Jesus Christ, however, in his miraculous person is the fulfilment of all that is alive in the human soul with longing and presentiment. The dispute, whether Jesus was a Jew or an Aryan does not at all affect the essence of Jesus. Jesus is not a human being but reveals in his person God's personality.

19. The German National religion can therefore be only a Christian one. Christianity is coined differently according to race and nationality. Therefore we struggle for the realization of a German Christianity.

20. This German Christianity we find embodied in Martin Luther. We perceive in Luther's reformation the break-through of a German Christian faith. German Christianity means Lutheranism. As German Lutherans we are wholly German and wholly Christians.

21. Presently a number of things are said about the human being which are deceptive. Deceptive is the assertion: The human being does not have any responsibility before God and therefore no debt before him. Deceptive is the assertion: The human being could conquer fate and death through his own power. Deceptive is the assertion that man is able to redeem himself.

22. The compulsion (*Sündengebundenheit*) of sin, fate and death can be conquered only and above through the faith in Jesus Christ. Through him we receive forgiveness of sin, the bond with God and everlasting life.

23. This does not mean that a lowering of man is pronounced, but pictures a sober opinion of man. His nobility is his close relationship to God, which is newly granted to him through Jesus.

24. This is the Christian gospel of salvation which man and people need all times. The Salvation is found firmly in the cross and resurrection of Jesus.

25. This pronouncement which takes equally seriously the real God and the real man prevents the recurrence of materialism and liberalism indirectly through religion.

26. Faith in Christ, which does not become active, is worthless in a people's church. The active faith in Christ is by all means a resolute struggle against everything evil and a courageous determination to service and sacrifice.

27. Therefore the National Church understands under positive Christianity (Point 24 of the Nazi Party Programme): Faith in Christ, Redemption through Christ, Action out of Christ.

28. This German Christianity creates the only foundation upon which German people can also unite themselves in faith.

Appendix 6: The Reich Youth Leader, Baldur von Schirach's Appeal to the German Catholic Youth

(Printed in J. Neuhausler, Kreuz und Hakenkreuz, pp. 168–70)

APPEAL TO THE GERMAN CATHOLIC YOUTH

Berlin, 15 March 1934

The official news service of the Youth Leader of the German Reich makes public the following ardent proclamation to Germany's Catholic Youth:

Loud and clearly, unmistakably and unequivocally we have again and again made known among the German people the goal of our struggle:

The unity of the youth – the unity of the Reich!

In thousands and thousands of meetings, rallies, and appeals, we have committed ourselves before the German nation to this goal of our struggle (*Kampfziel*). We have built the young united Germany in never-ceasing labour. Every step which we undertook in our action was to bring us closer to our goal, every one of our deeds was determined by the will to become a nation (*bestimmt vom Wille zur Nation*). The German people know today why we want to create and preserve German unity. The German people know why we are fighting so grimly and ruthlessly for the unity of the youth and the unity of the coming Reich; the German people know that we are prepared to make even the highest sacrifices for this.

The German people, however, still do not know why there can nevertheless be young Germans who close their eyes to the historic

358

greatness of this time of becoming a people (*Zeit der Volkswerdung*), who oppose this and who want to uphold their petty points of view at all costs.

The German people still do not know why a great portion of the German youth does not want to take part in the great enterprise of unification. The German people still do not know what they should think of your negative attitude.

Catholic youth! you run the risk of being looked upon as saboteurs by the German people some day, as your negative attitude could be interpreted as eccentricity and obstinacy. There is still time, the question is still unanswered, the question after the 'Why', which waits for its answer.

The die has not been cast.

Catholic youth! answer these questions! For only you still owe an answer to the people. Our reasons are known to the millions of our fellow Germans. The German people do not know your reasons, Catholic Youth. For the sake of the nation's future we demand of you to come out of the dark, in which you dwell in your hole in the corner existence (*Deine eigenen Süppchen Braust*)!!

For the sake of the honour of the German youth – for you also belong to it – we demand your answer.

The German youth has staked its honour on its ability to stand before the judgment of history as the creator and upholder of the unity of the Third Reich. Catholic Youth, do you want to adhere stubbornly to your special viewpoint, do you want to be branded in the judgment of history as the destructive force which sabotaged the unity of the Reich and the formation of its future?

We young millions still believe, our German people still believe, in your commitment to Germany which must be sublime and valuable to you when the interests of the nation are at stake. Catholic youth, our people are still waiting for the moment when you will let your commitment to Germany which so far you have confessed with your lips only, become a living deed, when you acknowledge the eternal Germany by aligning yourselves in the columns of our young nation and by abandoning every special viewpoint.

Catholic Youth! The German people are waiting for your historic step. They are waiting for your deed. The millions of our people want to hear out of your mouths why you still cannot force yourselves into line (*durchdringen*) with German unity.

Answer the silent question about the 'Why' which lies in the waiting looks of the German people. Our aims are clear. Our goal and our approaches to this goal are just as bright and clear. Out of your mouths, and only out of your mouths, Catholic Youth, not out of the mouths of your leaders and secretaries who have forced you into your exceptional position and who prove through their actions that they harbour no understanding for Germany and the unity of the Reich; out of your mouths, do our people want to hear whether you want any longer to stand outside our great society and for what reasons! The whole people will pass its judgment on you; this judgment shall be handed on to history! Catholic Youth! out with it!

Appendix 7: From the special issue of *Das Schwarze Korps* in honour of Hitler's fiftieth birthday, 20 April 1939

(a) My Führer!

So I stand on this day before your picture. This picture is colossal and without bounds, it is powerful, hard, beautiful and grand, it is so simple, good, plain and warm, more, it is father, mother, brother, in one, and it is still more. It bears the greatest years of my life, encompasses the quiet hours of meditation, the days of all difficulty and fears; it is the sun of most faithful fulfilment, the victory that was always the beginning of new duties and new fields of endeavour. The more I try to grasp it, the wider and brighter, without end, it is for me, yet never strange and far.

You are the Führer: without commanding, you live and are the law. You are love and strength, my heart is full in thinking of you on this day; too full to say all the best wishes and my thanks to you.

You are freedom, for you gave duty the meaning which imparts joy, strength and substance to all work. You took the curse of sweat, of hardship away from this nation which on this day holds its course in silent awe and is with you.

So you are now in a dome of millionfold love with its cupola arching up into luminous heights, millions of hearts beat faster and hotter on this high day in your life, and as your life is ours, it is a high day, a festive day for all Germans. And we who hoped to present you on this day with strength and blood from our love, we feel, as always, anew, even on this, your birthday, that your generous gift which makes us

N*

rich and strong, makes us happy deep in our hearts, and is without bounds.

How feeble are pen and tongue today to tell of what the heart is full, what almost painfully struggles for words and deeds, to tell you once, be it only this once, of that thankfulness which also in our hearts means real thankfulness.

We old comrades of your life's struggle who have often seen your vision on the way, we are on this day all with you, and with us the faithful dead and the million children waiting for the free life filled by you with sunshine and true meaning, for them and their later grand-children.

It is not much we have to say, we know that you shun idle words. And when we use words, you will know that they are true.

Führer – all the soldiers whom you have consecrated for battle through you – in good and in bad days we will remain the ones we have always been!

(b) 'Everything blossoms for him'

I have been asked to tell you what the Führer is to me.

Believe me, this question is very difficult to answer. How easily is one tempted to praise the person of the Führer, to flatter I mean. Yet he is actually above all praise after all. I will try to answer your questions as to which position the Führer has in my spiritual and material existence and in my strictly personal conceptions. In doing this, one can hardly make a distinction between the material and the spiritual, for the Führer is the preserver of my place of employment, he is the creator and the preserver, the protector of our magnificent, grand German Reich, and therewith also the preserver of my own small piece of land, of my garden.

Each flower that blossoms here blossoms in gratitude to him, each apple that ripens ripens in gratitude to him.

HERBERT G.,
SCHULZENDORF

Appendix 8: Himmler's Published Attitude towards Religion

(*From Die Schutzstaffel als antibolshewistische Kampforganisation*, (*Munich 1936*), *p. 27*)

I have put these questions and answers to you in order to show you clearly our attitude towards religion. You may be sure that we would not be capable of existing as a corps of sworn brothers if we did not have conviction and faith in a God who stands over us and our Fatherland, who created our people and this earth and sent us our Führer.

We are completely convinced that we shall be held responsible according to the eternal laws of this world for every deed, for every word and for every thought. Everything which our minds can think up, which our tongues speak and which our hands carry out is not a chance event, but a cause, which will have its effects, which will return in the inescapable unavoidable succession of events to be a blessing or a curse upon us and upon our people. Believe me, men with these convictions are anything but atheists. We object therefore to being called atheists, because as a society we are not bound to this or to that denomination, nor as individuals. But we do take it upon ourselves to draw a sharp and clear line between church and denominational activity on the one side, and political or ideological soldierliness on the other, and we will attack any overlap very sharply. At the same time, despite some very bad experiences and well-justified cause for exasperation which our people have had in the past in this area, we still teach our men to respect anything which is holy to our fellow citizens, from education to upbringing, which will be esteemed by us in words and deed.

Appendix 9: A Christmas Sermon 1936 preached in Solingen

(*Source: files of the Old Prussian Union Church, Berlin*)

Christmas is the feast of light of our ancestors, the ancient Germans, and so is several thousand years old. In the height of the winter solstice between 23–25 of the Yule month (December), the various members of each family came together under the leadership of the head of the family and met under a tree in the woods. The Winter man, Old Ruprecht, as the representative of the old dying year, appeared and gave out gifts. Burning torches were attached to a tree, and soon the night of deepest darkness was lit up by the burning flames of the Christmas tree. With wide open eyes, young and old stood around the tree. The deepest darkness of the longest night could not take away from them the hope of seeing again the light of the sun, which their God would give them in the coming year. And this is why we still give gifts around the Xmas tree.

Having sung some Xmas songs, our forefathers went home with the knowledge and the joy in their hearts, that despite the deepest night, despite the ice and snow and the darkness, they were not forgotten or forsaken by their God. From now on the sun rose higher day after day and brought warmth and joy into the hearts of our ancestors.

And just as our ancestors did not lose their faith in the coming light and the sun despite the ice and cold of the longest night, yes, indeed even celebrated the festival of light, so we took stand today in the light after long darkness.

Germany, after the Great War, was threatened with collapse. But then he came who, despite the great darkness in so many German hearts, spoke of light and showed them the way to the light. His appeal found an echo in thousands and hundreds of thousands of German souls, who carried the appeal further. It swelled out like a sweeping cloud and then happened that greatest miracle: Germany awoke and followed the sign of light, the Swastika.

The darkness is now conquered, now suffering is over, which so long gripped our people. The Sun is rising ever higher, with our ancient German symbol, the Swastika, and its warmth surrounds the whole German people, melts our hearts together into one great German community. No one is left out, no one needs to hunger or freeze, despite the deep night and snow and ice because the warmth from the hearts of the whole people pours out, in the emblems of the National Socialist Welfare programme and the Winter Help work and carries the German Xmas in the most forsaken German heart.

In this hour, Adolf Hitler is our benefactor, who has overcome the winter night with its terrors for the whole people and has led us under the Swastika to a new light and a new day.

Appendix 10: Two Nazi Party Directives from 1939 on the future of religious education in schools

(From the files of the American Document Centre, Berlin)

1. *Directive No. 79/39*   12 April 1939
The removal of denominational schools

There are still in various parts of the country a number of denominational schools, such as those run by monks and nuns, and various boarding schools. Until recently, the higher education for girls in several *Gaus* was almost completely a matter for conventual schools or for the orders of nuns.

In recent years it has been possible through the co-operation of the Party, the Education Ministry, and the individual provincial school administrations to dissolve many of these schools run by monks and nuns, in cases where their compulsory take-over by the State did not seem necessary. In the East Mark [Austria] almost all of these institutions have disappeared.

The creation of an ideologically objective school system is one of the most important tasks of the Party and the State. In order to achieve this goal, the remains of denominational influence must be completely removed from our German education system wherever it still appears. Not for nothing have the political Catholics, above all, realized the importance of teaching the young and controlling their spiritual growth and character building. Even though the official responsibility for carrying out the necessary measures belongs to the State and its responsible authorities, the Party, of course, and its local branches, is called upon to be the champions of political renewal, to point out circumstances which can no longer be tolerated on political or ideological grounds, and if necessary to bring about their alteration. I ask you, therefore, to observe the following instructions when carrying out these policies of the Party and to take care always in general or in particular cases to notify the State authorities.

1. Removal of monastic or conventual schools: in order to remove the influence of these schools once and for all, it will be necessary to establish how far denominational schools and other educational institutions are to be found outside the public schools system and in the hands of political Catholicism or other denominational groups. The removal of these institutions can then be undertaken along with State authorities along the following lines:

(a) the State ought to be the basic organizer and controller of the school system. In many cases, the private schools and institutions can be simply transferred from the Orders to the State. But look carefully to see whether there is not the danger of a continuing influence if the same buildings are used which may lie close to the monastery or convent. If necessary, transfer the school, as a State institution into other buildings. It is naturally pointless to transfer the ownership of such buildings to the State if the same teachers are to continue as before.

(b) in many cases, particularly where public schools are available, private schools can only be regarded as superfluous, especially those which cannot be considered ideologically objective. The pupils should be put in the public school system, and the private schools closed.

2. Hand-in-hand with the removal of the monastic and conventual schools, there is need to get rid of denominational boarding houses. These houses are particularly advantageous for the country people since they can send their children from country areas there to attend the secondary schools, and there they can get some attention and care during the time they are not in school. Of course these houses are useful for the churches, so that in many *Gaus* in the country there are only denominational boarding houses. All attempts to bring up these children in the schools as Nazi boys and girls is destroyed by the influence they get in the denominational boarding houses. In many cases these boys are prevented from entering the Hitler Youth or membership is permitted only as a disguise and as a purely external act.

I therefore recommend that the boarding houses should be completely removed and the instructions as in para. 1, followed. I should also like to point out that at the time of taking over these buildings by the State it is not entirely necessary to purchase the buildings outright, since the means for this will not always be there. The possibility should be looked into of renting the buildings. In some cases the appropriate rights of expropriation can be used, which will in most cases also mean a payment of rent. In these matters too, I recommend a good relationship with the authorities of the State.

3. Denominational Youth Holiday Camps: the denominations are gradually beginning to build up youth holiday camps, particularly during school holidays. It cannot be expected that these youth camps will be kept within the range of activities for which they have permission. I therefore ask you to ensure that such camps are not held any more in the future. Religious instruction of young people can always be carried out in the Churches, for which indeed they were built, but not in youth camps. The National Youth Leadership and the Gestapo are also asked to see that these camps are prohibited without exception. Such attempts by the denominations to get around the present situation cannot be allowed.

I would ask you to report on the measures you have taken to carry out these directives. Particularly, I should like to know when the last of these institutions in your area have been removed. Should you encounter difficulties, please refer to me again.

Signed
M. BORMANN.

II. *Directive No. 132/39*   9 June 1939
Removal of Church Influence from Education

In my directive No. 48/39 about the introduction of the community schools and 79/39 about the removal of denominational schools, I asked you to ensure that the Church influence in our German educational system should be removed through the introduction of community schools and the dissolution of monastic and conventual schools.

Several *Gaus* have reported to me that the necessary measures are already under way and partly are already completed. Most *Gauleiters* have not yet reported. I would like to draw your attention once again to the directives and ask you expressly to carry out the measures without question in the course of this year. It is urgently desired that by the end of the year no more denominational schools or monastic or conventual schools should exist. In many cases it should be possible to carry out these orders by the beginning of the second half of the school year 1939.

Further, you should take all other possible steps to remove denominational influences from the German educational system. By the end of the year, no educational institutions should exist which are under denominational influence. Particularly, this includes orphanages, foster homes, boarding-houses and hostels. Only in those places where the Church authorities have an overwhelming proportion of the facilities, such as kindergartens, nursing homes, etc., and where the take-over cannot be effected because of the lack of other resources and the necessary personnel within a short time, should the process be stretched out over a longer period. But even here the purpose must be clear that in the shortest possible time no more educational institutions should be left in the hands of the Church or under denominational influence. We have no interest of seeing the situation maintained where even the smallest part of the German Youth remains subordinate to Church or denominational influence.

Signed
M. BORMANN

Appendix 11: List of sects prohibited by the Gestapo up to December 1938

(*Source, Schumacher Collection, Berlin Document Centre*)

Gestapo Headquarters   Berlin
   II B2 – 127/39 S   7 June 1939

TO ALL POLICE HEADQUARTERS

RE: Listing of Prohibited Sects.

Enclosed is a list of sects which have been prohibited between 1933 and the 31.12.1938 in the Reich Territory, including those prohibited only in one Police District or in one place only.

A report should be submitted to me if further prohibitions during this period have been ordered in individual towns or administrative districts, which are not listed.

If any such sects have been finally dissolved since 1 January 1939, or will be dissolved in the future, this fact should also be reported to me. I do, however, draw to your attention that in principle such measures require my previous agreement.

                   Signed by order
                   Müller

LIST OF SECTS PROHIBITED SINCE 1933

No.	Name of Sect	Prohibited on . . . by . . . File no.	Area of Prohibition	Published in official record on . . .
1.	International Jehovah's Witnesses (International Bibelforscher Vereinigung)	24.6.33 by Prussian Minister of Interior order no. II 1316a/ 23.6.33	Prussia	Not published
2.	Fighting League for a German Ideology (Kampfbund für Germanische Weltanschauung)	19.10.33 by Gestapo II E/K 2.33	Prussia	Not published
3.	Gathering of Mankind's friends (Menschenfreundliche Versammlung)	13.1.34 by Gestapo II E 2–244/21S	Prussia	Not published
4.	Juda's Apostolate in the family of Jacob (Aposteleamt Juda in Jacobs Geschlecht)	5.11.34 by Gestapo II 1 B 1 2132/34	Prussia	Not published
5.	Union of Free religious communities in Germany (Bund freireligiöser Gemeinden Deutschlands)	20.11.34 by Gestapo II 1 B 1 60634/1860	Prussia	Not published
6.	Weissenberg Sect.	17.1.35 by Gestapo II 1 B 1 55237/786	Prussia	Not published
7.	Union of fighters for faith and truth (Bund der Kämpfer für Glaube und Wahrheit)	27.8.35 by Gestapo II 1 B 1 67109/ 4846/35	Prussia	Prussian official record p. 1109.
8.	God's Social Parish (Soziale Gemeinde Gottes)	28.8.35 by Gestapo II 1 B 1 65779/ 4568/35	Prussia	ditto
9.	Anabaptist Sect (Der Wiedertäufer)	24.8.35 by Gestapo II 1 B 1 67918/ 4687/35	Prussia	ditto
10.	Mazdaznan Movement (Mazdaznan Bewegung)	5.11.35 by Political Police Commissions and Gestapo II 1 B 1 76090/35 S 327	Reich	p. 1407
11.	Seventh Day Adventists – Reform Movement (Siebenten-Tags-Adventisten – Reformbewegung)	28.4.36 as before by II 1 B 1 S 213/36.	Reich	p. 675

Appendices

No.	Name of Sect	Prohibited on ... by ... File no.	Area of Prohibition	Published in official record on ...
12.	Mission for Awakening in Germany (Erweckungs-mission in Deutschland)	30.5.36 as before by II 1 B 1 S 672/36	Reich	p. 1703
13.	Tanatra Union of God (Gottesbund Tanatra)	10.7.36 as before by II 1 B 1 S 853/36	Reich	p. 1137
14.	Gnosis (Gnostics)	10.7.36 as before by II 1 B 1 835/35	Reich	p. 1138
15.	Community of Divine Socialism – Ruben family (Gemeinschaft des Göttlichen Sozialismus – Stamm Ruben)	22.1.36 Gestapo Breslau	District of Breslau Liegnitz	Not published
16.	Zionist Community (Zionsgemeinde)	27.10.36 Gestapo Darmstadt	Darmstadt	Not published
17.	Free Pentecostalists of Berlin (Freie Pfingst-gemeinde Berlin)	11.3.37 Gestapo Berlin	Berlin	Not published
18.	Free Pentecostalists of Salem (Freie Pfingst-gemeinde Salem)	7.11.36 Gestapo Kiel	Province of Schleswig-Holstein	Not published
19.	Study group for Psychic Research (Studienkreis für psychische Forschung)	23.1.37 Gestapo Düsseldorf	Düsseldorf	Not published
20.	Open Brethren (Offene Brüder)	12.4.37 Gestapo Liegnitz	Liegnitz	Not published
21.	Bible Faith fellowship (Biblische Glaubens-gemeinschaft)	10.4.37 Reich Leader SS and Chief of the German Police in the Ministry of the Interior S–PP (IIB) 2514/37	Reich	Prussian official record p. 623
22.	Christian Gathering (Christliche Versammlung)	13.4.37 as before by S PP (IIB) 570/36	Reich	p. 655
23.	Seventh Day Adventists – 3rd Division (Siebenten-Tags-Adventisten Vom III Teil)	19.4.37 as before by S. PP (IIB) 1867/36	Reich	p. 655
24.	Friends of Schopdach (Schopdacher Freundes-kreis)	24.4.37 as before by S PP (IIB) 23.49/36	Reich	p. 655

No.	Name of Sect	Prohibited . . . by . . . File no.	Area of Prohibition	Published in official record on . . .
25.	New Salem Company (Neu-Salem-Gesellschaft)	10.5.37 as before by S PP (IIB) 1169/36	Reich	p. 617
26.	Bahai Sect (Bahai-Sekte)	21.5.37 as before by S PP (IIB) 4030/37	Reich	p. 917
27.	Thabor Pentecostalists (Pfingstgemeinde Thabor)	16.4.37 Gestapo, Berlin	Berlin	Not Published
28.	Thanks be to Thee, dear Father (Lieber Vater habe Du Dank)	2.6.37 Reich Leader SS and Chief of the German Police in the Reich Ministry of the Interior S PP (IIB) 4291/37	Reich	Prussian official record p. 993
29.	German People's Church (Deutsche Volkskirche e. V. Dinter-Bewegung)	31.5.37 as before by S PP (IIB) 3495/37	Reich	Prussian official record p. 993
30.	The Church of the Apostle John (Apostelkirche Johannes)	26.6.37 as before by S PP (IIB) 4472/37	Reich	p. 993
31.	Darbyists – 2nd group, Infant Baptism (Darbysten – 2 Richtung Kindtäufer)	21.3.38 as before by S PP (IIB) 732/38	Reich	20.4.38 p. 698
32.	Möttling Movement (Möttlinger Bewegung)	30.10.38 Reich leader SS and Chief of the German Police in the Ministry of the Interior S PP (IIB) 7287/38	Reich	16.11.38 p. 1851
33.	Shepherd and Flock (Hirt und Herde)	28.8.33 Saxon Minister of Interior 11.9.33 Thuringia Minister of Interior	Saxony Thuringia	
34.	Free League of Jehovah's Witnesses (Freie Bibelforscher Vereinigung)	Nov. 1933 Gestapo Bielefeld 21.10.37 Governor of Thuringia	Thuringia	

Appendices

LIST OF LOCAL SECTS DISSOLVED BY THE POLICE

No.	Description of Sect	Dissolved by	Date	Reasons
1.	Nameless Sect – leader Josef Mahl (Namenlose Sekte)	Augsburg	10.2.38	Endangering public morality
2.	Christian Community (Christliche Gemeinschaft)	Osnabrück	17.5.38	Endangering public security
3.	Richard Wagner Fellowship – leader Karl Ernst Lange	Dresden	15.6.38	Endangering the National Socialist ideology
4.	Association for a common life (Vereinigung vom gemeinsamen Leben)	Nuremberg	5.12.38	Aims of the sect contradict the purposes of the National Socialist leaders.
5.	Bible Community – no. 213 (Biblische Gemeinschaft)	Hamburg	24.11.38	Faith healing

374

Appendix 12: Treatment of a Lutheran Pastor who protested against the persecution of the Jews in 1938

(Reprinted from a mimeographed newsletter of the Confessing Church)

Pastor Julius von Jan of Oberlenningen, Württemberg, in his sermon on the National Day of Contrition and Prayer, 13 November 1938, amongst other things spoke out in a clear and unmistakable manner against the pogrom against the Jews. He declared:

'A crime has been committed in Paris. The murderer will undoubtedly receive his due punishment, because he has offended against the divine law. All our people are saddened by the horror of this event, and express our sympathy with the victim of this criminal act. But who would have believed that this one crime in Paris could have resulted in so many crimes here in Germany as a result? Here we see the reckoning for the great apostasy from God and Christ, arising out of organized anti-Christianity. Passions have been unloosed, God's commandments have been despised, the houses of God, which were holy places to others, have been burned down, and the arsonists left unpunished. The property of foreigners has been confiscated or destroyed. Men who have served our people loyally and done their duty in all conscience, have been thrown into concentration camps, simply because they belonged to another race! Even if the authorities do not admit this wrong, our sense of decency is offended, even if no one dares to speak about it. And we Christians cannot fail to see how this injustice condemns our people in the sight of God, and must bring his justified punishment upon Germany. Since it is written: "Be not deceived; God is not mocked: for whatsoever a man soweth, that shall he also reap." Yes, this is the terrible seed of hatred, which is now once again being

375

sown. What a terrible harvest will ensue, if God does not grant to us and our people his grace through genuine contrition. . . .'

On 25 November, about 10.30 at night, a gang of approximately 500 demonstrators, who did not belong to the community, attacked Pastor von Jan with wild cries outside his vicarage, beat him up and severely injured him. He is now in prison under arrest in the County Prison at Kirchheim, Teck. The thugs, most of whom came from Nürtingen and neighbourhood arrived about 8 o'clock in trucks and private cars. When they found out that the Pastor was not at home, some of them searched the vicarage from top to bottom looking for him. Pastor von Jan was at the time in the nearby village of Schopfloch, where he and the village pastor were holding a bible study on the First Epistle of St Peter. When the mob found out where he was, a car with four persons in it was despatched there and brought von Jan back from Schopfloch to Oberlenningen. It was shortly after 9 o'clock, and the Pastor had just completed his talk on I Peter, chapter 4. When they arrived in Oberlenningen, he was forced out of the car, and the mob descended on him like wild animals. They threw him, half unconscious, on to the top of a nearby woodshed, in order to let him be seen and abused by the wild horde. After they brought him down, they dragged him through the ranks of the mob, which was screaming and howling, to the Town Hall, about 100 yards away. There an interrogation took place, which lasted about an hour, while outside the crowd gave vent to its indignation with bloodthirsty talk and shouting and swearing, denouncing Jan as a traitor to the people, and a slave of Judaism. All hell was let loose. About 11 o'clock Pastor von Jan was taken away in a car to Kirchheim and put in prison.

Appendix 13: Pro-Nazi sentiments by a Pastor from Schortens, Oldenburg

(*Reprinted from the Oldenburgischen Rundschreiben 85/1935, 7 October 1935*)

Dear Editor of the *Stürmer*,

Just today I received the August number of the *Stürmer*. As a Lutheran Pastor I must thank you for the courageous words with which you replied to the incredible statements of the Provincial Brethren Council [of the Confessing Church] in Saxony. We stand enthusiastically behind your struggle against the Jewish death watch beetles which are undermining our German nation. So too against those friends of Jewry which are to be found even in the ranks of the Protestant pastorate. We will fight alongside you and we will not give up until the struggle against all Jewry and against the murderers of Our Saviour has been brought to a victorious end, in the spirit of Christ and of Martin Luther.

In true fellowship, I greet you with Heil Hitler!

Yours,
Riechelmann,
Pastor.

Appendix 14: A directive signed by Heydrich ordering the immediate suppression of certain secret and religious societies, and the arrest and internment in concentration camps of all persons connected therewith

(*Translation of Nuremberg Document D–59*)

I In the present struggle for the fate of the German people, it is necessary to maintain not merely the physical but also the spiritual health of our people, both individually and collectively.
The German people can no longer be exposed to occultist teachings which pretend that the actions and missions of the human being are subject to mysterious magic forces.

II These immediate measures will be taken against the following:

Astrologers.
Occultists.
Spiritualists.
Followers of the Occult Theories of Rays.
Fortune Tellers, fake or otherwise (no matter which type).
Faith Healers (*Gesundbeter*).
Followers of Christian Science.
Followers of Anthroposophy.
Followers of Theosophy.
Followers of Ariosophy.

and also against their organizations, clubs, unions, circles, etc., as well as against leading and single persons as far as these teachings and sciences are their main occupation, or wherever they perform some special function or exert some special influence.

III *The Purpose of the Impending Action*

1) All organizations, clubs, unions, circles, etc., will

    a) without exception and simultaneously be purged; the existing material (particularly lists of addresses, card indexes, correspondence, apparatus, occult objects, written material and any existing property) will be confiscated.

    b) they will be dissolved and prohibited.

Since it must be assumed that such material has already been removed, a simultaneous search of all the houses of the leading persons of the circles and also of such persons who are in any way suspected of keeping any such material, will be conducted.

(Left marginal note: Special file has been prepared).

2) Publisher's and Printer's firms who have mainly been occupied with the publication of such literature will be purged and confiscated (with the object of closing them down) (for instructions seen enclosure 1). Where Publisher's and Printer's Firms have only dealt from time to time with the production of such material they will also be purged and the literature still existing will be confiscated. They will be prohibited from the further production of such literature under the threat of closing them down, should this be disregarded.

3) Persons who have devoted themselves to secret teachings and secret sciences as their main occupation, and who have therefore led the existence of a parasite at the expense of the people are to be arrested in every case. Persons who have occupied themselves with these teachings and sciences as a part-time occupation will be forbidden this activity with immediate effect, under the threat of the severest measures by the State police. They are to be sent, case by case, to a concentration camp or (in less serious cases) through the agency of the Labour Exchanges, to be directed to an occupation more useful to the German people.

    It is obvious that in their cases a thorough search of their houses is to be conducted and their existing material (lists of addresses, card indexes, correspondence, etc.) must be confiscated.

IV I therefore decree that: 1.) this action is to be carried out in the entire Reich territories (including OSTMARK, ALSACE,

LORRAINE, LUXEMBOURG, and the Protectorate) on the 9/6/41, if possible between 7 and 9 o'clock.

1) The Director of the State Police Office or State Police (Superior) Office is responsible for directing this action.

2) The Director of the State Police (State Police Superior) offices (Superior KRIPO Offices) and the leaders of the SD (Superior SD) sectors, to discuss and secure uniformity in carrying out the action, the assembling and readiness of the necessary force and the immediate exploitation of the confiscated material (for discovering further organizations, clubs, unions, circles, etc., and persons possibly not yet known).

Should the immediate exploitation produce further evidence, all necessary action will be taken within the framework of this decree.

Wherever it is a local necessity, immediate contact with the directors of the Health Department is to be established by the Health Department. The Reich Minister for the Interior has informed the Health Department accordingly.

Separate instructions will be issued after the conclusion of the action for the final exploitation of the material.

3) As far as is known here the lists of organizations, publishers and personalities concerning your district will be made known by express letter in the course of today. Where arrest appears necessary, this will be stated in each case (viz. further general instructions in following paragraph). (In addition to this, the State Police Offices (State Police (Superior) Offices), in close co-operation with the KRIPO Offices (KRIPO (Superior) Offices) and SD Sectors (SD (Superior) Sectors), will establish on their own part which organizations, clubs etc., as well as persons, should further be included in the section.

Should any of the persons named have moved in the meantime the State Police Office (State Police (Superior) Office) at their new domicile should be informed immediately, with reference to this decree.

4) Regarding the treatment of the persons concerned by this action, the following is laid down:

a) Thorough interrogation regarding their family circumstances, life history, occupation, profession and the type and degree of their participation with clubs, unions, circles and persons. Instructions for the interrogation of these persons will be sent in time by means of express letter.

b) Persons who have devoted themselves to these secret teachings or sciences as their main occupation or have already been previously sentenced in this connection, but have continued their activities, must on principle be arrested. Application for protective custody together with a comment as to whether transfer to a concentration camp appears necessary must be made after the subject has been clarified.

c) Such persons as have occupied themselves with these subjects as part-time work are likewise to be arrested, if they have been particularly active, or if the arrest appears essential for the prevention of an escape and the danger of removing or destroying materials etc.

Otherwise, it must be divulged to these persons after their interrogation that:

they are forbidden any further activity in these matters with immediate effect,

that until conclusion of the investigation they may only leave their domicile after previously obtaining permission.

that they must refrain from all applications to Party and State Departments until the final lawful ruling, and that they must not talk to third persons.

d) Wherever such persons are already under punitive arrest, interrogation arrest or protective custody, and wherever this has not already been carried out, their houses are also to be searched. An application has to be submitted for persons who are under punitive arrest or interrogation arrest for their re-transfer for the purpose of examining the case with a view to transfer to a concentration camp.

e) Before carrying out the action it will be established whether such persons are not at present doing duty with the Army or are active in the Party in leading positions (from *Ortsgruppenleiter* upwards or corresponding rank.)

The same applies to leading officials of the State; the existing regulations apply to proceedings against medium and lower ranking civil servants (Department Leaders to be informed).

If necessary I am to be informed immediately by means of a teleprinter message. No measures are to be taken until receipt of further instructions. The appropriate measures for the prevention of the removing of material will not infringe this.

V After the action has been carried out, a summary report will be submitted to me, by means of express letter, no later than 15.6.41. This will contain
1) The measures taken
2) The principal results.

a) Persons arrested
b) Organizations, Clubs, Unions, Circles, etc., dissolved.
c) Searches of houses carried out.
d) A list of confiscated material (as far as possible the most important results of the immediate exploitation).
e) Suggestions for further measures.
f) Experiences made.

VI A severe stand will be applied to all occurring decisions regarding the carrying out of this decree.

VII All correspondence referring to this action is to be addressed to me personally.

VIII Only extracts of this decree are to be used for the information of local Police Authorities (*KREIS* und *ORTSPOLIZEIBE-HORDEN*) (particularly regarding fortune tellers, fake or otherwise).

(Signed) HEYDRICH

Seal – A true copy: signed: HARTL,

4.6.41

To all Gauleiters
 Provincial Governments
 Police Headquarters

SS Sturmbannführer

Gruppenleiter IV B.

Appendix 15: Bormann's Circular on the Relationship of National Socialism and Christianity

(*Nuremberg document, 075–D*)

National Socialism and Christianity are irreconcilable. Christian churches build on the uncertainty of human beings and attempt to preserve this fear in as wide segments of the population as possible, for only in this way can Christian churches keep their power. In opposition to this, National Socialism is based on scientific foundations. Christianity has invariable tenets, which were set up almost 2,000 years ago and have petrified into dogmas incompatible with reality. National Socialism on the other hand must always, if it is to fulfil its job in the future, be organized according to the latest knowledge of scientific research.

Christian churches have long recognized the dangers which threaten their existence on account of exact scientific knowledge and therefore attempt by means of pseudo-science, such as theology, to suppress or falsify scientific research by means of the concepts of Christianity, which in their essential points have been taken over from Jewry. For this reason also we do not need Christianity.

No human being would know anything of Christianity if it had not been drilled into him in his childhood by pastors. The so-called dear God in no wise gives knowledge of his existence to young people in advance, but in an astonishing manner, in spite of his omnipotence, leaves this to the efforts of the pastors. If therefore in the future our youth learns nothing more of this Christianity, whose doctrines are far below ours, Christianity will disappear by itself.

It is also strange that before the beginning of the modern era nothing was known of this Christian God. At that time most inhabitants of the

383

earth never learned anything about Christianity and therefore according to the standard Christian concept were damned from the beginning.

When we National Socialists speak of a belief in God, we do not
understand by God, like naive Christians and their spiritual opportunists,
a human-type being, who sits around somewhere in space. We must
rather open people's eyes to the fact that besides our small universe,
there are an inconceivably large number of other bodies, innumerable
additional bodies, which like the sun are surrounded by planets, and
these in turn by smaller bodies, the moons. The force of natural law,
with which all these innumerable planets move in the universe, we call
the Almighty or God. The claim that this world force is concerned
about the fate of every single being, of every smallest earth bacillus,
or can be influenced by so-called prayers or other astonishing things, is
based on a proper dose of naivete or alternatively on a commercial
shamelessness.

In opposition to this, we National Socialists impose on ourselves the
demand to live naturally as much as possible, i.e., biologically. The more
accurately we recognize and observe the laws of nature and of life, the
more we adhere to them, so much the more do we conform to the
will of the Almighty. The more insight we have into the will of the
Almighty, the greater will be our successes.

It follows from the irreconcilability of National Socialist and
Christian concepts, that a strengthening of existing denominations and
every demand of the original Christian denominations is to be rejected
by us. A differentiation between the various Christian denominations
should not be made here. For this reason also the thought of creating a
National Evangelical Church by merging the various Evangelical
churches has been definitely given up, because the Evangelical Church
is just as inimical to us as the Catholic Church. Any strengthening of
the Evangelical Church would merely react against us.

It was a historical mistake of the German Emperors in the Middle
Ages that they repeatedly created order at the Vatican in Rome. It is
always an error into which we Germans unfortunately fall too often,
that we attempt to create order where we ought to have an interest in
disunion and separation. The Hohenstaufens would have had the
greatest interest in the disintegration of ecclesiastical power. From the
standpoint of the Reich it would have been most favourable if not one
pope but at least two, if possible even more popes had existed in mutual
conflict. Instead of this the German emperors and church helped one
pope to power over all other rivals, with such success that the emperors,

as soon as the pope was again strong enough immediately received the first blow from 'their' pope. The church however in strengthening its own position of power repeatedly used the particularism of the princes and later of parties and tied it up with all its strength.

In former generations leadership of the people lay exclusively in the hands of the church. The State limited itself to issuing laws and orders and primarily to administering. The real leadership of the people lay not with the State but with the church. The latter exerted via the priest the strongest influence on the life of the individual human being, of families and on the totality of things. Everything which did not suit the churches was suppressed with unprecedented ruthlessness. For centuries the State by the most various turns granted to the church the possibility of influence. It depended on the church whether it would help the state or oppose it. The State was reduced to the aid of the church, it was dependent on it. The struggle of the German Emperors against the pope failed in the Middle Ages and repeatedly in modern times, because not the emperor, but the church had the leadership of the people in its hand.

The ideological dependence of the State on the church, the yielding of leadership of the people to the church, had become a matter of course, so that nobody dared to oppose it seriously. To refuse to consider this as an incontrovertible fact from the beginning, passed as absurd stupidity until just before the *Machtuebernahme* [Hitler's rise to power, 1933].

For the first time in German history, the Führer consciously and completely has the leadership of the people in his own hand. With the Party, its components and attached affiliates, the Führer has created for himself, and thereby for the German Reich leadership, an instrument which makes him independent of the Church. All influences which might impair or damage the leadership of the people exercised by the Führer with the help of the NSDAP, must be eliminated. More and more the people must be separated from the churches and their organs, the pastors. Of course, seen from their viewpoint, the churches must and will defend themselves against this loss of power. But never again must influence in the leadership of the people be yielded to the churches. This (influence) must be broken completely and finally.

Only the Reich government and by its direction the party, its components and affiliates have a right to leadership of the people. Just as the deleterious influences of astrologers, seers and other fakers are eliminated and suppressed by the State, so must the possibility of church influence

Appendices

also be totally removed. Not until this has happened, does the state leadership have influence on the individual citizens. Not until then are people and Reich secure in their existence for all the future.

It would only repeat the fatal mistakes of past centuries, if we were to contribute in any way to the strengthening of one of the various churches, and they were to get to know about this. The interest of the Reich lies not in conquering but in preserving and strengthening ecclesiastical particularism.

(signed) M. BORMANN
Reichsleiter.

386

Appendix 16: Two of Bormann's decrees relating to the treatment of foreign workers in Germany

(*Source: Bundesarchiv*)

National Socialist German Worker's Party
The Deputy of the Führer

Muenchen 22, 27 January 1941.
Braunes Haus

Stabsleiter   III/04 – Wh

Circular
(Not for publication)

Highly Confidential!

Re.: Erection of brothels for foreign workers

Referring to my circular letter of 7 December 1940, I am sending you in the enclosure a compilation of the most significant points in a report from the NSDAP *Gauleitung* Oberdonau (Upper Danube) which was the first to arrange for the erection of brothels for alien labourers on a large scale.

The experiences gained in the *Gau* Oberdonau may be valuable for the realization of similar arrangements in other *Gaus*. Above all the vital point appears to me to be not to engage German-blooded girls in the brothels intended for foreign-workers and not to allow German citizens to frequent these houses.

Heil Hitler!
sgd. M. BORMANN

Appendices

1 *enclosure* on reverse
for the correctness:
....
Distribution:
Reichsleiter,
Gauleiter
Verbändeführer.

Enclosure to the circular letter of January 27th 1941

Extracts from the report from *Gauleitung* Oberdonau of 27 December 1940.

1. *Reasons for measures taken:*
   The workers in the Reichswerke Hermann Göring in Linz are to a considerable extent composed of Czechs, Slovaks, Bulgarians, and Italians. To counteract recurrent undesirable intercourse of these foreign workers with German women, the *Gauleitung*, assisted in particular by the *Rassenpolitisches Amt* and supported by the criminal investigation police, the Security Service (SD) and the municipality of Linz has envisaged the erection of a brothel.

2. *Ownership:*
   The municipality of Linz is the party who gives the building order. After completion the brothel will be leased by the municipality of Linz to a solvent as well as competent person suited for such an establishment.

3. *Erection:*
   Because of the special conditions and the location of the Hermann Göring works – work on a new construction was begun rather than reconstruction of an extant building. The site was chosen so as to be located in the vicinity of the largest hutted camp for foreign workers and to be easily secluded from the public. The required building estate of 3/4 of an acre belongs to the *Gau* Oberdonau and was taken on lease by the municipality of Linz for a period of five years with the promise of an extension of the lease for another five years. The Reich Labour Minister gave permission to start the project.
   In a great number of cases erecting adequately furnished wooden houses (huts) will be sufficient.

4. *Interior Decoration:*
   The most primitive requirements, as was planned in the beginning,

388

were not taken as a basis for the building; the establishment is rather built and furnished in such a way as to meet all the demands that can be made on houses of such a kind and in such surroundings. Sanitarily, all requirements were taken account of by installing several baths, supplying all rooms with running water, bidets, etc. etc. A room has been provided for the police. It will not be permanently occupied but will be at the disposal of the police, if they are compelled to intervene in an official capacity. Special value has been set upon the erection of a medical treatment centre.

5. *Financing:*
The costs for the erection of the rough brickwork amount to RM 78 000.—; another RM 40 000,— will be required for the interior decoration including garden landscaping. The owner procured the means by raising a loan from a banking institution. The future leaseholder has guaranteed the loan. The leaseholder has to pay the owner a monthly rent of RM 1200.—. If, as has been attempted, a licence for selling alcoholic liquor should be granted, the rent will be increased by RM 300.— a month.
In the event of the establishment being disposed of, the leaseholders, by contract, will have the right of pre-emption.

6. *Management:*
The leaseholder, who was selected with the approval of the criminal investigation police, is the manager of the brothel. His life companion assisting him is a former prostitute who speaks several Slavonic languages. The leaseholder owns real estate to such an extent that there has been and will be no danger of financial difficulties in this respect. Moreover, as a longtime manager of similar establishments, he has been in a position to gain extensive experience here and abroad during recent years.

7. *Occupants:*
The initial plans were for a house for 30 occupants. The restrictions imposed on constructions in general permit, however, only a building for 15 occupants, but the building will be constructed in such a way as to permit a replenishment up to the number of personnel originally provided for. The contract of lease provides that no German-blooded girls shall be admitted. The criminal investigation police will permit only the engagement of non-German-blooded occupants of Aryan descent.

8. *Separation according to nationalities:*

In course of time more houses will be established and so far as possible the houses will always be accupied by girls of *that* country, the nationals of which live next door. Thus, the Italians will probably have one or several houses, and, separated from them, the Balkan nations theirs as well. If foreigners do not go to the house intended for their nation but to a house for others, no offence shall be taken at this.

9. *Exclusion of German visitors:*

It is strictly taken care of that no Germans will go into houses occupied by foreign girls and that no foreign workers will come to German houses already existing in town.

National Socialist German Workers' Party
Party Chancellery
The Director of the Party Chancellery

(To Pg. Ohr
„ Meister
for information and return)
K.

Circular No. 126/41
(Not for Publication)

Führerheadquarters, 15 October 1941.

Re: Brothels for foreign workers.

As I have discovered, only an infinitely small number of brothels have been establshed so far. To remove the difficulties accounting for this situation the following has been arranged for:

I. *Organizational:*

In virtue of decrees issued by the particular Reich ministries and other Reich administrative departments, the directors of the head office of the criminal investigation department, the presidents of the regional labour offices and the municipal heads of the offices of the Reich *Mittelinstanz* of the general administration will convene in the near future in each *Gau* district, under the chairmanship of the German Labour Front *Gau* spokesmen, a meeting to ascertain the need of brothels, to take charge of the planning and to determine the basis of financing the project. According to the results of this conference, the decree will be carried out by the body appointed for conducting the operation. Responsible for the overall planning is the criminal investigations department.

II. *Financing:*

As listed below the following bodies will be called upon to finance the project:

1. the contractor of the building project who employs a large number of alien labourers or several of them combined. By decree of the Reich Labour Minister and the Reich Chamber of Economic Affairs the contractors have been urged to bear the expenses;

2. the municipalities (cities), so far as the means to 1. has been made impossible due to the dispersal of employment and so far as a municipality sufficiently solvent is available. In a circular letter the Reich Minister of the Interior called the attention of the municipalities to the significance of this task and urged them at all events to place land at the contractor's disposal.

3. If both means are not practicable, the project will be financed by the *Häuser- und Barackenbau-GmbH.* founded by the German Labour Front which has been endowed with advance means by the German Labour Front and the Reich.

III. *Allotments:*

For the present, Reich Minister Dr Todt has immediately placed 150 huts of the current production for disposal for the intended use as brothels. They may be called for by the Reich criminal investigation department on demand. For alterations necessary in existing buildings a special allotment of lumber, iron and cement has been set aside. The building projects have been classified into priority class O. Before falling back on this special arrangement, it has to be investigated in each individual case whether the brothel can be built out of the building material allotment of the respective contractors. For relief of the building material situation this means should be preferred in every case.

IV. *Administration and management:*

As a rule, the enterprise will be leased with the *Häuser- und Barackenbau-GmbH.* and the leaseholder being parties to the contract. The enterprise will be controlled by the criminal investigation police head offices. Licenses for selling alcoholic liquor will as a rule not be given. An admission fee will not be collected from visitors, rather the occupants of the brothels will have to pay a fixed rent to the leaseholders. How much they get from the visitors will be their own concern.

For particulars please look up the instructions received by the *Gau* spokesmen of the German Labour Front in an express letter of 24 September 1941 from the office for allocation of labour at the German Labour Front together with the relevant decrees of the Reich ministries. I emphasize once more that the speedy erection of brothels in order to avert the dangers threatening German blood has been ordered by the Führer himself and I ask all *Gauleiters* to see to it that the implementation of the Führer's order will take place without delay.

sgd. M. BORMANN

Appendix 17: Protest of the Austrian Bishops to the Minister of the Interior, 1 July 1941

(From the files of the Ministry of Justice)

In the course of recent months the Gestapo has again ordered the confiscation of the property of a great number of monasteries and nunneries in Austria. This is tantamount to the closure of the affected orders, since it has occurred in connection with the frequent compulsory eviction of the inhabitants of these institutions. Included were the monasteries of St Peter and Michelbeuern in the province of Salzburg, the monasteries of Hohenfurt, Kremsmunster, Schlogl, St Florian and Wilhering in the province of Upper Danube, the monastery of Klosterneuburg and St Gabriel's convent in Mödling, both in the Vienna District. In all cases, as was reported to the superiors of the institutions, these confiscations were justified 'for reasons of police measures against opponents of the State' (*Staatspolizeilichen Gründen*). In no case was the nature of these acts stated which were alleged to be hostile to the State, as supposedly undertaken by the monasteries and convents, or by their inhabitants. Nor did any judicial investigation, let alone any judicial sentence, follow for any of those concerned. On the contrary, only ridiculous rumours were frequently bruited abroad, to the effect that in one monastery weapons, in another a secret radio transmitter, had been found.

In Salzburg the Gestapo closed the archiepiscopal diocesan teachers' training college and the archiepiscopal theological seminary. On 4 May 1941 the Governor of Salzburg issued an order No. 5/5-52/41 (Rst. 147/41) which took away the administration of the property of the theological college (Fund for the priests' house) from the Church and transferred it to the Salzburg Party Region administration (*Reichsgau Salzburg – Gauselbstverwaltung*). This measure was also justified 'for reasons of police measures against opponents of the State'. That is, these accusations are raised against the whole community of professors, college administrators and alumni, accusing them of attitudes and activities hostile to the State, even at a time when 90 per cent of the alumni are serving with our armed forces and are loyally fulfilling their duty to people and Fatherland. It goes without saying that in this case too no judicial enquiry, nor any judicial proceedings, took place.

On 12 May the Gestapo ordered Canon Karl Dorr of the metropolitan cathedral of St Stephen in Vienna to be expelled from Austria with effect from 24 May, even though the Gestapo, which had put his preaching engagements in the cathedral under regular surveillance, had never had cause to take action against Dorr or even to give him a warning. Thousands of Viennese who attended his sermons know and can confirm that all his activity as a preacher and counsellor was always of a purely religious character. Finally the Gestapo itself expressly acknowledged to the representative of the archbishop's office in Vienna that Dorr had not been engaged in political activity. The real reason for the measures taken against Dorr, despite all the avoidance of the term, is clearly the circumstance that his sermons attracted such a large following.

Similar circumstances affected another Vienna preacher, Dr Diego Götz, a priest of the Dominican Order, who received an expulsion order from Austria on 18 June. So also Father Ernst Mayer from Piernitz in the Archdiocese of Vienna received the same eviction order as Dorr and Götz, for no other reason than that he is an effective priest and shepherd of his parishioners. So too Canon Martin Sturr of St Stephen's, whose expulsion was ordered on the grounds that in his pastoral care of the young men he led them away from the Nationalist Socialist spirit.

The legal restrictions presently in force throughout the whole Reich concerning Ascension Day and Corpus Christi Day, in so far as they forbid purely religious celebrations of the Church on these days, constitute an invasion of the internal and purely religious affairs of Church life. But the Gestapo in Austria has frequently gone beyond these regulations to forbid even those celebrations ordered within the framework of the weekday celebrations of the Liturgy. They have on occasions prohibited such services and in Vienna they in fact forbade and made impossible the public celebration of the Corpus Christi Day processions on 15 June. Even though these are protected by law, they ordered them to take place only on church property, despite the rights explicitly guaranteed by law. [i.e. permitting their appearance on the streets: translator's note.] This took place, even though special dispensations were issued for 22 May and 12 June from the general church injunctions for attendance at mass and for the stopping of work, so that there was no danger of any general disturbance of work requirements, and even though the holding of Corpus Christi Day processions on Sunday 15 June could not have caused any difficulties for the traffic police.

In view of these facts, to which others from the everyday events in church life in Austria could be added, we, the Catholic bishops of Austria, are obliged to raise our voices in protest. We do this in view of the fundamental importance which we attribute to these facts, and of the spirit which informs these measures, even if the action of the Gestapo has not been the same in all the dioceses of Austria. We have to state firmly that:

1. So long as the concrete evidence of guilt, upon which the monasteries have been ordered to be closed, is not made public, we must raise a protest against acts taken arbitrarily in what is supposed to be an orderly and legally established state, as bishops of a similarly legally recognized church. Unfortunately we have already had our suspicions raised for a long time that these closures of monasteries, even from the point of view of the State, have not been organized to protect the public order through disciplinary measures against monasteries for reasons of alleged misdemeanours of their inhabitants. Nor too have the confiscations without compensation of these properties by the State – even though the economic significance of the value of monastic property is grossly overestimated – been taken for these reasons. Rather we see here organized a deliberate attack against religious orders as such, which seeks to hit the Church itself through these branches of its institutions, which are designed to be the highest expressions of the Christian life.

2. The closure of the above-mentioned institutions in Salzburg can be regarded in no other way than as the desire of the State to make impossible the duty of the Bishops, which is firstly to our Lord Jesus Christ and to our Catholic people, in caring for the training of priests. The purpose can only be to prevent in the future a sufficient

supply of priests to proclaim the truths of salvation and to dispense the Sacraments and other necessary means of grace.

3. the expulsion of the above-mentioned priests from Austria is an open proof that the proclamation of the Word of God and of the Gospel of Jesus Christ, and the encouragement of the faithful to maintain a life of Christian faith and morality, whether these are directed to the faithful generally, to artistically-creative circles, to the student bodies or to young men or women, are all regarded in the National Socialist state as something which is damaging to the State and people, and worthy of punishment.

4. the measures, which have up to now been restricted only to the Vienna region during the last two feast days, will no doubt be extended to other services, and thus Christ will be banned from the streets of the Third Reich.

The sum of all these experiences, observations and facts forces us to declare firmly, and to announce publicly, that the measures taken by the State in the area of Church affairs are no longer concerned with individual institutions or organs of the Church. This is a struggle against the deepest and truest things of life, against the Church and religion as such, in order to separate our church from the people and to rob our Catholic people of their Church and their Catholic faith.

We must raise a strong protest in the name of the Church, which can not allow any earthly force to deprive it of its God-given task of bringing salvation to the world. We must protest in the name of the Catholic faith, whose moral value and ethical power has unconditional claims upon the respect and the protection of every ethical human society. We protest in the name of the Catholic people, whose faith is the most holy basis for the salvation of souls and the unchanging guarantee for all human prosperity. We protest in the name of the dignity and freedom of mankind, which are the foundation stones of all true community of peoples (*Volksgemeinschaft*) and have their deepest and truest roots in Christianity. We protest last but not least in the name of our German civilization, which is inseparately united to the nature of Christianity.

In view of the seriousness of the situation we demand that these actions hostile to our church and religion should be stopped. We demand for the Church and the Catholic Christian faith, law and justice and that respect from the State which Catholics, who cannot be and do not want to be second class citizens of the Reich, expect, and are entitled to expect, for their Catholic faith and their Church, which is for them the deepest and most holy possession, on a level with the Fatherland.

Up to now we have refrained from speaking of the distress of the Church and our religion in our dioceses to our parishioners, out of concern for the maintenance of the inner spiritual cohesion of the German people in these dangerous and difficult days when we are struggling for a secure future. We expressly declare our desire to continue this reserved attitude out of true love and genuine care for our people and Fatherland, up to the utmost limits of the needs of the State, as suggested at this time. But we see with concern, which is not for our own persons but for the religion of our people as entrusted to our care by God, the time drawing near in which we will be forced, by our consciences and because of our episcopal offices, to render an account to our faithful people of the state of affairs of their inherited religion and their Church in Austria. It is not we, who must carry the blame for this, but rather those persons who have brought about this intolerable situation by failing to recognize the true realities of life.

Reich Minister! We bishops of Austria, in deep concern of conscience have spoken serious and frank words to you, and we assure you that it has been hard for us to do so. Only our anxiety about the Catholic Church in Austria has caused us to take this step. This anxiety is finally a genuine concern, beyond all considerations of faith or ideology, for the welfare of the German people, which you, Reich Minister, will surely understand, even if you stand on another shore. In confidence of this understanding, we are sending to you, Reich Minister, as the responsible authority for the governmental administration of the Austrian provinces, our urgent request to grant law and justice to the Catholic Church in Austria in a manner different from heretofore. We ask you to grant us, the bishops and the whole Catholic population of Austria, the certainty that, in the greater united German Fatherland, for whom our Austrian Catholic soldiers have dedicated their health and lives in frequently praised and heroic service, our faith and our Church is not to be regarded as outlawed but has a true and lasting resting place.

Appendix 18: A Telegram from the Ecclesiastical Council of the German Evangelical Church to the Führer

(Printed from Kirchliches Jahrbuch 1933–44 (Gütersloh 1948) p. 478–9)

The Ecclesiastical Council of the German Evangelical Church, convened for the first time since the beginning of the decisive combat in the East, assures you, my Führer, in these fascinatingly stirring hours once again of the unshakable loyalty and readiness for service of the entire Evangelical Christendom in Germany. You have, my Führer, staved off the Bolshevist peril in our country and are now calling our nation and the nations of Europe to the decisive passage of arms against the deadly enemy of all order and all European–Christian civilization. The German nation and with it all its Christian members thank you for this deed. Since British policy now aligns itself as an ally of Bolshevism against the Reich, this is an ultimate sign that it is not concerned about Christianity, but only with the annihilation of the German nation. May Almighty God assist you and our nation against the double enemy. The victory shall be ours, to gain which must be the main point of our aspirations and actions.

In this hour the Evangelical Church in Germany honours the Baltic Evangelical martyrs of 1918; she thinks of the unspeakable affliction which Bolshevism wanted to inflict upon all other nations just as it had done with the nations in its own sphere of power, and in all her prayers she is with you and with our peerless soldiers who now are about to eliminate the root of this pestilence with heavy blows. She prays that under your leadership a new order may come into existence all over Europe and that an end will be put to all internal decomposition, to all soiling of the Holiest, and to all desecration of freedom of conscience.

Charlottenburg, 30 June 1941.

398

Biographical Notes

The names of some leading Nazis have been omitted since their personalia are readily available in most of the general histories. The books mentioned are those which had some bearing on Church–State relations in the period 1933–45. Those titles marked* are not mentioned in the post-1945 works of references, such as *Who's Who in Germany* or Kürschner's *Gelehrtenkalendar*.

ALTHAUS, PAUL Professor; b. 1888; 1920 Prof. in Rostock; from 1925 Prof. Systematic Theology in Erlangen, Bavaria; author of *Leadership and Authority (Führertum und Obrigkeit)*, 1936*, *Die deutsche Stunde der Kirche* 1935*, and other works, especially on Lutheranism; emeritus 1958; d. 1966.

BARTH, KARL Professor; b. 1886; Prof. of Reformed Theology, in Göttingen 1921–5; Prof. for Dogmatics and Exegesis of the N.T. in Münster 1925–30; Prof. of Systematic Theology in Bonn 1930–35; Prof. of Systematic Theology in Basle 1935; author of *Church Dogmatics* (1927–   ), *Theologische Existenz heute*, co-author of Barmen Declaration 1934.

BERNING, WILHELM Bishop; b. 1877; ordained 1900; Consecrated Bp. of Osnabrück 1914; appointed Prussian State Councillor by Goering, Sept. 1933; d. 1955.

BERTRAM, ADOLF Cardinal; b. 1859; ordained 1881; consecrated Bp. of Hildesheim 1906; appointed Archbishop of Breslau 1914; Cardinal 1919; Chairman of the Conference of German Bishops 1919–45; d. 1945.

BIBERSTEIN, ERNST Protestant pastor; b. 1899; original name Czymanowski; appointed to Parish of Kating, Schleswig-Holstein 1924; Member of NSDAP 1927; membership no. 272692; 1927–33 Pastor of Kaltenkirchen, Schleswig-Holstein; 1933–5 Provost of Bad Segeberg, Holstein; 1935 appointed to Reich Ministry of Church

Affairs; 1936 member of SS: membership no. 40718; 1940 drafted into army; served as corporal in Holland and France; Oct. 1940 transferred to serve under Heydrich as Chief of Security Police in Oppeln, Silesia; 1942–3 Leader of Einsatzkommando 6, in southern Russia; SS Obersturmbannführer (Lt.-Colonel); 1947 Condemned to death as a war criminal in Nuremberg Trials; 1951 sentence commuted; and later released.

BONHOEFFER, DIETRICH Protestant pastor; b. 1906; studied theology 1923–7; served in Barcelona; University Chaplain, Berlin 1931–3; Pastor of German Lutheran Church in London 1933–5; Director of illegal Preachers' Seminary in Finkenwalde, Pomerania 1935–41; arrested 1943; author of *Letters & Papers from Prison*; hanged in Flossenbürg Concentration Camp, 9 April 1945.

BORMANN, MARTIN Nazi leader; b. 1900; 1920–6 Member of the Society against the Presumptions of Jewry; 1924 sentenced to one year's imprisonment; 1927 Member of NSDAP: membership no. 555; SS no. 60508; 1928–30 on the Staff of Commander of the SA; 1930–41 Chief of Staff to Hess, Hitler's Deputy; 1941–5 Head of the Nazi Party offices; 1943, Secretary to Hitler; presumed killed 1945.

BÜRCKEL, JOSEF Nazi leader; b. 1895; from 1920 Teacher; 1921 Member of the NSDAP; membership no. 46975; 1930 Nazi member of the Reichstag; May 1933 *Gauleiter* of Palatinate and Saar; 1935 Governor of the Saar; 1938 *Gauleiter* of Vienna and 1939 Governor of Austria; 1940 Chief of administration of occupied Lorraine; ordered to commit suicide by Hitler after fall of Metz, Sept. 1944.

CLEMENS, JACOB Catholic priest; b. 1890; ordained 1914; officer of Catholic Action; vicar in Cologne from 1938; d. 1963.

DARRÉ, WALTHER Nazi leader; b. 1895; farmer; NSDAP membership no. 6882; author of *The Peasantry as the Source of Life for the Nordic Race*, 1929; Reich Minister for Agriculture and Nutrition 1933–42; dismissed from NSDAP 1942; condemned to 7 years' imprisonment at Nuremberg 1949; released 1950; SS membership no. 248256, Obergruppenführer (Lt.-General); d. 1953.

DIBELIUS, OTTO Bishop; b. 1880; ordained 1907; 1925–33 General Superintendent of Kurmark; 1933 retired; active in church resistance 1933–45; 1947 appointed Bishop of Berlin and Brandenburg, Chairman 1947–61 of Central Council of Evangelical Church in Germany;

President of World Council of Churches; 1965 retired from bishopric; d. 1967.

DOHRMANN, E. Bishop; b. 1881; ordained 1908; pastor in Stettin 1920–34; Military Bishop for the Evangelical Church 1934–45; 1946 pastor in Munich; since 1950 retired.

EBERLE, FRANZ Bishop; b. 1874; ordained 1897; provost of Augsburg 1933, Suffragan Bishop of Augsburg 1934; d. 1951.

EHRENFRIED, MATHIAS Bishop; b. 1871; ordained 1898; Prof. of Philosophical Theology, Eichstätt, Bavaria 1900–24; consecrated Bp. of Würzburg 1924; d. 1948.

FABRICIUS, CAJUS Professor; b. 1884; Prof. of Systematic Theology in Berlin 1921; ditto in Breslau 1935–43; Member of NSDAP 1932–40; Author of *Positive Christianity in the New State*, 1936*; d. 1951.

FAULHABER, MICHAEL Cardinal; b. 1869; ordained 1892; Professor of O.T. Exegesis, Strassburg 1903–10; Bishop of Speyer 1910–7; Archbishop of Munich 1917–52; author of *Judentum–Christentum–Germantum*, 1933; named Cardinal 1921; d. 1952.

FLORIAN, FRIEDRICH Nazi leader; b. 1894; Active in resistance against French occupation of Ruhr 1922; *Gauleiter* of Düsseldorf 1929; sentenced to 6 years' imprisonment for belonging to Nazi leadership 1949; released 1951; presently living in Rhineland.

FRICK, WILHELM Nazi leader; b. 1877; lawyer in Munich 1901; sentenced to 15 months' imprisonment for participation in 1923 revolution; Nazi member of the Reichstag 1924; 1933–43 Reich Minister of the Interior; 1945–6 tried and sentenced to death at Nuremberg Trials.

GALEN, COUNT CLEMENS AUGUST Bishop; b. 1878; ordained 1904; pastorates in Berlin & Münster; 1933 appointed Bishop of Münster; 1945 named Cardinal; d. 1946.

GERSTENMAIER, EUGEN Protestant Pastor; b. 1906; studied theology in Rostock, Zurich and Berlin; author of *Kirche, Volk und Staat* (*Church, Race and People*), 1936* member of the Evangelical Churches Foreign Relations Dept. 1936–44, also author of *France's Protestants and the War* (under pseud. Albrecht Allmann), 1940*; arrested and tried for complicity in 20 July 1944 plot and sentenced to 7 years' imprisonment; 1949 CDU member of Bundestag; 1954 speaker of the Bundestag.

GREISER, ARTHUR Nazi leader; b. 1897; officer in Freikorps 1918–9; NSDAP membership no. 166635; Deputy *Gauleiter* and leader of NSDAP Parliamentary party in Danzig 1930; President of Danzig Senate 1934; SS membership no. 10795, 1939 *Gauleiter* and Governor of newly created *Warthegau* carved out of occupied Poland; SS Obergruppenführer (Lt.-General) 1942; tried by the Poles 1946 and in Posen publicly hanged.

GRÖBER, CONRAD Archbishop; b. 1872; ordained 1897; Bishop of Meissen 1931; Archbishop of Freiburg 1932; d. 1948.

GROHE, JOSEF Nazi leader; b. 1902; Active in resistance to French occupation of the Ruhr 1922; *Gauleiter* of Köln–Aachen, Prussian State Councillor and member of the Reichstag Nov. 1933; 1944 Military Commander in Belgium and N. France; arrested 1946; sentenced in 1950 to $4\frac{1}{2}$ years' imprisonment; presently living in Cologne.

GRUNDMAN, WALTER Professor; b. 1906; ordained 1932; Professor of N.T. and *Völkische* Theology, Jena 1938; author of *Germanism, Christianity and the Jews**, 1943, and *Jesus the Galilean*, 1940*; General secretary of the Research Institute for the Eradication of Jewish Influences from the German Church, Eisenach 1941. Presently Prof. of N.T., Eisenach Theological Faculty since 1954.

HAHNENBRUCH, ERICH Nazi leader; NSDAP membership no. 272602; official of the Reich Security Main Office (*Reichssicherheitshauptamt*), responsible for Evangelical church affairs 1939–45; SS membership no. 4746795; Sturmbannführer (Major).

HART(E)L, ALBERT Catholic priest; b. 1904; ordained 1929; taught in Catholic schools; 1934 entered service of Himmler and suspended from priest's orders; NSDAP membership May 1933, no. 3,201,046; responsible for organization of spy service against Catholic Church 1935–41; SS membership, April 1934, no. 107050; Head of Dept. IVB (Religious opponents) in Gestapo HQ. and nominal superior of Eichmann, 1941; in Russia 1941–2, SS Standartenführer (Colonel); 1947 and 1951 witness at the trials of former Gestapo associates.

HECKEL, THEODORE Bishop; b. 1894; studied theology 1913–4 and 1920; ordained 1921; appointed head of Evangelical Church's Foreign

Relations Dept. 1934; in charge of aid for Interned people and
P.O.W.; Dean of Munich 1950–64; 1961 Member of Bavarian
Senate; 1953 Grosse Verdienstkreuz des Bundesrepublik; d. 1967.

HEYDE, WERNER Professor; b. 1902; participated in Kapp *Putsch*;
1933 member of the Nazi Party; 1939 Professor of Psychiatry,
Würzburg, and Head of University Clinic for Nervous Diseases;
1939–44 on staff of SS Hauptamt; SS membership no. 276656; 1943,
Obersturmbannführer (Lt. Col.); 1945 Standartenführer (Col.);
responsible for medical direction of euthanasia programme; 1945
arrested; 1947 escaped and took refuge in Schleswig-Holstein; 1948–
59 practised as medical doctor under false name of 'Sawada' despite
the fact of his real identity being known to senior officials of Schleswig-Holstein provincial government; 1959 rearrested; 1964 committed suicide shortly before his trial was due to begin.

HEYDRICH, REINHARD Nazi leader; b. 1904; naval officer 1922–31;
1931 joined Nazi Party, membership no. 544916. SS Sturmbannführer 1931, membership no. 10120; head of 'Security Service of the
Reich leader of the SS' 1932; assistant to Himmler, 1933 in Bavaria,
and 1934 for whole of Germany; Political Police Chief of the Security
police 1936–42; SS Obergruppenführer (Lt.-General) and Head of
Reich Security Main Office (RHSA); Deputy Protector for Bohemia
and Moravia, 1941; assassinated 5 June 1942.

HIMMLER, HEINRICH Nazi leader; b. 1900; farmer; took part in 1923
Revolution; joined Nazi party 1925, membership no. 168; 1926–30
Deputy *Gauleiter* of Lower Bavaria; from 1925 in SS, membership
no. 14304; 1929 Reichsführer of SS; 1933 Commander of Political
Police in Bavaria; 1934 for all German Police; 1943 Minister of the
Interior; also Reichskommissar für die Festigung deutschen Volks-
tums, Chef der Herresrüstung und Befehlshaber der Ersatzheeres;
Oberbefehlshaber der Heeresgruppe Oberrhein and Weichsel, Chef
des Kriegsgefangenenwesens etc.; committed suicide 1945.

HIRSCH, EMMANUEL Professor; b. 1888; 1915 lecturer in Bonn; 1921
Professor of Church History in Göttingen; one of the world-famous
German theologians; author of *Das kirchliche Wollen der Deutschen
Christen*, 1933*, and *Die gegenwärtige geistige Lage**, 1934; dismissed
1945; presently in Göttingen.

Biographical Notes

HOSSENFELDER, JOACHIM Protestant pastor; b. 1899; ordained 1923; participated in Freikorps; founder and 1st Reich leader of 'Faith Movement of German Christians', 1932; 1933 appointed General Superintendent of the Kurmark; Sept. 1933 appointed Bishop of Brandenburg; presently Pastor of Ratekau near Eutin, Schleswig-Holstein.

HUBER, JACOB Protestant pastor; b. 1908; formerly pastor for *Volks-deutsche* in Galicia; left the church to work for the SA; as Unter-sturmführer (2nd Lieutenant) belonged to Einsatzkommando in Russia; later, Hauptsturmführer (Capt.) in *Reichssicherheitshauptamt*; presently pastor in Hamburg.

JÄGER, AUGUST Lawyer; joined NSDAP March 1933; June 1933 appointed Commissioner for the Prussian Evangelical Church; 1939 Administrator and Deputy Governor of Warthegau; 1945 delivered to the Poles and sentenced to hanging.

KERRL, HANNS Nazi leader; b. 1887; after legal studies, entered Prussian Provincial Parliament; joined NSDAP 1925; April 1933–June 1934, Prussian Minister of Justice; 1934–5 Minister without portfolio in charge of town and country planning; July 1935 appointed Minister for Church Affairs; d. in Paris December 1941.

KUBE, WILHELM Nazi leader; b. 1879; joined NSDAP 1923, membership no. 9528; entered Prussian Provincial Parliament 1924; leader of Nazi Party in Prussian Parliament 1928–33; *Gauleiter* of Kurmark and *Oberpräsident* of Brandenburg 1933–6; dismissed 1936 for sending an anonymous letter accusing the wife of his colleague Reichsleiter Buch of being Jewish; SS membership no. 204233; 1941 appointed Commissioner for White Ruthenia in Minsk; Sept. 1943 assassinated.

LAMMERS, HANS HEINRICH Nazi leader; b. 1879; studied law at Breslau University; administration officer in German govt. of Poland during World War I; 1920 joined Reich Ministry of the Interior, despite hostility to the Weimar Republic; 1932 NSDAP, membership no. 1010355; 1940 SS Obergruppenführer (Lt.-General), membership no. 118404; Jan. 1933, State Secretary in Reich Chancellery; member of and secretary to the Secret Cabinet and the Ministerial committee for Reich Defence; Prussian State Councillor; member of Academy of German Law; lecturer at the Deutsche Hochschule für Politik; 1945 arrested and served as witness throughout trials of major war criminals; was himself indicted and tried in the so-called Wilhelmstrasse Trial in 1948–9 and was sentenced to 20 years' imprisonment. This was reduced to 10 years in 1951, and he was released in the Christmas amnesty of 1951; d. 1962.

LEFFLER, SIEGFRIED Protestant pastor; b. 1900; ordained 1925; 1927 pastor in the Werra Valley, Thüringen; leader of the 'German Christians'; author of *Christus im Dritten Reich der Deutschen**, 1935; Chairman of Institute for the Eradication of Jewish influences from the German Church; presently Pastor of Hengersberg, Bavaria.

LEUTHEUSER, JULIUS Protestant pastor; 1927 pastor in the Werra Valley, Thüringen; Leader of the 'German Christians'; died on war-service.

LICHTENBERG, BERNHARD Catholic priest; b. 1875; ordained 1897; Provost of St Hedwig's Cathedral, Berlin 1938; 1941 arrested by Gestapo for praying on behalf of Jews; d. in captivity 1943.

LORTZ, JOSEF Professor; b. 1887; ordained 1913; joined Nazi Party 1933; Professor of Church History, State Academy, Braunsberg 1929–35, Prof. of Ecclesiastical History, Münster 1935–50; author of *Katholischer Zugang zum Nationalsozialismus kirchengeschichtlich gesehen**, 1933; Professor of History of Western Religion, and director of the department in Institute for European History, University of Mainz 1950; awarded Bundesverdienstkreuz.

MEISER, HANS Bishop; b. 1881; ordained 1905; parishes in Munich; elected Bishop of Evangelical–Lutheran Church in Bavaria 1933; arrested and dismissed Oct. 1934, but reinstated; member of Central Committee of World Council of Churches 1948; retired 1955.

MEYER-ERLACH, WOLF Protestant pastor; b. 1899; radio pastor in Bavaria 1931; 1933 appointed Professor of Practical Theology, University of Jena, despite no academic degree; 1934 Dean of the Theological Faculty, and 1935 Rector of Jena University; instrumental in making Jena University the prototype of a Nazi University. 1961 awarded Bundesverdienstkreuz 1st class by President of Federal Republic, for services in the anti-communist cause. Last heard of as vicar of Wörsdorf, Ilstein, Hessen.

MUHS, HERMANN Nazi leader; b. 1894; joined Nazi Party 1929, membership no. 152594; 1932 *Gauleiter* of South Hannover–Brunswick; 1937 appointed State Secretary to Ministry of Church Affairs; SS Sturmbannführer (Major), membership no. 54402; 1941–5 took over responsibility after Kerrl's death for Ministry of Church Affairs; presently living in Bavaria.

Biographical Notes

MÜLLER, LUDWIG Bishop; b. 1883; 1914–26 Naval Chaplain; 1926–33 Army Chaplain in Königsberg; 1933 appointed Bishop of Prussian Evangelical Church and Bishop of Reich Evangelical Church; d. 1945.

MURAWSKI, FRIEDRICH Catholic priest; b. 1898; 1933 joined NSDAP, membership no. 3,215,779; 1934 suspended by his diocese; 1935 appointed to work for SS and its spy service (SD); 1937 SS no. 272,329, Untersturmführer; 1938 Obersturmführer; 1940 Hauptsturmführer (Capt.); 1941 Head of Section VII B.2 (Political Churches) *Reichssicherheitshauptamt*; expelled from SS and dismissed from RSHA after complaints by Prof. Grundmann (q.v.) of philo-semitic statements in his book *Jesus of Nazareth, King of the Jews* (Berlin 1943).

MURR, WILHELM Nazi leader; b. 1888; Joined Nazi Party 1923, membership no. 147545; businessman; 1928 appointed *Gauleiter* of Württemberg and 1933 Governor of Württemberg; Obergruppenführer (Lt.-General); committed suicide 1945.

MUTSCHMANN, MARTIN Nazi leader; b. 1879; joined Nazi Party; factory owner; 1925 *Gauleiter* of Saxony; 1930 member of the Reichstag; 1933 Governor of Saxony; noted for his brutality toward Jews; 1945 fell into the hands of the Russian occupation troops.

NIEMÖLLER, MARTIN Protestant pastor; b. 1892; served in Navy 1910–18; ordained 1924; pastor in Dahlem 1931–37; imprisoned in Sachsenhausen and Dachau 1937–45; leader of German Evangelical Church's foreign office 1945–56; Church President of Hessen 1948–62; President of World Council of Churches 1961– .

PREYSING, GRAF Bishop; b. 1880; ordained 1909; Canon of Munich; 1932 Bishop of Eichstätt, Bavaria; 1935 Bishop of Berlin; created Cardinal 1946; d. 1950.

ROSENBERG, ALFRED Nazi leader; b. 1893; architect; joined Nazi Party 1921–4; editor of Nazi newspaper *Völkischer Beobachter*; 1934 Hitler's delegate for the complete cultural and educational supervision and training of the Nazi Party; 1945–6 sentenced at Nuremberg trials to death as a war criminal.

ROTH, JOSEPH Catholic priest; b. 1897; ordained 1922; taught in Catholic schools in Munich 1922–36; given leave of absence from his diocese 1936; head of Catholic Section of Church Ministry 1936–41; drowned in River Inn 1941.

RUST, BERNHARD Nazi leader; b. 1883; schoolteacher; joined Nazi Party; 1933 appointed Prussian Minister of Education, Science and Popular Training; 1934 Reich Minister of Education; committed suicide May 1945.

SASSE, MARTIN Bishop; appointed Bishop of Evangelical Church of Thüringen 1934; d. 1941.

SAUCKEL, FRITZ Nazi leader; b. 1894; engineer; joined NSDAP 1921, membership no. 254890; 1927 *Gauleiter* of Thüringen; 1933 Governor of Thüringen; 1942 General Administrator for Labour; SS membership no. 1395; tried and sentenced to death at Nuremberg 1946.

SCHACHLEITER, ALBAN Catholic priest; b. 1861; Head of Benedictine Monastery of Emmaus, Prague; forced to leave Czechoslovakia 1918; active in public lecturing for the Nazi Party; suspended by the Vatican for publishing pro-Nazi article in *Völkischer Beobachter*, 1933; restored to office Sept. 1933; given personal pension by Hitler 1933; d. 1937.

SCHIRACH, BALDUR VON Nazi leader; b. 1907; 1925 joined Nazi Party; Reich Youth leader of NSDAP 1929 and later leader of German Youth 1933-9; 1940 *Gauleiter* and Governor of Vienna; 1946 tried in Nuremberg for war crimes and sentenced to 20 years. Released from Spandau Prison, Berlin, 1967.

SCHMAUS, MICHAEL Professor; b. 1897; ordained 1922; Professor at the German University in Prague 1929-33; Professor of Dogmatic Theology in Münster 1933-45; Munich 1945-62; author of *Begegnungen zwischen Katholischen Christentum und nationalsozialistischer Weltanschauung* 1933*; 1951-2 Rector of University of Munich; presently retired.

SPROLL, JOHN BAPTIST Bishop; b. 1870; ordained 1895; served in Württemberg Parishes; 1912 coadjutor and 1915 suffragan bishop of Rottenburg; 1926 Bishop of Rottenburg; 1938 subjected to mob violence and later banned from Württemberg; returned 1945; d. 1949.

STUCKART, WILHELM Nazi leader; b. 1902; lawyer; 1922-4 and again 1929 Nazi party member; membership no. 378144; 1922-3 served in the Freikorps as active participant in resistance to French occupation of the Ruhr; April 1933 appointed to Prussian Ministry of Education; June 1933 appointed State Secretary; dismissed on amalgamation of Prussian and Reich ministries; July 1934 given post as Joint State Secretary, but lost it in November; March 1935 appointed to Reich Ministry of the Interior in charge of Constitutional and Legislative Section, responsible for drawing up the Nuremberg Laws and other discriminatory legislation against the Jews; 1936 joined SS, membership no. 280042; 1936 Standartenführer; 1939 Brigadeführer, 1942 Gruppenführer, 1944 Obergruppenführer (Lt.-General); 1942 participated in notorious Wannsee Conference at which plans for the 'final solution of the Jew question' were discussed. He added the suggestion that compulsory sterilization of all half-Jewish Germans, approximately 70,000 should be undertaken, 'in order to solve the half-breed question'; 1946 tried at Nuremberg and sentenced to 3 years' imprisonment; 1951 elected as deputy vice-chairman of Provincial League of Refugees and Dispossessed Persons Party, in Hildesheim; 1953 fined 50,000 marks; died in car accident 1953.

WEIZSÄCKER, ERNST VON Civil servant; b. 1882; served in Navy; Joined Foreign Ministry; 1931 Minister to Norway; 1933 Minister to Switzerland; 1937–43 State Secretary under Ribbentrop; 1943 appointed Ambassador to the Vatican; 1948 Tried in Nuremberg and in 1949 sentenced to 7 years' imprisonment; 1950 released; d. 1951.

WERNER, FRIEDRICH Lawyer; b. 1897; appointed Provisional President of the Evangelical Church of Prussia June 1933; member of ecclesiastical council of German Evangelical Church; present address, Düsseldorf.

WIENEKE, FREIDRICH Protestant pastor; b. 1892; ordained 1919; Canon of Soldin, Province of Brandenburg; 1929 joined Nazi party, no. 159088; headed list of Nazi Party candidates for local office in Soldin; local speaker for Nazi Party, Soldin; author of *Christianity and National Socialism*, 1931, and *The Training of Character under National Socialism*, 1936; 1933 appointed to staff of Prussian Evangelical Church offices; responsible for educational questions; Vicar of Alt-Töplitz by Potsdam 1950; d. 1957.

WURM, THEOPHIL Bishop; b. 1868; appointed Church President of Württemberg, 1929; July 1933 took the title of Protestant Bishop of Württemberg; dismissed 1934 but reinstated; chosen as chairman of reconstituted Evangelical Church in Germany 1945; retired 1949; d. 1953.

Notes

INTRODUCTION

[1] An essay in English by Birger Forell, entitled 'National-Socialism and the Protestant Churches', and another by Robert d'Harcourt, 'National-Socialism and the Catholic Church in Germany', are to be found in *The Third Reich* (for UNESCO) (London 1955); partial studies are to be found in J. Donohoe, *Hitler's Conservative Opponents in Bavaria 1930–45* (Leiden 1961) and G. C. Zahn, *German Catholics and Hitler's Wars* (New York 1962). In 1964 there appeared Professor Guenter Lewy's brilliant polemic *The Catholic Church and Nazi Germany*, in which he used material from the diocesan archives to document the readiness of Catholics to collaborate with Nazism both in word and deed, which led to the failure, he believes, of the Catholic Church to take any co-ordinated stand against the spread of Nazi aggressions and atrocities. A more specialized study by S. Friedländer, *Pius XII and the Third Reich* (English ed. 1966) seeks to show that Pope Pius was reluctant to condemn the German misdeeds because of a predilection for Germany and a desire to avoid any increased persecution of the Catholic Church. On the Protestant side, Professor F. H. Littell, in *The German Phoenix* (New York 1960) discusses the background of the Church Struggle, the resistance of the Confessing Church, and the lay movements which have taken their rise as part of the post-war renewal. The paperback by E. H. Robertson, *Christians Against Hitler* (London 1963), is too short and insignificant to be of value to historians of this subject.

[2] A. C. Cochrane, *The Church's Confession Under Hitler* (Philadelphia 1962), p. 16. This is an excellent analysis in English of the Barmen Declaration of 1934, most sympathetically describing the position of the authors.

[3] This book was based on the collection of facts and documents, *The Persecution of the Catholic Church in the Third Reich* (London 1940). This work was actually prepared in Rome, but published in London and later in Buenos Aires. I learn from private sources that the previously unknown author was P. Walter Mariaux, SJ, who died in Munich, 30 April 1963.

[4] S. W. Herman, *It's Your Souls We Want* (London 1943); A. Frey, *Cross and Swastika* (London 1938); P. Means, *Things That Are Caesars's* (New York 1935); D. F. Buxton *The Religious Crisis in Germany* (London 1938); N. Micklem, *National Socialism and the Roman Catholic Church* (Oxford 1939).

[5] See E. Matthias and R. Morsey (Eds.), *Das Ende der Parteien 1933* (Düsseldorf 1960); and R. Leiber, SJ, 'Reichskonkordat und Ende der Zentrumspartei' in *Stimmen der Zeit*, 167 (1961), pp. 213 ff.

[6] See also F. J. Raddatz (Ed.), *Summa iniuria oder Durfte der Papst schweigen* (Hamburg 1963), which is a collection of press criticisms of the play. A collection in English of similar reactions to the play was published with the title *The Storm over the Deputy* (New York 1964).

[7] On this last point see the short but excellent analysis in *Der Ungekündigte Bund*, D. Goldschmidt and H.-J. Kraus (Eds.) (Stuttgart 1963).

[8] July 1963.

[9] Littell, Franklin H., 'Current Study of the Church Struggle with Nazism and its significance for Church History', a paper delivered at the American Society of Church History spring meeting, Southern Methodist University, 8 April 1960; in mimeographed form in Newsletter #4 of the American Committee on the History of the Church Struggle with Nazism (8 January 1960), edited by F. H. Littell.

CHAPTER 1

[1] Adolf Hitler, *Mein Kampf* (Eng. trans. London 1939), p. 289.

[2] Hermann Rauschning, *Hitler Speaks* (London 1939), p. 232.

[3] Innumerable remarks of a similar kind are to be found in the various editions of *Hitler's Table Talk*, the authenticity of which cannot be doubted.

[4] *Gutachten des Instituts für Zeitgeschichte* (Munich 1958), p. 364.

[5] For English translation of the Nazi Party programme, see M. Oakeshott, ed., *The Social and Political Doctrines of Contemporary Europe* (New York 1953), pp. 192–3.

[6] *Mein Kampf* (Note I/1) loc. cit.

[7] Loc. cit.

[8] H. Müller, *Katholische Kirche und Nationalsozialismus* (Munich 1963), p. 17.

[9] Count Galen, later Bishop of Münster, for example, openly attacked the liberal Weimar constitution as being 'godless'.

[10] For examples of Catholic anti-semitism, see G. Lewy, *The Catholic Church and Nazi Germany* (Boston 1964), pp. 271–4.

[11] For example, Abbot Alban Schachleiter, who had been 'retired' from his office by his superiors, was rewarded for his open Nazi sympathies by a personal pension of 300 marks a month, on Hitler's orders, from March 1933.

[12] See the Altona Bekenntnis of January 1933, quoted in K. D. Schmidt, *Die Bekenntnisse des Jahres 1933* (Göttingen 1934), p. 23.

[13] Following such a tradition, even such a widely respected figure as General Superintendent Otto Dibelius could send an Easter Greeting in 1928 to the clergy of his diocese, as follows:

General Superintendent
    of the Kurmark

Berlin-Steglitz
Kaiser Wilhelmstr 11
April 3rd 1928
Tel. Steglitz 2614

Confidential
1928 No. 2
My dear brothers,
We will all have not only understanding but also full sympathy for the final motives which have given rise to the nationalist movement. Despite the ugly sound which has often attached itself to the work, I have always regarded myself as an anti-semite. The fact cannot be concealed that the Jews have played a leading part in all the symptoms of disintegration in modern civilization . . . May God bless our Easter and our Easter message
With heartfelt greetings, your truly
Dibelius

For other examples see *The Strange Case of Bishop Dibelius* (Berlin n.d.).

[14] H. Buchheim, *Glaubenskrise im Dritten Reich* (Stuttgart 1953), p. 51.

[15] G. van Norden, *Kirche in der Krise* (Dusseldorf 1963), p. 181.

[16] See F. Baumgärtel, *Wider die Kirchenkampflegenden* (Neuendettelsau 1959).

[17] See Appendix 1. See also Muller (Note I/8), for these views as expressed by Hitler to the Bishop of Osnabrück.

[18] It is significant that in 1933 Rosenberg was deliberately not given Ministerial office of any kind in either the Reich or the provincial governments.

[19] Evangelische Nachrichten 21/2/1934, quoted in W. Niemöller, *Kampf und Zeugnis* (Bielefeld 1948), p. 102; see for example, Prof. J. M. Verweyen, 'Hitlers Lebensglaube' in *Pädagogische Warthe* 40/42 (Dec. 1933), 1061–2. 'The belief in God shown by Hitler and his government of national renewal demonstrates the particular impression of Christian faith.'

[20] Foreign Minister, June 1920–May 1921, and interim President 1925.

[21] C. S. MacFarland, *The New Church and the New Germany* (New York 1934), p. 15.

[22] *Dokumente der deutschen Politik*, ed. P. M. Benekenstein, Vol. I, (Berlin 1935), p. 4.

[23] H. Rauschning (Note I/2), p. 57.

[24] A. Hitler, *Table-Talk*, ed. A. Bullock (London 1953), entry for 13 December 1941.

[25] Rauschning (Note I/2), p. 58.

[26] *Völkischer Beobachter*, 9 February 1933.

[27] In the Cabinet meeting of 7 March, Hitler had stated: 'It would not be possible to win over the political support of voters of the Centre Party or of the Bavarian People's Party until the Curia dropped both parties.' Goering, however, believed that the Centre Party could be coerced by a ruthless dismissal of all its civil servants, unless it agreed to the proposed Enabling Bill. *Documents on German Foreign Policy* (DGFP) Series C.1, no. 54.

28 Müller (Note I/8), p. 72.

29 But see the excellent and suggestive analysis in Lewy (Note I/10), pp. 64–70.

30 For further details, see R. Morsey, *Das Ende der Parteien* (Düsseldorf 1960), pp. 358–63.

31 *Dokumente der deutschen Politik*, ed. Hohlfeld (Berlin 1954), vol. IV, p. 30.

32 Hitler (Note I/3), entry for 13 December 1941.

33 As a sign of this revocation, the sentence marked [ ] was not printed in the official text of Hitler's speech, nor in any later collected editions; see Buchheim (Note I/14), p. 82 and footnote 60 thereto.

34 Müller (Note I/8), p. 74.

35 See Lewy (Note I/10), pp. 30–1.

36 Müller (Note I/8), pp. 78–9.

37 Op. cit., p. 77.

38 Müller (Note I/8), p. 72.

39 There is still uncertainty as to where Papen got this idea. Some have suggested that he was put up to it by the Vatican itself, though that was strenuously denied by E. Deuerlein in his article, 'Die Lage der katholische Kirche 1933' in *Stimmen der Zeit* 168 (1960–1) 196. Nor is there yet any proof that Msgr Kaas was influenced towards supporting the Enabling Bill because of hints from the Nazi side about a possible Concordat. But see also Lewy (Note I/10), pp. 37–8, 66, 359.

40 Papen *Memoirs* (New York 1953), p. 278.

41 DGFP (Note I/27), C.1. no. 162.

42 Müller (Note I/8), pp. 116–20; DGFP (Note I/27) C.1, no, 188.

43 Müller (Note I/8), pp. 123–5.

44 Quoted in Lewy (Note I/10), pp. 54–5.

45 Müller (Note I/8), pp. 127–30.

46 Müller (Note I/8), p. 141.

47 DGFP (Note I/27), C.1. nos. 250, 319, 333, 347, 348, 349, 350, 351, 362.

48 Ibid., no. 347.

49 Bundesarchiv, Schumacher Akten (BA, Schu.), vol. 243/I/2/96–7.

50 Ibid., vol. 244.

51 Müller (Note I/8), p. 161.

52 *Documents on British Foreign Policy* (DBFP), Series II, vol. 5, no. 342.

53 For the pacifying gesture issued to the Press in which Hitler promised to annul all coercive measures against priests and other leaders of Catholic organizations, and to prevent their future repetition, see W. Conrad, *Kampf um die Kanzeln* (Berlin 1957), p. 43.

54 Quoted in Buchheim (Note I/14), p. 85.

55 See J. Goebbels, *Vom Kaiserhof zur Reichskanzlei* (Berlin 1934), pp. 29 ff.

56 See Appendix 2.

57 See W. Niemöller (Note I/19), p. 40.

58 He was allotted the provisional Party number 2, 816, 993, but his application was refused in February 1934. He was later to join the Confessing Church.

[59] Buchheim (Note I/14), p. 106.

[60] Unpublished diary of Dr W. Conrad.

[61] See F. Zipfel, *Kirchenkampf in Deutschland* (Berlin 1965), p. 35.

[62] Norden (Note I/15), p. 76.

[63] Bundesarchiv, Akten der Reichskanzlei (BA, R), 43, II, 162.

[64] Buchheim (Note I/14), p. 110.

[65] Quoted in A. Cochrane, *The Church's Confession under Hitler* (Philadelphia 1962), p. 105.

[66] A. Jäger, *Kirche im Volk* (Berlin 1936).

[67] See Buchheim (Note I/14), p. 75; several excursi of Dr Wieneke's views are to be found in the archives of the Prussian Evangelical Church in Berlin.

[68] An English translation of the Constitution of the Evangelical Church is to be found in Cochrane (Note I/65), pp. 224-8; and of the Reich Concordat in DGFP (Note I/27), no. 371; for discussion of its terms, see Lewy (Note I/10), pp. 79-86.

[69] DGFP (Note I/27), no. 362: As the official Nazi gazette, the *NS Korrespondenz* jubilantly claimed: 'the significance of the Reich Concordat lies above all in the fact that the Vatican has signed a treaty with the new Germany which means recognition of the Nazi State by the Catholic Church. By this treaty the world has been clearly and unmistakably shown that the idea that Nazism is opposed to religion is no more than a lie, invented for the purposes of political agitation': quoted in E. Deuerlein, *Das Reichskonkordat* (Düsseldorf 1956), p. 124.

[70] This law provided for the 'voluntary' sterilization of all persons suspected of having incurable or inheritable diseases, including mental diseases, and was in direct contradiction to the teachings of the Catholic Church. Further evidence on the results of this law was supplied in the journalistic account of G. Ziemer, *Education for Death* (Oxford 1941), pp. 24-8.

[71] DGFP (Note I/27), no. 371.

[72] *Nordische Zeitung*, 28 July 1933.

[73] This was not just opportunism. Many leaders of this movement, later to become stalwart fighters in the church struggle, continued to maintain an incredible sense of loyalty to Hitler as the duly authorized power in the State. *His* crimes could be no reason for *their* disloyalty.

[74] M. Niemöller, *First Commandment* (London 1937), p. 50.

[75] *Völkischer Beobachter*, 19 July 1933.

[76] This action drew a protest to Hitler from the official in the Reich Ministry of the Interior, who was officially responsible for ensuring the 'impartial' conduct of the elections. Hitler admitted that the Gestapo action was a mistake, and ordered the release of the literature. But, he added, the Nazi Party must naturally support those it favours. BA, R (Note I/63), 43, II, 161.

[77] J. Gauger, *Chronik der Kirchenwirren*, vol. I, p. 94.

CHAPTER 2

[1] See Appendix 3.

[2] J. Beckmann, *Artgemässes Christentum oder schriftgemässe Christenglaube* (Essen 1933), p. 11.

[3] Quoted in H. Schmid, *Apokalyptisches Wetterleuchten* (Münich 1947), p. 39–40. There were seventeen 'non-Aryan' pastors in the Prussian Evangelical Church.

[4] W. Niemöller (Note I/19), pp. 63–4. Nevertheless, many churchmen were appalled by Müller's appointment and his opinions. As one witness related: 'Throughout the whole of the rest of Protestant Germany that morning the churches were packed. They had come together to pray for the true Christianity that was being threatened by a false. They heard their pastors inveigh once more against a 'hybrid Nordic Christian religion'. Never before in history can the nominal head of a Church have been solemnly invested with the trappings of his high office while the vast majority of his following were gathered elsewhere, praying that their church might be saved from his activities.' Quoted in M. Power, *Religion in the Reich* (London 1939), pp. 130–1.

[5] G. Norden (Note I/15), p. 94.

[6] BA, Schu (Note I/54), 244/2/25.

[7] Gauger (Note I/77), vol. I, p. 98.

[8] BA, Schu (Note I/54), 245/1/48.

[9] BA, Schu (Note I/54), 245/1/47; but for the actual practice, see Appendix 4.

[10] BA, R (Note I/63), 43, II, 161, and Macfarland (Note I/21), pp. 52–4; but already in September, the Nazi governor of Schleswig had sought to interfere with Church doctrine by ordering the removal from the school curriculum of the story of Isaac's sacrifice, on the grounds that in its attitude towards God it was un-German.

[11] R. Krause, *Der Fall Krause* (Berlin 1933), p. 12.

[12] Gauger (Note I/77), vol. I, p. 103.

[13] This move found wide support throughout all sections of the Evangelical Church. Pastor Niemöller sent Hitler a telegram of congratulations on this occasion.

[14] See Buchheim (Note I/14), pp. 129–31. Krause's phraseology was in part taken over directly from Rosenberg's *Myth of the Twentieth Century*, ch. 5.

[15] Gauger (Note I/77), vol. I, pp. 114–16.

[16] Believing himself to have taken on the role of the 'Godly Prince', Kube ordered all the Church bells to be rung whenever he toured the villages of his *Gau*. See also Biographical Notes, p. 404.

[17] A Nazi charitable organization which took up door-to-door collections for the 'poor and needy'. The record of contributions was always used as a measuring standard for political reliability.

[18] In an interview with Hitler on 7 February, Cardinal Schulte of Cologne

complained about this recommendation, with the result that the book was later recommended 'for teachers only'.

[19] A Party office which, however, carried no governmental responsibility.

[20] See Appendix 5.

[21] After the war Meyer-Erlach fled to Bavaria. He has since been active in the service of the semi-official 'Committee for Undivided Germany' and in 1963 received a high decoration from the West German government. Grundmann is currently Professor of New Testament in Eisenach, East Germany. See Biographical Notes, pp. 402 and 405.

[22] BA, Schu (Note I/54), 244/2/30.

[23] Ibid., 244/1/163.

[24] BA, R (Note I/63), 43, II, 150.

[25] BA, Schu (Note I/54), 244/2/41.

[26] Müller (Note I/8), p. 55.

[27] Ibid., p. 168.

[28] See Lewy (Note I/10), pp. 103–110.

[29] Müller (Note I/8), p. 55.

[30] Ibid., p. 173.

[31] Müller (Note I/8), p. 161.

[32] The Reich Youth Leader, von Schirach, had issued an order on 17 June 1933 which prohibited dual membership in Catholic Youth groups and the Hitler Youth.

[33] Müller (Note I/8), pp. 184–90.

[34] Ibid., p. 186.

[35] DBFP (Note I/57), no. 342.

[36] BA, Schu (Note I/54), 243/I/2/98.

[37] This was later repealed on 2 November because of the desire to have Catholic support for the plebiscite of 12 November: BA, Schu, ibid., 101.

[38] DGFP (Note I/27), C.2, no. 17.

[39] For the Bishops' statement see Müller (Note I/8), p. 219; also the prohibition of the Chief of the State Chancellery of Bavaria, of 10 November; quoted in Conrad (Note I/58), p. 89; also the protest against this prohibition by Cardinal Faulhaber, Müller, 221–4. The fullest treatment is given in L. Volk, *Bayerns Episkopat und Klerus in der Auseinandersetzung mit dem Nationalsozialismus 1930–1934* (Mainz 1965).

[40] Müller (Note I/8), pp. 212–13.

[41] Goering on the other hand, did not scruple to make inflammatory speeches in which he spoke of the need to stamp out in Germany the underground activities of 'Red Rats and Black Moles'; DGFP (Note I/27), C.2, no. 96.

CHAPTER 3

[1] BA, Schu (Note I/54), 254/I/2/100.

[2] BA, Schu (Note I/54), 4.

³ Ibid., 244/I/125–6.

⁴ For example, the Vatican noted as early as January 1934, in an official protest to the German government, that: 'In many cases, a hostile surveillance surrounds every step and act, every word and every service.' Quoted in Albrecht, *Der Notenwechsel zwischen dem Heiligen Stuhl und der deutschen Reichsregienung* (Mainz 1965), vol. I, p. 61.

⁵ Nuremberg Documents (mimeographed but not printed), NG 4834.

⁶ BA, Schu (Note I/54), 254/I/1/84.

⁷ Bavarian Political Police records, 26 January 1934.

⁸ BA, R (Note I/63), 43, II, 161.

⁹ *Hitler's Table Talk* (Note I/3), p. 413.

¹⁰ *Kirchliches Jahrbuch 1933–44* (Gütersloh 1948), p. 39.

¹¹ The *Daily Telegraph*, however, rightly reported on 29 January: 'German Church surrenders. Under complete Nazi control. Primate Dictator of 20,000,000.

After a struggle lasting many months, the moderate opposition movement in the German Evangelical Church has been completely crushed. Three events during the week-end tell the story of this defeat.

(1) Dr. Niemöller, leader of the Pastors' Emergency League, and those pastors who read the defiant declaration from their pulpits on Jan. 14th have been suspended from church office. Later Dr. Niemöller was arrested, but released by the secret police on condition that he reported to them at stated periods.

(2) The Primate has promulgated a decree making himself dictator of the "Old Prussian Union". This church, with about 20,000,000 members is by far the largest of those united to form the National Evangelical Church. Dr. Müller's decree, issued in his capacity as Bishop of Prussia, allocates to himself the powers hitherto exercised by the Synod.

(3) The heads of the other churches, most of whom opposed the Primate, have capitulated to his authority.'

¹² These were the first occasions on which Evangelical Pastors were sent to concentration camps, but the instigation for such actions clearly came from Müller. Indeed one of his associates openly told a public meeting a few weeks later: 'The State has established a sanatorium for its opponents, i.e. the concentration camp. I would also like to establish such an institution for my clerical colleagues as a form of "Retreat", where they would first of all learn to get up at the proper time. For the Church always arrives too late. How much better off she would have been if she had participated in the [Nazi] Revolution from the beginning. Then the Pastors would have to learn to sing the Horst Wessel song. They would have to learn what true Nazism is all about . . .' Niemöller (Note I/19), p. 93.

¹³ BA, Schu (Note I/54), 245/1/49.

¹⁴ Bavarian Political Police records, 7 March 1934.

Special instructions were issued on 15 February limiting the circumstances under which priests could be taken into protective custody. See Zipfel (Note I/61), pp. 270–1.

¹⁵ BA, R (Note I/63), 43, II, 162.

¹⁶ Quoted in Schmid (Note II/3), pp. 61–2. The version of this interview given in Hermelinck *Kirche im Kampf* (Tübingen 1950), pp. 75–6 is much abbreviated but corroborates the verbal accuracy of the last paragraph.

¹⁷ See the illuminating article on the connection between pietism and political nationalism, by K. Scholder, 'Neuere deutsche Geschichte und protestantische Theologie' in *Evangelische Theologie* 23/10 (October 1963), 510–536.

¹⁸ Goebbels' speech in Hamburg, 25 June 1934, see Niemöller (Note I/19), p. 94.

¹⁹ BA, R (Note I/63), 43, II, 174.

²⁰ See the discussion of the alternatives in a letter of Archbishop Gröber of 27 October 1933, in Müller (Note I/8), pp. 213–15.

²¹ DGFP (Note I/27), C.2, 135, 136.

²² For the discussions on this point see the works of Amery, Böckenförde, Müller and Neuhäusler, quoted in the Introduction, p. xxii.

²³ The Archdiocese of Munich, for example, noted sixteen cases of such attacks in the period 2 to 25 April 1934 alone. In Oberaudorf, Bavaria, on 10 May 1934, SS men ambushed a truckload of Catholic children and forcibly removed the boys' blue shirts, while girls of the *Bund Deutsche Mädel* removed the white roses from the dresses of the Catholic girls. In the evening a victory celebration was held by SS, Hitler Youth and *Bund Deutsche Mädel* with a glorious bonfire of all the Catholic shirts and insignia.

²⁴ See Appendix 6.

²⁵ Conrad suggests that Müller was glad to have Jäger on his staff so that some of the outcry against his unscrupulous measures could be diverted on to the head of the infamous and much disliked Jäger: W. Conrad (Note I/53), p. 95.

²⁶ Gesetzblatt der Deutsche Evangelische Kirche, 10 July 1934.

²⁷ Niemöller (Note I/19), p. 104.

²⁸ Cochrane (Note I/65), p. 139.

²⁹ DGFP (Note I/27), C.3, 15.

³⁰ *Kirchliches Jahrbuch* (Note III/10), p. 65.

³¹ G. Zahn, *German Catholics and Hitler's Wars* (New York 1962), p. 73.

³² Zipfel (Note I/61), pp. 272–326.

³³ *Guide to Captured German Records, microfilmed at Alexandria, Virginia, no. 33. Records of the Reichsführer S.S. and Chief of the German Police*, Part II, microfilm no. T 175, Roll 193, frame nos. 2732631–42 and 2732650–704.

³⁴ The report continued: 'Because of the reaction among the Catholic population who have been for centuries brought up to a blind prejudice in favour of the priests, it would hardly seem feasible to carry out measures which attack the bodily existence or freedom of the priests. Many of them indeed would like to be thought of by their parishioners as "martyrs" ... Rather

measures should be taken which will be painful without increasing their status in the eyes of the people.

(1) The first measures should be that any priest who has made himself even in the slightest respect suspicious, shall lose the right to give religious instruction in the elementary and higher schools. Such priests shall be forbidden to enter the schools.

(2) The withdrawal of recognition to exercise pastoral care or to receive a stipend ... The final confirmation of this withdrawal should follow as a result of a legal hearing, but this should not be public. This last is suggested because the courts still have a reputation for objectivity at home and abroad....

(4) If this withdrawal is confirmed, it should be made irrevocable and for the duration of life....

(5) The priest, from the moment of the provisional withdrawal of his official status should be forbidden to return to his parish....

(6) The Parish should be informed that because of his political activities, the priest has been sent away, but has been spared the measures which would have been taken against hostile laymen (protective custody, trial and punishment by loss of freedom ... ?) Any mention of the case in the Parish is forbidden....

(10) Protective custody, imprisonment or concentration camps are much less suitable for the priests, since they are in the long run only temporary measures and allow the priests to return as "martyrs". A public trial is equally unsuitable since the possibility exists of sympathetic demonstrations. On the other hand, those who know the Catholic clergy will recognize that the previously suggested measures are more painful, since the priest prides himself on his status in the parish, on the comfort and freedom from care of the parish house and not least on his stipend. He will do everything to avoid being thrown out of these....

(11) Should the Church authorities prove difficult, the State authorities should be asked to help since they are responsible for the collection of the church taxes and the approval of the church budget. A light pressure will at the most be necessary in the first few cases.

As for measures against monks who have proved themselves politically suspect, the matter is simpler. They have no parish or its support. They can be forbidden to leave their monasteries, or prohibited from any preaching or writing engagements. The monasteries feel themselves far more isolated, and since they receive no stipends, but are dependent upon free gifts, the monks lay great stress on an atmosphere of goodwill and peace towards the public. Above all they want to have excellent relations with the State. So any Abbot would withdraw from the public eye a Father who had been put under the State's prohibition.'

(Records of the Reichsführer SS, loc. cit.)

35 See Röhm's communique to the SA of 10 June 1934, quoted in N. Baynes, *Hitler's Speeches* (London 1942), vol. I, p. 287.

[36] A. Rosenberg, *Das Politische Tagebuch* (Munich 1964), ed. H. G. Seraphim, p. 43.

[37] DGFP (Note I/27), Series C.3, no. 50.

[38] A comparison of the list of protected organizations as envisaged in this provisional settlement with the list of those held to be worthy of dissolution by Himmler's Security Service shows how far the Church had been able to resist the pressures from the Nazi negotiators to renounce their privileges voluntarily.
BA, R (Note I/63), 43, II, 176a and W. Conrad (Note I/53), pp. 140–1.

[39] Since on no account could he be accused of hostility to Nazism, the suspicion may not be unfounded that Fr Stempfle's murder was designed to destroy the possibility of his revealing how large a part he actually had in the writing of *Mein Kampf*.

[40] H. Trevor-Roper in the introduction to T. Prittie, *Germans Against Hitler* (London 1964).

[41] Müller (Note I/8), p. 295.

[42] Conrad (Note I/53), p. 103.

[43] Quoted in Niemöller (Note I/19), p. 136.

[44] The 'German Christians' declared in their congratulatory telegram that 'Justice, discipline and loyalty are the invisible pillars which alone can support a great nation. God will continue to bless the German people if they are obedient to His divine will and laws. The 'German Christians' see in the Leader of the German nation the guarantor of the Divine order of things, and the six million members of the Movement and the millions of its supporters representing all classes and provinces hold fast to him in unconditional loyalty. God save Germany and our Leader Adolf Hitler.'
(From the papers of Bishop Bell, Lambeth Palace, London.)

CHAPTER 4

[1] See Rosenberg (Note III/36), p. 53.

[2] BA, R (Note I/63), 43, II, 162.

[3] Quoted in Niemöller (Note I/19), p. 157.

[4] For example, the Gestapo in Neu Ulm reported as follows: 'Dr. Meiser of Munich came to preach in Neu Ulm. He was greeted with the Hitler salute and returned it. In his sermon he spoke about loyalty to the Church. On the one side a new Germany is being built, on the other the Church is being destroyed, But, let it be remembered, he said, that the power of the Church can not be compared to the power of the State and God can never be turned into an Aryan hero. If Dr. Wurm had been removed, it was necessary for him, Meiser, to witness in his place. After the service the crowd gave a rousing welcome to Dr. Meiser. *Ein Feste Burg* was sung and before his departure the whole crowd in front of the Parish house sang the Horst Wessel song.' (Files of the Bavarian Political Police.)

[5] DGFP (Note I/27), C.3, no. 213.

[6] DGFP (Note I/27), C.3, no. 245; BA, R (Note I/63), 43, II, 163.

[7] DGFP (Note I/27), C.3, no. 246.

[8] Ibid., no. 252.

[9] Ibid., no. 276.

[10] Hermelinck (Note III/16), p. 185.

[11] Rosenberg (Note III/36), p. 56.

[12] He issued a German Farmer's Calendar for 1935, from which all the Christian festivals were removed. Instead Germanic heroes and Gods were commemorated, for example, on Good Friday, which was dedicated to the 4,500 Saxons murdered by Charlemagne or Charles the Slaughterer as Nazi historians were bidden to call him. Similarly Christmas Eve was to be given over to the celebration of the birth of Baldur, the Guardian of Light.

[13] Rauschning (Note I/2), p. 61.

[14] BA, R (Note I/63), 43, II, 163.

[15] Few bishops can have received such an outspoken letter as the following from 610 students of the universities of Rostock and Erlangen:

For years now you and your fellow travellers have been defaming the desire to rebuild the Church as mere reaction, and you speak about your unity with the Führer. We laugh! Where in the world can you find the Evangelical youth, let alone the theological or the evangelical students behind you? The more we stand behind the Führer, the less we support you. . . . It is now clear to all that the core of the German Evangelical Church stands opposed to your leadership. It is now clear to all that those of our academic teachers whose reputation we respect stand solidly with us against you. You know that the situation has been made impossible by your behaviour. You know that you are hindering all the constructive forces from development. We therefore demand once again: resign! . . . Heil Hitler!

Signed: Gerstenmaier.   Signed: Seyferth.

Quoted in Niemöller (I/19), pp. 198–9.

[16] Niemöller (Note I/19), p. 203. The reply of the Confessing Church to this speech, issued in a circular on 13 December, was at once prohibited from publication in any form by order of the Ministry of the Interior on 15 December: BA, Schu (Note I/54), 244/1/148.

[17] Speech to a Party rally, 11 September 1935.

[18] Rosenberg (Note III/36), pp. 72–4.

[19] Quoted in Buchheim (Note I/14), pp. 186–7.

[20] BA, R (Note I/63), 43, II, 180.

[21] Buchheim (Note I/14), p. 199.

[22] *Guide to Captured German Records, microfilmed at Alexandria, Virginia,* (GCGR) no. 3: *Records of the N.S.D.A.P.,* microfilm copy no. T. 82, roll no. 75, frame nos. 86533–5.

Despite the very definite warning not to let anything said get out to the public, a theology student wrote a letter to a Darmstadt newspaper criticizing the Nazi Students' League for its anti-Christian sentiments. The Gestapo in turn prohibited the further publication of this letter, which was calculated to stir up resentments 'in a shocking manner hostile to the State', and justified its actions on the grounds that these indoctrination sessions were 'certainly not anti-Christian in tone, for, if they had been, a student of theology would not have been admitted': BA, Schu (Note I/54), 244/2/57.

But numerous prominent Nazis, such as Dr Ley, made equally inflammatory speeches using virtually the same phraseology.

[23] Bavarian Political Police decrees of 25 and 7 March 1935; Zipfel (Note I/61), pp. 327–8.

In answer to this latter decree, the Pastor of Eibelstadt, near Ochsenfurt, replied:

> It is not the attacks on Rosenberg's ideas which make confusion and disquiet, but rather the spreading of these ideas themselves. They are spread abroad despite the fact that the state rests on a basis of positive Christianity, and despite the repeated declarations of the Führer that the national government sees in the two Christian denominations the most important factors for the maintenance of our national way of life. . . . Catholics and Protestants alike wish to express their support of the State and devote their energy to its service, but they need freedom to do so from the side of the State. They can't understand why the authorities should seek to prevent by force the teaching and defence of true Christian doctrines while the enemies of Christianity who are the enemies of the State since this is after all a Christian country, are allowed to work undisturbed.

BA, Schu (Note I/54), 244/1/155.

[24] *Völkischer Beobachter*, 6 April 1934.

[25] Micklem, *National Socialism and the Roman Catholic Church* (London 1939), p. 126.

[26] *Guide to Captured German Records, microfilmed at Alexandria, Virginia,* (GCGR) no. 3: *Records of the N.S.D.A.P.*, microfilm copy no. T. 82, roll no. 9, frame no. 17628.

[27] BA, Schu (Note I/54), 243/I/2/135.

[28] BA, Schu (Note I/54), 244/1/146.

On 15 October 1934 Himmler issued an order to his own force, the SS, whereby 'in order to preserve peace and harmony between Church and State it is desirable that those few serving priests who are members of the SS should be released. This release should be honourable and tactfully carried out': BA, Schu 245/383.

Himmler's argument that the presence of priests in the SS would lead to differences of view within its ranks had apparently not been a significant hindrance in previous years. The execution of this order gave rise to a protest from the Evangelical Bishop of Nassau-Hessen, Dr Dietrich, who wrote to Himmler:

For me as the Nazi Bishop of Nassau-Hessen, this order causes a painful conflict, since it chiefly affects trustworthy Nazi pastors and theologians. On the one hand, as Bishop, I must stand up for my clergy, but on the other hand, as a Party member I have gladly given my contribution as a Contributing Member of the SS I am now forced most regrettably to give up my Contributing Membership of the SS.

BA, Schu 245/2/176.

[29] BA, Schu (Note I/54), 243/I/2/143.

[30] *The Persecution of the Catholic Church in the Third Reich* (London, 1940), p. 64.

[31] BA, Schu (Note I/54), 244/2/50. Such services continued to be held, and a year later the Bavarian Political Police informed its local detachments:

The Reich Minister for Church Affairs has decided not to take action against the holding of such services of intercession. However the personal details of such priests who conduct these services are to be sent in. Any attempt to publicise the prayers of intercession in the press, in leaflets or in parish magazines, is to be prevented, but no action should be taken against the official church gazettes.

Files of the Bavarian Political Police, 16 June 1936.

[32] Niemöller (Note I/19), p. 261.

[33] *Bayerische Rundschau*, 19 July 1935, reprinted in *Albrecht* (Note III/4), pp. 259–62.

[34] Niemöller (Note I/19), p. 262; for a similar use of economic pressure upon Catholic employees and parents in the Rhineland, Bavaria and Würzburg, see *Persecution* (Note IV/30), pp. 98–102.

[35] *Völkischer Beobachter*, 5 August 1935.

CHAPTER 5

[1] Rauschning, *Germany's Revolution of Destruction* (London 1939), p. 35.

[2] S. D. Lagebericht, submitted to the Reichsführer SS in May/June 1934, printed in Zipfel (Note I/61), pp. 272–326.

[3] BA, R (Note I/63), 43, II, 163.

[4] Unfortunately there were no vacancies for an ambitious young *Staatssekretär* with a previous record of insubordination. The incumbent in the Ministry of the Interior, Pfundtner, was too well established, and refused to hear of a joint appointment. Stuckart had to be content with the lesser post as head of the Constitutional and Legal division of the Ministry of the Interior, with the honorary title of *Staatssekretär* from March 1935. He was later responsible for framing the notorious Nuremberg Racial Laws, which deprived German Jews of their citizenship and property rights. See Biographical Notes, pp. 407-8.

[5] BA, R (Note I/63), 43, II, 163a.

[6] B. Rust in *Hochschule und Ausland* January 1935, quoted in Micklem (Note IV/25), p. 125.

[7] Niemöller (Note I/19), p. 206.

[8] For the text of the prohibition, see Zipfel (Note I/61), pp. 361–2.

[9] A. Rosenberg, *An die Dunkelmänner unserer Zeit, Eine Antwort auf die Angriffe auf den 'Mythus des 20 Jahrhunderts'* (Munich 1935).

[10] For the text see *Kirchliches Jahrbuch* (Note III/10), pp. 85–6.

[11] BA, R (Note I/63), 43, II, 175; Müller (Note I/8), pp. 337–8.

[12] *Persecution* (Note IV/30), p. 87.

[13] Circular issued on 27 August 1935, quoted in *Persecution* (Note IV/30), p. 96. Another circular issued in Düsseldorf at the same time made these instructions even more explicit:

1. Without exception all teachers are required to bring their whole personal influence to bear on all children above the age of ten, explaining the idea of, and encouraging them to join, the Hitler Youth. Henceforth, therefore, no teacher may in any way, directly or indirectly, encourage, work for, or give financial assistance to other youth associations.

In accordance with the above-mentioned decree it is a teacher's duty to see that his, or her, own children are members of the Hitler Youth and serve thus as an example for the rest.

It is furthermore an offence against the ministerial decree of 27 February 1935 (RU II G No. 1 882–34 K II 1), for teachers not to prevent children under the age of ten from being taken into any other groups or associations, and thus being influenced against the State Youth.

2. In every school and classroom posters are to be exhibited which effectively and vividly illustrate the necessity for unity among German youth.

3. In every classroom numerical statistics, which must be kept up to date by monthly revision, must be posted up in graph form in a prominent place, showing the number of children in the Hitler Youth.

4. Precautions are to be taken that no children in the preparatory classes are organised into any groups or associations. Parents who do not conform to this are to be sent for and informed that their behaviour is an offence against school regulations and discipline.

5. In order to accomplish the complete organisation of youth, heads of schools shall, from time to time as shall appear necessary, call the parents together and impress upon them the necessity for unity among the youth of Germany.

6. Teachers who do not show the necessary enthusiasm for this unification of youth are to be reported to me by Area School inspectors, so that disciplinary measures may be taken against them for negligence.

7. The clergy are to be informed immediately by the heads of schools that when giving religious instruction they are subject to school regulations, and in accordance with the decree mentioned above, must desist from promoting organisations other than that of the State Youth. The clergy are to make a written acknowledgment of the receipt of these instructions, which is to be preserved by head-masters in the school archives. Members of the clergy who

P*

offend against their duty as teachers will be deprived by me of the permission
to teach religion.

8. I shall hold the Area School Inspectors, in particular, responsible for the
carrying out of these regulations. Reports addressed to me are on each occasion
to contain details of the progress made.

Appendix for vocational and trade schools: The foregoing circular instruction
No. 1, paras 1 and 2, Nos. 2, 3, 7, No. 5 so far as applicable and No. 6 with the
additional regulation that the reports are to be brought to me in the normal
course, holds for vocation and trade schools.

By order.

(signed) PREMER

Quoted in *Persecution*, pp. 95–6.

[14] *Persecution* (Note IV/30), p. 105 with accompanying photograph.

[15] Müller (Note I/8), pp. 300–1.

[16] BA, Schu (Note I/54), 245/1/77.

[17] Müller (Note I/8), p. 351.

[18] See the report from the Minister of Justice Gürtner, to Hitler of 26 June
1935: BA, R (Note I/63), 43, II, 175.

[19] *Persecution* (Note IV/30), p. 268. The song exists in various versions, mostly
with pornographic emendations.

[20] See for example the remarks of the Aachen Gestapo in B. Vollmer,
Volksopposition im Polizeistaat (Stuttgart 1957), p. 212.

[21] Müller (Note I/8), pp. 343–4.

[22] Rosenberg's speech was later printed in *Gestaltung der Idee: Blut und Ehre*,
vol. 2, (Munich 1938), pp. 349–63.

[23] Vollmer (Note V/20), *passim*.

[24] BA, R (Note I/63), 43, II, 163a.

[25] D. C. Watt, book review in *History*, L/168 (Feb. 1965), 111.

[26] It was said that, because of his pious upbringing, Kerrl was the only Nazi
leader who could quote the Bible by heart. The following anecdote is recorded
in Himmler's personal files: On meeting Kerrl sometime after his appointment
as Church Minister, Himmler told him: 'I thought you were only acting
piously hitherto, but now I see that you actually are pious. I will treat you badly
in future.' When the astonished Kerrl asked why, the Reichsführer SS answered:
'Well, in your view, the worse you are handled here below, the better marks
you will receive later.' GCGR no. 32: *Records of the Reichsführer SS and Chief
of the German Police Part I*, microcopy no. T-175, roll no. 88, Frame 2611273.
A more tolerant view of Kerrl was that of the former Finance Minister,
Schwerin von Krosigk: 'He was a truly convinced Protestant, and had made
himself by his own efforts well acquainted with all of Luther's writings. He
even read deeply in the works of the church fathers, had a remarkable familiarity
with theological ideas and had created his own system of belief', S. v. Krosigk,
Es geschah in Deutschland (Tübingen 1951), p. 255.

[27] BA, Schu (Note I/54), 244/1.

[28] See speech of 27 November 1935, quoted in Niemöller (Note I/19), p. 303.

[29] See Biographical Notes, pp. 399–400.

[30] See report on 'Catholicism and National Socialism' in Himmler's files: *Guide to Captured German Records, microfilmed at Alexandria, Virginia* (GCGR), no. 39: *Records of the RFSS and Chief of the German Police Part III*, microfilm copy no. T. 175, roll 506, frame no. 9371712 ff.

[31] For the text see *Kirchliches Jahrbuch* (Note III/10), pp. 101–2.

[32] *Kirchliches Jahrbuch* (Note III/10), pp. 102–3.

[33] Ibid., p. 104.

[34] GCGR, no. 28; *Records of the Reich Ministry for the Occupied Eastern Territories 1941–1945*, microfilm copy no. T. 454, roll 62, frame no. 612 ff.

[35] Niemöller (Note I/19), p. 282.

[36] GCGR, no. 3 (Note IV/22): *Records of the N.S.D.A.P. Part I*, microfilm copy no. T. 81, roll no. 21–2, frame no. 18875–7, *Monatsbericht der Reichsleitung der NSDAP, Abteilung für den kulturellen Frieden*, July 1935.

[37] Niemöller (Note I/19) p. 293.

[38] Ibid., p. 289.

[39] K. J. B. (Note III/10), pp. 105–7.

[40] GCGR, no. 3 (Note IV/22), roll no. 151, frame no. 154735 ff.; see Kerrl's letter of 5 September 1935 to all provincial governments and police officers claiming sole authority for police measures against clergymen. On 12 December 1935, the Bavarian Political Police sent a circular to its local detachments to state that the arrests of clergymen of both denominations should be undertaken only with the permission of Headquarters. 'It should be noted that for these purposes only members of your forces who are really trustworthy and used to handling political affairs should be employed. It is not something which could be left to the older men.' BA, Schu 244/1/171.

[41] *Frankfurter Zeitung*, 16 January 1938.

CHAPTER 6

[1] The transportation of thousands of Nazis from all over the country was also an opportunity to test the efficiency of the railway system and to prepare it for eventual mobilization procedures.

[2] H. Frank, *Im Angesicht des Galgens* (Neuhaus 1955), p. 296.

[3] Ibid., p. 298; for other examples of these sentiments, see H. Müller, 'Der Pseudoreligiöse Charakter der Nationalsozialistischen Weltanschauung', in *Geschichte in Wissenschaft und Unterricht*, 6/1961, 339–40; and Neuhäusler (note Introduction, p. xvi), pp. 111–12.

[4] M. Domarus, ed., *Hitler Reden und Proklamationen 1932–45*, vol. I (Würzburg 1963), p. 745.

[5] G. L. Mosse, *The Crisis of German Ideology* (New York 1964), p. 301. Typical invocations of this cult were issued on the occasion of Hitler's birthdays, as for example in the *Schwarze Korps* for 20 April 1939; see Appendix 7.

[6] *Persecution* (Note IV/30), p. 480; in this, he was only echoing the words of Hitler himself:

The greatness of every powerful organisation which embodies a creative idea lies in the spirit of religious devotion and intolerance with which it stands out against all others, because it has an ardent faith in its own right. ... The greatness of Christianity did not arise from attempts to make compromises with those philosophical opinions of the ancient world which had some resemblance to its own doctrine, but in the unrelenting and fanatical proclamation and defence of its own teaching. *Mein Kampf* (Note I/1), p. 294.

[7] Loc. cit.

[8] See Appendix 8.

[9] BA, Schu (Note I/54), 245/127.

[10] W. Hofer, *Der Nationalsozialismus* (Frankfurt-am-Main 1961), p. 15.

[11] I.e. 'Deutschland, Deutschland über alles', and the 'Horst Wessel Lied': *Persecution* (Note IV/30), p. 494.

[12] *Persecution* (Note IV/30), p. 493; for other examples of Nazi 'creeds' see S. W. Herman, *It's Your Souls We Want* (London 1942), p. 55.

[13] *Schulungsbriefe der NSDAP* 4.1937; see also Goebbels' remark: 'The Faith in the Führer in the Ranks of the National Socialists may be described as partaking of a secret and enigmatical Mysticism', *Kampf um Berlin* (Munich 1934), p. 39.

[14] *Persecution* (Note IV/30), p. 494.

[15] H. J. Gamm, *Der Braune Kult* (Hamburg 1962), p. 141.

[16] Mosse (Note VI/5), pp. 309–311.

[17] Quoted in Micklem (Note IV/25), pp. 163–4.

[18] Rauschning, (Note I/2), p. 237.

[19] B. v. Schirach, *Revolution der Erziehung* (Munich 1938), p. 21.

[20] See Appendix 9 for the text of a Nazi Christmas sermon.

[21] An order issued by the SS Headquarters in September 1935 forbade the singing of anti-clerical songs, such as the 'Currency smuggling song' (see p. 126 *supra*). In Himmler's view, anti-clericalism should have a certain style and not sink to the level of such disreputable vilification. Nevertheless the practice was already widespread: BA, Schu (Note I/54), 245/2/134.

[22] BA, Schu (Note I/54), 245/2/136, and see Appendix 4.

[23] From the Süddeutsche Korrespondenz-Büro, quoted in Micklem (Note IV/25), p. 130. On such occasions it was usual to present the happy pair with a copy of *Mein Kampf* or of Rosenberg's *Myth*. In answer to a protest about such ceremonies from a Protestant pastor, Himmler replied in March 1937 to say that this was purely a voluntary act, and in no way replaced the legal obligation of a registry office wedding. It was merely a gesture of acceptance by the SS of the bride; files of the Evangelical Kirche der Union, Berlin. See also Herman, (Note IV/12), p. 38.

[24] BA, Schu (Note I/54), 446: see also *Persecution* (Note IV/30), pp. 503–4. For similar rituals, see also Herman (Note VI/12), p. 32.

[25] Quoted in K. Immer, *Entchristlichung der Jugend* (Barmen 1936). The Gestapo was immediately ordered to confiscate all copies of this pamphlet; files of the Bavarian Political Police, 16 March 1936.

[26] From H. Adam, *Weihnacht im Dritten Reich* (Berlin 1933).

[27] For examples of Nazi funeral customs see Herman (Note VI/12), pp. 45–7; Although Nazi units were forbidden from November 1937 to take part in church ceremonies in uniform, the SS headquarters, commenting in 1941 on a funeral where this ruling had been contravened, remarked that as long as high-ranking SS officers asked to be buried according to Christian rituals, it was hardly possible in an overwhelming Catholic area to prohibit the same for men in the ranks. GCGR: no. 33 (Note III/33): *Records of the Reichsführer SS and Chief of the German Police* Part II, microcopy T. 175, roll 149, frame no. 2677284 ff.

[28] G. Zahn (Note III/29), p. 189.

[29] Lewy (Note I/10), pp. 174–5.

[30] 'It is the pestilential stench of a putrefying world; it stinks to heaven. We are referring to all those scandalous proceedings in those Church circles, both within and without the monasteries, in the midst of which not one crime is lacking, from perjury through incest to sexual murder ... Behind the walls of monasteries and in the ranks of the Roman brotherhood what else may have been enacted that is not publicly known and has not been expiated through this world's courts?' *Schwarze Korps*, 15 April 1937.

Of the far more numerous cases in which Nazi Party members were accused of similar offences, no mention appeared in the Press.

[31] R. Knox, *Nazi and Nazarene* (London 1940), p. 25; for the Vatican protests against such special treatment being given to clerical offenders, see Albrecht (Note III/4), pp. 330–1, 333–4. At the same time, Heydrich acknowledged that random acts of violence by individual Nazis would cause disquiet, and therefore forbade any such action against church institutions such as monasteries, convents, denominational hospitals etc. Several such cases had been notified arising from the heated anti-clericalism stirred up during the immorality trials. 'I do not deny that some necessary measures will be taken against the unsavoury state of affairs in various institutions as revealed in these trials, but before anything is done, my final decision should be obtained': BA, Schu (Note I/54), 245/II/1/41.

[32] Ibid., p. 24. Rosenberg noted in his diary that 'The Party members at the local level are furious because the Church Commissions in the provinces are attempting to replace Nazi sympathisers with those who are true to the gospel (*bekenntnistreue*)'; *Das politische Tagebuch* (Note III/36), 25 April 1936.

[33] Micklem (Note IV/25), p. 159. On 24 July 1936 the Foreign Ministry noted that Hitler had ordered the cessation of any new large-scale immorality trials of Catholic priests.

[34] See Zipfel (Note I/61), p. 449.

[35] For example, from the decrees of 27 April and 18 June 1936, issued by the Bavarian Police; BA, Schu (Note I/54), 244.

[36] Files of the Evangelische Kirche der Union, Berlin; in the same month an SA leader reporting on the proceedings at the Nazi training school, the Ordensburg Vogelsang, stated:

1. A Nazi can't be a Catholic;

2. We are not interested whether Jesus was an Aryan or a Jew. In any case he wasn't a German.

3. Hitler's book *Mein Kampf* is the book of the present, Rosenberg's *Myth* is the book of the future.

4. We must be clear. Only the tactics of our struggle have changed. The end remains the same.

Quoted in BA, R (Note I/63), 43, II, 156.

[37] This division finally became too wide to be healed; see Niemöller (Note I/19), pp. 315 ff, and KJB (Note III/10), pp. 123 ff.

[38] BA Schu (Note I/54), 244/2/63. The Gestapo was also to note if they saw any duplicating machines in the houses they searched, and to report this information confidentially.

[39] W. Niemöller, *Die bekennende Kirche sagt Hitler die Wahrheit* (Bielefeld 1954), p. 18; for the full text of the memorandum, see pp. 9–18.

[40] W. Niemöller, *Kampf und Zeugnis* (Note I/19), p. 348.

[41] Quoted in Niemöller, *Die bekennende Kirche sagt Hitler die Wahrheit*, p. 24.

[42] BA NS 10.109. On the other hand, in December 1936, nine Confessing Church pastors were expelled from Lübeck for having refused to accept the authority of the 'German Christian administration'. The justification according to the Gestapo, was that in Lübeck, 'Party, State and Church are one'. E. Klügel, *Die Lutherische Landeskirche Hannovers und ihr Bischof 1933–45* (Berlin 1964), p. 229.

[43] For the English text see *Persecution* (Note IV/30), pp. 523 ff. According to Fr Angelo Martelli, SJ, Cardinal Faulhaber was mainly responsible for writing the first draft of this encyclical in January 1937: *Archivum Historiae Pontificiae* 2 (1964), pp. 303–20; for a comparative treatment of the texts, see Albrecht (Note III/4), pp. 402 ff. See also W. M. Harrigan, 'Pius XI and Nazi Germany 1937–9,' in *Catholic Historical Review* 51 (1965–6), 457–86.

[44] DGFP (Note I/27), D. 1.638; see also 632, 635, 639, 640, 641, 642, 643, 646.

[45] Ibid., 661.

[46] Zipfel (Note I/61), pp. 450–1.

[47] Loc. cit.

CHAPTER 7

[1] See Biographical Notes, p. 402.

[2] See Biographical Notes, p. 406.

[3] Reprinted in full in J. Neuhausler, *Kreuz und Hakenkreuz* (note Introduction, p. xvi), pp. 371–82.

[4] Loc. cit.

[5] W. Adolf, *Hirtenamt und Hitlerdiktatur* (Berlin 1965), p. 61.

[6] BA, Schu (Note I/54), 243/1/11–24.

[7] Lewy (Note I/10), p. 132.

[8] See the directive from Hess, BA, Schu (Note I/54), 243/I/189.

[9] BA, Schu (Note I/54), 243/2/1.

[10] See the figures given in Zipfel (Note I/61), p. 124.

[11] According to one source there were 261 German Catholic priests incarcerated in Dachau: H. Mohr, *Katholische Orden und deutscher Imperialismus* (East Berlin 1965), p. 135; Reimund Schnabel in his book *Die Frommen in den Hölle* (Berlin 1966) lists the names of 340. The Catholic Year book of 1947 gives the figures for imprisoned members of monastic orders as: Benedictines 4, Dominicans 5, Jesuits 23, Capuchins 4, Missionaries of the Sacred Heart 6, Oblates of the Immaculate Conception 1, Pallottines 32, Salesians 3, Steyler Missionaries 42, Franciscans 13.

[12] *Nationalsozialistische Erziehung*, II/7, 15 April 1933.

[13] See also his interview with the Bishop of Osnabrück, Berning, quoted in Müller (Note I/8), p. 120.

[14] Bracher, Sauer and Schulz, *Die Nationalsozialistische Machtergreifung* (Cologne 1960), p. 570.

[15] Zipfel (Note I/61), pp. 450–1.

[16] Quoted in *Persecution* (Note IV/30), p. 118; see also Minister Rust's statement quoted in Micklem (Note IV/25), p. 147.

[17] BA, Schu (Note I/54), 245/189; for the full text see Appendix 10.

[18] Micklem (Note IV/25), p. 145. For an account of the Nazi campaign in one local area, see F. Teping, *Der Kampf um die Konfessionelle Schule in Oldenburg während der Herrschaft der NS-Regierung* (Münster 1949).

[19] BA, R (Note 1/63), 43, II, 177a.

[20] *Persecution* (Note IV/30), p. 144; for a similar description of these events by the Evangelical Church, see *Kirchliches Jahrbuch für die Evangelische Kirche in Deutschland 1950* (Gütersloh 1950), p. 414; for the protest note from the Vatican, see Albrecht (Note III/4), pp. 346 ff.

[21] BA, Schu (Note I/54), 243/II/1/38.

[22] *Persecution* (Note IV/30), p. 158.

[23] BA, Schu (Note I/54), 245/192; for the full text see Appendix 10.

[24] *Persecution* (Note IV/30), p. 137.

[25] BA, Schu (Note I/54), 243/II/1/130.

[26] *Völkischer Beobachter*, 13 December 1937.

[27] For examples, see *Persecution* (Note IV/30), pp. 181–2.

[28] K. Ludecke, *I Knew Hitler* (London 1938), p. 466.

[29] Micklem (Note IV/25), p. 204.

[30] *Persecution* (Note IV/30), p. 164. The same note was repeated in a widely distributed book entitled *Gott und Volk*, published in 1941: 'The education of the youth is to be confined primarily to the teacher, the officer, and the leaders

of the Party. The priests will die out. They have estranged the youth from the *Volk*. In their places will step the leaders. Not deputies of God. But anyway the best Germans. And how shall we train up our children? Thus as though they had never heard of Christianity! We will take them out into nature and show them God's wonders. We will teach them our sacred history.'

[31] BA, R (Note I/63), 43, II, 177; 12 February 1937.

[32] KJB (Note III/10), p. 466.

[33] From the files of the Evangelische Kirche der Union, Berlin; on the other hand, in view of the complaints received about such activities, Hess, early in 1939, issued a directive to all Party branches in which he restated the need for a complete neutrality on the part of the Party, which should not get involved in denominational preferences. The Churches' wishes that religious instruction should be given in a manner which was in agreement with their teachings should be observed. It was not the task of National Socialism, nor of the Nazi State, to decide which of this stuff was actually national socialist or not. Explanations, justifications or other misleading arguments tending to support the views of one or other of the denominational positions should be avoided: BA, Schu (Note I/54), 245/173.

[34] From the files of EKU, Berlin.

[35] 098–PS, *Nazi Conspiracy and Aggression* (Washington 1946), Vol. III, pp. 152–7.

[36] In his reply to this suggestion, Rosenberg stated that he had launched a large-scale project for the writing of a directive with the title 'German Piety' which should search out from German history suitable examples of the desired kind of conduct: GCGR no. 28 (Note V/34), microcopy T. 454, roll 62, frame nos. 612 ff.

[37] BA, R (Note I/63), 43, II, 165a.

[38] GCGR no. 28 (Note V/34), microcopy T. 454, roll 62, frame nos. 612 ff.

[39] BA, R (Note I/63), 43, II, 156.

[40] NG–1755, unpublished Nuremberg document.

[41] Zipfel (Note I/61), pp. 485–91.

[42] For a description of the seizure of this college at the end of 1938, written by an American exchange student, see *Persecution* (Note IV/30, pp. 49–50. The College staff fled to Switzerland, leaving their German and Austrian students behind.

[43] 116–PS, *Nazi Conspiracy and Aggression* (Note VII/35), vol. III, pp. 165–7.

[44] Ibid., p. 167.

[45] Zipfel (Note I/61), p. 490.

[46] Ibid., p. 493. As part of their planned series of confiscations at the beginning of 1941 the Gestapo seized no less than five of the Catholic diocesan seminaries, at Innsbruck, Salzburg, Trier, Bensberg near Cologne, and Berlin-Bohnsdorf, using the grounds of hostility to the Reich: BA, R (Note I/63), 43, II, 172a.

[47] 123–PS, *Nazi Conspiracy and Aggression* (Note VII/35), vol. III, pp. 175–9.

[48] GCGR no. 3 (Note IV/22), microcopy T. 81, roll 7–8, frame nos. 15430 ff.

[49] GCGR no. 28 (Note V/34), microcopy T. 454, roll 62, frame nos. 612 ff.

[50] GCGR no. 3 (Note IV/22), microcopy T. 81, roll 7-8, frame nos. 15430 ff. See also E. Hegel, *Geschichte der katholischtheologischen Fakultät Münster 1773–1964*, vol. I (Münster 1966), p. 496.

[51] For the statistics of 1940, see NG–1755, unpublished Nuremberg document; for 1942, see the secret SD report, *Meldungen aus dem Reich*, no. 291: the Development of Theological Studies, in BA, R (Note I/63), 43, II, 156. Also alternative figures for 1942 given in GCGR no. 3 (Note IV/22), microcopy T. 81, roll 7-8, frame nos. 15448 ff.

[52] Dieter Schwarz, 'Die Grosse Lüge des politischen Katholizismus', in *Schwarze Korps* (Berlin 1938), pp. 21, 30, 40.

[53] See Zipfel (Note I/61), pp. 175–203, for a masterly analysis of their situation in German life. I am indebted in what follows to his insights here.

[54] For a Nazi description of the Jehovah's Witnesses' theories, entitled *The Bible in the service of world revolution: the political Background of the Jehovah's Witnesses*, see Zipfel (Note I/61), pp. 366–71.

[55] Zipfel (Note I/61), p. 203.

[56] BA, Schu (Note I/54), 267/1/33.

[57] BA, Schu (Note I/54), 267/1/35.

[58] Zipfel (Note I/61), pp. 193–4.

[59] In contrast, only seven Catholics in the whole country were known to have been conscientious objectors: for an account see G. Zahn, *In Solitary Witness* (New York 1964), *passim*.

[60] From Himmler's personal files, quoted in Zipfel (Note I/61), p. 200.

[61] Zipfel (Note I/61), p. 483.

[62] See the list in *Gutachten des Instituts für Zeitgeschichte* (March 1956), pp. 45–7; but also a more complete list in Appendix 11.

[63] BA, Schu (Note I/54), 267/2/81; see also Chapter IX below.

CHAPTER 8

Quoted in Hermann (Note VI/12), p. 15.

[2] W. Adolf (Note VII/5), p. 59.

[3] Micklem (Note IV/25), p. 222.

[4] Speech at Hagen, 30 November 1937; also in Berlin, 15 January 1938.

[5] *Völkischer Beobachter*, 25 November 1937.

[6] Ibid., 13 February 1937.

[7] KJB (Note III/10), p. 153.

[8] Niemöller (Note I/19), pp. 379–80.

[9] Reprinted in Hofer (Note VI/10), p. 77.

[10] See Rosenberg's diary for 18 February 1937: quoted in R. Kempner, 'Der Kampf gegen die Kirche' in *Der Monat* I (July 1949); for a Nazi evaluation of the situation in the Evangelical Church, see *N. S. Monatsheft*, March 1937.

[11] Herman (Note VI/12), p. 144; on 20 February, however, the Bavarian

Political Police issued orders that in view of the approaching election, all church services and meetings of Evangelical Church groups were to be put under surveillance and a report was to be submitted on any statements made in connection with the election: files of the Bavarian Political Police.

[12] KJB (Note III/10), pp. 158–61.

[13] Ibid., p. 160; this letter evinced an interesting comment from a member of Rosenberg's staff, the Party Propaganda Indoctrination officer for Berlin:

'... for us the fact remains that the discussion of religious and church questions is spread widely not only in the general public but in party circles too, where the uncertainty on such matters is shockingly great.

I personally believe that it is fundamentally impossible to get rid of these questions by recourse to superficial methods of speech or with slogans or by pointing to certain individuals or events. ... This could induce a dangerous underestimation of the enemy and is not likely to lead to the mobilisation of energies which would be necessary if we are going to achieve anything new in the religious sphere within the probable period of generations, so that within that long-range period, the over-priested Christianity of the Churches will be replaced by something superior.' Zipfel (Note I/61), p. 378.

[14] KJB (Note III/10), pp. 165–6.

[15] For a description of the scene, see KJB (Note III/10), p. 193.

[16] BA, R (Note I/63), 43, II, 156; Klügel (Note VI/42), p. 328.

[17] Files of the Evangelische Kirche der Union, Berlin.

[18] For the public letter to Hitler from Bishop Marahrens protesting against these plans, see Hermelinck (Note III/16), pp. 446–9.

[19] In a telegram to Hitler on 8 April 1938, the Bishop of Mecklenberg, Schultz, declared:

'My Führer, in this great historical hour I can announce to you that the whole clergy of the Mecklenburg Evangelical Church, obedient to an inward law, have taken their oath to the Führer and the Reich with joyful hearts. May God the Almighty be with you always. Our loyalty to you is our thanks for the providence which sent you to be the saviour and founder of our country in the hours of its greatest need. One People, One Reich, One Führer, One God, one obedience in Faith. Hail to you my Führer.' BA, NS 10.109.

[20] Rundschreiben 87/38, quoted in KJB (Note III/10), p. 262; naturally this decree was highly embarrassing for Kerrl, who was anxious to brand those who refused to take the oath as 'traitors and enemies of the Reich'.

[21] For examples of the trials of clergymen and their acquittal by certain judges, see H. Schorn, *Der Richter im Dritten Reich* (Frankfurt 1959), pp. 504 ff.

[22] A notable exception was the attitude of the Anglican Bishop of Gloucester, who expressed the view in *The Times* that Niemöller was a trouble-maker who deserved what he got.

[23] See W. Niemöller, *Macht geht vor Recht, der Prozess Martin Niemöllers* (Munich 1952), and for a brief description of the legal situation, Schorn (Note VIII/21), pp. 589–96.

[24] When, in 1939, Niemöller's wife made a personal plea for her husband, Hitler wrote back to say that if Niemöller was set free, he would very soon again become the centre of a circle of persons who were opposed to Nazism and whose activities would only endanger the unity of the German people and the Nazi State. In view of this, the request was refused: BA, R (Note I/63), 43, II, 156.

It should however be pointed out that Niemöller himself, despite this ill-treatment, nevertheless still professed his loyalty to Hitler's political leadership of the German nation. In September 1939, he offered, as a former U-boat Commander, to serve in Hitler's navy 'in any capacity'. This was certainly not intended just to enable him to be released from custody.

[25] For the text of the Confessing Church's declaration on the outcome of Niemöller's trial see KJB (Note III/10), p. 235; some Nazis also had doubts about the wisdom of the flagrant injustice; see the report to Rosenberg from one of his collaborators: unpublished Nuremberg document, NG–910, reprinted in *Vierteljahrshefte für Zeitgeschichte* 1956, pp. 307–15.

[26] Files of the Kirchliche Hochschule, Berlin.

[27] BA, R (Note I/63), 43, II, 169.

[28] GCGR no. 32, *Records of the RFSS and Chief of the German Police, Part I*, microcopy no. T. 175, roll no. 124, frame no. 2647772; see also Bormann's comments in the same vein, BA, R (Note I/63), 43, II, 169.

[29] Unpublished Nuremberg document, 005–PS.

[30] DGFP (Note I/27), D. 1, no. 681.

[31] Micklem (Note IV/25), pp. 223–4; a fuller text of this speech, with suitable commentary, was circulated secretly in Catholic and Evangelical parishes in the following months where it was used as prime evidence of the Nazi intentions for the eradication of the Churches. A copy came into the hands of the police and was sent to Bormann and Rosenberg, asking whether it described accurately what had been said.

[32] Unpublished Nuremberg document NG–4604. Similar views had been embodied in instructions sent out to all provincial governors in September 1938, see GCGR no. 39 (Note V/30), roll no. 409, frame no. 2933384 ff.

[33] PS–117, NCA. Vol. III (Note VII/35), p. 169.

[34] Quoted in Zipfel (Note I/61), pp. 458–9.

[35] Ibid., p. 464; see also Heydrich's report to the Reich Chancellery of 8 November entitled 'The attitude of the Churches in the time of foreign political tension', BA, R (Note I/63), 43, II, 169.

[36] M. Domarus, *Hitler Reden und Proklamationen 1932–45* (Würzburg 1963), vol. II, pp. 1,058–61.

[37] Loc. cit.

[38] Quoted in Zipfel (Note I/61), p. 458.

[39] *New York Times*, 27 March 1938; in the Church Ministry a survey was compiled of the reactions of the Catholic bishops of Germany to the plebiscite noting the very favourable response; see H. Mohr, *Katholische Orden*

und deutscher Imperialismus (East Berlin 1965) (Note VII/11), pp. 292–3.

[40] BA, R (Note I/63), 43, II, 160.

[41] For the full text see KJB (Note III/10), pp. 262–4.

[42] 117-PS NCA. Vol. III (Note VII/35), p. 169.

[43] BA, R (Note I/63), 43, II, 177a.

[44] BA, R (Note I/63), 43, II, 169. This statement was formulated by Kerrl personally.

[45] BA, R (Note I/63), 43, II, 169.

[46] On the other hand, the distinguished historian, Gerhart Ritter, commented later: 'After the Crystal Night, there arose in church circles a fundamental consciousness that the Christian's duty to obey had limits when authority not only ignored God's commandments but placed itself like a gang of thugs above and outside the law; there had been so such phenomenon before in the history of German Protestantism ... No one who did not live as a German through those dark November days can really measure the depths of the anger and impotent despair in the hearts of countless Germans. For many who hesitated there was now no possibility of reconciliation with the regime of violence.' *The German Resistance* (London 1958), p. 115; but see Appendix 12 for an example of what happened to those who did speak out. The pastor involved, von Jan of Oberlenningen, Württemberg, was later summoned to appear before a Special Court, was sentenced to 1½ years' imprisonment and was expelled from Württemberg. On the other hand this attitude was not unanimous amongst the clergy; see Appendix 13.

[47] See *An der Stechbahn: Erlebnisse und Berichte aus dem Büro Grüber in den Jahren der Verfolgung* (Berlin n.d.).

[48] *Judennot und Christenglaube* (Zurich 1943), p. 7.

[49] DGFP (Note I/27), series D. 1, nos. 707, 709, 713, 717, 719, 720, 721, 722, 723.

[50] Ibid., D. 1, nos. 725, 726.

[51] BA, R (Note I/63), 43, II, 154.

[52] Unpublished Nuremberg Document, NG–1755; for an example of the Nazi defence of their anti-clerical measures, see Power (Note II/4), pp. 216–20.

[53] Unpublished Nuremberg Document PS–424, 27 October 1938.

[54] See also the secret directive signed by Bormann of 9 May 1939, BA, Schu (Note I/54), 245/1/199.

[55] Micklem (Note IV/25), pp. 227–9.

[56] Unpublished Nuremberg document PS–1718.

[57] Quoted in Lewy (Note I/10), p. 218.

[58] For the text see A. Giovanetti, *Der Vatikan und der Krieg* (Cologne 1961), pp. 36 f. This gesture was not reciprocated. Far from welcoming Pacelli as the new Pope, it was reported to Rome that 'an absolutely fanatical hatred against Cardinal Pacelli fills the Party'. *Le Saint Siège et la Guerre en Europe 1939–40* (Vatican City 1965), p. 4.

[59] DGFP (Note I/27), D. 6, no. 65.

[60] See *Kampf und Zeugnis* (Note I/19), p. 467, for praise of Hitler on his birthday.

[61] Reprinted in L. Poliakov and J. Wulf, *Das Dritte Reich und seine Denker* (Berlin 1959), p. 193. It is noteworthy, however, that despite Kerrl's enthusiastic endorsement of the Declaration, Heydrich wrote to Rosenberg suggesting the suppression of its publication. In June 1939 the leaders of the Church in Hanover, Brunswick and Hessen issued a statement, which ran: The National Socialist ideology fights with all its might against the political and spiritual influence of the Jewish race on our people's life. In obedience to the divine laws of creation the Evangelical Church approves the need to preserve the racial purity of our community. Quoted in K. Meier, 'Kristallnacht und Kirche—Die Haltung der evangelischen Kirche zur Judenpolitik' in *Wissenschaftliche Zeitschrift der Karl-Marx-Universität Leipzig* XIII/1 (1964), 102.

[62] See Biographical notes; for a short description of the Institute's objectives see K. Weinreich, *Hitler's Professors* (New York 1946), pp. 62–7. The foreword to the Report of the Second Conference of the Institute, entitled *Germantum, Christentum Judentum* edited by Walter Grundmann, Professor of Jena University, stated:

> The research and publications work of the Institute is not tied to any one denomination or religious group, but only to the pious German way of life. In the fateful struggle in which Greater Germany is engaged now, which is a struggle against world Jewry and all other anarchistic and nihilistic forces, the work of the Institute plays its part. It is a weapon for the overcoming of all religious alienation internally and serves the faith of the Reich. So it makes its contribution to the war effort of the German scholars of religion.
>
> The motto of our work runs: Now and always for the Reich and its Führer.

Printed in *Die Evangelische Kirche in Deutschland und die Judenfrage* (Geneva 1945), p. 188.

[63] A remarkable instance followed the eirenical and ecumenical request to the Confessing Church from the Archbishop of Canterbury, suggesting that a continent-wide service of prayer for peace be held in all Protestant churches of western Europe at Whitsuntide, 1939. In reply Bishop Marahrens of Hanover stated that 'if the English really wanted peace they would not have associated themselves with atheistic and Bolshevist Russia, in seeking to thwart the just demands of Germany to overcome the shackles of the Versailles Treaty. All Germans stood unitedly behind their Führer in his attempt to put this situation right. Only thus would true peace prevail.' This exchange of correspondence fell into the Gestapo's hands and was forwarded to the Reich Chancellery for Hitler's perusal. BA, R (Note I/63), 43, II, 154.

CHAPTER 9

[1] Quoted in a circular from the Chief of the Race and Settlement Headquarters, 8 September 1939, unpublished Nuremberg Document NG–1392.

[2] Unpublished Nuremberg document NG–1755.

[3] International Military Tribunal, trial of the major German war criminals, vol. IX, p. 271.

[4] *The Goebbels Diaries 1942–3*, ed. Lochner (New York 1948), *passim*.

[5] Herman (Note VI/12), p. 20.

[6] GCGR no. 39 (Note V/30), roll 250, frame no. 2741718 ff. A month later another circular stated that the churches were not to be denied their right, in the services or in the sermons, to take note of the war and to hold services of thanksgiving, or to pray for the victory of German arms or for those who had fallen in battle: BA, R (Note I/63), 43, II, 150.

[7] Niemöller (Note I/19), p. 487. A copy of this proclamation was sent to the Reich Chancellery for Hitler's perusal. BA, R (Note I/63), 43, II, 150.

[8] Quoted in Lewy (Note I/10), p. 226.

[9] Niemöller (Note I/19), p. 488.

[10] Quoted in Lewy (Note I/10), p. 229, for a fuller discussion see G. Zahn, *German Catholics and Hitler's Wars* (note III/31).

[11] BA, R (Note I/63), 43, II, 169, in part used as unpublished Nuremberg document NG–4968.

[12] For other reports on Catholic opinions to this effect see H. Boberach ed., *Meldungen aus den Reich* (Neuwied 1965), p. 39.

[13] In December 1939, in a circular to all Party offices, Bormann noted:

Complaints have been received from many regions that our comrades at the front have been sent literature from various sources which is not designed to strengthen their national socialist convictions but may in part contribute to the confusion of the steadfastness and *völkisch* attitude of our soldiers . . . the sending of such printed matter which will only give rise to denominational arguments amongst the troops will not strengthen the fighting morale of the men at the front, but rather weaken it. . . .

It is necessary that our soldiers should be given good literature free from ideological objections. I can recommend strongly: *The Soldier's Faith – The Soldier's Honour, a German Breviary for Hitler's Soldiers*.

Rundschreiben 236/39, files of the Institut für Zeitgeschichte.

[14] BA, Schu (Note I/54), 244/2/115.

[15] See Neuhäusler (note Introduction, p. xvi), pp. 159–64 for details of this persecution.

[16] Zipfel (Note I/61), pp. 504–6.

[17] Unpublished Nuremberg document PS–410.

[18] For Heydrich's report on the Corpus Christi celebrations, see BA, R (Note I/63), 43, II, 1266.

[19] GCGR no. 28 (Note V/34), roll 65, frame no. 232 ff.

[20] BA, R (Note I/63), 43, II, 153a.

[21] BA, R, cited in S. Friedländer, *Pius XII and the Third Reich* (London, 1966), p. 38.

[22] Loc. cit.

[23] Unpublished Nuremberg document NG–4604.

[24] Loc. cit., also NG–2063.

[25] Unpublished Nuremberg document NG–4603.

[26] DGFP (Note I/27), series D. VIII, no. 668; for the Papal version of this conversation see *Le Saint Siège et la Guerre en Europe 1939–40* (Vatican City 1965), pp. 384–87; see also DDI 9th Series III, no. 536 and FRUS 1940, vol. I, pp. 107–8, and G. O. Kent, 'Pope Pius XII and Germany: Some aspects of German-Vatican Relations 1933–45' in *American Historical Review*, LXX, 1 (October 1964), 66–7.

[27] Loc. cit. A secret SD report submitted to Himmler on 15 March 1940 stated:

The visit of Foreign Minister von Ribbentrop to the Pope aroused considerable astonishment in the public mind. Particularly in Catholic areas, it was frequently mentioned and in some cases gave rise to certain rumours and speculations about the contents of the conversations. In particular, it was rumoured that the Pope was trying to arrange peace. In Catholic circles, the Foreign Minister's visit to the Pope and the Führer's telegram of congratulations on the occasion of the anniversary of the Pope's coronation were occasionally regarded as a victory for the Vatican. Boberach (Note IX/12), p. 53.

[28] Unpublished Nuremberg documents NG–1776, 1740, 1737, 1741.

[29] Unpublished Nuremberg document NG–2808.

[30] On 19 January 1940 Weizsäcker noted: For quite a time now the Nuncio has come to me almost every week at least once in order to bring half-a-dozen Verbal Notes or declarations and equally numerous reminders of unsettled complaints. These conversations with the Nuncio have often little result because of the tardy and frequently negative handling of these things. The chief point of concern to the Nuncio at present is the condition of the Church in the former Poland. German Foreign Ministry archive, Pol. AA: Staats. Vatikan Vol. I, reprinted in Broszat, p. 164.

[31] Reprinted in J. S. Steward, *Sieg des Glaubens* (Zurich 1946), pp. 18–19.

[32] GCGR no. 33 (Note III/33), roll. no 187–8, frame no. 2726178.

[33] Neuhäusler (note Introduction, p. xvi), p. 125.

[34] GCGR no. 33 (Note III/33), roll 187–8, frame no. 2726180–1.

[35] BA, R (Note I/63), 43, II, 177a.

[36] See microcopy 'Weltanschauung und Religion' in Institut für Zeitgeschichte.

[37] GCGR no. 3 (Note IV/22), roll no. 184, frame no. 335261 ff; see also H. Brunotte, 'Der Kirchenpolitische Kurs der Deutschen Evangelischen Kirchenkanzlei' in *Zur Geschichte des Kirchenkampfes: Gesammelte Aufsätze* (Göttingen 1965), pp. 107–8.

[38] Unpublished Nuremberg document 129–Ps.

[39] Unpublished Nuremberg document 067–PS.

[40] Ibid.

[41] Rosenberg (Note III/36), p. 90.

[42] Ibid., pp. 105–6.
[43] 128–PS, quoted in Rosenberg, pp. 177–80.
[44] Unpublished Nuremberg document NG–1283.
[45] Unpublished Nuremberg document NG–4548.
[46] Unpublished Nuremberg document NG–4840.
[47] BA, R (Note I/63), 43, II, 150.
[48] Ibid.
[49] Rosenberg (Note III/36), p. 118. Later in the same month, Kerrl wrote again to Lammers on another issue. 'Particularly against the Catholic Church with its unified chain of command we need a unified governmental Church policy; this unified policy is however frequently and dangerously destroyed because all sorts of offices (*Stellen*) continually usurp competence in this area, which ought not to belong to them as long as my office exists. I would be grateful if you would bring to the notice of the Führer on a suitable occasion how matters stand in the area of church policy and how it is impossible for me to take the due steps because of a lack of full authority. I am quite ready to send you full details, should you so desire.' Quoted in Mohr (Note VII/11), p. 314.
[50] GCGR no. 28 (Note V/34), roll 62, frame no. 612 ff; see also Bormann's letter to *Gauleiter* Sprenger, unpublished Nuremberg document 097–PS.
[51] BA, R (Note I/63), 43, II, 150a.
[52] Loc. cit.
[53] BA, R (Note I/63), 43, II, 153a.
[54] In June 1941 Kerrl wrote to Lammers: 'I must make it clear that I am fundamentally an opponent of monasteries and monastic life, and that I welcome the disappearance of these outdated forms of church life. Nevertheless, I believe the methods used to remove these monasteries during the war are very doubtful for reasons both of internal and external policy. I feel myself bound to say this and must also refuse to accept the consequences for the spoliations already carried out or now planned.' See BA, R (Note I/63), 43, II, 1,271a; and Mohr (Note VII/11), p. 328.
[55] BA, R (Note I/63), 43, II, 1,272; Lewy (Note I/10), p. 254.
[56] *Hitler's Table Talk* (Note I/3), 14 December 1941.

CHAPTER 10

[1] Herman (Note VI/12), p. 216.
[2] NCA (Note VII/35), Vol. VIII, R–146, p. 250.
[3] Unpublished Nuremberg document, PS–1224.
[4] In May 1941 Ley circulated to all the *Gauleiters* lists of suitable monasteries —no less than 125 in all—which he would like to have confiscated for this purpose: unpublished Nuremberg document, PS–1232.
[5] BA, R (Note I/63), 43, II, 158A.
[6] BA, NS 6/223.
[7] GCGR no. 32, (Note V/26) roll no. 21, frame no. 2526105. For an example

of the effects of this decree in Bavaria, see S. Altmann, *Bayerns Benediktiner unterm Hakenkreuz* (Feldafing 1964).

⁸ Unpublished Nuremberg document NO–1886.

⁹ Unpublished Nuremberg document NO–1887; GCGR no. 32 (Note V/26), roll no. 21, frame no. 2526068.

¹⁰ GCGR no. 3 (Note IV/22), roll no. 123, frame no. 145233–4.

¹¹ BA, Schu (Note I/54), 243/II/2/68.

¹² Early in 1942, at Ribbentrop's request, a list was drawn up of all the instances about which the Vatican had protested. Out of 35 cases, 8 had been settled to the Church's satisfaction, one had been partly successful, but in 24 the seizures had been upheld. Two cases were still unsettled. Unpublished Nuremberg document NG–5431, cited in G. Kent (Note IX/26), pp. 67–9.

¹³ NCA (Note VII/35), vol. V, PS–3261, p. 1,011.

¹⁴ BA, R (Note I/63), 43, II, 159.

¹⁵ See Lewy (Note I/10), pp. 147–50.

¹⁶ BA, Schu (Note I/54), 243/II/2/67. Priests were not allowed to visit other patients than those who had specifically requested their services, nor were they allowed access to hospital lists. The nursing personnel, such as nuns and deaconesses, were forbidden to exercise 'spiritual functions'. If services were permitted, these could only be held in separate rooms, and no loud-speakers were to be used. Baptism could only be administered in an emergency.

¹⁷ For the effects of this decree and the considerable resistance it encountered, see H. Huber, *Dokumente Christlichen Widerstandes: Gegen die Entfernung der Kruzifixe aus den Schulen 1941* (Munich 1958).

¹⁸ Nazi Party Circular no. 11/41 secret: Release of Jesuits from the Armed Forces, reprinted in Zipfel (Note I/61), p. 516. Plans had already been considered a year earlier for the complete prohibition of the Jesuit order in Austria. Kerrl's view on this proposal was sent to Lammers on 24 May 1940:

Prohibition of the Jesuit Order not only in Austria but throughout the whole of Germany would be looked on favourably by me for fundamental reasons. On the other hand at the present time I regard such a prohibition inopportune on general political grounds. In Germany proper [*Alt-Reich*] the terms of the Reich Concordat do not allow such a prohibition, and while in Austria no such scruples arise over the legal provisions of a concordat, they may well do so for general political reasons. In my opinion, particularly now during the war, measures should be avoided which would give the Catholic Church (both inside and outside the country) welcome propaganda material against the Reich. The Jesuit Order has a great significance in the Catholic Church both because of numbers and of power, and the Pope has a particular relationship of confidence to it. I would therefore advise postponing the prohibition of the Order in Austria until the restoration of peace, when the whole ecclesiastical and religious problem will have to be settled clearly and finally.

Lammers replied on 15 June 1940 that he had raised the matter with Hitler, who 'wished at the present time no prohibition of the Jesuit Order in Austria should be enforced, since he wanted to avoid during the war all measures, unless definitely necessary, which might cause the relationship of the State and the Party to the Church to deteriorate ...' Quoted in Mohr (Note VII/11), pp. 314–15.

[19] J. S. Steward, *Sieg des Glaubens* (Zurich 1946), p. 13. A few weeks later *Gauleiter* Adolf Wagner of Munich declared: 'By the end of August we shall have won the Russian campaign and that will be the end of the Jesuits'—a sentiment shared by Regierungsrat Schiml of the Munich Gestapo who stated: 'At the latest by 1942 the Society of Jesus will be sent eastwards to the camps.'

[20] Unpublished Nuremberg document D–59; for the full text see Appendix 14.

[21] GCGR no. 32 (Note V/26), roll no. 65, frame nos. 2581292 ff.

[22] Nuremberg document D–75; for the full text see Appendix 15.

[23] Lewy (Note I/10), p. 295; 'among the Christians a few courageously helped the persecuted, but the large majority failed disgracefully in the face of this unheard-of provocation of the merciful God.'

The fullest discussion of the reactions of the Church to these tragic events is to be found in D. Golschmidt and J. J. Kraus (eds.) *Der Ungekündigte Bund* (Stuttgart 1962), a summary of public discussions held at a church congress in 1961, but which also includes a most valuable collection of documents compiled by Renate Heydenreich. See also Otto Elias, *Der Evangelische Kirchenkampf in seinen Verhältnis zur Judenfrage und zu den Juden*, manuscript 104, Institut for Zeitgeschichte, Munich; *Das Christentum und die Juden* (Cologne 1966), pp. 188 ff; and K. Kupisch, *Durch den Zaun der Geschichte* (Berlin 1964), pp. 371 ff, and Lewy (Note I/10), chapter 10.

[24] Other draconian measures followed; all Jews were to include the name Israel or Sarah to all official documents; various occupations were declared closed to Jews; Jewish precious metals and art objects were to be 'redeemed' by the authorities; no Jews were allowed to attend cultural festivities, or to use sleeping and restaurant car facilities on the trains; public parks and baths were closed to them; Jewish school children were excluded from the schools; higher taxes were imposed on Jews; Jews were not allowed to possess cars or own driving licences; Jewish organizations were dissolved, their publications prohibited and their officers arrested; the wave of emigration was at first encouraged, but finally, on 1 October 1941, this too was forbidden: see K. Meier, 'Kristallnacht und Kirche' (Note VIII/61), 94.

[25] KJB (Note III/10), p. 481.

[26] Hermelinck (Note III/16), p. 651.

[27] KJB (Note III/10), pp. 432–3.

[28] Hermelinck (Note III/16), pp. 654–5.

[29] Quoted in Lewy (Note I/10), p. 289; for Cardinal Bertram's instructions to the clergy issued on 17 September 1941, advising against any pastoral measures which might hurt Catholics of Jewish origin, see *Meldungen aus dem Reich* (Note IX/12), p. 196.

[30] Lewy (Note I/10), p. 294.

[31] KJB (Note III/10), pp. 399–402.

[32] A. Mitscherlich and F. Mielke, *Wissenschaft ohne Menschlichkeit* (Heidelberg 1949), p. 176.

[33] NCA (Note VII/35), Vol. III, p. 451; H. Hase, ed., *Evangelische Dokumente zur Ermordung der 'unheilbareKranken' unter der nationalsozialistischen Herrschaft in den Jahren 1939–45* (Stuttgart 1964), p. 8. This directive was to be carried out by a special office under Hitler's personal command, through a Party official, Bouhler, and Hitler's own doctor, Brandt. Bouhler instructed his assistant, SS *Oberführer* Brack, in collaboration with a Würzburg psychiatry professor Dr Werner Heyde, to take all necessary measures to establish this programme.

[34] Bouhler committed suicide in 1945; Brack was sentenced to death at the Nuremberg trial of Nazi doctors and hanged; Doctor Brandt was likewise condemned to death and hanged; for Professor Heyde, see Biographical Notes, p. 403.

[35] Busloads of mental patients were stripped naked at Brandenberg on the Havel before they were gassed; see *The Times*, 5 October 1966.

[36] Neuhäusler (note Introduction, p. xvi), pp. 357–9.

[37] *Evangelische Dokumente* (Note X/33), p. 12.

[38] Neuhäusler (note Introduction, p. xvi), p. 356. See also the protest from the Evangelical Churches' national office in Berlin: mentioned in Brunotte (Note IX/36), p. 125.

[39] PS-615, NCA (Note VII/35), vol. III, pp. 449–51; also unpublished Nuremberg document PS-616.

[40] Quoted in *Die Briefe Pius XII an die deutschen Bischöfe 1939–44*, ed. Schneider (Mainz 1966), p. 133.

[41] See his account of his actions and the text of his memorandum to Hitler of 9 July 1940 in *Evangelische Dokumente* (Note X/33), pp. 14 ff and 108 ff.

[42] Unpublished Nuremberg document NG-265; see also the protest of Magistrate Lothar Kreyssig, reprinted in *Evangelische Dokumente* (Note X/33), pp. 31 ff.

[43] Unpublished Nuremberg Document NO-018.

[44] For more details on 'Lebensborn' see the files of the Wiener Library Bulletin, XVI/3 (July 1962), 52–3, from which the information in this paragraph is taken.

[45] GCGR no. 33 (Note III/33), roll no. 128, frame no. 2654114.

[46] *Völkischer Beobachter*, 25 December 1939.

[47] Files of the Wiener Library Bulletin XVI/3 (July 1962), 52–3.

[48] E. Kogon, *Der SS-Staat* (Frankfurt 1946), p. 1.

[49] It was noted, for example, in a report to the Nazi headquarters in Baden, only two days after the Russian campaign began, that: 'the outbreak of war with Russia had only made worse the already bad feelings of the population. At the early service the pious people could hardly enjoy the sermon, they were so busy whispering to each other about the poor prospects which Germany had

in this war . . . the business about Hess had naturally harmed the Party considerably although it might be of some advantage that the outbreak of the Russian war has pushed this affair into the background.' Steward (Note X/19), p. 31.

[50] On 16 July Cardinal Bertram sent to Hitler a long memorandum of complaints which called for an end to the infringements on the Church's freedom and on its institutional life. On 4 August Kerrl replied expressing the resentment of the government at the attitude of the German Bishops. Kerrl declared: 'The German People is now entering into a life and death struggle with the enemy of humanity, which has persecuted not only the Christian churches but all religion with fanatical hatred. Surely it could be expected that this could have aroused the flames of indignation in the hearts of the bishops. Then they could have used their wholehearted efforts to influence their faithful followers to an assurance of victory and the will to win. Instead of that they made no mention of this great fact.' (Unpublished Nuremberg document PS-2139.) In the secret weekly report, *Meldungen aus dem Reich* prepared by the SD for 21 July 1941, especial attention was given to the popular reaction to the Bishops' pastoral letter. It noted the extraordinary disquiet aroused and quoted verbally many of the unwelcome sentiments expressed by the congregations: BA, R (Note I/63), 58/162. For the letter of complaint sent by the Bishops of Austria on 1 July 1941, see Appendix 17.

[51] For the full text, see Appendix 18.

[52] Rundschreiben 53/41: BA, NS 6/335.

[53] Unpublished Nuremberg Documents NG–4531 and 4533.

[54] DGFP (Note I/27), D. XIII, no. 340, enclosure 2; the text is reproduced in H. Portmann, *Der Bischof von Münster* (Münster 1947), p. 166. Despite the fact that Hitler's decree was circulated only to the *Gauleiters*, it soon became known to a wide circle of Church authorities. The Bishop of Trier mentioned having heard about it in a letter to the Reich Chancellery on 22 August. Bishop Preysing wrote to the Pope on 28 August to say: 'Hitler ordered Bormann to write to all the *Gauleiters* to tell them to stop operations against the monasteries. In fact no more confiscations seemed to have taken place since then. Even if this is only a postponement, we can thank God for it': *Die Briefe Pius XII an die deutschen Bischöfe 1939–1944*, p. 155. On the other hand, neither the Foreign Ministry nor the Church Ministry was informed. On 16 August Lammers wrote to Bormann to say that he had not notified Kerrl of Hitler's decision because he was awaiting Bormann's view on how to tell him. The Church Ministry first heard about the decree from a copy of the Bishop of Trier's letter. Kerrl had earlier complained that he had neither been consulted nor informed beforehand about the seizures of Church properties. Now it was clear that he and his Ministry played no part whatsoever in the unfolding or the stopping of the whole process. No wonder he could write to Lammers on 2 August to say: 'I cannot believe that the manner in which the confiscation of monasteries is now being carried out during the war is in line with the will

of the Führer. .... I cannot believe that the Führer believes that the present
moment is especially appropriate. .... I feel myself obliged to make you aware
of my express disapproval of these measures, so I will not have to carry the
responsibility for these measures in the eyes of the Führer.' Quoted in Mohr
(Note VII/11), p. 328. On 12 September the Nuncio approached Weizsäcker
to find out if such a directive had been issued. Weizsäcker 'acted as if I were not
informed in the matter'. DGFP (Note I/27), D. XIII, no. 307.

⁵⁵ See also the letter of *Gauleiter* Wahl of Augsburg to Bormann, dated 6
August 1941: BA, R (Note I/63), 43, II, 1,272.

⁵⁶ Portmann (Note X/54), pp. 174–5.

⁵⁷ Ibid., p. 191.

⁵⁸ Ibid., pp. 182–4.

⁵⁹ NCA (Note VII/35), vol. VI, PS–3701, pp. 406–8.

⁶⁰ BA, R (Note I/63), 43, II, 153A.

⁶¹ Domarus (Note VI/4), vol. II, p. 1,777.

⁶² *Table Talk* (Note I/3); two years later, while still trying to influence the
populace against their Bishop, Himmler gave orders that on the death of the
next clergyman in Münster, 'it should be said that the person in question was
murdered by his adherents because he said this or that at some time against the
Bishop. Please inform the *Reichsführer SS* as soon as a death occurs which
should be exploited in this manner.' Unpublished Nuremberg Document
NO–1613.

⁶³ Lewy (Note I/10), p. 266.

⁶⁴ On the same day the removal of crucifixes from Bavarian schools was
halted.

⁶⁵ In November 1941 an interesting comment on the Catholic Bishops was
made by Ulrich von Hassell, formerly German Ambassador in Italy: 'The
majority under the leadership of the old pacifist cardinal, Bishop Bertram of
Breslau, was opposed to an open struggle and against "political" rather than
religious methods. The proponents of drastic action, Galen and Preysing, were
therefore in the minority. People such as Bertram will get nowhere at all with
men such as Hitler and Himmler. Bishop Gröber of Freiburg, once dubbed
"Brown Konrad", is now completely disillusioned by the regime ...': *The
von Hassell Diaries* (New York 1947), p. 223. And Goebbels noted in his diary:
'I took the position in talking with the Führer that the old cardinals of the
type of Faulhaber and Bertram are much less dangerous than the young clergy
who are serving at the front as army chaplains and even wear the Iron Cross of
the First Class.' *The Goebbels Diaries* (Note IX/4), entry for 12 May 1943.

⁶⁶ Von Papen, *Memoirs*, p. 482.

⁶⁷ BA, R (Note I/63), 43, II, 173a.

⁶⁸ Nazi Party Circular 22/43 Secret: Bundesarchiv NS 6/344.

⁶⁹ Ibid.

⁷⁰ Hitler's *Table Talk* (Note I/3), 14 October 1941, see also similar remarks
made 21, 24, 25 October, 11 November, 13 and 14 December, 27 January

1943, 27 February, 9 April, 1 August 1942, 17 May 1944, 29 November 1944; see also *The Goebbels' Diaries* (Note IX/4), entry for 12 May 1943.

[71] *Table Talk* (Note I/3), 9 February 1942; see also *The Goebbels' Diaries* (Note IX/4), entries for 20 March 1942 and 9 March 1943.

[72] *The Goebbels' Diaries* (Note IX/4), 12 March 1942; for similar remarks see entries for 26 March and 8 May 1942 and 3 March, 25 April and 16 May 1943; according to Goebbels, this was also Goering's view, see entry for 21 March 1942.

[73] See this author's 'Pius XII and the German Church: an unpublished Gestapo Report' in *Canadian Journal of History*, vol. I, no. 1, 1966.

[74] PS–1815, International Military Tribunal, Trials of the Major War Criminals (Nuremberg 1948), vol. XXVIII, p. 448.

[75] Loc. cit.

[76] Ibid.

[77] GCGR no. 39 (Note V/30), roll no. 409, frame nos. 2932521 ff.

[78] For example, Hitler refused to sanction one of Heydrich's schemes whereby young and fully convinced Nazis should be deliberately enrolled as ordinands in the theological colleges in order to be able to subvert the church from within; W. Hagen, *Die Geheime Front* (Linz 1950), p. 35.

[79] Loc cit.

[80] In his diary for 7 March, Goebbels noted: 'I am now going to have a number of the clergymen, who read Mölders' letter from their pulpits and who refused to publish a denial despite being taught the facts, taken into a concentration camp. I shall then publish a bulletin about it. If I were Minister of Justice I would find a passage somewhere in the thousands of existing regulations which would enable me to fight such infamous conduct by the Church.' *The Goebbels' Diaries* (Note IX/4), 7 March 1942. See also entries for 2, 16 and 21 March.

[81] BA, R (Note I/63), 43, II, 173a.

[82] GCGR no. 32 (Note V/26), roll no. 38, frame no. 2547948.

[83] Steward (Note X/19), pp. 55–6; see also numerous other reports contained in Boberach (Note IX/12), passim. For example a Party official in Karlsruhe in 1943 commented: 'The struggle in this war is not only very difficult on the Eastern Front; at home the power of the clergy is become more and more like a fungus that causes cleavages (*Spaltpilz*) among the people. The clergy is the greatest destroyer of our confidence in victory. That is where the liberal bourgeoisie which is impregnated with the spirit of Freemasonry finds its best representatives. Earlier these circles used to despise the "parsons"; now they see in them the pioneers of their attitude of hostility to the State, and the clergy are glad to stand in well with these circles, and hope, after the defeat, to get their old political power back again. That is how the rival fronts have changed. A large part of our war effort must be devoted to the home front. What a pity that so much effort must be squandered where there ought to be only a policy of eradication ... !'

[84] Quoted in *Dying We Live*, ed. Gollwitzer, Kuhn and Schneider (London 1956), p. 121.

[85] *Spiegelbild einer Verschwörung*, ed. K. H. Peter (Stuttgart 1961), pp. 167–8; Gerstenmaier's part in this movement has long been a subject of acrimonious debate; see *Karl Barth zum Kirchenkampf* (Münich 1956), pp. 84–9, and F. Schlabendorff, *Eugen Gerstenmaier im Dritten Reich: Eine Dokumenenentation* (Stuttgart 1965).

[86] *Dying We Live* (Note X/84), p. 140.

CHAPTER 11

[1] Typical of Hitler's threats was the following:

The war will be over one day. I shall then consider that my life's final task will be to solve the religious problem. Only then will the life of the German nation be guaranteed once and for all.

I do not interfere in matters of belief. Therefore I can not allow churchmen to interfere with temporal affairs. The organised lie must be smashed. The State must remain the absolute master.

The final state must be: in the pulpit, a senile officiant; facing him, a few sinister old women, as gaga and as poor in spirit as anyone could wish. *Table Talk* (Note I/3), 13 December 1941.

[2] In Rosenberg's view this would present 'a great and positive opportunity for German colonization, which would not be directed against the Russian people but would restore the old links between the ancient land of the Goths and would remove forever the political pressure felt by Germany from the East.'

[3] See Biographical Notes, pp. 401–2.

[4] This first contact had the effect, however, of teaching the good bishop 'about the subtlety of the snake as well as the gentleness of the dove'. See B. Höye and T. M. Ager, *The Fight of the Norwegian Church against Nazism* (New York 1943), p. 8.

[5] 'The Bishops want to maintain their ridiculous attitude of pride, thinking that they alone hold the key to salvation, thus terrorizing the most courageous in our midst. As prelates, they may not be vulnerable, but when they openly sympathize with secret and cunning saboteurs, thwarters, and liars, when they continue to show animosity against those who defend this country with their lives, they will be despised and finally removed from this soil.' (From the Dutch Nazi newspaper, *Volk en Vaderland*, cited in E. Castonier, *The Eternal Front* (London 1943), p. 59. For a Norwegian example of the same thing, see Höye (Note XI/3), p. 44.

[6] Höye (Note XI/4), p. 46.

[7] 'Today we can definitely assert that it is National Socialism which defends our western civilization and with it, the Christian religion, which will be mercilessly wiped out if Bolshevism is victorious, despite all the fantasies of an

Q

Archbishop [sic] of Canterbury who believes Bolshevism to be a lighthouse in the darkness of the night.' A. Seyss Inquart, *Vier Jahre in der Niederlanden* (Amsterdam 1944), p. 158.

[8] To be sure, Seyss Inquart also admitted that some priests had been imprisoned, but only because they had attacked the Nazi political leadership or were spies or had helped the enemy. The tolerance of the Nazi authorities, he claimed, was to be seen in the freedom the Church had to publish critical pastoral letters.

On the other hand, in Norway when Bishop Berggrav, in a remarkably frank interview with no less a person than Himmler, sought to persuade the *Reichsführer SS* that repression would inevitably lead to the creation of a martyr church, Himmler darkly hinted:

'Today it is no longer possible to have martyrs. We will take care of that. We will see to it that such people are forgotten. Think for example of Niemöller. . . . In Germany no one thinks of him. Only abroad is his name banded about. And I can promise you, he will never come out again.' A. Johnson, *Eivind Berggrav* (Göttingen 1960), p. 188.

[9] Goebbels (Note IX/4), diary entry for 13 February 1942.

[10] DGFP (Note I/27), D. XIII, no. 114.

[11] Hitler's *Table Talk* (Note I/3), 25 October 1941.

[12] See J. Piotrowski, *Hans Franks Tabeguch* (Warsaw 1963), pp. 190–1.

[13] Unpublished Nuremberg Document NG–962, cited in M. Broszat, *Nationalsozialistische Polenpolitik 1939–45* (Stuttgart 1961), p. 20.

[14] B. M. Kempner, *Priester vor Hitlers Tribunalen* (Munich 1966), p. 10. At the risk of giving offence in certain quarters, I have quoted the place-names as found in the sources, but have tried to give the Polish names wherever possible at the first reference.

[15] I am indebted for this information to my colleague, Dr William Rose.

[16] *The Nazi Kultur in Poland* (London 1942), pp. 30–1.

[17] For the telegram from four Ukrainian bishops thanking Hitler for their liberation from Bolshevism, see files of the German Foreign Ministry, microcopy T. 120, roll 314, frame no. 240074.

[18] For example, in Norway, in order to prevent an all-out Church struggle which would have jeopardized the German military position, Bishop Berggrav of Oslo was placed in complete isolation and house arrest in the countryside for the next three years. His probable execution on the orders of Quisling and Reich Commissar Terboven was only stopped by the intervention of other German authorities, at the urging of Graf von Moltke, one of the later conspirators against Hitler. Commenting on this matter, Goebbels noted in his diary: 'Terboven acts like a bull in a china shop. Evil consequences resulted in Norway, and Terboven is now the most hated man in Scandinavia' (diary entry for 22 May 1943).

[19] PS–998, International Military Tribunal, *Trial of the Major War Criminals* Nuremberg 1948), vol. XVI, p. 474.

[20] *The German New Order in Poland* (London 1941), p. 331.

[21] *The Nazi Kultur in Poland* (Note XI/16), p. 13. Despite the fact that this and the preceding source were written on behalf of the Polish government in exile in London, the accuracy of the information contained therein was to be confirmed after the liberation of Poland in 1945. In fact, the later revelations were to disclose in even greater detail the full extent of the Nazi atrocities.

[22] He demanded that the legal officers 'should take account of the dangerous agitation of many of the priests . . . and of the fact that the majority of priests are in opposition to the present State. This fact alone should be sufficient to put the utterances of priests in their correct context. . . . All too often the lenient sentences of the courts make necessary forcible measures by the Gestapo.' Kempner (Note XI/14), p. 11. See also Kempner, *passim*, for short biographies of 130 priests who were condemned to death by Nazi tribunals.

[23] Writing to the Papal Secretary of State, Cardinal Maglione, in December 1942, Cardinal Bertram stated: 'About the concentration camps. Up to this point, we have been able to learn little, because we know scarcely anything of the reasons why the individuals are sent there, of the treatment they receive, of their fate, their health or their needs. Those who are put into the camps are compelled by threat of the severest penalties to maintain the strictest silence about all that happens in the camps; as a result, they dare not say anything. All the bishops feel a deep sympathy and a keen sense of pity for those in concentration camps, especially as we are persuaded that the great majority of those held there are innocent. Many of the clergy have died there – men whom I held in special esteem and love for their upright life and conduct, known to the whole people.' PS-3266, NCA (Note VII/35), pp. 1035–6.

The Nazi authorities were adamant in their refusal to release these priests, though they were prepared to allow certain facilities in Dachau for the saying of Mass. However, a year later, Cardinal Bertram told his superiors in Rome: 'On 2 July 1938, 4 December 1940 and 3 June 1942, I made an urgent appeal to the authorities of the concentration camps that the celebration of Mass should be allowed in other camps as in Dachau and that spiritual ministry should be allowed, especially amongst the sick and the dying. I also presented a petition that the bodies of those who die should not be indiscriminately burnt, but should be given due burial whenever they had asked for it. This petition was rejected.' Ibid.; see also *Christ in Dachau* (Oxford 1952), *passim*.

[24] See R. Schnabel, *Die Frommen in der Hölle* (Note VII/11). Among the useful statistical data is the following division of the total by nationality:

Albania	2	Lithuania	3
Austria	105	Luxemburg	17
Belgium	47	Netherlands	62
Czechoslovakia	122	Norway	1
Denmark	5	Poland	1,773
France	156	Roumania	1
Germany	390	Switzerland	2

Great Britain	2	Spain	1
Greece	2	Stateless	2
Hungary	3	Yugoslavia	46
Italy	29		
		TOTAL	2,771

[25] Kempner (Note XI/14), p. 8.

[26] E. von Weizsäcker, *Memoirs* (London 1951), p. 281. From the context, the date of this remark is not clear.

[27] *Hans Franks Tagebuch* (Note XI/12), p. 181.

[28] PS-3266, NCA (Note VII/35), vol. V, p. 1,032.

[29] *The persecution of the Catholic Church in German-occupied Poland* (London 1941), pp. 25–6; the report continued: 'The Churches between Bydgoszcz (Bromberg) and Gniezno (Gnesen) with a very few exceptions have been closed, the property of the Church in most cases has been sequestrated, religious services no longer take place, Church funds have been confiscated, people are dying without the Last Sacraments. His Excellency, the Vicar General, cannot send new priests here because at once they are arrested, driven out, even often insulted and beaten. A certain number of the parishes are considered as suppressed or as having ceased to exist.'

A month later another report stated: 'The following priests have been shot: The Reverend Fathers, Zablocki, Rolski, Ladislaus Nowicki, Casimir Nowicki, Niziolkiewicz, Janke, Jakubowski, Lewicki, and two Lazarist Fathers of Bydgoszcz. The Rev. Fr. Breczewski was killed by a bomb. Rev. Frs. Domeracki and Jaskowski died in prison. Some priests are in hiding among the people, fearing the same fate. A certain number of priests have been deported to Germany, others are either in prison or in concentration camps at Gorna Grupa, at Gniezno and in Germany. The number of priests exiled into "Central Poland" [the Government General] is continually increasing. . . . Mass deportations of Poles into Central Poland are now being carried out; due to this the deported lose all that they possess: land, houses, furniture, business, clothes, linen, and money. In an instant they have been turned into beggars. Thus stripped of all, they are driven to the central regions, where people are already suffering from a lack of every day necessities: in the spring many will die of hunger. . . .' Ibid., pp. 29–30; for a fuller account of these atrocities, see *The German New Order in Poland* (Note XI/20), pp. 331–56.

[30] *The German New Order in Poland* (Note XI/20), p. 321.

[31] Hitler's *Table Talk* (Note I/3), 29 August 1942.

[32] Ibid., 4 July 1942.

[33] Loc. cit.

[34] Loc. cit.

[35] Loc. cit.

[36] Quoted in Friedländer, *Pius XII and the Third Reich* (London 1966), p. 169.

[37] See the letter from Weizsäcker to *Gauleiter* Greiser, dated 7 January 1942, unpublished Nuremberg document NG-5004.

[38] According to Ambassador Bergen, 'the Vatican was stunned by this news': unpublished Nuremberg document NG 4043. In February 1940, the Nuncio was informed that the Chief of the Security Police refused to give details about the condition of Catholics in Poland so long as the Vatican continued to recognize the jurisdiction of Cardinal Hlond: unpublished Nuremberg document NG 1777.

[39] Unpublished Nuremberg document NG 4605, quoted in Friedländer (Note XI/36), p. 39.

[40] Unpublished Nuremberg document NG 4604.

[41] See NCA (Note VII/35), vol. V, p. 1037.

[42] DGFP (Note I/27), D. XIII, no. 148; and D. XIII, no. 241.

[43] PS-3261, NCA (Note VII/35), vol. V, pp. 1,009–15.

[44] *Die Briefe Pius XII* (Note X/40), p. 142.

Three months later, in an interview with the Italian Ambassador to the Holy See, Attolico, the Pope is reported as saying: 'the situation in Germany, he told me [Attolico] has become infinitely worse since the day of his departure from Berlin. Even if the Führer has ordered the "suspensions" of the persecutions, this does not mean that Christ has been readmitted to the schools from which he was removed and that the numerous convents and religious institutions now closed will be reopened, or that the German children will no longer be made to recite that parody of the Our Father in which they thank Hitler for their daily bread.'

The Pope dwelt on this point for about thirty minutes. In fact, he said that he was glad of an opportunity to ask me a question: 'I was told that long ago in Germany they already had it in mind to do away with the Vatican, because there was no place for it in the European order, etc., etc. Now I am assured that even in his meeting with Mussolini the Führer stated that it was necessary to "put an end to" the Vatican. Is that true? . . .'

The Ambassador's negative reply 'seemed to make the Pope feel glad and almost relieved thus showing how much his conviction, I might almost say his nightmarish fear, of new and more ruthless persecutions weighs on his mind. He speaks as though one day he might, *manu germanica*, be driven out of Rome. But – mark me – he does not speak of it out of fear. . . .

Continuing his conversation the Holy Father said:

"I, too, feel that, in view of the long duration of the war with Russia, a word from me on Bolshevism, would be most beneficial and timely in Italy and the entire world; but have I said anything or perhaps published anything in *L'Osservatore Romano* about the Pastoral Letter of the Bishop of Münster or that of the German Bishops? However, if someday I 'must' speak, I shall speak, but I will say everything . . . O, if only Germany had left me in peace . . . my attitude towards this war, especially at this time, would have been quite different . . ." ' DGFP (Note I/27), D. XIII no. 330.

[45] *Die Briefe* (Note X/40), pp. 155–6. As briefly mentioned in the Introduction, it is the contention of Hochhuth and other critics, such as Friedländer,

that the Pope's protests were never as forceful as they should have been They point to his omission of more outspoken proclamations against the Nazi persecutions, especially of the Jews, and his apparent readiness to favour concessions to Nazism because of an alleged desire to create a bulwark against the danger of Bolshevism in Western Europe. For this author's critique of these views, see J. S. Conway, 'The Silence of Pope Pius XII' in *Review of Politics*, vol. 27, no. 1, January 1965, pp. 105–31, and *Times Literary Supplement*, 1 December 1966, pp. 1,109–11.

46 These representations form the bulk of the material to be found in the 5 volumes of the Handakten of State Secretary Weizsäcker relating to Vatican affairs 1937–43, comprising in all approximately 2,500 pages. They were all reproduced on microcopy T. 120, rolls 314, 315, 364 and 361. It was Weizsäcker's habit to prepare a minute on each representation made by the Nuncio, and in many cases a copy of any verbal note left by the Nuncio is appended; frequently the Nuncio would raise a dozen or more matters each of which was minuted by the State Secretary on a separate sheet of paper. Following the capture of the German Foreign Ministry documents at the end of the war, approximately a hundred of the more significant of these minutes were used at the Nuremberg Trials and were allotted numbers from the NG series, though only a few have since been published. These documents can be easily found in the microfilms mentioned above, which are arranged in chronological order. I have therefore omitted cross-references. In his discussion of German-Vatican relations, Friedländer (see Note XI/36), has omitted the vast majority of these representations, and has referred only to certain unsuccessful gestures by the Nuncio – an omission which conceals the range and extent of the interventions made by the Vatican throughout the years of Nazi persecution. He has also chosen to overlook the most significant of the Papal protests, which, despite his contention, are to be found in the sources he used. This arbitrariness in selection is matched by a bias in interpretation which extends even to the translations in the various editions of his book.

47 Unpublished Nuremberg document NG 4445.

48 See Note IX/28, and also unpublished Nuremberg documents NG 1738, 1757, 1758, 1776, 4443, 4444, 4459, 4521, 4532; see also PS–3265, NCA (Note VII/22), vol. V, p. 1,029.

49 Unpublished Nuremberg documents NG 4533, 4531, 4565, 4574.

50 Unpublished Nuremberg documents NG 4517, 4577, 1933, 4512, 4519, 5124–6.

51 Unpublished Nuremberg Document NG 4567.

52 Unpublished Nuremberg document NG 4447.

53 Unpublished Nuremberg document NG 4571.

54 For further details on Weizsäcker's personal attitudes, see an unpublished article by L. E. Hill.

55 Unpublished Nuremberg document NG 5004.

56 *Table Talk* (Note I/3), 4 July 1942.

⁵⁷ Ibid.

⁵⁸ Unpublished Nuremberg document NG 4576.

⁵⁹ Unpublished Nuremberg document NG 4576, dated 11 June. On 22 June a conference was held in the Foreign Ministry to discuss the implementation of Hitler's decision: unpublished Nuremberg document NG 4570; on the same day Weizsäcker informed Bergen of the decisions: Friedländer, pp. 160–1. On 19 August Weizsäcker sent a circular to all German missions abroad informing them of the decision: unpublished Nuremberg document NG 5443. A month later, on 23 September, Weizsäcker suggested to the Reich Chancellery that all governmental agencies should be informed by their respective ministries: unpublished Nuremberg document NG 4575; and on 18 October, Lammers sent out such a circular obviously prepared by the Foreign Ministry: unpublished Nuremberg document NG 1466. This was then taken by Bormann at the Party Chancellery who gave it a covering letter and sent copies to all *Reichsleiters, Gauleiters,* and Associated Leaders as circular no. 51/42 secret, dated 22 October 1942; unpublished Nuremberg document NG 1466.

⁶⁰ Unpublished Nuremberg document NG 4569 and PS–3262, NCA (Note VII/35), vol. V, p. 1,015. On 24 July and 17 August Weizsäcker again reminded the Nuncio of the limitations on his competency: unpublished Nuremberg document NG 4569 and 5443.

⁶¹ Broszat (Note XI/13), p. 175.

⁶² Unpublished Nuremberg document PS–361.

⁶³ Telegram to Ambassador Bergen, 13 January 1943. This telegram was first drafted in October 1942, but was not sent; see unpublished Nuremberg document NG 4571. Both the draft and the later telegram are discussed in G. Kent, 'Pope Pius XII and Germany: some aspects of German–Vatican relations 1933–1943', in *American Historical Review*, vol. LXX, no. 1 (October 1964), pp. 73–4. The telegram is printed in excerpts only by Friedländer, *Pius XII und das Dritte Reich* (Cologne 1964), pp. 119–20, where a passage in the draft dealing with the cessation of seizures of church property is indicated only as paragraph 2, which is not cited. In the English edition of Friedländer's book, even this citation is omitted and the paragraphs are renumbered, see *Pius XII and the Third Reich* (Note XI/36), pp. 167–8. The originals are to be found in the files of the German Foreign Ministry: *Politische Archiv, Staatsekretär Vatikan*, vol. 4.

⁶⁴ PS–3263 and 3264, NCA (Note VII/35), vol. V, pp. 1,017–29.

⁶⁵ *Die Briefe* (Note X/40), pp. 240–1.

⁶⁶ *Ostdeutscher Beobachter*, 26 October, quoted in P. Gürtler, *Nationalsozialismus und Kirchen im Warthegau* (Goettingen 1958), p. 39. I am indebted for much of what follows to Gürtler, to B. Stasiewski, 'Die Kirchenpolitik der Nationalsozialisten im Warthegau 1939–45', in *Vierteljahreshefte für Zeitgeschichte*, 7/1959, 46–74, and to M. Broszat, *Nationalsozialistische Polenpolitik 1939–1945* (Stuttgart 1961).

⁶⁷ Gürtler (Note XI/66), p. 39.

⁶⁸ *Table Talk* (Note I/3), 12 May 1942.

⁶⁹ BA, R (Note I/63), 43, II, 153.

⁷⁰ In February 1940 Himmler wrote to Greiser giving his warm approval of Greiser's determination to treat the churches in a novel and unprecedented manner: GCGR no. 32 (Note V/26), roll 69, frame no. 2585629, quoted in Broszat (Note IX/66), p. 167.

⁷¹ BA, R (Note I/63), 43, II, 170.

⁷² PS–66, NCA (Note VII/35), pp. 112–14. Gürtler suggests four reasons why this draft decree for Danzig–West Prussia was not implemented: first, the close and unbroken connections between the German Evangelical Church and its representatives in Danzig; second, the much more public notice which was taken of the state of affairs in Danzig. Experiments could be more easily conducted in the less-publicized Warthegau; third, the small number of original German inhabitants in the Warthegau could allow radical changes in the position of the Churches to be disguised as part of the recolonization procedures; fourthly, the personality of the *Gauleiters* was markedly different. Greiser also possessed in Jäger a man who had experience in 'dealing with' Church problems: Gürtler (Note XI/66), pp. 33–4.

⁷³ PS–117, NCA (Note VII/35), vol. III, p. 168; see also Chapter X above, p. 260.

⁷⁴ Party Records NS VI/24. Two further circulars ordering the same central control over all relations with the Churches were issued on 1 August 1942; see GCGR no. 3 (Note IV/22), roll nos. 184–5, frame nos. 335247 ff.

⁷⁵ BA, R (Note I/63), 43, II, 170, quoted in Broszat (Note XI/13), p. 169.

⁷⁶ GCGR no. 32 (Note V/26), roll 69, frame nos. 2585629 ff.

⁷⁷ See Bormann's remark in a letter to Lammers, dated 22 October 1941: 'already last winter – the date at the moment escapes me – *Gauleiter* Greiser outlined his plans to the Führer': BA, R (Note I/63), 43, II, 170b; also a note in Rosenberg's diary, dated September 1940: '*Gauleiter* Greiser reported on regulations in the Warthegau: the denominations to become private associations. The Führer raised no objections to there being quite different regulations in force in the *Gaus*.' Rosenberg (Note III/36), p. 148.

⁷⁸ Quoted in Broszat (Note XI/13), p. 165.

⁷⁹ See Greiser's telegram to the German Foreign Ministry, 28 April 1941; film of the German Foreign Ministry, microcopy T. 120, roll 315, frame nos. 835–6.

⁸⁰ Gürtler (Note XI/66), p. 52.

⁸¹ GCGR no. 32 (Note V/26), roll 69, frame nos. 2585629 ff.

⁸² For the text, see Gürtler (Note XI/66), p. 200. As Gürtler and Stasiewski note, certain authorities have mistakenly stated that these thirteen points were issued as an official decree in March 1940. In fact, it was not until the following September that a revised statement in legal phraseology was issued; see p. 320.

⁸³ In May 1940 the SS had already issued a decree forbidding Catholic

priests to receive permits to enter or leave the two regions of Danzig–West Prussia and the Warthegau, quoted in Broszat (Note XI/13), p. 165.

[84] Gürtler (Note XI/66), p. 55.

[85] Gürtler (Note XI/66), p. 214.

[86] BA, R (Note I/63), 43, II, 170a.

[87] For the antecedents of this decree and Bormann's support of Greiser see GCGR no 28 (Note V/34), roll 65, frame nos. 232 ff. The prohibition of public collections at the end of church services led to remarkable counter-measures by churchmen. In many parishes, processions around the altar were formed to hand over their offerings, and many rectories received secret gifts which as much as doubled the previous contributions from the laity: Gürtler (Note XI/66), p. 65.

[88] Quoted in Gürtler (Note XI/66), p. 144; see also a verbal note to the Nuncio from the German Foreign Ministry, May 1941, justifying the confiscations; files of the German Foreign Ministry microcopy, T. 120, roll 315, frame nos. 239825-7.

[89] In Konstantinow for example, such a placard was affixed on the church door immediately under the inscription 'Come unto me all ye who travail or are heavy laden'; Gürtler (Note XI/66), p. 141.

[90] For the text, see Gürtler (Note XI/66), p. 260.

[91] Stasiewiski (Note XI/66), p. 58.

[92] BA, R (Note X/63), 43, II, 170b.

[93] Broszat (Note XI/13), p. 172.

[94] See Appendix 4b.

[95] After numerous protests, this regulation was eventually withdrawn in July 1944.

[96] For the text, see Gürtler (Note XI/66), pp. 269-71.

[97] Quoted in Gürtler (Note XI/66), p. 148.

[98] For the protests from the Evangelical leaders see Gürtler (Note XI/66), pp. 256-9 and 265-9; the Papal Nuncio protested to the German Foreign Ministry on 16 August, 2 September, 29 September and 5 December 1941; see DGFP (Note I/27), D. XII, nos. 272, 368 and 547.

[99] See Gürtler (Note XI/66), pp. 256 ff.

[100] BA, R (Note I/63), 43, II, 170b.

[101] See Gürtler (Note XI/66), p. 277.

[102] Schnabel (Note VII/11), p. 97.

[103] See Broszat (Note XI/13), p. 161.

[104] Quoted in Broszat (Note XI/13), p. 162.

[105] See above footnote 24.

[106] Report by Fr Hilarius Breitinger, quoted in Broszat (Note XI/13), p. 173.

[107] Broszat (Note XI/13), p. 173.

[108] See unpublished Nuremberg document NG 4571; the figures are taken from a draft telegram from the German Foreign Ministry to its Embassy in Rome, dated October 1942; in March 1942, the Papal Nuncio complained

Q*

bitterly to the Foreign Ministry that in Posen so many churches had been closed by order of the *Reichsstatthalter* that churchgoers were unable to find places in those that remained open.

[109] Ibid., quoted in Stasiewski (Note XI/66), p. 65.

[110] Unpublished Nuremberg Document NG 5003.

[111] See footnote 64 above, and also references in the Verbal Note of the Vatican to the German Embassy, January 1942, quoted in PS 3261, NCA (Note VII/35), vol. V, p. 1,011; for the situation in October 1943 see Unpublished Nuremberg Document PS-2132; see also Superintendent Blau's protests of 1943, unpublished Nuremberg Document PS-2134; and the complaint submitted to the Reich Chancellery by the Bishop of Hanover, in June 1943: BA, R (Note I/63), 43, II, 172.

[112] Neuhäusler (note Introduction, p. xvi), vol. II, p. 68.

[113] PS-3264, NCA (Note VII/35), vol. V, pp. 1,018–29.

[114] This brutal treatment of the nuns had already been the subject of a protest by the Nuncio, see unpublished Nuremberg Document, NG-4459.

[115] When the Nuncio presented this mordant commentary upon Nazi Church policy to the German Foreign Ministry, Ribbentrop refused to accept it, but curtly replied that it concerned matters which did not relate to the German Reich. 'As the result of this, it would be best if, in this case, the letter would be regarded as non-existent by all concerned.' PS-3269, NCA (Note VII/35), vol. V, p. 1,045.

[116] Allocution of His Holiness Pope Pius XII to the Sacred College of Cardinals, June 1945, quoted in PS-3268, NCA (Note VII/35), vol. V, pp. 1,038–41.

[117] Ibid.

[118] Stasiewski (Note XI/66), p. 74.

CONCLUSION

[1] New Cambridge Modern History, vol. IX, *War and Peace in an Age of Upheaval* (Cambridge 1965), p. 148.

[2] Loc. cit.

[3] Ibid., p. 152.

[4] Quoted in S. Herman, *The Rebirth of the German Church* (London 1946), p. 137.

[5] Ibid., p. 132.

[6] Ibid., p. 131.

[7] Lewy (Note I/10), p. 338.

[8] D. Bonhoeffer, *Letters and Papers from Prison* (London 1959), pp. 137–8.

Bibliography

As already mentioned in the Introduction, a vast literature on the German church struggle has already appeared in German, the titles of which, up to 1958, were published in the bibliography by Otto Diehn, *Bibliographie zur Geschichte des Kirchenkampfes 1933–45* (Goettingen 1958). Since then much of the vast quantity of governmental and Nazi Party records for the period 1933–45 has become available to scholars, either in the archives of Western Germany or through microfilm collections prepared in Great Britain and the United States. The following bibliography does not attempt to be comprehensive. Only the main works and sources used have been cited, and much of the ephemeral literature which appeared during the period of the Church struggle has been omitted.

I

UNPUBLISHED SOURCES

A. *Records of the German Government Ministries*

Records of the Reich Chancellery R 43 II 149–178a.
Records of the German Foreign Ministry, Politisches Archiv, Staatssekretär, Vatikan and Pol. III, Vatikan.
Records of the Reich Ministry of Justice.
Records of the Reich Ministry of the Occupied Eastern Territories, 1941–5.
Records of the Reich Ministry of Education.

B. *Records of Nazi Party organizations*

Records of the NSDAP, Part I–III.
Records of the Reichsführer SS and Chief of the German Police, Part I–III.
Sammlung Schumacher, Berlin Document Centre.
Ordinances and Directives of the Nazi Party Chancellery.

Bibliography

Documents prepared for the Nuremberg Trials 1946–8, Institut für Zeitgeschichte.
Miscellaneous German Records, Part I–III.
Records of the Bavarian Political Police, Institut für Zeitgeschichte.

C. *Records of various Church authorities*

Archive of the Landeskirche Westphalia, (Niemöller collection).
Archive of the Evangelische Kirche der Union, Berlin.
Archive of the German Church Struggle, Berlin.

II

PUBLISHED SOURCES

Adam, H. *Weihnacht im Dritten Reich.* Berlin 1933.
Adolph, Walter. *Im Schatten des Galgens.* Berlin 1953.
——. *Hirtenamt und Hitlerdiktatur.* Berlin 1965.
Albrecht, D. *Der Notenwechsel zwischen dem Heiligen Stuhl und der Deutschen Reichsregierung.* Mainz 1965.
Altmann, Sigrid. *Bayerns Benediktiner Unterm Hakenkreuz.* Feldafing 1964.
Altmeyer, K. A. *Katholische Presse unter NS-Diktatur.* Berlin 1962.
Amery, Carl. *Die Kapitulation.* Hamburg 1963.
Barth, Karl. *Eine schweizer Stimme 1938–1945.* Zurich 1945.
——. *The German Church Conflict.* Richmond, Virginia 1965.
Baumgaertel, Friedrich. *Wider die Kirchenkampflegenden.* Neuendettelsau 1959.
Beckmann, J. *Artgemässes Christentums oder schriftgemäss Christenglaube.* Essen 1933.
——. *Kirchliches Jahrbuch für die Evangelische Kirche in Deutschland 1950.* Gütersloh 1950.
——, (Ed.). *Kirchliches Jahrbuch für die Evangelische Kirche in Deutschland 1933–1944.* Gütersloh 1948.
Benekenstein, P. M. (Ed.). *Dokumente der deutschen Politik* Vol. I. Berlin 1935.
Bergmann, Ernst. *Die deutsche Nationalkirche.* Breslau 1934.
——. *Die 25 Thesen der Deutschreligion.* Breslau 1934.
Bielefeldt, Johann. *Der Kirchenkampf in Schleswig-Holstein 1933–1945.* Goettingen 1964.
Boberach, H. *Meldungen aus dem Reich.* Neuwied 1965.

Böckenförde, E. W. 'Der deutsche Katholizismus in Jahre 1933: Stellungnahme zu einer Diskussion' in *Hochland* 54 (1961–2).

——. 'Der deutsche Katholizismus in Jahre 1933' in *Hochland* 53 (1960–1).

Bonhoeffer, Dietrich. *Letters and papers from Prison*. London 1959.

——. *Gesammelte Schriften*, vols. 1–4. Munich 1961.

Bracher, K. D., Sauer, Wolfgang, and Schulz, G. *Die National-sozialistische Machtergreifung*. Cologne 1960.

Die Briefe Pius XII an die deutschen Bischöfe 1939–44 ed. Schneider, B. Mainz 1966.

Broszat, M. *Nationalsozialistische Polenpolitik 1939–45*. Stuttgart 1961.

Brunotte, H. (Ed.). *Zur Geschichte des Kirchenkampfes: Gesammelte Aufsätze*. Goettingen 1965.

Buchheim, H. 'Der deutsche Katholizismus in Jahr 1933' in *Hochland* 53 (1960–61).

——. *Glaubenskrise im Dritten Reich: drei Kapitel nationalsozialistischer Religionspolitik*. Stuttgart 1953.

Buxton, D. F. *The Religious Crisis in Germany*. London 1938.

Castonier, E. *The Eternal Front*. London 1943.

Catholic Church in Germany. Zeugnis und Kampf des deutschen Episkopats. Freiburg 1946.

Catholic Church in Germany. Berlin, Bischoefliches Ordinariat. Dokumente aus dem Kampf der Katholischen Kirche in Bistum Berlin gegen der Nationalsozialismus. Berlin 1948.

Christ in Dachau. Oxford 1952.

Das Christentum und die Juden. Cologne 1966.

Cianfarra, Camille Maximilian. *The Vatican and the War*. New York 1944.

Cochrane, Arthur C. *The Church's confession under Hitler*. Philadelphia 1962.

Conrad, Walter. *Der Kampf um die Kanzeln*. Berlin 1957.

——. *Kirchenkampf (Zeitpolitisches Archiv)*. Berlin 1947.

Conway, J. S. 'Pius XII and the German Church: an unpublished Gestapo Report' in *Canadian Journal of History* I/1 (1966).

Corsten, Wilhelm, (Ed.). *Kölner Aktenstücke zur Lage der Katholischen Kirche in Deutschland*. Cologne 1949.

Delp, Alfred. *Im Angesicht des Todes*. Frankfurt 1947.

Deuerlein, E. *Der deutsche Katholizismus 1933*. Osnabruck 1963.

——. 'Die Lage der Katholische Kirche' in *Stimmen der Zeit* 168 (1960–1).

——. *Das Reichskonkordat*. Düsseldorf 1956.

Bibliography

Deutsche Evangelische Kirche. *Die erste Bekentnissynode der Deutschen Evangelischer Kirche zu Barmen.* Goettingen 1959.

Deutsche Evangelische Kirche. *Der Altpreussischen Union: 4 Bekenntnissynode, Halle, 1937.* Niemoller, Gerhard, (Ed.). Goettingen 1963.

Dibelius, Otto. *In the service of the Lord.* New York 1964.

The Strange Case of Bishop Dibelius. E. Berlin, n.d.

Diehn, Otto. *Bibliographie zur Geschichte des Kirchenkampfes 1933–45.* Goettingen 1958.

I Documenti Diplomatici Italiani Ottava and Nona Serie. Rome 1952– .

Documents on British Foreign Policy 1919–39 Series II and III. London 1949– .

Documents on German Foreign Policy Series C and D. London–Washington 1950– .

Dokumente der Kirchenkampfes II Die Zeit der Reichskirchenausschusses 1935–7. 2 vols. Goettingen 1965.

Domarus, M., (Ed.) *Hitler Reden und Proklamationen 1932–45* 2 vols. Würzburg 1962 and 1964.

Donohoe, James. *Hitler's Conservative Opponents in Bavaria 1930–1945.* Leiden 1961.

Drummond, Andrew L. *German Protestantism since Luther.* London 1951.

Duncan-Jones, Arthur Stuart. *The Crooked Cross.* London 1940.

——. *The Struggle for Religious Freedom in Germany.* London 1938.

Elias, Otto. *Der Evangelische Kirchenkampf in seinen Verhältnis zur Judenfrage und zu den Juden.* (Unpublished manuscript, Institut für Zeitgeschichte.)

Die Evangelische Kirche und die Judenfrage. Geneva 1945.

Faulhaber, Michael von, Cardinal. *Judaism, Christianity and Germany.* New York 1934.

Frank, H., *Im Angesicht des Galgens.* Neuhaus 1955.

Frey, A. *Cross and Swastika.* London 1938.

Friedlander, Saul. *Pius XII and das Dritte Reich.* Hamburg 1965; also Engl. ed. London 1966.

Gallin, Mary Alice. *The German Resistance: Ethical and Religious Factors.* Washington, D.C. 1961.

Gamm, Hans-Jochen. *Der braune Kult. Das 'Dritte Reich' und seine Ersatz-religion.* Hamburg 1962.

Gauger, J. *Chronik der Kirchenwirren* 3 vols. Elberfeld 1934–6.

Geiger, M., (Ed.). *Der Deutsche Kirchenkampf, 1933–1945.* Zurich 1965.

Gerlich, F. *Prophetien Wider das Dritte Reich.* Munich 1948.

The German New Order in Poland. London 1941.

Giovannetti, Alberto. *Der Vatikan und der Krieg*. Cologne 1961.

The Goebbels Diaries (Ed.) Lochner, J. New York 1948.

Goebbels, J. *Vom Kaiserhof zur Reichskanzlei*. Berlin 1934.

——. *Kampf um Berlin*. Munich 1934.

Goldschmidt, D., and Kraus, H. J. (Eds.). *Der Ungekündigte Bund*. Stuttgart 1963.

Gollwitzer, H., Kuhn, K. & Schneider, R. *Dying we live*. London 1958.

Grundmann, Walter. *Wer ist Jesus von Nazareth?* Weimar 1940.

Gurian, Waldemar. *Hitler and the Christians*. London 1936.

Gürtler, Paul. *Nationalsozialismus und Evangelische Kirchen im Warthegau*. Goettingen 1958.

Gutachten des Instituts für Zeitgeschichte. Munich 1958.

Hagen, W. *Die Geheime Front*. Linz 1950.

Harder, Gunther & Niemoller Wilhelm. *Die Stunde der Versuchung: Gemeinden im Kirchenkampf 1933–1945*. Munich 1963.

Harringan, W. M. 'Nazi Germany and the Holy See: The Historical Background of "Mit brennender Sorge". 1933–6' in *Catholic Historical Review* 47 (1961–2).

——. 'Pius XI and Nazi Germany 1937–9', in *Catholic Historical Review*, 51 (1965–6).

——. 'Pius XII's efforts to effect a Detente in German–Vatican relations 1939–40' in *Catholic Historical Review*, 49 (1963).

Hase, Hans Christoph von. *Evangelische Dokumente zur Ermordung der 'unheilbare Kranken' unter der nationalsozialistischen Herrschaft in den Jahren 1939–45*. Stuttgart 1964.

Hauer, Jakob Wilhelm. *Germany's New Religion*. Abingdon 1937.

Hegel, Eduard. *Geschichte der Katholisch-Theologischen Fakultaet Münster, 1773–1964*. Münster 1966.

Heine, Ludwig. *Geschichte des Kirchenkampfes in der Grenzmark Posen-Westpreussen 1939–40*. Goettingen 1961.

Herman, S. W. *It's Your Souls We Want*. London 1943.

——. *The Rebirth of the German Church*. London 1946.

Hermelink, Heinrich (Ed.). *Kirche im Kampf; dokumente des Widerstands und des Aufbaus in der evangelischen Kirche Deutschlands von 1933 bis 1945*. Tübingen 1950.

Hitler, Adolf. *Hitler's Speeches*. Ed. N. Baynes. London 1942.

——. *Mein Kampf* (English trans. London 1939).

——. *Hitler's Table Talk* (A. Bullock, ed.) London 1953.

Hochhuth, Rolf. *The representative*. London 1963.

Hofer, W. *Der Nationalsozialismus*. Frankfurt-am-Main 1961.

Bibliography

Hohlfeld, E. (Ed.). *Dokumente der deutschen Politik*, Vol. IV. Berlin 1954.

Höye, B. and Ager, T. M. *The fight of the Norwegian Church against Nazism*. New York 1943.

Huber, H. *Dokumente Christlichen Widerstandes: Gegen die Entfernung der Kruzifixe aus den Schulen 1941*. Munich 1958.

Immer, Karl. *Entchristlichung der Jugend*. Barmen 1936.

International Military Tribunal. *Trial of the Major War Criminals*, 42 vols. Nuremberg 1947–9.

Jaeger, A. *Kirche im Volk*. Berlin 1936.

Jannasch, Wilhelm. *Deutsche Kirchendokumente; die Haltung der Bekennenden Kirche im Dritten Reich*. Zurich 1946.

Johnson, Alex. *Eivind Berggrav. Mann der Spannung*. Goettingen 1960.

Judennot und Christenglaube. Zurich 1943.

Kempner, B. M. *Priester vor Hitlers Tribunalen*. Munich 1966.

Kempner, R. 'Der Kampf gegen die Kirche' in *Der Monat* I (1949).

Kent, G. O. 'Pope Pius XII and Germany: Some Aspects of German–Vatican Relations 1933–45' in *American Historical Review* LXX. 1964.

Kinder, C. *Neue Beiträge zur Geschichte der Evangelische Kirche in Schleswig-Holstein und im Reich 1924–45*. Flensburg 1964.

——. *Die Deutschen Christen. Die Reden des Reichsbischofs und des Reichsleiters der Deutschen Christen*. Berlin 1934.

Kinkel, Walter. *Kirche und Nationalsozialismus*. Düsseldorf 1960.

Kluegel, Eberhard. *Die lutherische Landeskirche Hannovers und ihr Bischof 1933–1945*. Berlin 1964.

Knox, Arbuthnott Ronald. *Nazi and Nazarene*. London 1940.

Kogon, E. *Der SS-Staat*. Frankfurt-am-Main 1946.

Krause, R. *Der Fall Krause*. Berlin 1933.

Kupisch, Karl. *Durch den Zaun der Geschichte*. Berlin 1964.

——. *Studenten entdecken die Bibel Die Geschichte der DCSV*. Hamburg 1964.

——. *Quellen zur Geschichte des deutschen Protestantismus 1871–1945: Quellensammlung zur Kulturgeschichte*. Vol. 11. Goettingen 1960.

Leber, Annedore. *Conscience in Revolt*. London 1957.

Leiber, Fr E., S.J. 'Reichskonkordat und Ende der Zentrumspartei' in *Stimmen der Zeit*, 167 (1961).

Lewy, Guenter. *The Catholic Church and Nazi Germany*. New York 1964.

Littell, F. H. *The German Phoenix*. New York 1960.

Lortz, Joseph. *Katholischer Zugang zum National-sozialismus kirchengeschichtlich gesehen.* Muenster 1933.

Ludeke, K. *I Knew Hitler.* London 1938.

Lueken, W. *Kampf, Behandlung und Gestalt der Evangelische Landeskirche Nassau-Hessen.* Goettingen 1964.

MacFarland, Charles. *The New Church and the New Germany.* New York 1934.

McGovern, William. *From Luther to Hitler: A History of Nazi Philosophy.* New York 1941.

Martin, Hugh. *Christian Counter-Attack.* London 1943.

Marty, Martin (Ed.) *The Plan of Bonhoeffer.* New York 1962.

Means, Paul Barnwell. *Things that are Caesar's.* New York 1935.

Matthias, E., and Morsey, R. (Eds.). *Das Ende der Parteien 1933.* Düsseldorf 1960.

Meier, Kurt. *Die Deutsche Christen.* Goettingen 1965.

——. 'Kristallnacht und Kirche- Die Galtung der Evangelischen Kirche zur Judenpolitik' in *Wissenschaftliche Zeitschrift der Karl-Marx-Universität Leipzig* XIII/1 (1964).

Micklem, Nathanial. *National Socialism and the Roman Catholic Church 1933–38.* Oxford 1939.

——. *National Socialism and Christianity.* Oxford 1939.

Middendorff, Friedrich. *Der Kirchenkampf in einer reformierten Kirche.* Goettingen 1961.

Mitscherlich, A., and Mielke, F., *Wissenschaft ohne Menschlichkeit.* Heidelberg 1949.

Mohr, H. *Katholische Orden und deutscher Imperialismus.* E. Berlin 1965.

Mosse, G. L. *The Crisis of German Ideology.* New York 1964.

Muckermann, Fr H., S.J. *Der Deutscher Weg.* Zurich 1946.

Müller, Hans. *Katholische Kirche und Nationalsozialismus.* Munich 1963.

——. 'Der Pseudoreligiöse Charakter der Nationalsozialistischen Weltanschauung' in *Geschichte in Wissenschaft und Unterricht* 6/1961.

Natterer, Alois. *Der Bayerische Klerus in der Zeit dreier Revolutionen 1918–1933–1945.* Munich 1946.

Nazi Conspiracy and Aggression, 8 vols. with Supplement A and B. Washington 1946–7.

The Nazi Kultur in Poland. London 1942.

Neuhaeusler, Johann B. *Kreuz und Hakenkreuz.* Munich 1946.

Niemöller, Gerhard. *Die Erster Bekenntnissynode der DEK zu Barmen.* 2 Vols. Goettingen 1959.

Bibliography

Niemöller, Martin. *Bielefelden Dokumente*. Bielefeld 1947.

———. *First Commandment*. London 1937.

Niemöller, Wilhelm. *Bekennende Kirche in Westfalen*. Bielefeld 1952.

———. *Die bekennende Kirche sagt Hitler die Wahrheit*. Bielefeld 1954.

———. *Die Evangelische Kirche im Dritten Reich*. Bielefeld 1956.

———. *Hitler und die Evangelischen Kirchen-fuehrer*. Bielefeld 1959.

———. *Kampf und Zeugnis der Bekennenden Kirche*. Bielefeld 1948.

———. *Kirchenkampf im Dritten Reich*. Bielefeld 1946.

———. *Karl Koch: Präses der Bekenntnissynoden*. Bielefeld 1956.

———. *Macht geht vor Recht; der Prozess Martin Niemöllers*. Munich 1952.

———. (Ed.) *Texte zur Geschichte des Pfarrernotbundes*. Bielefeld 1958.

———. *Die vierte Bekenntnissynode der deutschen Evangelischen Kirche zu Bad-Oeynhausen*. Goettingen 1960.

———. *Die zweite Bekenntnissynode der deutschen Evangelischen Kirche zu Dahlem*. Goettingen 1958.

Van Norden, Guenther. *Kirche in der Krise – Die Stellung der Evangelischen Kirche zum nationalsozialistischen Staat im Jahre 1933*. Düsseldorf 1964.

Oakeshott, M. *The Social and Political Doctrines of Contemporary Europe*. New York 1953.

Oertel, Ferdinand. *Jugend in Feuerofen die Katholische Jugend im Dritten Reich*. Recklinghausen 1960.

Papen, Franz von. *Memoirs*. New York 1953.

Pelke, Else. *Der Luebecker Christenprozess, 1943*. Mainz 1961.

Perau, Joseph. *Priester im Heere Hitlers*. Essen 1963.

The Persecution of the Catholic Church in German-Occupied Poland. London 1941.

The Persecution of the Catholic Church in the Third Reich; facts and documents translated from the German. London 1940.

Piotrowski, S. *Hans Franks Tagebuch*. Warsaw 1963.

Poliakov, L., & Wulf, J. *Das Dritte Reich und seine Denker*. Berlin 1959.

Portmann, Heinrich. *Der Bischof von Muenster*. Muenster 1946.

Power, M. *Religion in the Reich*. London 1939.

Priepke, Manfred. *Die evangelische Jugend im Dritten Reich*. Hannover 1960.

Prittie, T. *Germans against Hitler*. London 1964.

Raddatz, F. J. (Ed.). *Summa Iniuria oder durfte der Papst schweigen*. Hamburg 1963.

Rauschning, H. *Germany's Revolution of Destruction*. London 1939.

———. *Hitler Speaks*. London 1939.

Reimers, Karl F. *Lübeck im Kirchenkampf des dritten Reiches.* Goettingen 1965.

Ritter, Gerhard. *The German Resistance: Carl Goerdeler's struggle against tyranny.* London 1958.

Robertson, E. H. *Christians against Hitler.* London 1963.

Rosenberg, Alfred. *An die Dunkelmänner unserer Zeit.* Munich 1935.

——. *Gestaltung der Idee: Blut und Ehre.* Vol. 2. Munich 1938.

——. *Mythus des 20 Jahrhunderts.* Munich 1930.

——. *Das Politische Tagebuch 1934-5 und 1939-40*, ed. H. G. Seraphim, Munich 1964.

Le Saint Siège et la Guerre en Europe 1939-40. Vatican City 1965.

Schirach, B. von. *Revolution der Erziehung.* Munich 1938.

Schlabrendorff, F. *Eugen Gerstenmeier im Dritten Reich: Eine Dokumentation.* Stuttgart 1965.

Schmid, H. *Apokalyptisches Wetterleuchten.* Munich 1947.

Schmidt, Dietmar. *Niemöller.* London 1959.

Schmidt, Kurt-Dietrich. *Die Bekenntnisse und grundsätzlicher Äusserungen zur Kirchenfrage.* Vols. 1-3. Goettingen 1934-6.

——. *Dokumente des Kirchenkampfes II: Die Zeit des Reichskirchenausschusses 1935-7.* 2 vols. Goettingen 1964.

Schnabel, R. *Die Frommen in der Hölle.* Berlin 1966.

Schneider, Paul. *Der Prediger von Buchenwald: Das Martyrium Paul Schneider.* Berlin 1964.

Scholder, Klaus. 'Die Evangelische Kirche und das Jahr 1933' in *Geschichte in Wissenschaft und Unterricht* 11/1965.

——. 'Neuere deutsche Geschichte und Protestantische Theologie' in *Evangelische Theologie* 10.1963.

Scholl, Inge. *Die Weisse Rose.* Munich 1955.

Schorn, H. *Der Richter im Dritten Reich.* Frankfurt-am-Main 1959.

Seyss Inquart, A. *Vier Jahre in der Niederlanden.* Amsterdam 1944.

Spiegelbild einer Verschwörung (Ed.). K. H. Peter, Stuttgart 1961.

Stasiewski, B. 'Die Kirchenpolitik der Nationalsozialisten im Warthegau 1939-45' in *Vierteljahrshefte für Zeitgeschichte* 7 (1959).

An der Stechbahn: Erlebnisse und Berichte aus dem Büro Grüber in den Jahren der Verfolgung. Berlin n.d.

Steward, John S. *Sieg des Glaubens.* Zurich 1946.

Stoevesandt, Karl. *Bekennende Gemeinden und deutsch-glaeubige Bischofsdiktatur.* Goettingen 1961.

Stoll, Gerhard E. *Die evangelische Zeitschriftenpresse im Jahre 1933.* Witten 1963.

Bibliography

Streisand, J. 'Die deutsche Evangelische Kirchen und die faschistische Diktatur' in *Zeitschrift für Geschichtswissenschaft* 4/1966.

Teping, Franz. *Kampf um die Konfessionelle Schule in Oldenburg während der Herrschaft des NS Regierung*. Muenster 1949.

The Third Reich (for UNESCO). London 1955.

Tilgner, W. *Volksnomostheologie & Schöpfungsglaube*. Goettingen 1965.

Viereck, Peter R. E. *Metapolitics: The Roots of the Nazi Mind*. New York 1961.

Volk, Ludwig. *Bayerns Episkopat und Klerus in der Auseinandersetzung mit dem Nationalsozialismus 1930–4*. Mainz 1965.

Vollmer, Bernhard. *Volksopposition in Polizeistaat*. Stuttgart 1957.

Weinreich, K. *Hitler's Professors*. New York 1946.

Weizsäcker, Ernst von. *Memoirs*. London 1951.

Wolf, Ernst. *Die Evangelische Kirchen und der Staat im Dritten Reich*. Zurich 1963.

——. *Kirche im Widerstand*. Munich 1965.

——. *Zeugnisse der Bekennenden Kirche*. Tübingen, 1946.

——. *Barmen – Kirche Zwischen Versuchung und Glaube*. Munich 1957.

Zahn, Gordon C. *German Catholics and Hitler's Wars*. New York 1962.

——. *In Solitary Witness*. New York 1964.

Ziemer, G. *Education for Death*. Oxford 1941.

Zipfel, F. *Kirchenkampf in Deutschland*. Berlin 1965.

Index

Althaus, P., 399
Amery, C., xxiv, xxvii
Asmussen, Pastor, 333
Austria, 211, 220, 224, 252, 309, 320, 366, 379; Nazi persecution in, 182, 224–8, 393–7, 452; confiscations in, 255, 256, 393–7

Backhaus, H., Pastor, 37
Bares, Nicholas, Bishop, 93
Barmen Declaration or Confession, xx, 83–4, 87, 335
Barth, Karl, xviii, xix, xx, 86, 191, 222–3, 334, 338, 399; theological influence of, 10; attacks 'Deutsche Christen', 10; author of Barmen confession, 83
Bauer, Munich School Inspector, 185
Baumgärtel, Friedrich, xxi
'Bekennende Kirche', see Confessing Church
Bell, George, Bishop of Chichester, xvii, 83, 100
Bergen, D. von, German Ambassador to the Vatican, 100, 304, 459, 461
Berggrav, E., Bishop, 293, 456
Berning, Wilhelm, Bishop, 25–6, 246, 399
Bertram, Adolf, Cardinal, 26, 166, 399, 453; warns against Nazism, 6–7, 22, 26; expresses concern about Nazi policy, 18, 22; gives support to the Nazi Government, 26, 229; urges acceptance of Concordat, 63; protests to the Government, 165, 179,

224, 256–8, 266, 288, 324, 452; and failure of complaints, 300; on concentration camps, 457
Biberstein, E., 133, 399–400
Böckenförde, E. W., xxii–xxiv
Blau, Superintendent, 318
Bodelschwingh, F. von, 35, 37
Bohm, W., 33
Bonhoeffer, Dietrich, xv, xvii, 290, 337–8, 400
Bormann, Martin, 50, 59, 60, 133, 178, 387–92, 400; institutes measures against the Churches, 67, 160, 192–4, 239, 287, 368–9; anti-clerical attitudes, 188–9, 203, 217, 221, 277, 314; and Oath of Loyalty, 211; appointed Hitler's secretary, 251; and seizure of church properties, 255–6, 279–80; institutes measures against clergy, 258; Circular to *Gauleiters*, 259–60, 330, 383–6; orders cessation of seizures of church properties, 279; and Galen, 280–1; orders postponement of church settlement, 284; supports forcible suppression, 291, 294; opposes Kerrl, 132, 139, 188, 214, 228, 249, 251–2; opposes other Nazis, 303; and Warthegau, 313, 314, 318, 320, 462; and Greiser, 313
Bornewasser, Franz, Bishop of Trier, 127, 279
Bouhler, Philipp, Chief of the Führer's Office, 267, 451
Brack, SS Leader, 271, 451
Brandt, Dr, 267, 451

465

Index

Index